The Social History of Human Experience

General Editor: Neil McKendrick

Marriage and Society:
Studies in the Social
History of Marriage

Marriage and Society

Studies in the Social History of Marriage

Edited by R. B. Outhwaite

St. Martin's Press   New York

© the Authors 1981

All rights reserved. For information, write:
St. Martin's Press, Inc., 175 Fifth Avenue, New York, NY 10010
Printed in Great Britain
First published in the United States of America in 1982

ISBN 0-312-51595-2

Library of Congress Cataloging in Publication Data
Main entry under title:

Marriage and society.

   Includes bibliographical references and index.
   1. Marriage—History—Addresses, essays,
lectures.   I. Outhwaite, R. B.
HQ503.M3   1982   306.8'09   81–18362
ISBN 0-312-51595-2   AACR2

Contents

Notes on Contributors

Lloyd Bonfield is Research Fellow in History at Trinity College, Cambridge. He received a law degree from the University of Iowa and a doctorate in history from Cambridge. He has just completed a monograph entitled *Marriage Settlements, 1601–1740: the Development of the Strict Settlement*.

Christopher N. L. Brooke held chairs in Liverpool University and London University and is now Dixie Professor of Ecclesiastical History at Cambridge, where he is also a Fellow of Gonville and Caius College. He has edited, with W. J. Millor and H. E. Butler, *The Letters of John of Salisbury* (1955–79), and with Dom Adrian Morey, *The Letters and Charters of Gilbert Foliot* (1967). His recent books include *The Monastic World* (1974), and, with G. Keir, *London 800–1216: the Shaping of a City* (1975).

Roger Lee Brown read history at St David's University College, Lampeter, and held the Goldsmiths Company's Studentship in London history at University College, London during 1964–65. He is now vicar of Tongwynlais near Cardiff, and currently studying the history of the nineteenth-century church in Wales.

L. A. Clarkson is Reader in Economic and Social History at Queen's University, Belfast. He is the author of *The Pre-industrial Economy in England, 1500–1750* (1971) and *Death, Disease and Famine in Pre-industrial England* (1975).

Kathleen Davies is Head of Subject Studies at Westminster College of Education, Oxford. She graduated in history at St. Anne's College, Oxford, and in law at London University. Publications include a school textbook, articles on teaching history and on social history.

Vivien Brodsky Elliott is Lecturer in History at the University of Adelaide, South Australia. She studied with the Cambridge Group for the History of Population and Social Structure and completed her Cambridge Ph.D on 'Mobility and Marriage in Pre-industrial England' in 1978.

Penina M. Glazer is Professor of History at Hampshire College, Massachusetts, and has a doctorate from Rutgers, the State University. She has written on social movements and the history of reform. She is the co-author of *Sociology, Inquiring into Society,* and, with M. Slater, of *Unequal Colleagues: Women's Entrance into the Professions.*

Olwen Hufton is Professor of History at the University of Reading. Her works include *The Poor of Eighteenth-Century France* (1974), which won the Wolfson Award for 1975, and *Europe: Privilege and Protest, 1730–1789* (1980). She has also written on women and work in eighteenth-century France, on crime and popular culture, and is currently working on *mentalités populaires* during the *ancien régime.*

Martin Ingram graduated at Oxford and is Lecturer in Modern History at the Queen's University of Belfast. His research interests include the history of climate and various aspects of social history, and he is currently preparing for publication his doctoral thesis on the church courts' work relating to sex and marriage in early modern England.

R. B. Outhwaite graduated at Nottingham University, held lecturing posts at Manchester and Leicester Universities, and is now Lecturer in History at Cambridge University and a Fellow of Gonville and Caius College. He has written *Inflation in Tudor and Early Stuart England* (1969) and articles on the economic and social history of early modern England.

Miriam Slater is Professor of History at Hampshire College, Massachusetts, with a doctorate from Princeton University. Her book on the Verneys, *Family Life in the Seventeenth Century,* will be published by Routledge and Kegan Paul. Her contribution, with P. Glazer, 'Natural and Sacred Professions: Motherhood and Medicine in America' is part of a larger study, *Unequal Colleagues: Women's Entrance into the Professions.*

Christopher Smout studied at Clare College, Cambridge. He is Professor of Scottish History at the University of St. Andrews and was formerly Professor of Economic History at the University of Edinburgh. His publications include *Scottish Trade on the Eve of Union* (1963), *A History of the Scottish People* (1969), with M. W. Flinn *et al., Scottish Population History from the Seventeenth Century to the 1930s* (1977), and, with Ian Levitt, *The State of the Scottish Working Class in 1843.*

E. A. Wrigley is Professor of Population Studies at the London School of Economics and a director of the S.S.R.C. Cambridge Group for the History of Population and Social Structure. He has written *Industrial Growth and Population Change* (1961), *Population and History* (1969), and (with Roger Schofield), *The Population History of England 1541–1871* (1981); and has published as editor *English Historical Demography* (1966), *Nineteenth Century Society* (1972), *Identifying People in the Past* (1973), and (with Philip Abrams) *Towns in Societies* (1978).

Introduction:

Problems and Perspectives in the History of Marriage

R. B. OUTHWAITE

Marriage is a near universal human experience: all societies recognize it in some form, though not all eligible members of society enter into it. Its functions and purposes are many but primacy may perhaps be given to the need to regulate sexual activity: it is, as Margaret Cole once drily remarked, the *maison tolérée* of the human race.[1] Despite any 'convergence' deriving from modern economic development, and despite the march of the great world religions, it still exists in a bewildering variety of forms. To describe the present is difficult enough; to describe and explain the past even more so. 'A social history of marriage' is a near impossible task, and no one book can do justice to the complexities of spatial variety and historical change. This book compromises, and compromises severely, by looking at particular facets of the western European experience of marriage as revealed to historians working in periods from the Middle Ages to relatively modern times. To give the work greater coherence it looks in particular at the experience of England and some of its nearest geographical and cultural neighbours—Scotland, Ireland, France and the United States.

Twelve scholars known to have interests in the institution were invited to contribute essays. Some of these authors were chosen because they were developing new approaches to the subject, in some cases by exploring hitherto lightly used historical sources; other because they were knowledgeable about aspects of great intrinsic interest; yet others for their ability to cut their way clearly through complexities in areas that have become contentious. The essays thus range from the narrowly specialized to the broadly general. All of them, it is hoped, will be of interest, not just to specialists in the history of the family but to all who profess a broad interest in social history.

The contributors were offered the loosest of guide reins. Although it would not have been difficult to produce some list of problems with which contributors might have wrestled—some taxonomy of subject matter—it would have been difficult to find contributors willing and able thus to confine themselves, and impossible to find historians willing to subject themselves to any one particular conceptual approach to these problems. Although there might be broad agreement about what are the important questions that should be

[1] M. Cole, *Marriage Past and Present* (London, 1938), p. 51.

1

asked, the hope for agreement on methodological approaches to these questions must be remote.

Indeed the history of marriage has long been characterized by the very great variety of approaches made to it. If one looks very briefly at the historiography of English marriage, for instance, one can see a number of traditions: the Malthusian, social-statistical, the demographic; that deriving from the preoccupations of economic historians; those influenced by forces as different from one another as feminism and anthropology; and a powerful juristic one, influenced by both English legal history and Germanic intellectual preoccupations with orderly stages of human evolution. A series of specialist trickles always joining and parting has now coalesced into a raging and perhaps unmanageable torrent, one not yet successfully dammed by the sociologists.

Thomas Malthus's gloomy prognostications about population behaviour, first issued in his *Essay on the Principle of Population* in 1795, provoked a barrage of critical retorts which, along with a visit to Norway in 1799, drove him to modify his views about the supreme importance of the positive checks—famine, disease and war—and to elevate in importance those preventive checks, such as the tendency to delay marriage, that enabled men to stave off economic and demographic disaster.[2] Not only did his assertions raise important questions about rates of marriage and ages at entry into that state, they also brought into contention the influence of a whole number of institutions, such as the Poor Law and education, which were thought to influence these things. Debate has continued ever since and is still vigorous today. Indeed a recent copy of *The Economic History Review* contains an essay entitled 'The demographic impact of the Old Poor Law: more reflexions on Malthus'.[3] The ghost of Malthus is still being invoked and exorcized.

Opportunities to measure English marital behaviour more perfectly were opened up from 1839 with the publication of the first of the Registrar General's *Annual Reports . . . of Births, Deaths and Marriages in England,* and these opportunities were seized by social statisticians, often to illustrate pro- or anti-Malthusian propositions. At first the emphasis was perhaps laid upon differential life expectation,[4] but the emphasis shifted gradually to take

---

[2] *Introduction to Malthus,* ed. D. V. Glass (London, 1953) contains several illuminating studies including 'A list of books, pamphlets and articles on the population question, published in Britain in the period 1793 to 1880' (by J. A. Banks and D. V. Glass). See also D. E. C. Eversley, *Social Theories of Fertility and the Malthusian Debate* (Oxford, 1959), esp. ch. IX, and M. Drake, 'Malthus on Norway', *Population Studies,* XX (1966–67), 175–96.

[3] By J. P. Huzel, *Economic History Review,* 2nd ser., XXXIII (1980), 367–81. See also Huzel's 'Malthus, the poor law, and population in early nineteenth-century England', *Economic History Review,* XXII (1969), 430–52; and J. W. Leasure, 'Malthus, marriage and multiplication', *Milbank Memorial Fund Quarterly,* XLI (1963), 419–35.

[4] A good example is F. Galton, 'The relative supplies from town and country families, to the population of future generations', *Journal of the Royal Statistical Society,* XXXVI (1873), 19–26.

in questions of differential nuptiality as marriage rates apparently declined in later Victorian England.[5]

With the very much more marked decline in the crude birth rate in the 1930s came modern demography, with its careful conceptualization and sophisticated measurements, especially of nuptiality and fertility. Workers in this tradition confined their attention very largely, however, to recent—late nineteenth- and twentieth-century—developments in these areas, and they displayed little interest in earlier eras for which accurate statistics were unavailable.[6]

Such difficulties had not deterred economic historians, however, for they had long been locked in debate about the relative contributions of mortality and fertility to population changes in the English industrial revolution. Early opinion was on the whole in favour of falling mortality as the principal determinant of change, though note should be taken of T. H. Marshall's important warning that we should pay as much attention to the forces that kept the birth rate up as to those that pulled the death rate down.[7] It was, however, in the 1950s that emphasis shifted more firmly towards the possibility that high and rising fertility was the dynamic demographic element in the late eighteenth and early nineteenth centuries. Important here were the arguments of K. H. Connell, H. J. Habakkuk and J. T. Krause who in different ways suggested that falling marriage ages and rising nuptiality were key elements in this expansion.[8] Debate has continued ever since,[9] and it is sure to be further stimulated by Professor Wrigley's essay

[5] See, for example, C. Ansell, *On the Rate of Mortality at Early Periods of Life, the Age at Marriage, the Number of Children to a Marriage, the Length of a Generation, and Other Statistics of Families in the Upper and Professional Classes* (London, 1874), and W. Ogle, 'On marriage-rates and marriage-ages, with special reference to the growth of population', *Journal of the Royal Statistical Society*, LIII (1890), 253–80.

[6] J. H. C. Stevenson's 'The fertility of various social classes in England and Wales from the middle of the nineteenth century to 1911', *Journal of the Royal Statistical Society*, LXXXIII (1920), 401–32, can be offered as an interesting link between the studies of authors such as Ansell and Ogle and the more modern demographic studies of D. V. Glass, 'Changes in fertility in England and Wales, 1851 to 1931', in *Political Arithmetic*, ed. L. Hogben (London, 1938), pp. 161–212, and J. W. Innes, *Class Fertility Trends in England and Wales, 1876–1934* (Princeton, 1938).

[7] M. C. Buer, *Health, Wealth and Population in Eighteenth-Century England* (London, 1926), G. T. Griffith, *Population Problems of the Age of Malthus* (Cambridge, 1925), and T. H. Marshall, 'The population problem during the industrial revolution', *Economic History*, I (1929), 429–56, and 'The population of England and Wales from the industrial revolution to the world war', *Economic History Review*, V (1935), 65–78.

[8] Their writings were many but key ones were K. H. Connell, 'Some unsettled problems in English and Irish population history, 1750–1845', first published in *Irish Historical Studies*, VII (1951) and reprinted in *Population in Industrialization*, ed. M. Drake (London, 1969), which, incidentally, gives a much fuller picture of this debate; H. J. Habakkuk, 'English population in the eighteenth century', *Economic History Review*, VI (1953), 117–33; and J. T. Krause, 'Some neglected factors in the English industrial revolution', *Journal of Economic History*, XIX (1959), 528–40.

[9] The state of play by 1970 is very ably summarized in M. W. Flinn, *British Population Growth 1700–1850* (London, 1970).

in this volume which tilts the balance decidedly towards earlier marriage and increasing tendencies to marry as explanations of the eighteenth-century population rise. Questions are sure to be asked about the typicality of his dozen communities, about what happened in the large and expanding industrial towns, and about what happened later. Debate could profitably shift to the first half of the nineteenth century. Although mean ages at first marriage, calculated from national (and perhaps not random) samples, may hide rather more than they reveal, the Registrar General's returns suggest that spinsters were in the 1850s on average a year older at marriage than they were in Tony Wrigley's parishes in 1800–24.[10] Wrigley himself suggests that nuptiality began to fall around the end of the eighteenth century. If these trends are corroborated, what is it that caused nuptiality to rise and marriage ages to fall for much of the eighteenth century but at various times soon thereafter apparently sent these tendencies into reverse?

Tony Wrigley is a founder member of the Cambridge Group for the History of Population and Social Structure, set up in the early 1960s to reconstruct the demographic history of the English past, and recent developments have owed much to this group and its refinement of the technique of 'family reconstitution', developed originally by French demographers attempting to discover the dimensions of 'natural' fertility.[11] Wrigley's discovery that in the Devon community of Colyton there were marked shifts in female age at marriage—a pronounced rise in the second half of the seventeenth century followed by a great fall to the early nineteenth[12]—provoked a reassessment of English population behaviour over the whole early modern period and certainly fuelled the industrial revolution debate. Continental historians meanwhile appear always to have been very much more interested in early modern developments, and the implications of some of this work were brought sharply into focus with the publication in 1965 of Professor Hajnal's important short study of European marriage patterns. North-west Europe had by the sixteenth century a pattern of marriage decidedly different from that prevailing in much of the modern 'third world'; it had a pattern of late female age at marriage and a high proportion of people who never married at all.[13] Hajnal's study, arguably one of the most influential of recent times, further concentrated attention on

---

[10] See, for example, *Twentieth Annual Report of the Registrar-General* (London, 1859), p. vii, where spinsters were reported as marrying in 1857 at an average age of 24.7 years; and *Fifty-ninth Annual Report* (London, 1897), pp. ix–xi, where averages are returned as 23.0, 25.0, 24.9 for the three registration years 1858–60.

[11] The origins and development of the technique are explained in *An Introduction to English Historical Demography*, ed. E. A. Wrigley (London, 1966), ch. 4.

[12] E. A. Wrigley, 'Family limitation in pre-industrial England', *Economic History Review*, XIX (1966), 82–109.

[13] J. Hajnal, 'European marriage patterns in perspective', in *Population in History*, ed. D. V. Glass and D. E. C. Eversley (London, 1965), pp. 101–43.

pre-eighteenth-century nuptiality, and also initiated a search for medieval origins for this peculiar behaviour.[14]

The acquisition of empire in the nineteenth century, and the development of social anthropology which was nurtured by it, fed other traditions, although it must be pointed out that an interest in alien marriage behaviour antedated both developments, as Lady Augusta Hamilton's *Marriage Rites, Customs and Ceremonies: of all Nations of the Universe,* published in London in 1822, suggests. Keith Thomas's proposition in 1963 that 'historians might profit from an acquaintance with anthropology' had earlier been profitably demonstrated in his own illuminating short study of the 'double standard' in action.[15] History and anthropology have since married in the person of his one-time pupil, Alan Macfarlane, and from him has flowed a stream of interesting findings and thought-provoking suggestions about the nature of early modern marriage and family life.[16]

With a few conspicuous exceptions, such as Dr. Macfarlane and Professor Goody, the traffic from anthropology to history has been light: anthropologists have been resolutely attached to the study of contemporary but 'non-modern' cultures and have largely ignored the potentialities of historical research. Much the same is true of sociology. Obsessed with theoretical positions, and frequently disdainful of historical analysis, it has made a disappointingly meagre contribution to our understanding of the history of marriage, though the excellence of some sociological work in this field is a reminder of these lost opportunities.[17]

Far more fruitful, and appearing very much earlier, were the efforts of legal historians, such as Pollock and Maitland, and Dibdin, which expounded and clarified the development of marriage law.[18] This legal tradition fused with others, notably Germanic preoccupations with stages of social development, in works such as G. E. Howard's early and monumental *History of Matrimonial Institutions*[19] and W. Goodsell's later and lesser *History of Marriage and the Family.*[20] The best part of these works dealt with the evolution of medieval and early modern marriage law, the weaker parts with dimly observed early practices in chapters labelled 'Primitive matrimonial

[14] A valuable discussion of recent work and current thinking is R. M. Smith, 'Some reflections on the evidence for the origins of the "European marriage pattern" in England', in *The Sociology of the Family,* ed. C. Harris (Keele, 1979), pp. 74–112.

[15] K. Thomas, 'History and anthropology', *Past & Present* (1963), 3–24, and the 'The double standard', *Journal of the History of Ideas,* XX (1959), 195–216.

[16] See, in particular, *The Family Life of Ralph Josselin* (Cambridge, 1970), and *The Origins of English Individualism* (Oxford, 1978).

[17] Especially interesting have been works such as J. Banks, *Prosperity and Parenthood* (London, 1954); and M. Anderson, *Family Structure in Nineteenth-Century Lancashire* (Cambridge, 1971), and 'Marriage patterns in Victorian Britain: an analysis based on registration district data for England and Wales 1861', *Journal of Family History,* I (1976), 55–78.

[18] Sir F. Pollock and F. W. Maitland, *The History of English Law* (Cambridge, 1895); Sir L. Dibdin, *English Church Law and Divorce* (London, 1912).

[19] 3 vols., Chicago and London, 1904.

[20] New York, 1934.

institutions', 'Horde and mother-right', 'Original pairing' and so on. These dimly observed early stages could hardly survive another of Margaret Cole's taunts:

> ... the theory of an original state of promiscuity, a sort of glorious state of things where any man cohabited with any woman at will within, as it were, the twelve-mile radius, and any resultant children were put in a common stock if not a common stock pot, has now ceased to be respectable.[21]

Other traditions exist. As marriage and motherhood were long viewed as the only worthwhile careers for women, the institution was bound to attract the attention of women themselves. From Mary Wollstonecraft onwards one can discern a stream of critical feminist writing, focusing successively on married women's property rights, access to divorce, and the rights to work and vote. Whatever their critical stances, the institution and its development have exercised a fascination for women, and it is perhaps no accident that women scholars contribute so prominently to this book. In more recent times the women's liberation movement has boosted this tradition and in Miriam Slater's and Penina Glazer's reproachful reminder of how 'the blemish of gender' hindered work opportunities for modern American women we hear its authentic rumbles. How would they respond, one wonders, to the categorization of the wife's role that came from that seventeenth-century 'male chauvinist', perhaps not inappropriately called Bacon, 'Wives are young men's mistresses; companions for middle age; and old men's nurses'?[22]

The most prolific stream of all was probably work of a casual antiquarian kind, designed to satisfy curiosity in a general reading public about what was a fundamental human institution. Good examples can be found in E. J. Wood's *The Wedding Day in all Ages and Countries* (London, 1869), J. C. Jeaffreson's *Brides and Bridals* (London, 1872), and W. Tegg's *The Knot Tied* (London, 1877); and that simple desire to communicate to a general public what is likely to be of interest in the past still happily survives. It has been accompanied, moreover, by an extraordinary enlargement of what is deemed to be of interest, a subject worthy of discussion in its own right. Nineteenth-century writers, such as Lady Hamilton, felt impelled to write, 'Whatever might give offence to delicacy has, in the following pages, been carefully avoided—the object being not to inflame the passions, but to render the thirst of curiosity subservient to the ends of rational enjoyment and the Christian character',[23] and Jeaffreson prefaced his book with the remark, 'I shall in some places speak with the greatest reserve, in order that my pages may contain no single sentence calculated to disincline an English gentlewoman to place them in her daughter's hands.'[24] How shocked they would be with Professor Stone's recent *The Family, Sex and Marriage in*

---

[21] Cole, *Marriage,* p. 10.
[22] *Essays of Francis Bacon,* ed. O. Smeaton (London, 1906), p. 23.
[23] Hamilton, *Marriage Rites,* p. viii.
[24] Jeaffreson, *Brides and Bridals,* I, 11.

England 1500–1800,[25] where reference to the letter 'B' in the index would give immediate access to sections dealing with 'bagnio', 'ballads, obscene', 'bastards', 'bed-wetting', 'bestiality', 'bigamy', 'birth-control', 'bi-sexuality', 'brothels', 'buggery' and much else besides.[26]

Professor Stone's book is a monument in more senses than one. Extremely fertile in ideas, and a testimony to the author's astonishingly wide reading, yet it has been criticized for papering over very large areas of ignorance and for embodying erroneous conceptions of social and familial development.[27] Dr. Macfarlane obviously doubts that 'England changed from a society in which the individual was subordinated to a group of some kind, whether the family, village, religious congregation or estate, to that described by Hobbes in the seventeenth century in which society was composed of autonomous individuals'[28] and would prefer to substitute a view of England which, even by 1400, was intensely individualistic in its fundamental economic and social arrangements. We should resist the temptation to substitute one extreme stereotype for another, however, and it is perhaps unfair to dismiss the work of the past generation of economic and social historians as having been built on 'an optical illusion created largely by the survival of documents and the use of misleading analogies'.[29] But whatever the outcome of this larger debate about social change, we can be certain that many of Professor Stone's statements about the particular institution of marriage will be challenged. Indeed a number of them are challenged in the essays collected here. Thus his remark, 'Whether in Anglican or Puritan households, there was in varying degrees, a new emphasis on the home and on domestic virtues, and this was perhaps the most far-reaching consequence of the Reformation in England', rests partly on changes discerned in the advice tendered in domestic conduct books in the sixteenth and early seventeenth centuries.[30] Kathleen Davies, however, finds rather more evidence for continuity than change, and some of the latter can also be accounted for by concurrent alterations in the character of both authors and audience. We must be careful, she insists, to 'compare like with like . . .', to 'compare Puritan sermons and works of moral instruction with earlier works about marriage and family life, also addressed to the married laity', and must remember that early works were 'written for priests, who needed to know about canon law and theological

---

[25] London, 1977.
[26] That this permissiveness has arrived with some suddenness, however, is suggested by G. R. Scott's *Curious Customs of Sex and Marriage* (London, 1953), a limited edition of 975 copies supposedly restricted to purchase by 'Anthropologists, Ethnologists, Psychologists, Sociologists, the Clergy, [and] Members of the Medical and Legal Profession' (found by the author in the library of the English Folk Lore Society).
[27] See, in particular, the important review by Alan Macfarlane in *History and Theory*, XVIII (1979), 103–26.
[28] Macfarlane (pp. 104–5) summarizing Stone's view of early modern social change.
[29] Macfarlane, p. 125.
[30] Stone, *The Family,* p. 141.

interpretation', while 'most late sixteenth-century books on marriage were written for the general market'.

Professor Stone tells us on several occasions that marriage ages rose in the eighteenth century among the lower classes.[31] In the 12 communities surveyed by Professor Wrigley, however, the trend appears to be the reverse of this: taking all 12 together, and comparing the first quarter of the century with the last, age at first marriage for men dropped by 1.5 years and for women by 2.2 years.

Here then are two judgements which are challenged directly by our contributors, and there are many more in his stimulating book which could be challenged. The combination of Professor Stone's vivid style, teetering often towards hyperbole, and the relative absence of solid investigative work in many of these areas produces statement after statement that cry out for further research. One can list some of them:

1. bigamy . . . [in early-modern England] seems to have been both easy and common (p. 40)

2. the possibility of female or child employment facilitated early marriage (p. 52)

3. The decline of the adult mortality rate after the late eighteenth century, by prolonging the expected duration of marriage to unprecedented lengths, eventually forced Western society to adopt the institutional escape-hatch of divorce (p. 56)

4. A final effect of the Reformation [? in England] was to reduce the incest taboos . . . to close blood relatives limited to the Levitical degrees. . . . The purpose of this change was to block the scandalous divorce proceedings of the pre-Reformation church, as well as to return to sound biblical precedent (pp. 138–9)

5. Only a handful of children resisted parental dictation [about marriage] before the end of the sixteenth century (p. 183)

6. In the eighteenth century the importance of money was far less generally accepted as a crucial factor in marriage than it had been in the seventeenth (p. 290)

7. The urban tradesmen and artisans and the rural smallholders of the late eighteenth century were thus probably largely unaffected by the new demands of love, generated among their betters by the romantic movement of the age (p. 366)

Such statements will at least be welcomed by the setters of examination papers; they are all of that familiar variety that invites the appendage 'Discuss'. In relation to the first of them, it is true that deserted wives are commonly encountered in the Poor Law records of the period, but can this support the notion that bigamy was therefore easy? Does the relative absence

[31] Stone, *The Family*, pp. 296, 375.

of prosecutions for bigamy also betoken its ease? As for the second, while it is tempting to associate female employment with early marriage, and one can find examples where it does appear to have stimulated early and greater nuptiality, such an association is not an invariable one. In mid-Victorian England, for example, domestic service for girls clearly diminished nuptiality, and the effects of other female employments on marriage appear very much more debatable.[32] The conjunction in the third statement of life expectation and divorce is an arresting one, but does it seriously explain the appearance of, say, the Matrimonial Causes Act of 1857?[33] As for the fourth, the reason for the frequently bewildering changes in the prohibited degrees that took place in England between 1533 and 1540 was surely not 'to block the scandalous divorce proceedings of the pre-Reformation church' but to further Henry VIII's own equally scandalous divorce proceedings. Confusion was produced, it has been suggested, by that monarch's penchant for incest.[34] If 'only a handful of children resisted parental dictation before the end of the sixteenth century' then some of that handful is to be found in F. J. Furnivall's famous *Child Marriages, Divorces, and Ratifications, etc. in the Diocese of Chester . . . 1561–6*,[35] where the espousals of young children, arranged by their parents, were set aside on their reaching the age of consent (12 for girls, 14 for boys). The fourth case cited there is particularly illuminating. John Bridge, aged 13–14, had been forced by his father 'for saving his father of a bond' into an espousal with Elizabeth Ramsbotham, aged 11–12. She complained formally, as the law required her to, that he never treated her lovingly, but then she added

> insomuch that the first night they were married, the said John would eat no meat at supper, and when it was bed time the said John did weep to go home with his father, he being at that time at her brother's house. Yet nevertheless, by his father's intreating, and by the persuasion of the priest, the said John did come to bed to this respondent far in the night, and there lay still till in the morning, in such sort as this deponent might take unkindness with him, for he lay with his back toward her all night.

Here, apparently, was one little boy who proved remarkably resistant to the pressure of both father and priest. Joan, aged 11–12, could have married Rafe Whittall, of about the same age, and 'she should have had by him a pretty bargain', because he had about 40s. a year of land, 'if they could have loved one the other'. Ellen Dampart and John Andrew were espoused by their parents, to settle some dispute over the ownership of a tenement, but the young people 'never consented thereunto'.[36] A law of marriage which, as Professor Brooke reminds us, was grounded early on a doctrine of consent

[32] M. Anderson, 'Marriage patterns', pp. 65–9.
[33] 20 and 21 Vict. c. 85.
[34] L. B. Smith, *Henry VIII: the Mask of Royalty* (London, 1971), p. 65; H. A. Kelly, *The Matrimonial Trials of Henry VIII* (Stanford, 1976), *passim*.
[35] Published by the Early English Text Society in 1897.
[36] Furnivall, *Child Marriages*, pp. 6, 12, 13.

lay uneasily with the resolve of parents to match their children, sometimes (as in the Furnivall cases) for mercenary reasons. To argue also, as Professor Stone does, that large groups were unaffected by pressures of love is to fly in the face of opinion both modern and contemporary. Love is frequently the art of the possible, and both Dr. Ingram and Professor Hufton detect signs of its presence, operating sometimes in the most restrictive of personal circumstances. Miles Coverdale might insist in the sixteenth century that a mate was to be chosen for true riches of mind, body, and temporal substance, and 'if beside these, thou findest other great riches (beauty and such like gifts) . . . thou hast the more to thank God for'.[37] But that arch-complainer, the Elizabethan Philip Stubbes, moaned about feckless young matches: boys matching themselves without sufficient maintenance for marriage, not caring so long as 'he have his pretty pussy to huggle withall'.[38] Finally, if it is true that money was less generally accepted as a crucial factor in marriage in the eighteenth century, how did this affect the size of portions (dowries) for brides? Professor Stone's own evidence relating to aristocratic portions suggests that they continued to rise in the early eighteenth century.[39] What happened to them thereafter?

Stone's touch is most sure when he directs his attention to elites, to the noble and greater gentry families of England. His account of marital and familial changes among the greater landed families in the eighteenth century, and especially the development of a more domestic and affectionate life style, is of great value and has received powerful corroboration in the recent work of Professor Ralph Trumbach.[40] His touch is less sure, however, when he directs his comments at the propertyless and poor. Here there are any number of provocative judgements.[41] Given the absence of historical work across the broad front of marital history, Professor Stone's book must be regarded, as presumably it was partly intended, as a *ballon d'essai*—though one of dirigible dimensions.

One has only to chart the subjects appropriate to the history of marriage to confirm the vast areas of ignorance and uncertainty that still prevail. Our knowledge is still extraordinarily patchy: good in some areas, sadly deficient in others. Among the subjects open for discussion would be such things as the esteem in which the institution and its obverse—celibacy—were held, along with changes through time and across cultures; the degrees to which those eligible were willing and able to enter into it; the relationships between law and social practice; ideal and aberrant matrimonial forms; the nature and significance of ritual and ceremony; the ages at which marriage took

---

[37] Cited in C. L. Powell, *English Domestic Relations, 1487–1653* (New York, 1917), p. 115.
[38] Cited in Furnivall, *Child Marriages,* p. xxxiv.
[39] L. Stone, *The Crisis of the Aristocracy, 1558–1641* (Oxford, 1965), p. 790.
[40] R. Trumbach, *The Rise of the Egalitarian Family* (London, 1978).
[41] Such as: 'They procreated extensively, partly because of social tradition, and partly for lack of forethought and self-control'; or 'After marriage, fairly brutal treatment of wives by husbands was normal' (*The Family,* pp. 393, 421).

place; the costs of matrimony, and who bore them; and the extent of what the sociologists call endogamy and exogamy. The last hinges on a wide range of relevant issues: not least on what qualities were considered desirable in a potential spouse, and by whom. Much might depend on who made the important decisions, whether parents, other kin, or the parties themselves. This, in turn, might determine the nature of courtship and other preparations for marriage, including perhaps complex property arrangements. The whole question of the role of husbands and wives is virtually open-ended in its potentialities. Less so are those questions relating to the termination of matrimony: the legal and other devices available; the degree to which they were resorted to; and the attitudes with which termination, and perhaps re-entry into matrimony, are regarded. At almost every point marriage practices are revealing of society and its attitudes. This is because marriage is a social act: it involves more than two people; it is hedged by law and custom; it is subject to often intense feelings of approval and disapproval; it profoundly alters the status of the parties, especially women and any children they might bear; and it is nearly always accompanied by transfers of legal rights and, frequently, of property.

The essays collected here touch on many of these issues and, it is hoped, make valuable contributions to our understanding in particular areas. An equally important product of a collection such as this, however, is the way in which these separate essays interact in the reader's mind. Although each was designed as a separate, self-contained study, and individually they repair deficiencies in our knowledge and extend our awareness of the scope and complexities of the subject, they do also mutually reinforce each other in various ways. This is not only because there are themes common to several of these studies but also because discussion of a particular problem in one place and time raises questions about its existence in other places and at other times.

The laws relating to the formation of marriage, their evolution and application, are themes which engage many of these contributors.[42] Christopher Brooke's study deals with that shadowy period from which the canon law of marriage emerged more sharply defined; Martin Ingram deals with

---

[42] The development of marriage law is one of the more brightly illuminated areas in the history of English marriage, but dark patches remain, especially on the subject of why Parliament came to intervene in this one-time clerical preserve. There have been valuable studies recently of the background to the Abduction Act of 1487 in E. W. Ives, '"Agaynst taking awaye of women": the inception and operation of the abduction act of 1487' in *Wealth and Power in Tudor England,* ed. E. W. Ives. R. J. Knecht and J. J. Scarisbrick (London, 1978), pp. 21–44; and of the Commonwealth Act of 1650 'for suppressing the detestable sins of incest, adultery and fornication' in K. Thomas, 'The puritans and adultery: the act of 1650 reconsidered' in *Puritans and Revolutionaries,* ed. D. Pennington and K. Thomas (Oxford, 1978). But good subjects remain. Similar work now requires to be done, for example, on such measures as the Bigamy Act of James I's first parliament (1 Jac. I, c. 11), and that curious measure, the 'Act for granting to his Majesty certain rates and duties upon marriages, births and burials, and upon bachelors and widowers' (6 & 7 Wm. & Mary, c. 6).

questions of how that law was practised in provincial English ecclesiastical courts between the late Middle Ages and the seventeenth century. If the first study reveals the law in a state of flux, the second indicates how a relatively unchanging law could be used in different ways over time, both by those who resorted to it and those who administered it. What is also immediately noticeable is how different are the *dramatis personae* of these studies. In Brooke's essay it is kings, queens, nobles and other high-placed persons who occupy the stage. Their marital ambitions and machinations are undoubtedly important. They help to shape that law at decisive points, as he reminds us, and as Henry VIII's difficulties were subtly to shape English marriage law in the sixteenth century. The rich and powerful play a dual role, as law-breakers and law-makers. It is noteworthy, for example, that it was high-placed courtiers, like Sir Ralph Sadler and William Parr, Marquis of Northampton, who in the mid sixteenth century were first able to secure private acts of parliament confirming second, but strictly speaking bigamous, marriages, and later seventeenth-century parliamentary divorces were also instituted on the marital difficulties of well-placed males.[43] It is a wider cross-section of society which troops, however, through Ingram's provincial courts, though with noticeably diminishing frequency by the early seventeenth century. Annulment cases were never frequent, and spousal cases fell to a trickle. Both authors see clerical successes and failures in the developments they attempt to trace, and the Church's role in the history of marriage is throughout a curious mixture of both. The Church's insistence on the notion that marriage was grounded essentially in the free consent of both parties to it, and the failure in Protestant England to adopt in the mid sixteenth century the principle then adopted in the Catholic world that marriages to be valid must be conducted publicly by priests, made clandestinity the curse of the future. There is evidence that the second half of the seventeenth century witnessed something of a flight from regular marriage—that conducted strictly according to the canons of the established Church. The evidence for this lies not in prosecutions for clandestinity but in the suspicious falls of entries of marriages in parish registers, in the rise of notorious irregular marriage centres, and in contemporary complaints about the flight from regular marriage.[44] The attitude of the ecclesiastical courts may be partly responsible for this development but the responsibility was not theirs alone. Some blame must also be attached to the disruptions

[43] These early cases are discussed briefly by Dibdin, *English Church Law,* pp. 62–9, and the Sadler case more fully by A. J. Slavin, *Politics and Profit: A Study of Sir Ralph Sadler, 1507–1547* (Cambridge, 1966), pp. 212–18.

[44] A. Tindal Hart, *Clergy and Society 1600–1800* (London, 1968), p. 57; *Seventeenth-Century Economic Documents,* ed. J. Thirsk and J. P. Cooper (Oxford, 1972), p. 742; E. A. Wrigley, 'Clandestine marriage in Tetbury in the late seventeenth century', *Local Population Studies,* 10 (Spring 1973), 15–21; P. Laslett, *Family Life and Illicit Love in Earlier Generations* (Cambridge, 1977), pp. 125–32.

of tradition that occurred in the Interregnum, the growth of both Non-conformity and irreligion, settlement laws that penalized married labourers, taxes on marriage licences and certificates, and perhaps also, as war and emigration reduced the supply of eligible young men, a sex balance which tilted against the marriage chances of young women.[45]

The story of the rise and fall of the most notorious of the irregular marriage centres, the Fleet Prison and its precincts, is related here by Roger Lee Brown. The most impressive feature of this extraordinary episode is the sheer number of couples apparently resorting to the Fleet—well over 6,000 a year by 1740. If most of these couples were currently residing in the metropolitan area, this would suggest that a high proportion of London's population was marrying in this peculiar institution.[46] If these assumptions are correct it might even suggest that regular marriage in the London of the first half of the eighteenth century was a minority practice, and as such worthy of special investigation. There are strong reminders in this episode that the poor, and perhaps the urban poor especially, were laws unto themselves. It raises questions also about some of their other marital practices, such as the curious custom of wife-selling that occasionally surfaces in the record.[47]

Clandestine marriage in England was curbed by Lord Hardwicke's Act of 1753,[48] a measure of fundamental importance in the development of English marriage law. No such measure was passed in Scotland, however, and Christopher Smout here describes how English couples made their way to Scotland in increasing numbers, until that flow was curbed by Lord Brougham's Act in 1856, a measure hastened by the arrival of the railway at Carlisle. The notion that marriage required little more than attested consent and eligibility remained the basis of Scottish marriage law until 1940, a constant reminder of the separateness of Scottish law and custom, though the growth of irregular marriage there clearly had affinities with marriage by ecclesiastical licence in eighteenth-century England and with civil marriage after 1837.[49] The potentialities for future cross-cultural comparisons are manifold. Leslie Clarkson deals in this volume with the Irish conundrum of how what one commentator has called 'the most de-sexed

---

[45] Some of this is hinted at in the document printed in Thirsk and Cooper (note 44 above); D. Marshall, *English Poor in the Eighteenth Century* (London, 1926), pp. 206–7, 223–4; R. Thompson, *Women in Stuart England and America* (London, 1974), pp. 21–59.

[46] E. A. Wrigley, 'A simple model of London's importance in changing English society and economy', *Past & Present* (1967), p. 44, places London's population in 1750 at *c*. 675,000. Even assuming a high marriage rate of 10 per 1,000 population this would give only 6,750 metropolitan marriages a year.

[47] Discussed briefly in Stone, *The Family*, pp. 40–1.

[48] 26 Geo. II, c. 33.

[49] R. B. Outhwaite, 'Age at marriage in England from the late seventeenth to the nineteenth century', *Transactions of the Royal Historical Society*, 23 (1973), 55–70; O. Anderson, 'The incidence of civil marriage in Victorian England and Wales', *Past & Present* (1975), 50–87.

nation on earth',[50] a people with the latest ages of marriage of which we have record, and some of the lowest rates of nuptiality, nevertheless contrived to produce some of the highest rates of age-specific marital fertility. In his own agenda for future research he draws attention to the need to examine Irish communities elsewhere, but our understanding could also be increased by comparing post-famine Ireland with, for example, the northern Scottish highlands. There too the population actually fell, though not as drastically; there too emigration was pronounced; there too there were marked imbalances between the sexes (but in the highlands a preponderance of females in the reproductive age groups); and there too marriage was delayed, for men as well as women.[51] The principal difference, and it is this feature of Irish life which exercises Dr. Clarkson, is that the Irish combined all this with very high rates of marital fertility, while in the Scottish highlands rates were by contrast extremely low.[52]

A good many of these authors address themselves also to the circumstances controlling entry into marriage. One problem derives from the fact that for much of this period girls and boys were legally able to marry at very early ages (12 and 14 respectively) but in the European societies considered here the women appear on average to have delayed marriage for a decade at least, men for rather longer. Custom combined itself with economic conditions to dictate, for the bulk of ordinary people, that they lived separately from their parents and in these circumstances some measure of financial independence was necessary. Olwen Hufton here describes vividly for us the trials and tribulations of poor French girls, desperately striving to accumulate dowries to attract husbands. How much of this behaviour could be replicated in eighteenth-century England? It must be hoped that English archives, perhaps Poor Law records especially, will supply materials for comparable studies, for many important questions remain unanswered. How far down the social scale, for example, did the institution of the dowry descend? What is noticeable in Professor Hufton's study is how necessary it apparently was for these French girls to migrate in search of economic opportunity and husbands, a need shared not only by nineteenth-century Irish girls but also by Vivien Elliott's newcomers to seventeenth-century London. Dr. Elliott's skilful and persistent analysis is important in uncovering the different domestic circumstances and marriage opportunities of migrant and non-migrant girls. The death of a parent, she suggests, may well have precipitated a good deal of this female migration to London. Once there, the absence of nearby kin, and consequent family support and influence, meant more menial

---

[50] D. S. Connery, *The Irish* (London, 1968), p. 161. An interesting discussion of some of the mechanics and manifestations of this desexualization in one remote Irish island community is J. C. Messenger, 'Sex and repression in an Irish folk community', in *Human Sexual Behaviour*, ed. D. S. Marshall and R. C. Suggs (New York, 1971).

[51] Cf. *Scottish Population History*, ed. M. Flinn *et al.* (Cambridge, 1977), pp. 301–34, and R. E. Kennedy, *The Irish: Emigration, Marriage, and Fertility* (Berkeley, 1973), pp. 139–72.

[52] Flinn, *Scottish Population*, pp. 335–48, and Kennedy, *The Irish*, pp. 173–205.

employments and later marriages. They married later than London-born girls, a higher proportion of whom were living with kin—kin who may also have been anxious to see them settled in life before they themselves died in that unhealthy urban environment. What comes out of many of these studies is the complexity and interrelation of the circumstances governing the opportunities and incentives to marry. Far too often also attention has been focused on men, and subjects such as the ages at which women marry have been analysed by reference to male employments.[53] Now women are being considered as something more than mere male appendages. Things like the sex ratio and the nature of female employments are clearly important conditioners but they must also be joined by other things, such as whether parents were actually alive at the crucial time when marriage could be considered. Peter Laslett, in particular, has reminded us of the importance of orphanhood in these early modern societies, and a fresh reminder of its importance comes here in Lloyd Bonfield's finding that a high proportion of landed gentry fathers in the later seventeenth century were not alive at the time when their eldest sons came to be married themselves. The 'strict settlement' was adopted by these sons, and not always thrust upon them by fathers determined to perpetuate the patrimony. What Dr. Bonfield has succeeded in doing is to put marriage back into these marriage settlements: they now look rather less like devices designed to ensure the perpetual integrity of property and rather more like devices designed to ensure that jointures for widows were fixed and portions and pensions for other family members would be found. There is perhaps some evidence here for that growth of 'affect'—affection between the spouses and between parents and children—that Professor Stone has documented in other ways.

Affection in courtship and marriage was not, however, an invention of the seventeenth century. Christopher Brooke makes valiant attempts to explore the boundaries of marital sentiment in medieval times. His materials have perforce to be mainly literary ones, but they are accompanied by important caveats as to their purpose and use: literature depends for its success, he reminds us, on reversing values. But not always: Kathleen Davies insists, for example, that her matrimonial conduct books described an already established behaviour pattern. Much obviously depends on the literary form. Quite clearly also letters, diaries and personal memoirs offer the best hope of making real progress in this difficult field. Miriam Slater's and Penina Glazer's unearthing of the refreshingly candid recollections of two nineteenth-century American physicians trying to resolve the conflicting demands of being both wife and professional pioneer, suggests the very great possibilities for illumination of attitudes and behaviour that lie in the modern period. Nineteenth- and twentieth-century marital history need not be severely statistical; nor are these insights only possible in modern times, as

---

[53] The editor pleads guilty: Outhwaite, 'Age at marriage', pp. 60-2.

Miriam Slater's earlier study of the seventeenth-century Verney family has revealed.[54] A fresh attack on such personal materials is called for, if only to attempt to discover what discretion the doctrine of consent gave to young people and what role sentiment played in their choices. Love is a very inexact term and without careful definition its use must be more of a handicap than a help. People can be chosen for very different qualities, and attempting to discern and categorize the bases of such choices must be one of the priorities for future research.

---

[54] M. Slater, 'The weightiest business: marriage in an upper-gentry family in seventeenth-century England', *Past & Present* (1976), 25–54. That even with a well-documented family like this there are difficult problems of interpretation can be seen in the lively debate which followed: *Past & Present* (1979), 126–40.

I

Marriage and Society in the Central Middle Ages

CHRISTOPHER N. L. BROOKE

'Marriage is a sin which it is sinful to repent of.' Thus John Henry Newman when he learned of the engagement of Henry Wilberforce, youngest son of the great evangelical emancipator, William Wilberforce;[1] it was the ironic comment of an exasperated celibate who had seen most of his closest disciples, one by one, fall for matrimony. So close was Henry to Newman that he let some months pass after his engagement before telling his friend. When Newman eventually learned at second hand of the happy, or unhappy, event, he wrote a highly characteristic letter to Hurrell Froude in which annoyance and amusement were equally mingled, concluding with the sentence quoted above. It might have passed as the signature tune of the attitude of the ascetic theologians of the eleventh and twelfth centuries in whose hands marriage became a Christian sacrament.[2]

[1] M. Trevor, *Newman, The Pillar of the Cloud* (London, 1962), p. 159, cited in D. Newsome, *The Parting of Friends* (London, 1966), p. 154.

[2] This chapter is based on lectures I have given in a number of universities in England, Canada and Germany, and I owe much to friends and colleagues, and to the audiences which have listened to them, and helped me with advice and criticism: most recently, a version of it was presented as part of my programme as Snider Visiting Professor in Scarborough College, University of Toronto, at the generous invitation of the Principal and under the guidance of my friend Professor Michael Gervers. My earlier debts include especially kind help at various stages from my wife, Dr. Rosalind Brooke, and from Frau B. Hesse and Professor Nicolai Rubinstein. Recently I have benefited from discussions with my pupil, Miss Carolyn Moule, who is studying the entry into marriage in the eleventh and twelfth centuries. Pp. 27–8 are based on my Inaugural Lecture at Cambridge, *Marriage in Christian History* (Cambridge University Press, 1978), with the kind consent of the Syndics of the Press; and some of the legal aspects and examples here cited are explored rather more fully in 'Aspects of marriage law in the eleventh and twelfth centuries', *Proceedings of the 5th International Congress of Medieval Canon Law* (Salamanca, Sept. 1976; publ. Vatican City, 1980), pp. 333–44. In a brief survey it has been impossible to enter more than summarily into the vital issues of feudal inheritance and aristocratic succession: for England, for example, see S. F. C. Milsom, *The Legal Framework of English Feudalism* (Cambridge, 1976), ch. 5.

There is an admirable brief bibliography of the whole field in *Family and Marriage in Medieval Europe: a working Bibliography*, ed. M. M. Sheehan and K. D. Scardellato (Toronto, 1976); another by J. Gaudemet and M. Zimmermann has just been published: J. Gaudemet, *Sociétés et mariage* (Strasbourg, 1980), pp. 454–77. For the background, see esp. *Il matrimonio nella società altomedievale* (XXIV Settimana di Studio del Centro Italiano sull'Alto Medioevo, 2 vols., Spoleto, 1977) and now also Gaudemet; on theology and law, G. Le Bras and others, in *Dictionnaire de Théologie Catholique* (henceforth *DTC*), IX (Paris, 1926), coll. 2044-2317; on canon law also R. Naz in *Dictionnaire de Droit Canonique*

A former generation of scholars noted the extreme caution and conservatism of the eleventh- and twelfth-century theologians on marriage—their tendency to prefer the celibate life, and to countenance sexual relations even between husband and wife only if the sole purpose was the procreation of children, and so long as they took no pleasure in the act itself. In a world of such ideas it seemed hard to understand how marriage came to find a place among the seven sacraments at all; and the story is indeed paradoxical. But more recently many scholars have observed that in all sorts of ways the twelfth century marked a turning point: social historians, with Georges Duby among the foremost, have stressed how great a change came over the attitude of the landed aristocracy of western Europe; historians of the Church and of canon law, led by Michael Sheehan and others, have stressed the change in ecclesiastical attitudes, the new role accorded to consent and choice.[3] A world of new ideas has been discerned, almost to the point that we may be in danger of forgetting how much remained as before: how narrow a view the theologians continued to take of the purpose and nature of the sacrament; how little real choice or freedom most women could hope to enjoy. The theme of this chapter is indeed that many of the old attitudes remained unchanged, and that beside them a whole world of fresh ideas grew up, which were to live for centuries in uneasy harmony with the old. Much work on later periods indeed turns on questions to which the evidence of the central Middle Ages offers no answers: such as the age at which partners entered marriage, the proportion of the men and women in an age group who married, movements in fertility and the like. Our information is confined for the most part to the aristocracy, and even there it is relatively unusual to know a bride's precise age.[4] Yet if we spread our net wide and deep, there is a great deal about the marriage customs of this age which can be known. Much recent work on the later history of marriage has been concerned to find greater freedom of movement or choice in this or that century—sometimes the nineteenth, sometimes the eighteenth, sometimes the seventeenth.[5] Some of these new beginnings had been in a measure anticipated long before; and a good case can be made for reckoning the twelfth century a time of more substantial change. But in truth I am a little in rebellion

---

(henceforth *DDC*), VI (Paris, 1957), coll. 740–87; J. Dauvillier, *Le mariage dans le droit classique de l'Eglise* (Paris, 1933); on liturgy, J. B. Molin and P. Mutembe, *Le rituel du mariage en France du XIIe au XVIe siècle* (Paris, 1974); all with references to the earlier literature. The subject of medieval marriage, long neglected, has blossomed into a copious literature in recent years; only skeletal reference to this can be given in a brief article.

[3] See esp. M. M. Sheehan, 'Choice of marriage partner in the Middle Ages: development and mode of application of a theory of marriage', in *Studies in Mediaeval and Renaissance History*, new series, I (1978), 3–33; Brooke, 'Aspects of marriage law'.

[4] Before 1200, very rare indeed: for exceptional cases see below, pp. 19–20, 31.

[5] See esp. Lawrence Stone's *The Family, Sex and Marriage in England 1500–1800* (London, 1977), a book which is perhaps excessively given to find change where only variety can be seen, but has provided a notable stimulus to all students of the history of marriage.

against the whole conception of novelty and change: for what is striking is the way in which different attitudes can live together; what happened in the twelfth century, and perhaps in the seventeenth and eighteenth, was a widening of the variety of sentiment, rather than the total *bouleversement* of human attitudes.

But all this is very abstract, and one can make sense of the history of marriage only in periods like the twelfth century, when statistics are lacking and whole strata of society banned from view, by concrete illustration.

On 18 May 1152 Henry, Duke of Normandy and Count of Anjou, and pretender to the throne of England, married Eleanor, Countess of Poitou and Duchess of Aquitaine, ex-wife of Louis VII, ex-Queen of France.[6] Henry was 19 at the time; a few months later he assumed the title Duke of Aquitaine; when he was 21 he became King of England. The young King Henry II must have been deeply impressed by the importance of the marriage bond as a key to everything that made his world what it was. It was a world in which both the Church and secular society—for quite different reasons, at least in large measure—had come to take strict monogamy, and the larger idea of legitimate marriage, more seriously than western Christendom had taken it for many centuries. Henry's great-grandfather, William I, the Conqueror, was known to contemporaries as Willelmus Notus, the bastard; he was illegitimate. Yet his youngest son Henry claimed England and won Normandy, basing his claims on a plea of strict legitimacy; and Henry II likewise claimed, through his mother the Empress Matilda, to be King of England and Duke of Normandy, and through his father to be Count of Anjou—claimed and realized his claims. This illustrates some of the ways in which legitimate inheritance had taken on a new lease of life; and it would be highly surprising if Henry had not meditated deeply on this fact. His treatment of his children reveals that he had learned the lesson far too well. The younger Henry, his eldest surviving son, he betrothed when he was three and a half to the French Princess Margaret, who was younger still. When the next boy, Richard, was just four an arrangement was made for his marriage to Alice, Margaret's younger sister, who was perhaps two. Next Geoffrey was betrothed when he was seven to the heiress of Brittany, and John, aged four, was the subject of one of Henry II's most dazzling schemes, which (if it had come to pass) would have made him lord of a string of castles from the Alps to Turin.[7] As for the daughters, Matilda, aged 11, was sent to marry Henry the Lion, Duke of Saxony, and to become

---

[6] On Henry II and his family, see W. L. Warren, *Henry II* (London, 1973); for some of the details cf. *The Letters of John of Salisbury,* II, ed. W. J. Millor and C. N. L. Brooke (Oxford Medieval Texts, 1979), pp. 6–7, 638–9 and nn.

[7] Warren, *Henry II,* pp. 101, 563 (Geoffrey), 117, 221 (John); on the negotiations with Savoy, see esp. C. W. Previté-Orton, *The Early History of the House of Savoy* (Cambridge, 1912), pp. 337–41. Professor Warren seems to me to take too limited a view of Henry's intentions in 1173; but he rightly points out that the bride's death need not have ended the plan, had not the great rebellion of 1173–74 diverted Henry's attention elsewhere.

a few years later the mother of the future Emperor Otto IV. Eleanor, at eight or nine, was betrothed to the King of Castile; Joan at 11 became Queen of Sicily. Not all the schemes for the sons came to fruition, and in principle the Church always insisted that the partners must give their own consent when they reached the age of puberty (approximately 14 for the husband, 12 for the wife).[8] The whole basis of Henry II's system was legitimate monogamy; yet in few other respects did his attitude to marriage conform to the Church's; and he certainly paid little attention either to his children's consent or to domestic bliss in his matrimonial arrangements. Nor, it must be said, did his rival, the more conventionally pious Louis VII, who seems to have been content to see two little daughters pass into Henry's power—a complaisance more incomprehensible in human terms than Henry's absurd haste in marrying off his children almost before they were born. Louis' acceptance of these arrangements meant that one of the little girls was in the charge of her stepmother, Eleanor, Henry's queen, and formerly Louis'.[9] For this is the fundamental irony of the whole story: that all Henry's schemes depended on his marriage to Eleanor. This was in the first place a perfectly correct marriage by the Church's law, yet to a woman whose first husband still lived;[10] so that the legitimacy of both the English and the French lines depended on the rather frail grounds of consanguinity for the annulment of the marriage of Louis and Eleanor: they were third cousins once removed. And the second irony of the story is that Henry neglected two crucial elements in marriage: good relations with his wife, and reasonable understanding with his children. Henry's empire was built up on marriage alliances; and in the case of his own parents, strained relations between the spouses actually helped their dynastic schemes forward. But in his own family, after 15 years or so of successful partnership with Eleanor and the birth of eight children, the domestic scene became a battle-ground, and the failure of Henry to keep on reasonable terms with wife and sons was the principal cause of the collapse of his empire.

---

[8] *DDC*, I (ed. R. Naz, Paris, 1935) coll. 343–8; cf. Dauvillier, *Le mariage,* pp. 37–9, 43 ff.; *Decretalium Gregorii pp. IX compilatio* in *Corpus Iuris Canonici,* ed. Friedberg, II (Leipzig, 1881), 4, 2, cc. 3, 11, 14. It is evident that these ages were normally treated as approximate. For the details on Henry II's daughters, see R. W. Eyton, *Court, Household and Itinerary of King Henry II* (London and Dorchester, 1878), pp. 18, 54–5, 86, 108–9, 209, 211; Warren, *Henry II,* esp. p. 117.

[9] *Letters of John of Salisbury,* II, 6–7 (no. 136). Louis VII is usually reckoned more conventionally pious and (within limits) humane than Henry II.

[10] I.e. their marriage had been annulled; annulment was the only form of 'divorce' normally recognized in medieval canon law, although 'divorce' by separation (i.e. without the possibility of remarriage) was permissible if both partners entered religion, as in the case of Heloise and Abelard. See in general *DDC*, IV (1949), 1315 ff.; *DTC*, IV (1924), 1455–78; Dauvillier, *Le mariage,* pp. 279–367 (who also deals, pp. 279–80, 301 ff., with the curious problem of divorce 'pour cause d'absence'; for the special problems of crusaders' wives, see J. A. Brundage in *Studia Gratiana,* XII (1967)(= *Collectanea S. Kuttner,* II), 425–41, XIV (1967)(= *Collectanea S. Kuttner,* IV), 241–51).

Henry II of England is an extreme example of a familiar figure in twelfth-century society: the head of a great landed family to whom marriage is first and foremost a vehicle for dynastic, and landed, ambition. My second example illustrates quite a different area of the marriage market. In 1118 Heloise and Abelard went through a form of marriage service and received a priestly blessing.[11] The full significance of this extraordinary event has never been expounded, for to most modern commentators it seems perfectly natural that a man and woman deeply in love, who have just had a child, should wish to get married. But it was not so obvious at the time. As the law then stood, it should not have happened: Abelard was probably in higher orders and certainly a canon;[12] anyone with any serious knowledge of the laws of marriage and celibacy almost certainly knew that marriage was forbidden to canons, quite certainly that it was forbidden to all clergy in the orders of subdeacon or above. But as the law was then drawn, such a marriage, though illegal, was probably reckoned—again, by anyone with serious knowledge of the law—as valid. The date is striking, for it was probably a few years later that the decree or decretal was promulgated which destroyed the validity of clerical marriages as well as confirming that they were illegal.[13] So far as our evidence goes, it was quite normal, even common, for canons in the cathedral closes of western Christendom to have spouses: doubtless they had often been treated as wives, even though the Church had officially designated them concubines.[14] To Abelard, an eminent career ecclesiastic and a canon, and Heloise, a girl brought up in a cathedral close, the customary relationship would have been familiar, and (one might have supposed) entirely acceptable. Both Abelard and Heloise, in their subsequent correspondence, strongly emphasize that this was so—that Heloise would have preferred to be called mistress, strumpet, what-have-you, to being condemned for bringing Abelard's ecclesiastical career to a disastrous end by submitting him to the marriage bond. He himself relates with some complacency how he had explained to Heloise's outraged uncle, Canon Fulbert, that there was nothing in the event to astonish a man who knew anything of love's power, or had pondered on the frequency with which women, from the very origin of the human race, had brought men to ruin; and how, none the less, he had offered Fulbert something far more than he could have expected: to marry the girl.[15] Even more striking is the space

[11] Abelard, *Historia Calamitatum*, ed. J. Monfrin (2nd edn., Paris, 1962), p. 79; cf. Brooke, *Medieval Church and Society* (London, 1971), pp. 74–5n.; and Brooke, 'Aspects of marriage law', pp. 341–2.

[12] Brooke, *Medieval Church and Society*, loc. cit.

[13] Gratian, *Decretum*, D. 27 c.8 (ed. E. Friedberg, *Corpus Iuris Canonici*, I, Leipzig, 1897, p. 100); on this decree see J. Alberigo *et al.*, *Conciliorum Oecumenicorum Decreta* (3rd edn., Bologna, 1973), p. 194, c.21 and cf. p. 188; Brooke, 'Aspects of marriage law', p. 342 n.

[14] See Brooke in *Cambridge Historical Journal*, XXI, i (1956), 1–21, esp. 10–18, 20 (repr. *Medieval Church and Society*, pp. 69–99); on celibacy in general, *DTC*, II (1923), 2068–88; on concubinage see esp. J. A. Brundage in *Journal of Medieval History*, I (1975), 1–17.

[15] *Historia Calamitatum*, ed. Monfrin, pp. 74–9.

Abelard then devotes to Heloise's arguments against the fatal step. These arguments are extremely revealing; for the moment their importance to us lies in this fact—that they show a powerful awareness of the difference, not so much in law as in Christian faith and practice, between the permanent bond of marriage and the freely terminable bond of canon and concubine.

These two examples have revealed how men of very different cast of mind and background could none the less, in the same century, find extremely powerful reasons for taking the marriage bond more seriously than their ancestors had done.[16] If we look deeply into these examples, and the areas of marriage custom and sentiment which they illustrate, we can roughly separate four themes which will be the centre of our enquiry: marriage as the basis for the inheritance of land; marriage in the law and theology of the western Church; marriage in the liturgy; and the relation of marriage to the literary themes and cult of courtly love in the lyrics and romances of the twelfth and early thirteenth centuries.[17]

Of these perhaps the best known is the growing importance of inheritance as a central pillar in landholding and the social structure of the upper classes. In his brilliant lectures on *Medieval Marriage* Georges Duby set out to describe three aspects of the changing world of marriage in the French high aristocracy.[18] First of all, the older view in which 'marriage . . . regulated the sexual impulses, but only in the interests of a patrimony', and young men unpossessed of land, the *juvenes* to whom M. Duby has so often returned, had to make do with less formal liaisons; and coming into increasing evidence in the twelfth century, a new situation in which domesticity, settled landholding by married couples, could be spread more widely in a more prosperous society.[19] In his second lecture he concentrates more precisely on the specific case of the French royal house, which on the one hand achieved a reputation in the eyes of the Church and the Papacy for piety, and on the other hand consistently broke the Church's rules, as king after king divorced his wife with impunity. In this respect the French kings marked an extreme; and their 'divorces' or annulments belong to the most tangled area of the Church's law.[20] In the English royal house annulment or divorce was much

---

[16] It is true that both Abelard and Henry of Anjou came from northern France; my examples have ranged only over the Anglo-French world so far, and only among the aristocracy and the moderately well-to-do. But their attitudes reflect something which was happening over western Christendom at large, and I shall say a little about Germany below.

[17] For the social and geographical limitations of this study, see n. 16; but see also below n. 59 for some of the recent literature on peasant marriage.

[18] G. Duby, *Medieval Marriage: Two Models from Twelfth-Century France* (trans. E. Forster, Baltimore and London, 1978).

[19] Duby, *Medieval Marriage,* ch. I, esp. pp. 7, 11 ff.; see also Duby's *discorso inaugurale* to the Spoleto Settimana, *Il matrimonio,* I, 13–39.

[20] Duby, *Medieval Marriage,* ch. II. But his account of the changing attitude of Bishop Ivo of Chartres needs some revision (now being undertaken by Miss C. Moule: see n. 31, and see also the criticisms, which are, however, in my view much exaggerated, of J. C. Moore in *American Historical Review,* LXXXIV (1979), 440).

less common, and reliance on marriage to sustain and extend the heritage relatively greater, than in the French; but this is a political not a moral judgement, for neither Henry I nor Henry II was noted for his marital fidelity.[21] In his third lecture Professor Duby unfolds one of the remarkable case histories in which the French chronicles of this period are exceptionally rich: the chronicle of the house of Guînes, in which we see marriage as an aristocratic institution firmly established at the centre of a world in which love and lust and informal liaisons and the social institutions of household, estate and inheritance, are all reflected in rich and varied tones.[22] To discern in this field how much is old, how much new, is a very delicate matter. Kingdoms and estates had in some measure turned on marriage and inheritance time out of mind, yet no social historian doubts that rules of inheritance had developed—further in some areas of Europe than in others, with many varieties of local custom—and that some principles of succession by inheritance counted more strictly in the twelfth century than before, almost everywhere. The example of Henry II is an extreme case, but not uncharacteristic of its age.

It is in the strange and often strained relations between the Church's teaching and the landed nobility's practice of marriage that we see this sharpening of focus most clearly: for it is evident in a variety of ways that in the late eleventh and twelfth centuries there was a new emphasis on monogamy both in social custom and in canon law.[23] In this period of the Middle Ages more land passed by inheritance than heretofore, more by some kind of primogeniture:[24] unambiguous legitimacy came increasingly to be the key to landed estates. The Church in a sense had always insisted on monogamy: it is a fundamental element in Christian teaching in the New Testament and the Fathers. But in two ways the edge of canon law became sharper in this period. The distinction between a wife and a concubine had commonly in the past been somewhat ambiguous. In the social custom of the later Roman empire the concubine had a perfectly acknowledged status, but no security. The celebrated story of Augustine's concubine illustrates this: she lived with him and she was faithful to him, and was rudely cast aside

---

[21] Henry I acknowledged over 20 illegitimate children (GEC, *Complete Peerage*, revised edn., ed. V. Gibbs *et al.*, London, 1910–59, XI (ed. G. H. White, 1949), Appendix D, pp. 105–21); on Henry II's mistresses see Warren, *Henry II*, pp. 119, 601, 611.

[22] Duby, *Medieval Marriage*, ch. III, based on Lambert of Ardres, *Historia comitum Ghisnensium (Monumenta Germaniae Historica, Scriptores*, XXIV).

[23] Cf. the discussion in my *Marriage in Christian History*; for canon law, Dauvillier, *Le mariage*. But for a corrective to such general statements, see the Spoleto *Settimana, Il matrimonio*.

[24] Needless to say, custom varied greatly in different parts of Europe, and primogeniture only won a secure hold in north-western Europe. For the general context, see M. Bloch, *Feudal Society* (Eng. trans., London, 1961). Even where primogeniture was in the ascendant, many subtle problems were disputed: the arguments as to whether John or the son of his elder brother, Prince Arthur, should succeed to the English throne and the Angevin dominions in 1199 richly illustrate the development of these problems.

when Augustine, still unregenerate, prepared to marry the little girl his mother had chosen to be his wife.[25] In the early Middle Ages canonists recognized even certain affinities between concubinage and marriage; and King Cnut was not exceptional in living openly with a Norman wife in England and an English concubine in Denmark.[26] These relationships show that marriage had not acquired the unique quality it was later to have; and many an early medieval nobleman seems to have assumed that he was free to end an uncongenial marriage. The canon lawyers, needless to say, contested this view. But for two reasons the prohibition of divorce could be fairly blunt. First of all, there was great ambiguity in the teaching and practice of the early Church on the conditions under which marriages could be dissolved. It was always held that marriage between a Christian and a pagan could be broken by consent, and it was not until the twelfth and thirteenth centuries that the Church attempted seriously to defend the freedom of slaves to make effective marriages.[27] The ancient tradition that adultery was sufficient ground for divorce also took an unconscionable time in dying.[28] But more significant for the eleventh and twelfth centuries was the ecclesiastical hierarchy's deep-rooted horror of incest. Secondly, the Church was never able to prevent irregular matrimonial practices among the very great: the French royal house, with its numerous broken marriages, or the marriages arranged between princes and princesses across the frontiers of Byzantium, illustrate this.[29] In 1092 Philip I of France repudiated his first wife and married the Countess of Anjou in her husband's lifetime. The reactions to this blatant event have been finely analysed by Duby;[30] and he has shown in particular how the eminent canonist Bishop Ivo of Chartres—while always admitting the complexity of marriage law—gradually shifted his ground for condemning Philip's marriage from adultery or bigamy (which anyway ceased to be relevant when the first wife died in 1094) to incest.[31]

---

[25] Augustine, *Confessions*, vi, 15, 25 (cf. iv, 4, 7–9; iv, 2, 32): P. Brown, *Augustine of Hippo* (London, 1967), pp. 61–3, 88–9; Brooke, *Marriage in Christian History*, pp. 5–8.

[26] L. M. Larsen, *Canute the Great* (New York and London, 1912), pp. 128–30.

[27] The revolutionary decree of the (English) Pope Hadrian IV (1154–59) making valid marriages of unfree persons without their lords' consent, and its slow acceptance by canonists and theologians in the twelfth and thirteenth centuries, is discussed by P. Landau in *Studia Gratiana*, XII (1967), 511–53. On peasant marriage see also E. Searle in *Past & Present*, LXXXII (1979), 6.

[28] See *DDC*, I, 221–50, esp. 243–50.

[29] See esp. D. M. Nicol, 'Mixed marriages in Byzantium in the thirteenth century', *Studies in Church History*, I (1964), 160–72.

[30] Duby, *Medieval Marriage*, pp. 29–54.

[31] Ibid., pp. 30 ff.; but see above, n. 20. Professor Duby's discussion perhaps fails to do justice both to the consistency and lucidity of Ivo's position, since he notes the change in his ground without explaining the crucial relationship of the chronology of his letters to the turning point in 1094 when Bertha died and the marriage with Bertrada was 'solemnized'. It is clear that Ivo was always rigorist on adultery and incest, and that he condemned the marriage with Bertrada (in modern terminology) because they were third cousins once removed. He was both subtle and prudent in handling disputed questions, such as the effect of former

The Church had over many centuries promulgated an exceedingly elaborate and confusing table of prohibitions, which forbade a man to marry his third cousin (or in the view of the more rigid interpreters, a much more remote relation), and a number of women connected to him by affinity, which could be the result of marriage, fornication, adultery or godparenthood.[32] The last was to give rise to Gratian's famous, and absurd, *causa*, of the unfortunate man who acted godfather to his own child in a crowded baptistery by accident, and so incurred a relationship which might dictate formal separation from his wife.[33] Meanwhile, social custom was ambiguous on Philip's marriage: most of his subjects seem to have accepted it as necessary to keep up the supply of male children; the one boy born of the first marriage, when he became King Louis VI, encouraged posterity to condemn his father's outrageous conduct.[34] The Church tried to condemn, though with little practical effect.

We have shifted our ground, from social custom to canon law; and it is essential, if we are to understand the story of Philip I's marriages, to see why men of such scrupulous moral standards as Pope Urban II, Pope Paschal II and Bishop Ivo could be in any doubt on the issues. Our essential difficulty in understanding their viewpoint is that we find it hard to take seriously their table of prohibited degrees: we have inherited taboos against the marriage of very close relations, but find their objection to more distant marriages hard to fathom. Yet the point is fundamental. Ivo was shocked by bigamy and adultery; but on reflection reckoned that incest mattered more; and so apparently did Pope Urban.[35] His predecessors in the 1050s had set their faces against the marriage of William Duke of Normandy and Matilda of Flanders; and the two great abbeys in Caen are a monument to the penance they were compelled to perform for this act of indiscretion. There is, however, no agreement among modern historians as to how they were related.[36] In the present state of knowledge, it is reasonable to say that at the turn of the eleventh and twelfth centuries, annulment of marriages on the grounds of consanguinity—especially in situations where the wife was failing to produce a suitable heir—was common. In the French royal house it remained common; but not elsewhere. It is easy to be cynical about the

---

liaisons on the validity of subsequent marriages, and capable of using the word 'uxor' with extreme care in referring to Bertrada, without committing himself to its true significance; but on questions of law which he thought undisputed he was firm and clear and his great prestige at the time owed much to his reputation for integrity and firmness. I owe help in this problem to Miss C. Moule.

[32] Dauvillier, *Le mariage,* pp. 143–200.

[33] Gratian, *Decretum, Causa* 30.

[34] Cf. Duby, *Medieval Marriage,* pp. 35–6, 38.

[35] Duby, *Medieval Marriage,* pp. 33–4 and nn. (p. 120).

[36] See D. C. Douglas, *William the Conqueror* (London, 1964), pp. 391–3; *The Carmen de Hastingae proelio of Guy bishop of Amiens,* ed. C. Morton and H. Muntz (Oxford Medieval Texts, 1972), p. 63 n. 3, and refs.

frequency of annulment; but in the present state of knowledge it seems really to have suffered a marked decline in the twelfth century; and in ranks of society below the high aristocracy. Professor Helmholz's striking demonstration of the rarity of nullity cases in the English Church law courts in the late Middle Ages at present suggests a quite dramatic success in the campaign to make marriage a stable institution: stable at least in the sense that annulment or divorce seem to have been relatively rare.[37] Death, however, took its toll, and the expected length of marriage was probably much shorter in the Middle Ages than in most western countries even now, after the rapid recent rise in the divorce rate.[38]

If it be true that annulment became rarer in the twelfth century, the explanation seems tolerably clear: on the one hand, social custom and the common law made inheritance, and the whole ethos of family and household, depend more precisely than hitherto on legitimate marriage; and the Church had finally decided that incest was of less consequence than broken marriages, adultery or divorce. But this is only part of a new attempt by theologians, canon lawyers—the distinction had little meaning before the mid twelfth century[39]—and many of the more conscientious bishops and popes, to clarify the nature of marriage and defend it both as a sacrament and as a human institution.

Bishop Ivo shifted his ground in the 1090s and 1100s. So did Pope Alexander III in the 1160s and 1170s on the precise relation between consent and public ceremony in the entry to marriage.[40] In both cases it is clear that a conflict of precedents and pressures made consistency at first intolerably difficult for men of the highest standards. Pope Alexander tried for a time to enforce marriage *in facie ecclesiae*—that is to say, in some kind of ecclesiastical presence or ceremony—as an essential part of the marriage-making process.[41] But he was defeated by the flow of cases to Rome which revealed that many more informal processes of match-making flourished about Europe; and too premature or rigid a definition might well have unmade innumerable stable marriages. We encounter here another vital element in our story: the development of canon law, or papal jurisdiction, and above all of the system of appeals and decretals, makes the mid and late twelfth century a turning point in the practice of the courts; marriage became

---

[37] R. H. Helmholz, *Marriage Litigation in Medieval England* (Cambridge, 1974), esp. chs. II–III; cf. Brooke, 'Aspects of marriage law', p. 340 and n. 17. A rather rapid survey of the relevant information in the *Complete Peerage* (n. 21) confirms the impression that annulment for consanguinity was commoner in the early twelfth century, at least among the English nobility, than later.

[38] Cf. L. Stone, *The Family, Sex and Marriage in England 1500–1800* (London, 1977), esp. pp. 54–60.

[39] Cf. esp. S. Kuttner in *Studia Gratiana*, I (1953), 24; D. E. Luscombe, *The School of Peter Abelard* (Cambridge, 1969), ch. IX, 'Abelard and the *Decretum* of Gratian'.

[40] Dauvillier, *Le mariage*, pp. 17–54.

[41] Ibid., pp. 23–8.

subjected to the Church courts as never before.[42] This made it possible for the Pope to promulgate, after some changes of heart, a single doctrine for the first time in the history of the western Church. From the late twelfth century until the Council of Trent it was unambiguously the case that at the heart of every marriage lay an act of consent; and that consent *de praesenti* in the presence of witnesses—'to take you to wife here and now'—made a marriage which could not be dissolved, even if no religious ceremony, and no consummation, had taken place.[43]

Consent is of the essence of this doctrine, as a number of scholars have pointed out; most recently and effectively Professor Michael Sheehan.[44] By a strange paradox the clearest evidence that the idea of consent had won a new place in the eyes of responsible churchmen comes from the history of the monastic orders, the heart and hearth of an ascetic doctrine which took it for granted that marriage was a second best.[45] So far as our evidence goes, the normal age of entry to a monastery in the tenth and eleventh centuries lay between five and ten.[46] In a famous passage written in 1141 the Anglo-Norman monk Orderic Vitalis, who flourishes anew in our own day in Marjorie Chibnall's great edition, looked back to his childhood in Shropshire nearly 60 years before, when he was ten years old.[47] 'And so, O God of glory, who ordered Abraham to leave his country, his father's house and kindred, you inspired my father Odeler to give me up and surrender me wholly to you. Weeping, he gave a weeping child to Rainald the monk, and sent me into exile for your love—nor ever after saw me. A small boy did not presume to contradict his father, but I obeyed him in all things, since he promised me that I should possess paradise with the innocent.' Orderic's life as a monk was happy; but he was aware that he had lived in a time of changing notions, for by 1141 new orders had arisen which insisted that monks must enter only at the age of consent (14 at least) of their free will; and such ideas had begun to enter deep into the homes of traditional observance too.[48] Not only so, but Orderic's 56 years as a monk had witnessed an enormous expansion of monastic vocations, in a proportion far beyond

---

[42] Ibid., loc. cit. The evidence will be much clarified when the late Walther Holtzmann's corpus of twelfth-century decretals has been fully published: see meanwhile, *Studies in the Collections of Twelfth-century Decretals*, ed. W. Holtzmann, C. R. and M. G. Cheney, *Monumenta Iuris Canonici*, Series B, III (Vatican City, 1979).

[43] Dauvillier, *Le mariage*, pp. 76 ff.

[44] See esp. M. Sheehan, 'Choice of marriage partner in the Middle Ages: development and mode of application of a theory of marriage', *Studies in Medieval and Renaissance History*, new ser., I (1978), 3–33; Brooke, *Marriage in Christian History*, pp. 14 ff.

[45] This paragraph repeats my *Marriage in Christian History*, pp. 24–6 (with the kind permission of the Cambridge University Press).

[46] Cf. C. Brooke and W. Swaan, *The Monastic World 1000–1300* (London, 1974), pp. 87–8, 122; see below, at n. 48.

[47] *Ecclesiastical History of Orderic Vitalis*, ed. M. Chibnall, VI (Oxford Medieval Texts, 1978), 552–3; the translation is my own (cf. *Europe in the Central Middle Ages*, 2nd edn., London, 1975, p. 14; Brooke, *Marriage in Christian History*, p. 25).

[48] Cf. Brooke and Swaan, p. 88; *DDC*, I, 324–5, s.v. 'age'.

any conceivable increase in the population of western Europe. The idea that adult men could choose their own way of life acquired a grip scarcely conceivable a century earlier. This is really the most remarkable indicator of change that we have; and one of many signs that the choices open to men had substantially increased.

On the specific relation of consent to marriage, there is a characteristic canon of the Council of Westminster of 1175 which repeated an earlier text in revised form, stating that 'where there is no consent, there is no marriage', and went on to condemn the marriage of children under the age of consent—save in urgent necessity to preserve the peace; a face-saving clause made necessary, no doubt, by the presence of King Henry II and the young King Henry at the promulgation of the canons.[49] Political power still played a significant part in the marriage market; but the Church had taken secure hold of the law of marriage. And not only of the law; for the celibate theologians of the eleventh and twelfth centuries had by some mysterious alchemy turned marriage into a sacrament, set a mark of divine blessing on it which may not in essence have been new, but gave a new precision to its theological significance.[50] Indeed the careful reader of the correspondence of Heloise and Abelard will observe that the deepest theological insights could be affected by the direct experience of marriage and of human relations.[51] Heloise in particular clearly adumbrates the later doctrine that marriage is a sacrament made between the partners. Indeed she says in effect that the heart of her relationship to Abelard was an inner consent, a total surrender to him; and her celebrated outburst that she would rather have been his mistress than his wife crystallized the problem—what difference did it make?[52] This is one of the supreme moments of medieval theological debate: it is like the moment in the *Willehalm* of Wolfram von Eschenbach two generations later when the poem breaks off unfinished leaving the question ringing in our ears—what difference does baptism make?[53] The other deep and thorny issue raised by Heloise's letters is revealed by her clear assumption that the relation between them is eternal. Their marriage had actually been dissolved by both partners entering religious orders; but in truth she was still his wife in her own eyes. Her faith inspired the Abbot of Cluny, Peter the Venerable, to the famous vision in his letter to her on Abelard's death, of Abelard waiting to be reunited to her in Heaven.[54] But what happens to

[49] *Councils and Synods with other Documents relating to the English Church,* I, ed. D. Whitelock, M. Brett and C. N. L. Brooke (Oxford, 1981), p. 991; see meanwhile *Gesta Regis Henrici II . . .,* ed. W. Stubbs (London, Rolls ser., 1867), I, 83–4, 89.

[50] *DTC,* IX (1926), 2196 ff., XIV (1939), 546–9.

[51] Brooke, *Marriage in Christian History,* pp. 28–34 and references (p. 35).

[52] Letters, ed. J. T. Muckle, in *Mediaeval Studies,* XV (1953), 71.

[53] See Brooke in *The Layman in Christian History,* ed. S. C. Neill and H.-R. Weber (London, 1963), pp. 125, 133, referring to the work of Professor H. Sacker.

[54] Peter the Venerable, *Letters,* ed. G. Constable (Cambridge, Mass., 1967), no. 115, I, 307–8; quoted in translation in Brooke, *Medieval Church and Society,* p. 33. Cf. the comments of P. Dronke, *Abelard and Heloise in Medieval Testimonies* (Glasgow, 1976), pp. 22–3.

those who legitimately remarry after their partner's death? To this, and to all the host of questions her probing inspired, neither she nor any other theologian of the central Middle Ages gave any effective answer. But her letters show a depth and a sophistication which lifts the theology of marriage on to a new plane. They were not read at the time; but those about her were affected, as Abbot Peter shows.

Heloise and Abelard received a priestly blessing: there is a nice touch of idealism about this; and also a sign of changing fashions. Heloise was brought up in the cathedral close, in a world where the informal liaison of canons and concubines was assuredly still familiar. Not far away from Paris, on the shores of the English Channel, and in the course of Abelard's lifetime, a new liturgical tradition seems to have been born. In their remarkable study of marriage rites, *Le rituel du mariage en France du XIIe au XVIe siècle*,[55] Pères J.-B. Molin and P. Mutembe have argued that it was precisely in these regions and in this period that one can first discern the union of all the rituals of marriage in a single rite recorded in surviving liturgical books. The elements—the gift-giving, exchange of oaths and presents, the blessing and giving of the ring, the nuptial mass, the blessing of the couple, the blessing of the bedchamber—are all more ancient; but their union in a single liturgical whole seems to have been new. The liturgical evidence clearly confirms the importance of this age in developing practice: it was not until the Council of Trent that marriage in church, or at church door, in the presence of a priest, was enforced.[56] But in the eleventh and twelfth centuries it was evidently a growing, developing fashion; and Abelard's insistence on priestly blessing underlines this. There is much that is still obscure about this movement. But it seems likely that the development of splendid church porches in the twelfth and thirteenth centuries owed something to new matrimonial fashions.[57] The point is hard to prove: porches can provide shelter for any kind of gathering from the cradle to the grave; above all, to church processions and burials. But it is at least a hypothesis worth considering that one of the prime functions of many stately porches from now on, in the eyes of their builders, was for a setting of the life story of such as Chaucer's Wife of Bath, of whom he said that 'husbands at church door she had five'.[58]

The liturgical evidence is, however, ambiguous: Pope Alexander's retreat from marriage *in facie ecclesiae* to marriage by consent *de praesenti* as the basis of the institution strongly suggests that these new liturgical fashions left many unmoved; that more informal arrangements often prevailed.[59]

[55] Paris, 1974.
[56] *DTC*, IX, esp. 2246-7.
[57] This appears to be a relatively neglected topic; see meanwhile J. C. Wall, *Porches and Fonts* (London, 1912): I owe this reference to Professor G. Zarnecki.
[58] *Canterbury Tales, Prologue*, l.460; cf. *Wife of Bath's Tale*.
[59] Especially perhaps among the peasantry, though this is conjecture in the present state of knowledge. For recent attempts to penetrate the veil which covers marriage among the

Similarly ambiguous is the fourth element in our story: the rise of courtly love. In recent years Dr. Peter Dronke and others have argued with much cogency that the sentiments reflected in the lyrics and romances of the twelfth century were not entirely novel.[60] We are dealing with a group of attitudes in fact which had a very long history before and after the central Middle Ages. Furthermore, though no one doubts that the romantic tradition became fashionable in the twelfth and thirteenth centuries as never before, its relationship to marriage was ambivalent. It was at least a literary convention—and perhaps something more—to debate whether the two were compatible. Chrétien of Troyes showed in his *Erec* married love triumphing over remarkable obstacles: the reader is in doubt whether to wonder more at the ultimate triumph of fidelity and affection or at the obstacles.[61] In his *Chevalier de la Charrette* there is no such doubt: in spite of the poet's unconvincing disclaimer that it was his patroness, Marie de Champagne, and not he, who chose the theme, he presents in the sharpest light the romance of adultery. Harsher still are the portrayals of love as fate and doom in the Tristan legend, in which the lovers' adultery is explained in all the early versions of the story as made necessary and inevitable by the force of a love potion.[62] There are many hints of a happier attitude to married love in the romances, but we have to wait for the *Parzival* of Wolfram von Eschenbach before its idealization is entirely clear.[63] Furthermore, the relationship of the romances and of the social life of those for whom they were written is equally ambiguous. In the romances, broadly speaking, a woman is an object of a quest and of a cult; her knight must do deeds in her honour, and serve her as a slave. He must even undergo disgrace on her behalf: when Lancelot hesitated—though only for an instant—to climb into the cart in his quest for Guinevere, he offended against knightly gentility in mounting the cart, but even more against the cult of love for hesitating; and he was duly punished for it. This is all very well; but it is obvious enough

---

peasantry and unfree, see n. 27 above; J. Scammell in *Economic History Review*, 2nd ser., XXVII (1974), 523–37, XXIX (1976), 487–90; but see also E. Searle, ibid., XXIX (1976), 482–6 and in *Past & Present*, LXXXII (1979), 3–43. For the late Middle Ages, in this as in other areas of the social history of marriage, the work of Dr. Richard Smith is opening new horizons: see e.g. Smith in *The Sociology of the Family*, ed. C. Harris (Keele, 1979), pp. 74–112.

[60] See esp. P. Dronke, *Medieval Latin and the Rise of the European Love-Lyric* (2 vols., Oxford, 1965–6; 2nd edn., 1968); on related themes, cf. his *Poetic Individuality in the Middle Ages* (Oxford, 1970); J. Leclercq, *Monks and Love in Twelfth-century France* (Oxford, 1979).

[61] Cf. Leclercq, *Monks and Love*, pp. 129–32, 136.

[62] For the early versions of the Tristan legend, see *Arthurian Literature in the Middle Ages*, ed. R. S. Loomis (Oxford, 1959), chs. 13 (F. Whitehead) and 14 (W. T. H. Jackson); G. Weber, *Gottfried von Strassburg* (Stuttgart, 1962); and the many editions of Gottfried (e.g. by F. Ranke, Berlin, 1930); also A. T. Hatto's translation of Gottfried's *Tristan* with the Anglo-Norman poem by Thomas, with introduction (Penguin Classics, 1960).

[63] See below.

that it bears little relation to actual social life—its success indeed depends on reversing the normal values of the society for which it was written, in which many women were slaves of the marriage bond, at board and bed. Perhaps we may doubt if these poems could have been recited, read and relished without having some effect on the attitude of men to women; but even then the modern advocates of women's rights and freedoms would hardly approve the role allotted to women in the romances.

At the outset we considered two examples of the marriage market and the marriage bond in the twelfth century; and it may help to give some actuality to this analysis if we end with two more. About 1151 or 1152 was born Agnes, daughter of Henry of Essex, Royal Constable to King Henry II of England, and a leading baron and landholder.[64] When she was three years old a marriage was apparently planned between the little girl and Geoffrey de Vere, brother of Henry's neighbour in Essex and East Anglia, Aubrey de Vere, the first Earl of Oxford. The alliance seemed highly advantageous to both parties. As a guarantee of the arrangement (which the Church would not allow to be binding on Agnes for another nine years) she was removed to the household first of the Earl, then of Geoffrey de Vere, and brought up there. In 1162 or 1163, when she had attained the advanced age of 11 or 12, she was moved back to Aubrey's own household; the plan had changed, and, when she was just on the age of consent, she was betrothed to the Earl himself, evidently by *verba de praesenti*. Aubrey had been married twice before, but both his wives had died without leaving him an heir; and as he was well into his forties it was time for him to take further measures. But in 1163 Henry of Essex, Agnes' father, suddenly fell from power. He was accused of having fled from a Welsh ambush six years before and having abandoned the royal standard; the case was tried by battle and Henry lost. His lands were forfeit; his daughter, in the marriage market, became worthless. The Veres naturally set about disposing of her; and it is likely enough that she would have been cleared from their path without much difficulty a generation earlier. They had indeed no scruples about trumping up a case for annulment. They alleged that she had previously been betrothed to Geoffrey de Vere and could not therefore legally marry Aubrey (an ironical reminder to the modern student of the case of Henry VIII and Catherine of Aragon 250 years later). When this failed, because she had palpably been too young to give her consent, the Earl imprisoned her in a tower to make her see sense. She was not entirely friendless, and it is evident that the Church courts were not prepared to be complaisant. They were, however, in no hurry. The case was embarrassing; they could proceed against the Earl only by excommunicating him, and the Bishop who tried the case,

---

[64] For this case, see *Letters and Charters of Gilbert Foliot . . .*, ed. A. Morey and C. N. L. Brooke (Cambridge, 1967), pp. 214–18, nos. 162–4; Morey and Brooke, *Gilbert Foliot and his Letters* (Cambridge, 1965), pp. 236–7; *Complete Peerage,* revised edn., X, 205 ff.; Brooke, 'Aspects of marriage law', pp. 338–9. (What follows somewhat corrects this account.)

Gilbert Foliot of London, Thomas Becket's chief opponent among the bishops, knew the danger even for so staunch a friend of Henry II in excommunicating a tenant-in-chief in flagrant breach of the Constitutions of Clarendon at the height of the Becket dispute.[65] He moved, but extremely slowly. In 1166 he heard the case, and Agnes appealed to the Pope. The Bishop wrote to the Earl and urged him to treat her gently while the case lasted; but there is no reason to suppose that the Earl did anything of the kind. The case dragged on for over five years more, and then came to a dramatic climax. In January 1172 the Pope was preparing for the final agreements which made peace between himself and Henry II after Becket's murder, and he felt free to act in such a case as this. He wrote to the Bishop taking him to task for not acting more firmly with the Earl in the case of Agnes, who was still imprisoned; he evidently took it for granted (from the evidence he had received, doubtless, in 1166) that the marriage had been valid; and he told the Bishop to instruct the Earl to take Agnes back as his wife within 20 days under pain of excommunication. The Earl complied. He was by now over 60, she about 20; but they were married for over 20 years, and had at least four or five children.[66] It was a real marriage; whether it was a happy marriage, heaven knows. All that we know is that after Aubrey's death in 1194, the Countess remained a widow till her death.

This is a preposterous story, reflecting many of the harshest elements in the marriage customs of the day. But it has a happier side, both in the heroic determination of the little girl to vindicate her rights and her family name, and in the interest which the Pope took, however tardily, in her case and her fortunes. This was one of the cases which seems to have determined Alexander III to insist that *verba de praesenti*, immediate consent, made a marriage which could not be broken—and that this was binding on the Earl whether Agnes had in fact been technically at the age of consent when they were betrothed, or not. Agnes evidently accepted the fundamental arrangement: that she should be the victim of a marriage treaty made by her parents when she was too young to be consulted; she may even have accepted the view propounded by Lady Bracknell in *The Importance of Being Earnest* that a young lady's engagement should come to her as a surprise. But she reckoned that once married a wife had rights. One would dearly like to have comparable cases from less powerful families than the Veres, and the case law of the late twelfth century does include a certain number which are now being explored.[67] The best known so far, however, comes from the *Life of Christina of Markyate,* daughter of worthy citizens of Huntingdon in the early twelfth century, whose parents took it for granted that her marriage was their affair,

---

[65] Cf. Morey and Brooke, *Gilbert Foliot and his Letters,* ch. IX, esp. pp. 184–5 and nn. (corrected by M. D. Knowles, A. J. Duggan and C. N. L. Brooke in *English Historical Review,* LXXXVII (1972), 757–71).

[66] *Complete Peerage,* loc. cit.

[67] See nn. 2, 20.

and her early vocation to celibacy childish nonsense.[68] They married her off to a young man of good estate, who soon found that she was radically opposed to consummating the marriage—and after various attempts he became her ally in seeking its annulment. A similar conflict of social custom and human nature confronts us here; but in this case it is the ideal of celibacy, not marriage, which was the victor.

The Countess Agnes died in the early years of the thirteenth century; and at much the same time Wolfram was composing his *Parzival*.[69] Most of my examples have been chosen perforce from France and England; and so it is appropriate to end with one from Germany. The German poets differed from the French in working within a milieu which in some sense took it for granted that love and marriage were entirely compatible: at least, one word, *Minne,* could do service for both. This did not prevent Gottfried von Strassburg from propounding the most ironical, and perhaps the most cynical, surviving version of the story of Tristan and Isolde;[70] and even in Wolfram's poem it serves to underline some profound ambiguities. The highest form of love he portrays—and however briefly portrayed it is central to our understanding of the poem—is the married love of Parzival and Condwiramurs.[71] In none of his marriages does the Church play any visible part, although in a moral sense his idea of marriage as sacramental goes far beyond the normal teaching of the official theologians of his day. This attitude is quite characteristic of Wolfram: there is nothing clerical in his poem at all; priests are rarely mentioned; the most clerical figure, the hermit Trevrizent, is not in orders. Nor is the Church the only absentee from the marriage feast of Condwiramurs: there is some idea of a marriage settlement, clearly important yet quite informally arranged; there is no hint of any formal statement of consent; and it is made quite clear that she is married in her own eyes before consummation takes place. Two points seem to emerge from imaginative reflection on this episode. First, it is emphasized that marriage lies within: it is a deep compact between the partners—in theological terms, the sacrament is made by God between husband and wife, not by the clergy or the visible Church: and that for true marriage (and here Jane Austen would have agreed) deep, personal consent, sincere love, the will at least for consummation, are all needed, as well as the worldly arrangements which are its natural, social setting. The second point is that

---

[68] *The Life of Christina of Markyate,* ed. and trans. C. H. Talbot (Oxford, 1959), esp. pp. 44–55.

[69] On which see esp. H. Sacker, *An Introduction to Wolfram's Parzival* (Cambridge, 1963); M. F. Richey, *Studies of Wolfram von Eschenbach* (Edinburgh, 1957); M. Schumacher, *Die Auffassung der Ehe in den Dichtungen Wolframs von Eschenbach* (Heidelberg, 1967); H. E. Wiegand, *Studien zur Minne und Ehe im Wolframs Parzival und Hartmanns Artusepik* (Berlin, 1972): I owe these last two references to Dr. Marianne Wynne.

[70] See above, n. 62.

[71] *Parzival,* IV, 199–202; cf. the books cited above, n. 69; Brooke, 'Aspects of marriage law', pp. 334–5.

Wolfram can hardly be supposed to have sketched a marriage in all points out of line with social custom in his world. Evidently consent and consummation were the centre of some at least of the normal marriage customs that he knew; evidently, too, men and women in that world were not wholly at the beck and call of their fathers. He wrote above all for people to whom it was natural to see in the marriage settlement and the marriage bed the centre of the institution. Beyond that much is obscure.

Marriage is always a complex institution with many faces: social custom, religious doctrine, legal sanctions and human nature have always played their ambivalent roles in its formation; and men and women have enjoyed the delights of heaven and the pains of hell within it. Three strands were evidently woven into the thread of medieval marriage from the twelfth century on: the strength of parental control; the insistence of the celibate clergy that marriage was a second best; their equal insistence that consent not parental authority made a marriage—consent and human affection—*affectus,* in the cool Latin of the canonists,[72] *Minne* in the much stronger language of the German poets. All coexisted and in some measure influenced and coloured one another. Sometimes their relations were ironical: never more so, one may suppose, than in the mind of the Countess Agnes, who would have agreed with the celibate Newman that 'Marriage is a sin which it is sinful to repent of'.

[72] See J. T. Noonan, 'Marital affection in the canonists', *Studia Gratiana,* XII (1967), 479–509, a very interesting study, indicating some of the ambiguities and developments in the use of the phrase in both Roman and canon law.

II

Spousals Litigation in the English Ecclesiastical Courts c.1350–c.1640[1]

MARTIN INGRAM

Any investigation of the nature and significance of marriage in late medieval and early modern England should include the study of the matrimonial business of the ecclesiastical courts. It is true that the archiepiscopal, episcopal, archidiaconal, and peculiar tribunals of the provinces and dioceses of England did not enjoy a complete monopoly of litigation relating to matrimonial matters. Many other courts, including Chancery, Star Chamber, Requests, Wards, Common Pleas, and King's Bench, with greater or lesser frequency handled problems arising from the complex institution of marriage, especially those which had to do with property rights.[2] However, it was firmly established that all matters which essentially concerned the existence of the marriage bond were cognizable only in the courts Christian.[3]

Today the bulk of matrimonial litigation—no longer handled, of course, by the church courts, which lost their marriage jurisdiction in 1857—relates to divorce. In late medieval and early modern England the situation was very different. It is true that, although legal divorce in the modern sense was unknown, it was possible on rigorously specified grounds to bring actions for the annulment of marriage or for separation from bed and board.[4] However, all the available evidence indicates that, throughout the period

---

[1] For much help and many kindnesses I should like to thank Mr. Keith Thomas, who supervised the thesis on which some of the contents of this paper are based; Miss Pamela Stewart, until her recent retirement Assistant Archivist for the diocese of Salisbury; and the staffs of the University Library, Cambridge, and of other libraries and record offices which I have had occasion to use. I should also like to thank Miss Jean Potter for permission to quote from her unpublished dissertation, 'The ecclesiastical courts in the diocese of Canterbury, 1603–1665' (London University M.Phil. thesis, 1973).

[2] W. J. Jones, *The Elizabethan Court of Chancery* (Oxford, 1967), pp. 391–5; A. R. Winnett, *Divorce and Remarriage in Anglicanism* (London, 1958), pp. 46–7; J. Hurstfield, *The Queen's Wards: Wardship and Marriage under Elizabeth I* (London, 1958), ch. VIII; Sir F. Pollock and F. W. Maitland, *The History of English Law Before the Time of Edward I* (2 vols., Cambridge, 1968 edn.), II, book 2, ch. VII, *passim*. Cf. below, p. 52.

[3] Pollock and Maitland, *History of English Law*, II, 367. In the period of their existence in the late sixteenth and early seventeenth centuries, the courts of High Commission (which were technically not church courts but secular bodies empowered by statute to deal with matters of church discipline) also had jurisdiction over marriage cases; see P. Tyler, introduction to R. G. Usher, *The Rise and Fall of the High Commission* (Oxford, 1968 edn.), pp. v–vi, xxix–xxx.

[4] The grounds for action are surveyed in R. H. Helmholz, *Marriage Litigation in Medieval England* (Cambridge, 1974), ch. III.

from the fourteenth to the seventeenth centuries, such suits were comparatively infrequent: cases concerning the *formation* of marriage, not marital
breakdown, normally constituted the bulk of matrimonial litigation in the
English ecclesiastical courts.[5] A large proportion of them were actions for
the enforcement of marriage contracts, or spousals. What was generally at
issue in such suits was not simply a breach of promise[6] but the actual
existence of a binding state of marriage; and the study of spousals cases, and
of other aspects of court business relating to the formation of marriage, can
shed floods of light on the nature of, and attitudes to, entry into the marital
state in this period.

Certain broad questions present themselves in studying these aspects of
the business of the church courts. Firstly, what was the ecclesiastical law
relating to marriage formation and how was it administered in the courts?
This question may be answered in part by reference to the body of canon
and statute law which governed the church courts' actions. But a full answer,
taking account of local custom in the application of the law, requires the
study of the actual records of the courts—the books of acts and decrees, the
files of citations and sentences, the volumes or bundles of libels (statements
of a plaintiff's case), answers, interrogatories, depositions of witnesses, and
other cause papers, the surviving originals of which are to be found in
numerous local record repositories under county or diocesan administration
throughout England.[7] Such study will in addition provide an answer to a
second set of questions: how common spousals litigation and related court
business actually was, and how the pattern varied from period to period and
place to place. The study of actual cases can also furnish information about
yet another area of interest, the social circumstances which underlay
suits—though the wary researcher will recognize at the outset that court
records invariably give both an incomplete and a distorted impression of
underlying circumstances, and must be interpreted with the utmost caution.

This chapter offers a brief introduction to these issues. In order to provide
a long chronological perspective, some attention is given to the situation in
late medieval and early to mid sixteenth-century England, so far as it has
been revealed in published work. In addition the essay provides new evidence

---

[5] Helmholz, *Marriage Litigation,* p. 25; R. Houlbrooke, *Church Courts and the People
During the English Reformation 1520–1570* (Oxford, 1979), pp. 55–6; M. J. Ingram,
'Ecclesiastical justice in Wiltshire 1600-1640, with special reference to cases concerning sex
and marriage' (Oxford University D.Phil. thesis, 1976), pp. 114, 138, 142, 146.

[6] As in the common law action for the recovery of damages for the breach of promise of
marriage. On the origins of this action, see below, p. 52; the action was abolished by the
Law Reform (Miscellaneous Provisions) Act, 1970, c. 33.

[7] For an excellent introduction to the nature of ecclesiastical court records and procedure,
with examples and list of locations, see D. M. Owen, *The Records of the Established Church
in England* (British Records Association, Archives and the User, no 1, 1970), pp. 36–45,
58–60. For more detailed treatment, see Helmholz, *Marriage Litigation,* ch. I; Houlbrooke,
Church Courts and the People, pp. 38–54; Ingram, 'Ecclesiastical justice in Wiltshire', pp.
23–37, 53–61.

on the nature and significance of the church courts' matrimonial business in the late sixteenth and early seventeenth centuries. Obviously no one has yet succeeded in reading, far less analysing, all the relevant surviving ecclesiastical court records for this latter period: their bulk is enormous. This study relies on extensive samples of material from the diocese of Ely (covering the Isle of Ely and most of Cambridgeshire)[8] and from the western part of the diocese of Salisbury (covering most of the county of Wiltshire).[9] Analysis of the experience of these two fairly widely separated areas reveals certain differences, but far more prominent are major similarities. This convergence suggests that the conclusions drawn from the Wiltshire and Ely material are in their main outlines more widely applicable: and this view is further supported by the concurrence of such fragmentary evidence as is available for other English dioceses in the same period.

*   *   *

The Church's law on the definition of a valid marriage was in essence fixed in the twelfth century; in Catholic Europe it was altered only in the sixteenth century, and in England only in 1753.[10] The fundamental principle was that an indissoluble bond was created (assuming that no basic impediment existed to bar the marriage[11]) solely by the present consent of the parties, rather than by the act of coitus—which an older tradition supported by Gratian had held to be requisite in addition to consent—or by solemnization in church.[12] Thus the essence of a legally valid marriage was a contract in which the couple accepted each other as man and wife in words of the present tense (contract or spousals *per verba de praesenti*).

[8] The records of the diocese of Ely are located in the University Library, Cambridge, and are listed and described in D. M. Owen, *Ely Records: A Handlist of the Records of the Bishop and Archdeacon of Ely* (n.p., 1971). The sample of manuscript material used in this study mainly comprises the surviving instance act books and related volumes of the consistory court and of metropolitical jurisdiction within the see for the period 1574–1640, listed ibid., pp. 21–2, 65.

[9] The records of the diocese of Salisbury have recently been removed from the Wren Hall, Salisbury, to the Wiltshire Record Office, County Hall, Trowbridge, and are listed and described in P. Stewart, *Diocese of Salisbury: Guide to the Records of the Bishop, the Archdeacons of Salisbury and Wiltshire, and Other Archidiaconal and Peculiar Jurisdictions . . .* (Wiltshire County Council, Guide to the Record Offices, part IV, 1973). This list excludes the records of the archdeaconry of Berkshire (now in the diocese of Oxford), which are located in the Bodleian Library, Oxford, and which have not been used in this study. The conclusions presented here are based on a complete search of the surviving Wiltshire court records for the period 1601–40 (see Ingram, 'Ecclesiastical justice in Wiltshire', for a full discussion of these materials), supplemented by additional samples of material for the period 1560–1600.

[10] See below, p. 40.

[11] The principal impediments were consanguinity, affinity, and precontract. For changes in the law relating to these impediments, see Edmund Gibson, *Codex Juris Ecclesiastici Anglicani* (2 vols. consecutively paginated, Oxford, 1761 edn.), I, 408–18.

[12] Helmholz, *Marriage Litigation,* pp. 26–7 and the references there cited. Cf. J. A. Brundage, 'Concubinage and marriage in medieval canon law', *Journal of Medieval History,* I (1975), 1–17.

The law recognized other forms of spousals besides the immediately binding *de praesenti* contract. Spousals could be made in words *de futuro*, signifying a promise of future performance. A contract *de futuro* did not at once create an irrevocable union; it could be dissolved by the mutual consent of the parties, by the continued absence of one of them, and by fornication with a third party, and it had to give place to any subsequent *de praesenti* contract. Sexual intercourse between the parties, however, gave immediate binding force to an existing *de futuro* contract. Matrimonial contracts could also be made subject to certain conditions, notably the consent of parents or others and the provision of an adequate settlement of lands, goods, or money. The binding force of such contracts was suspended till the specified conditions were fulfilled, and if in the interim one party withdrew consent the contract had no force. A conditional contract, moreover, was superseded by one made unconditionally; the second, unconditional contract prevailed even if the conditions of the first contract were later fulfilled. Sexual intercourse between the parties, however, immediately made a conditional contract fully binding.[13]

Thus a legally valid marriage could be made by the sole consent of the parties, in whatever circumstances. But in order to limit the opportunities for fraud and self-deception, to minimize uncertainty about the validity of unions, and to prevent couples contracting marriages when basic impediments existed, the Church tried to ensure that marriages were made publicly, with due formality, and with ecclesiastical blessing. According to the most rigorous interpretation of the law as expressed in a series of medieval provincial canons, diocesan statutes, and other legislative enactments, the following formalities had to be observed.[14] The couple should initially betroth themselves only by means of a promise to marry (spousals *per verba de futuro*). The next step was the threefold publication of the banns of marriage in the parish church of each of the parties on three Sundays or major feasts. This was to allow the discovery of any impediment which might prevent the marriage, or (if no bar existed) to safeguard the future existence of the union by making it a matter of public knowledge. However, by the end of the Middle Ages it had become established that bishops could grant licences to marry without the publication of banns; the procedures involved in the issue of such licences, and the necessary safeguards to prevent abuse, were eventually codified in the canons of 1604.[15] Assuming that no impediment was found, the couple were publicly to take each other as man and wife by the exchange of consent (contract *per verba de praesenti*) at the church door.

---

[13] For the English reader the most convenient authoritative text setting forth the complex law of spousals is Henry Swinburne, *A Treatise of Spousals or Matrimonial Contracts* (London, 1686).

[14] The brief account which follows inevitably oversimplifies an exceedingly complex set of regulations, discussed at length in M. M. Sheehan, 'Marriage theory and practice in the conciliar legislation and diocesan statutes of medieval England', *Medieval Studies*, XL (1978), 408–60.

[15] Canons 101-4, printed in Gibson, *Codex*, I, 428–9.

This solemn act, the actual marriage, was to take place in the presence of witnesses and of a priest, and the verbal expression of consent was to be accompanied by the giving of a ring and other rituals. Finally the couple were to participate in a nuptial mass. Essentially this scheme survived the Reformation; the forms laid down in the sixteenth- and seventeenth-century Books of Common Prayer and in post-Reformation canons altered it only in details.

Though these procedures for ensuring that unions were made publicly and in a liturgical context were not essential to marriage—as we have seen, the exchange of consent alone was sufficient to create a valid and binding union—they were required to make a marriage fully licit. Any union which involved substantial deviation from the prescribed regulations was irregular, and referred to as clandestine. To neglect the solemnization of a contract was definitely illicit. This was so even if the contract had been witnessed. But unions which were both unattested and unsolemnized—the most extreme variety of clandestine marriage—were in the eyes of the law particularly reprehensible since they were so vulnerable to abuse and repudiation.[16] On the other hand, it seems in practice to have been generally accepted that couples might contract a binding union before they got married in church or even before the banns were read, so long as the contract was adequately witnessed and the couple proceeded to the publication and solemnization of their union without undue delay.[17] However, even in the Middle Ages, sexual intercourse between contract and solemnization was discouraged, or even absolutely forbidden, by legal commentators and moralists;[18] while in the early modern period many churchmen firmly denounced the practice whereby individuals took 'liberty after a contract to know their spouse'. William Gouge, for example, regarded this as 'an unwarrantable and dishonest practice'.[19]

To solemnize a marriage without observing the various safeguards for ensuring that the union was adequately publicized was also illegal, indeed an offence of great gravity in ecclesiastical law. Thus, *Humana Concupiscentia*, a canon of Archbishop John Stratford's provincial council of London (1342), forbade on pain of the greater excommunication the practice whereby couples who sought the respectability of a solemnized union but who were aware of impediments to bar their marriage evaded opposition by going to distant places and procuring marriage before a priest without the banns

---

[16] William Lyndwood, *Provinciale, (seu Constitutiones Angliae)* ... (Oxford, 1679), p. 276, s.v. *clandestina, statutis a jure.*

[17] H. A. Kelly, 'Clandestine marriage and Chaucer's "Troilus"', *Viator,* IV (1973), 441–2. In the early modern period some writers not only tolerated but actually recommended the practice of entering into a contract before the church ceremony, e.g. William Gouge, *Of Domesticall Duties* (London, 1622), pp. 196–202.

[18] Kelly, 'Clandestine marriage', pp. 440–1.

[19] Gouge, *Of Domesticall Duties,* p. 202.

being asked and at unsuitable times and seasons.[20] Subsequently, clandestine solemnization was more extensively defined to include the celebration of marriage without the threefold publication of banns or the issue of a valid licence, a ceremony conducted outside the diocese in which the couple dwelt, or solemnization within certain prohibited seasons (principally Advent and Lent), outside specified hours, or in any circumstances save within a lawful church or chapel and in the presence of a properly constituted minister of the Church of England. Ministers who conducted clandestine marriage ceremonies were liable to suspension from their benefices for three years; while laymen who procured a secret solemnization or who even attended a clandestine marriage ceremony incurred *ipso facto* the sentence of greater excommunication. Nevertheless, clandestine marriage ceremonies could create a valid union.[21]

Thus ecclesiastical law proscribed unsolemnized or irregularly solemnized unions, yet at the same time was prepared to regard them as creating a valid marriage. In retrospect this situation appears highly anomalous and bound to lead to confusion, and it might seem that the Church would have done better if it had at the outset made the due solemnization of marriage in church a necessary condition for the recognition of a valid union. It would seem, indeed, that Pope Alexander III wished to do this, but was deterred by the fact that, given the diversity and informality of marriage practices in twelfth-century Europe, the step would have rendered a massive proportion of marriages invalid.[22] In Catholic Europe the law was eventually rationalized by the decree *Tametsi* of the Council of Trent, which invalidated marriages not performed in public before the parish priest.[23] In England the projected *Reformatio Legum Ecclesiasticarum,* drawn up in the reign of Edward VI, included a provision to make clandestine marriages invalid.[24] But in fact the law remained unchanged until Lord Hardwicke's Marriage Act was passed in 1753.[25]

Thus throughout the period under review the church courts were faced with the duty of adjudicating disputes over unsolemnized marriage contracts. When contracts were alleged in the courts, the judge had the task of deciding whether they had in fact taken place, and if so in what form. Contracts had in general to be proved either by the confession of the parties or, in case of dispute, by the testimony of two unexceptionable witnesses. *De praesenti*

---

[20] Lyndwood, *Provinciale,* pp. 274–7; cf. M. M. Sheehan, 'The formation and stability of marriage in fourteenth-century England: evidence of an Ely register', *Medieval Studies,* XXXIII (1971), 240.

[21] Gibson, *Codex,* I, 424–5, 428-30. Clandestine marriages were not, of course, valid if basic impediments existed.

[22] C. N. L. Brooke, *Marriage in Christian History: An Inaugural Lecture* (Cambridge, n.d. [1978]), pp. 22-3.

[23] *Canons and Decrees of the Council of Trent,* ed. and trans. H. J. Schroeder (St. Louis, Mo. and London, 1960 edn.), pp. 454–6, translation pp. 183–4.

[24] *Reformatio Legum Ecclesiasticarum* (London, 1640), pp. 37–8.

[25] 26 George II c. 33, printed in Gibson, *Codex,* II, 1274-7.

contracts, if proved, were confirmed by an *adjudicatory* sentence which pronounced the parties man and wife, and were enforceable on pain of excommunication. In the case of conditional contracts, account had to be taken of whether the parties had subsequently made the spousals binding by the act of sexual intercourse or whether the specified conditions had been fulfilled. *De futuro* promises of marriage were, if proved, also enforceable, subject to the provision that if the recalcitrant party remained obdurate he might eventually be absolved on condition of performing penance. If no contract was proved at all, an *absolutory* sentence freed the parties from obligation; or, in cases of doubt, the parties might be referred to their consciences.[26]

At its simplest, an action over a disputed contract (*causa sponsalitica*) involved only two parties. But three or more people could take part when more than one person claimed the existence of a binding union with a certain individual. Such suits required the judge to decide which of the contracts (if any) was valid and which null; they were variously referred to as causes of 'spousals and nullity' or 'marriage and divorce'. Obviously cases of this type implied conscious or unconscious bigamy; and, though it is appropriate to deal with them in an essay on the formation of marriage, technically their determination involved annulment or divorce.[27]

The normal roles of the parties in spousals suits were reversed in another form of action over disputed marriage contracts—the cause of jactitation of matrimony. This enabled an individual to sue someone who untruly 'boasted and affirmed' that a contract or marriage existed between them. A successful action was supposed to dispose of all claim to and fame of the pretended marriage, and a defeated defendant was enjoined to keep perpetual silence on the matter.[28]

All these types of cause were characteristically prosecuted as 'instance' causes—suits between parties in which the judge acted as an adjudicator rather than as an initiator of proceedings. But since contract suits were so closely involved with matters of morality they inevitably had some disciplinary content. Accordingly, judges sometimes took the initiative and, acting on information from court officers, from 'detections' framed by churchwardens or ministers, or from an interested party, cited *ex officio*[29] couples who were in dispute over spousals or appeared to be reneging on contracts. Depending on the circumstances, such cases might be handled summarily, or they might develop into formal actions similar to those initiated by instance

---

[26] Swinburne, *Treatise of Spousals,* pp. 231–3.

[27] Helmholz, *Marriage Litigation,* pp. 57–9; Houlbrooke, *Church Courts and the People,* p. 59.

[28] Francis Clarke, *Praxis . . ., tam Jus Dicentibus quam Alijs Omnibus qui in Foro Ecclesiastico Versantur Apprime Utilis* (Dublin, 1666), pp. 145–7.

[29] I.e. by virtue of the office of the judge, the characteristic mode of procedure in disciplinary cases.

procedure.[30] Judges might also take disciplinary action *ex officio* against individuals involved in disputes over banns or in the irregular solemnization of marriage.

Such, in outline, was the ecclesiastical law of marriage contracts. How frequently did cases come before the courts? The indications are that in the fourteenth century spousals suits occurred in significantly large numbers. By the end of the fifteenth century they were already a far less prominent form of ecclesiastical court business, and by the seventeenth century the flow of causes had been reduced almost to a trickle. The fragmentary nature of the available evidence and the difficulties of presenting meaningful statistics, given the problems of changing population levels and shifts in the pattern of activity of courts exercising overlapping jurisdictions, make it impossible to offer a comprehensive series of figures which adequately demonstrate the decline. A few suggestive statistics must suffice. In the consistory court of Canterbury in the early 1370s, an annual average of about 30 contract cases were heard; but in 1485 only 12 or fewer contract suits were pending, and 9 or fewer in 1497.[31] The numbers of contract cases may have picked up somewhat in the early sixteenth century,[32] but in the early seventeenth century the Canterbury court rarely handled annually more than 10 matrimonial causes, including marriage suits other than contract cases.[33] The decline relative to population was presumably much greater than the absolute figures would indicate: the area of Kent included in the diocese of Canterbury, like other parts of England, undoubtedly experienced in the sixteenth and early seventeenth centuries a considerable demographic increase above the relatively low levels prevailing in the late Middle Ages.[34] The consistory court of the diocese of Ely in the period 1374–82 appears to have handled an average of about 6 instance spousals suits per annum, and a yearly average of about 5 cases which began as *ex officio* investigations and developed as suits to prove the existence of a marriage.[35] By the 1580s the consistory court was dealing with an average of something over 9 cases a year recorded in the instance act books, with a significant number of additional cases occurring in the records of *ex officio* prosecutions.[36] At first sight these figures

[30] Helmholz, *Marriage Litigation*, pp. 70–2; Houlbrooke, *Church Courts and the People*, p. 56; Ingram, 'Ecclesiastical justice in Wiltshire', p. 114.

[31] Calculated from figures given in Helmholz, *Marriage Litigation*, pp. 25, 166.

[32] B. L. Woodcock, *Medieval Ecclesiastical Courts in the Diocese of Canterbury* (London, 1952), p. 85.

[33] J. M. Potter, 'The ecclesiastical courts in the diocese of Canterbury 1603–1665' (London University M.Phil. thesis, 1973), p. 23.

[34] P. Clark, *English Provincial Society from the Reformation to the Revolution: Religion, Politics and Society in Kent 1500–1640* (Hassocks, Sussex, 1977), p. 6; cf. J. D. Chambers, *Population, Economy, and Society in Pre-Industrial England* (London, Oxford and New York, 1972), pp. 20–2.

[35] Calculated from figures given in Sheehan, 'Formation and stability of marriage', pp. 256–61.

[36] Based on analysis of Ely Diocesan Records, University Library, Cambridge, D/2/12–15, 18a; B/2/12; Norwich Diocesan Records, Norfolk and Norwich Record Office, Norwich, ACT 21/24a (stray Ely act book 1588–90).

might seem to indicate that contract litigation had increased rather than decreased over these 200 years; but it has to be borne in mind that before about 1400 a significant (but unfortunately unknown) proportion of matrimonial causes was handled in the archdeaconry court,[37] and also that the population of Ely diocese may have increased between the 1370s and the 1580s.[38] In any event a marked decline in contract litigation in this diocese is plainly evident by the early seventeenth century; the surviving records indicate that in that period an annual average of fewer than 3 contract cases were entered in the instance act books, with only a trickle of cases occurring in the registers of *ex officio* prosecutions.[39]

A decline in the incidence of contract litigation from the sixteenth to the seventeenth centuries has been noted for a number of areas. The Norwich consistory court handled an annual average of about 11 contract cases in the period 1520–70 (a slighty higher number than the consistory court of Winchester at the same time);[40] but in the legal year 1623–24 the Norwich consistory is known to have handled only one matrimonial cause, and none at all in 1636–37.[41] In the consistory court of the huge diocese of York, an average of 30 matrimonial causes (all types, not just contract cases) were entered in four sample years in the period 1561–1600. By contrast, the average number for six sample years in the period 1601–40 was 10, the figures for the individual years showing a clear downward trend.[42] Until the matrimonial business of the York consistory court has been analysed in more detail, it is impossible to be certain how far this decline was due to a reduction in contract litigation as opposed to a fall in numbers of separation and annulment suits. But, as Houlbrooke has argued, in the light of extensive evidence from other dioceses that divorce suits were relatively uncommon throughout the late Middle Ages and early modern period, it seems likely that the major factor was a reduced incidence of spousals causes.[43] As regards the Wiltshire portions of the diocese of Salisbury, the statistics of contract litigation in the early seventeenth century show no marked contrast with those of the later sixteenth. This is simply because the incidence of suits was already quite low in the Elizabethan period. Thus, sampling of the surviving

---

[37] Sheehan, 'Formation and stability of marriage', pp. 232–3.

[38] M. Spufford, *Contrasting Communities: English Villagers in the Sixteenth and Seventeenth Centuries* (Cambridge, 1974), pp. 3–28.

[39] Based on analysis of Ely D. R., D/2/22, 24, 27, 30, 31, 31a, 33, 34, 36–8, 40, 42–5, 47, 49, 50; B/2/34–6.

[40] Calculated from figures given in Houlbrooke, *Church Courts and the People,* pp. 276–7.

[41] R. A. Marchant, *The Church under the Law: Justice, Administration and Discipline in the Diocese of York 1560–1640* (Cambridge, 1969), p. 20. Since the Norwich act books at this period do not normally specify the nature of causes, the figures for these years are based on analysis of volumes of articles and replies in contested causes (ibid., p. 17). Possibly a few additional matrimonial causes occurred among the uncontested cases (about 25 per cent of the total) but cannot now be identified.

[42] Calculated from figures given in Marchant, *Church under the Law,* p. 62.

[43] Houlbrooke, *Church Courts and the People,* p. 65. Cf. above, p. 35–6.

Wiltshire records for the late sixteenth century, and a search of all the extant materials for the early seventeenth, indicate that there were rarely more than about 5 contract cases entered per annum throughout the period 1560–1640.[44]

Throughout the period from the fourteenth to the seventeenth century, contract causes of the jactitation type appear to have been relatively uncommon.[45] Thus in the great majority of spousals suits the plaintiff was trying to secure the enforcement of a disputed contract. In the century after 1350 a high proportion of cases—up to 50 per cent—were multi-party suits in which bigamy and annulment were potentially at issue; but thereafter the incidence of multi-party litigation appears to have declined. Nevertheless, multi-cornered contract causes were still reasonably prominent in the sixteenth and seventeenth centuries. In Wiltshire in the period 1600–40, about 14 per cent of suits for the enforcement of marriage contracts were of the spousals and nullity type.[46]

*   *   *

Evidence about the social status of parties in spousals suits is imperfect but not entirely lacking. For late medieval England, Helmholz concludes that members of the highest classes and those of servile condition did not generally figure among litigants in matrimonial causes, but otherwise all stations in life were represented. But Sheehan's analysis of the Ely consistory court register for 1374–82 indicates that the social status of the parties in marriage cases formed a spectrum which, apart from the possible underrepresentation of the upper classes, fairly accurately reflected the structure of non-clerical Cambridgeshire society as a whole, including the unfree; and he believes that Helmholz is in error in supposing that people of servile status did not participate in matrimonial causes in late medieval England generally. Houlbrooke implies that in the dioceses of Norwich and Winchester in the sixteenth century, the parties in matrimonial suits came from a broad social spectrum, ranging from servants and relatively poor people to members of the lesser gentry. Strictly speaking all these indications relate to matrimonial litigation generally, not just to contract suits; but given the preponderance of the latter in the marriage business of the church courts they can probably be taken to represent the social status of parties in spousals causes alone. Information relating specifically to contract litigation is available for early seventeenth-century Wiltshire: it closely parallels the findings for the earlier

---

[44] For the early seventeenth-century evidence, see Ingram, 'Ecclesiastical justice in Wiltshire', pp. 111, 114, 131; the conclusions for the late sixteenth century are based on analysis of Salisbury Diocesan Records, Wiltshire Record Office, Trowbridge, Bishop's Act Books (Instance) 3, 13–15.

[45] Houlbrooke, *Church Courts and the People,* p. 59; Ingram, 'Ecclesiastical justice in Wiltshire', p. 114.

[46] Helmholz, *Marriage Litigation,* pp. 58–9; Ingram, 'Ecclesiastical justice in Wiltshire', p. 114.

periods, indicating that most ranks of society were represented among contract litigants except for the very rich and the desperately poor.[47]

The evidence at present available on the relative proportion of males and females among plaintiffs in contract causes is both imperfect and inconclusive. The published material for the later Middle Ages and the sixteenth century is silent on this point. However, it is known that in the diocese of Ely in the 1580s, male plaintiffs outnumbered women in a ratio of about 2:1, the preponderance of men increasing in the early seventeenth century to about 3:1. In early seventeenth-century Wiltshire, on the other hand, there were about three female plaintiffs to every two males. The significance of this contrast is at present unclear, and further research is necessary to establish the situation in other areas.

What circumstances led to involvement in contract litigation? It seems clear that one basic problem was the prevalence of some degree of uncertainty among the population at large about what constituted entry into a binding state of marriage. Perhaps at the beginning of the period under review there was a reluctance among laymen to admit that any union should invariably be a lifelong obligation or to recognize the Church's right to exercise control over the institution of marriage.[48] Later, certainly by the sixteenth and seventeenth centuries, the problem seems rather to have been that, to many, a solemnized marriage seemed a more binding affair than an earlier unsolemnized and perhaps unconsummated union. In any event, throughout the period a proportion of the population remained convinced, or at a pinch were prepared to act as though they believed, that an unsolemnized marriage contract was merely an agreement to perform a marriage, which (like other forms of contract) might in certain circumstances be broken.[49]

This confused situation was encouraged by a number of circumstances. The first was the lack of any clear indication of precisely what words and acts could and could not constitute a marriage. Admittedly the canonists discussed these issues at length. But the niceties of their distinctions between words *de praesenti* and *de futuro* were, it is commonly accepted, over-subtle to the point of artificiality.[50] The lack of a single, plain, obligatory formula inevitably allowed scope for uncertainty and dispute.

These possibilities were enlarged by the fact that a binding contract could be made without safeguards for ensuring the publicity of the act and in circumstances inappropriate to the gravity of the occasion. Perhaps the

---

[47] Helmholz, *Marriage Litigation*, pp. 160–1; Sheehan, 'Formation and stability of marriage', p. 234; idem, review of Helmholz, *Marriage Litigation*, in *Speculum*, LII (1977), 986–7; Houlbrooke, *Church Courts and the People*, p. 75; Ingram, 'Ecclesiastical justice in Wiltshire', pp. 114–15.

[48] Helmholz, *Marriage Litigation*, pp. 4–5, 59.

[49] Ibid., pp. 27–33.

[50] Pollock and Maitland, *History of English Law*, II, 368–9; Helmholz, *Marriage Litigation*, pp. 34–45; Houlbrooke, *Church Courts and the People*, p. 57.

dimensions of this problem should not be exaggerated. It seems clear that both in the late Middle Ages and the early modern period, even when binding contracts were entered into before the ecclesiastical ceremony, they were often—perhaps normally in the case of contracts which did not lead to court action—of a highly ceremonious nature. They could involve lengthy preliminary discussions, a formal setting, and the presence of witnesses, and might be presided over by an individual (sometimes but not invariably a priest) acting as a kind of master of ceremonies who would make sure that the couple knew what they were doing and were content with the arrangement, and would minister the words of contract to them.[51] Yet even such relatively formalized contracts could prove vulnerable, and court records are littered with cases in which contracts were made in far less satisfactory circumstances. In many instances the contract (if it existed at all) had been made quite without witnesses, or with only a single witness present. Sometimes spousals were made on the spur of the moment, or effected in barns, streets, or fields.[52] In such circumstances the possibilities of fraud, deceit, and confusion were immense.

In legal theory and (it would seem) popular estimation, at least a partial presumption of the existence of a contract could be based on evidence other than that relating to the actual words of contract. A plaintiff's libel normally included allegations that the parties had exchanged gifts or tokens symbolic of a binding union, including in some cases the bestowal of a ring by the man; that the couple had acknowledged the existence of a contract to neighbours or friends; that they had called each other 'wife' or 'husband'; and that they were commonly reputed and taken to be man and wife by their neighbours, or that there existed a 'common fame' to that effect. Rituals such as the exchange of tokens, the sealing of a contract with a loving kiss, and the public acknowledgement of spousals were evidently common in relatively formal, adequately witnessed contracts; they added to the solemnity of the occasion and furthered the publication of the proceedings. But as supports for unwitnessed or inadequately witnessed contracts, their evidential power was slight and was generally so regarded by the courts.[53] In practice these circumstantial rituals and observances probably did little to safeguard contracts. On the contrary, they could help to create confusion, deluding the naive or unwary into assuming that a contract existed when none had in fact been made. The act of giving and receiving such presents as a pair of gloves

---

[51] Sheehan, 'Formation and stability of marriage', pp. 244–5; Ingram, 'Ecclesiastical justice in Wiltshire', pp. 115–18. For alleged examples of relatively formal contracts, see Ely D. R., D/2/11, fos. 55–6, 64–7v (*Ellys v. Scott,* 1575); Salisbury D. R., Bishop's Deposition Book 26, fo. 168 (*Monday v. Pile,* 1609); Dep. Bk. 28, fo. 81v (*Weare v. Graye,* 1611).

[52] Helmholz, *Marriage Litigation,* p. 29; Houlbrooke, *Church Courts and the People,* p. 58; Ely D.R., D/2/11, fos. 182–3 (*Meten v. Cropwell,* 1577), fo. 337v (*Stacye v. Searle,* 1580); Salisbury D.R., Bishop's Dep. Bk. 10, fo. 30v (*Slye v. Estcourt,* 1589).

[53] Helmholz, *Marriage Litigation,* pp. 46–7; Houlbrooke, *Church Courts and the People,* pp. 60–2.

or a broken coin was particularly ambiguous, because gifts could be made merely as 'tokens of goodwill' rather than as symbols of a binding union.[54]

Reluctance to accept that an unsolemnized contract actually created an indissoluble union, and confusion over what words and acts were sufficient to make a binding marriage, were thus the basic reasons for the incidence of contract suits. But a whole range of additional factors were involved in the creation of situations and disputes leading to litigation.

Some plaintiffs plainly had no shadow of a real case. They were naive, hopeful, scheming, or (especially in the case of women made pregnant by their lovers) desperate.[55] Some suits were probably malicious, intended to put the defendant to trouble and expense and not undertaken with the serious intention of securing the enforcement of the alleged marriage.[56] In the majority of cases, however, the plaintiff probably had at least some reasonable grounds for action (though not necessarily, of course, the means of proof), the defendant appearing as the fraudulent or capricious partner. Sometimes, the defendant had apparently made a promise of marriage without any intention of sticking to it: often the motive for such deception had been simply to gain sexual gratification. In other cases, the original promise had been genuine, but the defendant had subsequently undergone a change of heart. Sometimes altered circumstances or mere caprice were at issue. Frequently, however, the change of mind had deeper implications—it was related to a conflict between the individual's personal freedom to choose a marriage partner and the pressures of family or other interests. This issue is of such importance as to warrant extended discussion.

From the basic position that the mutual consent of the couple alone made a valid marriage, the Church developed the principle that the consent of no other person was necessary.[57] Sheehan stresses the highly individualistic implications of this idea,[58] but the point should not be pressed too far. The principle of freedom of consent was developed primarily to ensure freedom from positive compulsion. Medieval canonists accepted that in normal circumstances it was desirable for children to follow their families' wishes, especially when the latter were objecting to an individual's choice of partner rather than trying to impose one.[59] In the sixteenth century the desire to safeguard parental influence in this respect may have intensified. Protestant

---

[54] For cases which reveal the ambiguity of gifts with particular clarity, see Ely D.R., D/2/11, fo. 12 (*Kyng v. Angoulde,* 1574), fo. 263 (*Lucas v. Newman,* 1578); Salisbury D.R., Bishop's Dep. Bk. 28, fo. 1 (*Hayter v. Markes,* 1612).

[55] For example, Salisbury D.R., Bishop's Dep. Bk. 43, fos. 27v–29 (*Hobbs v. Locke,* 1629) (naive/hopeful); Dep. Bk. 26, fo. 115 (*Hunt v. Chipet* alias *Samson,* 1609) (scheming); Dep. Bk. 26, fos. 136v–137v (*Diar v. Rogers,* 1609) (desperate).

[56] For example, Salisbury D.R., Bishop's Dep. Bk. 46, fo. 208 (*Middlecot v. Abathe,* 1631).

[57] Sheehan, 'Marriage theory and practice', p. 458.

[58] Idem, 'Formation and stability of marriage', pp. 229, 263.

[59] J. T. Noonan, 'Power to choose', *Viator,* IV (1973), 419–34; Helmholz, *Marriage Litigation,* p. 91.

churchmen strongly denounced the selection of marriage partners in defiance of the family's wishes,[60] and the projected *Reformatio Legum* would have made marriages contracted by children without the consent of their parents invalid.[61] In the event, the canons of 1604 merely forbade marriage without parental consent for children under 21, and for the issue of marriage licences required the consent of parents irrespective of the age of the parties (unless they were in widowhood), but did not declare marriages made in contravention of these regulations to be invalid.[62] Thus throughout the period under review, an anomalous situation existed in that the Church recognized the desirability of parental consent, but did not make the validity of marriage dependent upon it lest the principle of the free consent of the couple should be violated.

Sheehan's study of the Ely register for 1374–82 revealed little evidence of family control over choice of spouse.[63] However, Helmholz and Houlbrooke report ample evidence of familial involvement in the background to contract causes,[64] while the records of the diocese of Ely and the Wiltshire parts of the diocese of Salisbury in the late sixteenth and early seventeenth centuries include numerous references to the intervention of the relatives, guardians (including masters and mistresses acting *in loco parentis*), and 'friends' of the parties.[65] The precise dimensions of these interest groups are somewhat unclear, but evidently in some cases they were extensive. Certainly in the sixteenth and seventeenth centuries, perhaps earlier, parents and guardians figured most prominently. But other kin and affines were also to some extent in evidence, sometimes (but by no means invariably so) when either or both parents were dead.[66] The precise standing and role of individuals referred to as 'friends' or *amici* is uncertain. Sometimes, throughout the period, the term clearly meant relations by blood or marriage. Thus in a Rochester case of 1438, *amici* denoted a litigant's father and uncles.[67] But, both in the Middle Ages and later, 'friends' could include intimates unrelated by blood or marriage.[68]

How far could these interests affect the individual's freedom to choose a marriage partner? The evidence of depositions suggests the existence among laymen of a set of ideals which prescribed, albeit loosely, how the issues of

---

[60] Thomas Becon, *The Worckes* ... (3 vols., London, 1560–64 edn.), I, fos. dcxviii–dcxxi; Gouge, *Of Domesticall Duties,* pp. 446 ff.; John Dod and Robert Cleaver, *A Godly Forme of Houshold Government* (London, 1630 edn.), sigs. I1v–I3v. Cf. Houlbrooke, *Church Courts and the People,* pp. 62–3.

[61] *Reformatio Legum,* p. 39.

[62] Canons 100, 102–4, printed in Gibson, *Codex,* I, 421, 428–9.

[63] Sheehan, 'Formation and stability of marriage', p. 263.

[64] Helmholz, *Marriage Litigation,* pp. 47–50; Houlbrooke, *Church Courts and the People,* pp. 62–4.

[65] Ingram, 'Ecclesiastical justice in Wiltshire', pp. 117–18.

[66] Ibid., p. 117.

[67] Helmholz, *Marriage Litigation,* p. 47n.

[68] Ingram, 'Ecclesiastical justice in Wiltshire', p. 118.

individual choice and family interest should be handled. However, the indications at present available are in several ways imperfect. It is uncertain how far attitudes varied at different social levels; in particular, it is doubtful how far the ideas discussed below were applicable to the upper classes who were poorly represented in the matrimonial business of the church courts.[69] Nor is it clear how much depended on the age of the individuals contemplating matrimony, a subject on which the court records provide little information.[70] Moreover, the conclusions which follow are based largely on later sixteenth- and seventeenth-century evidence, though it is possible that they are applicable also to earlier periods.

The indications are that it was not normally considered right for parents or others to arrange marriages wholly without reference to the wishes of their children, though certainly they might vigorously assert their preferences. Indeed, it was apparently not uncommon at the social levels generally represented in contract suits for the young people themselves to take the initiative in seeking out a potential mate and commencing courtship. However, this did not imply complete freedom of choice: it seems to have been conventional wisdom that in normal circumstances children were duty-bound to marry only with the consent of their parents or other governors, who had the right to veto alliances which could be reasonably regarded as unsuitable. Likewise, it seems to have been conventionally accepted that, in cases where parents or others did take the initiative in urging a particular match, the individuals concerned should be allowed to reject the proposed union if they were opposed to it on reasonable grounds.[71]

These ideas imply the existence of conventional criteria for judging the suitability or reasonableness of proposed marriages. Despite the opinion of

---

[69] For a discussion of marriage practices in an upper-class family, see A. S. Haskell, 'The Paston women on marriage in fifteenth-century England', *Viator,* IV (1973), 459–71. For a more general discussion, see L. Stone, *The Family, Sex and Marriage in England 1500–1800* (London, 1977).

[70] Demographic studies have revealed that in the later sixteenth and seventeenth centuries the mean age of first marriage was in the mid to late 20s, and there are indications that a relatively high age of marriage may also have prevailed in the late fourteenth century (P. Laslett, *Family Life and Illicit Love in Earlier Generations* (Cambridge, 1977), pp. 39–40, 46–7). It is at present uncertain whether the ages of the parties in spousals suits conformed to these norms, but it may be significant that the depositions in the few later sixteenth- and early seventeenth-century cases which refer to one or other of the parties being much below the age of 21 do so in terms which suggest that the circumstance was unusual: see, for example, Salisbury D.R., Dean's Dep. Bk. 5, fos. 26v, 28v, 29 (*Fry v. Tuck*, 1604); Bishop's Dep. Bk. 24, fos. 106, 107v (*Waterman v. Nicholas* and *Jeay,* 1607); Bishop's Dep. Bk. 47, fo. 138 (*Burden v. Ogbourne,* 1631).

[71] Ingram, 'Ecclesiastical justice', pp. 118–19. Nevertheless, some cases of parents coercing children into marriages which were distasteful to them undoubtedly occurred. Some instances came to light in church court actions for the annulment of marriages vitiated by the impediment of force and fear. However, the fact that such actions were very rare cannot be taken as an index of the incidence of parental coercion since the law was only prepared to entertain the most extreme cases of duress (Helmholz, *Marriage Litigation,* pp. 90–4; Noonan, 'Power to choose', pp. 432–4).

some modern historians that marriages tended to be loveless affairs before the eighteenth century,[72] it seems clear that one generally recognized criterion was mutual personal attraction between the potential spouses, to enable them to 'love' one another.[73] (Indeed, something very close to our idea of 'romantic love', with all its heartaches and inconstancies, emerges quite strongly from the pages of depositions in matrimonial suits.)[74] Other criteria were a rough equality between the couple in terms of age, 'ancestry' or family background (apparently relevant even in cases which did not involve gentry), reputation, and wealth. In practice, wealth seems to have been by far the most important.[75]

In reality these ideals were not sufficiently compelling or unambiguous to preclude conflict in particular cases, some of which led to contract litigation. Examination of the depositions in spousals suits illustrates a variety of disputes. In certain cases the defendant's withdrawal from the alleged contract was in conflict with the wishes of his own family; in some instances of this type, it would appear that the defendant had initially agreed to marry the plaintiff in compliance with the desires of his parents or other kin, but had reneged on the contract when such circumstances as the death of his father or a split of opinion among his relatives had provided the opportunity to exercise greater freedom of personal choice.[76]

However, cases in which the alleged contract went against the wishes of the defendant's family or friends appear to have been commoner than those in which the opposite was true. Sometimes both plaintiff and defendant really desired the alleged match, but family pressure prevented the latter from acknowledging the fact. To safeguard the freedom of individual consent in such cases, the law provided a specific procedure: if the plaintiff could show that it was necessary, the judge could order the defendant to be 'sequestrated' on neutral ground to prevent the application of undue influence.[77] Certainly, on occasion, the courts were willing to adjudicate in favour of contracts made against the wishes of the family, so long as the couple themselves were willing.[78] However, suits in which the defendant persisted in defying parents or other relatives were less common than cases in which the use of the family's veto had successfully dissuaded an individual from honouring a contract. The efficacy of family pressures is hardly surprising

---

[72] For example, Stone, *Family, Sex and Marriage,* pp. 102–5. For a different view, see A. Macfarlane, 'Modes of reproduction', *Journal of Development Studies,* XIV (1978), 109–10.

[73] Ingram, 'Ecclesiastical justice in Wiltshire', p. 119.

[74] For particularly vivid cases, see Ely D.R., D/2/11, fos. 202–6 (*Wynster v. Ritche* alias *Kellogge,* 1577); Salisbury D.R., Bishop's Dep. Bk. 30, fos. 95–6 (*Smith v. Head,* 1615).

[75] Ingram, 'Ecclesiastical justice in Wiltshire', pp. 119–20.

[76] For example, Salisbury D.R., Bishop's Dep. Bk. 30, fos. 50–5v, 90–102 (*Hussy v. Flower,* 1616) (death); Dean's Dep. Bk. 5, fos. 14v–16, 24–30 (*Fry v. Tuck,* 1604) (divided opinion).

[77] Houlbrooke, *Church Courts and the People,* p. 63. Sequestration was also used to prevent a defendant solemnizing a marriage with a third party in an attempt to prejudice the suit.

[78] Houlbrooke, *Church Courts and the People,* p. 63.

given the range of sanctions at their disposal, apart from conventional acceptance of their authority. The most widely used tactic seems to have been to threaten to deprive recalcitrant children of financial support or of their rights of inheritance; but moral and even physical pressures were sometimes applied.[79]

Further complexities in the matter of consent are illustrated by cases in which the plaintiff was a woman made pregnant by her lover. The wider community, having regard both to the morality of the situation and sometimes also to the fear that a bastard child would burden the poor rates, might regard the man as duty-bound to marry the woman and might exert considerable pressure on him to do so, while his own family might encourage him to resist if the match seemed imprudent.[80] Community pressures in such cases could be strongly supported by the secular authorities: it is known that, in the early modern period, Justices of the Peace (either at the petition of the pregnant woman, her representatives, or local Poor Law officers) sometimes coerced men into marrying women they had made pregnant as an alternative to being dealt with under the bastardy statutes.[81] Occasionally the circumstances underlying suits involved such forced marriages, and more commonly the more general issue of the problem of pregnancy was at issue. Ecclesiastical law prevented the church courts from responding to community pressures to enforce men to marry women whom they had seduced; cases had to be decided on the issue of consent.[82]

*   *   *

Since contract suits—like other matrimonial causes—had important disciplinary implications, the courts could not in theory leave them undecided: the relationship between the parties had to be clarified.[83] In theory this marked them off from most other types of medieval and early modern litigation, the abandonment or out-of-court settlement of which was common and legally admissible.[84] In practice, at all periods from the later Middle Ages onwards, the judges allowed a considerable proportion of contract cases to remain undetermined. Some suits were simply abandoned, others settled out of court with or without the help of arbitrators and mediators. In some instances

---

[79] Houlbrooke, *Church Courts and the People*, pp. 62–4; Haskell, 'Paston women', pp. 467–8; Salisbury D.R., Bishop's Dep. Bk. 26, fo. 169 (*Monday v. Pile*, 1609); Dep. Bk. 30, fo. 102 (*Hussy v. Flower*, 1616); Dep. Bk. 24, fos. 93–4, 108 (*Waterman v. Nicholas* and *Jeay*, 1607).

[80] For example, Salisbury D.R., Bishop's Dep. Bk. 36, fos. 125v, 137v, 139 (*Chisleton v. Maundrell*, 1620); Dep. Bk. 24, fo. 94v (*Waterman v. Nicholas* and *Jeay*, 1607).

[81] For example, Ely D.R., B/2/36, fo. 146; Salisbury D.R., Bishop's Act Book (Office) 9, 19 July 1619, *Office v. Foster;* Archdeacon of Wiltshire's Act Bk. (Office) 1, 15 Feb. 1602/3, *Office v. Sawier.*

[82] Houlbrooke, *Church Courts and the People*, p. 64.

[83] Helmholz, *Marriage Litigation*, p. 135.

[84] M. J. Ingram, 'Communities and courts: law and disorder in early seventeenth-century Wiltshire', in J. S. Cockburn (ed.) *Crime in England 1550–1800* (London, 1977), pp. 125–7.

abandoned or informally concluded cases ended with a marriage between the parties,[85] but the indications are that this was not true of the majority. Many suits probably remained in a totally indeterminate state. In others, the plaintiffs evidently renounced their claims, either freely or in consideration of an apology or, in some cases, of a payment in money or goods.[86] (The practice of settling causes for cash invites comparison with the common law action for breach of promise of marriage, the earliest cases of which apparently date from the sixteenth century.)[87]

To the extent that they condoned the abandonment or compromise of spousals suits, the church courts were tacitly ignoring the strict letter of their own law on marriage contracts. There are indications, moreover, that the abandonment or compromise of suits became relatively more frequent as time went on. In the later Middle Ages, according to Helmholz, 'most' suits were actually determined by the judges. In the Ely diocesan court in the late fourteenth century, the proportion of suits which came to sentence was apparently very high, and it was still impressive (over 70 per cent) in Ely diocese in the 1580s. In the dioceses of Norwich and Winchester in the period 1520–70, however, only about half the contract suits which came before the consistory courts ended in a sentence or final decree; while in the early seventeenth century, in Ely diocese and in the Wiltshire portions of the diocese of Salisbury, the proportion was below 40 per cent.[88]

The proportion of final sentences in favour of marriage contracts alleged by plaintiffs also declined from the late fourteenth to the seventeenth centuries. In the diocese of Ely in the 1370s and 1380s, over 50 per cent of plaintiffs in suits which came to sentence were successful. In the dioceses of Norwich and Winchester in the period 1520–70, plaintiffs securing successful sentences were outnumbered by unsuccessful ones in determined suits in a ratio of about 3:7. In the diocese of Ely in the 1580s, barely more than 20 per cent of sentences were favourable to plaintiffs, while in a sample of early seventeenth-century cases the plaintiff won in only 1 case out of 9 determined suits. The situation in Wiltshire in the period 1601–40 was even more extreme. In only 1 case out of a total of 26 which are known to have come to sentence was an adjudicatory decree awarded, and this was a suit in which

---

[85] For example, Salisbury D.R., Bishop's Act Bk. (Instance) 35, fo. 84 (*Holloway v. Leazie alias Hedges*, 1607); Act Bk. (Instance) 36, fo. 141v (*Browne v. Miles*, 1608); Act Bk. (Instance) 38, fo. 13 (*Gale v. Scott*, 1610).

[86] For example, *Child-Marriages, Divorces, and Ratifications, etc. in the the Diocese of Chester, A.D. 1561–6*, ed. F. J. Furnivall (Early English Text Society, Original Series, CVIII, 1897), 59–60; Salisbury D.R., Dean's Dep. Bk. 6, fo. 88 (*Matravers v. Miles*, 1609); Bishop's Dep. Bk. 46, fo. 196v (*Middlecot v. Abathe*, 1631). Cf. Helmholz, *Marriage Litigation*, pp. 135–7; Houlbrooke, *Church Courts and the People*, p. 67.

[87] S. T. C. Milsom, *Historical Foundations of the Common Law* (London, 1969), p. 289.

[88] Proportions taken or calculated from information in Helmholz, *Marriage Litigation*, p. 135; Sheehan, 'Formation and stability of marriage', pp. 257–61; Houlbrooke, *Church Courts and the People*, pp. 267–7; Ingram, 'Ecclesiastical justice in Wiltshire', p. 124; and sources listed in notes 36 and 39.

the defendant himself admitted the alleged contract but was being prevented by his family from solemnizing it.[89]

Variations in the proportion of adjudicatory sentences awarded may partly reflect the changing nature of the cases which came before the courts, but is seems likely that a more important conditioning factor was the attitude of the judges. The church courts gradually became more reluctant to confirm disputed marriage contracts, to the extent that eventually, at least in early seventeenth-century Wiltshire, adjudicatory sentences were exceedingly difficult to obtain. This development, coupled with the growing willingness to allow cases to be compromised or to remain undetermined, suggests that ecclesiastical lawyers were gradually turning their backs on the ancient law of spousals to the extent of treating unsolemnized unions, at least in cases of dispute between the parties, as virtually unenforceable.

At first sight this development may seem a gross dereliction of duty, but it needs to be understood in the light of the Church's long-term success in securing recognition of its authority in matrimonial matters and in fostering the acceptance of ecclesiastical solemnization in church as the normal mode of entry into the married state. The Church's task was aided by the fact that for certain purposes the common law, faced with problems which depended on the existence or otherwise of a marriage but unable itself to determine the validity of unions, used the ceremony in the face of the Church as a convenient touchstone for presuming that a marriage existed. In particular, it was established that no woman could claim dower unless she had been endowed at the church door.[90] For the property-owning classes at least, this was a powerful incentive towards acceptance of solemnization in church as the normal practice.

It is true that Sheehan's analysis of the late fourteenth-century Ely register indicates not only that a considerable proportion of cases involved unsolemnized unions, but also that the court in that period did not show much urgency in ordering contracted couples to proceed to solemnization. In the diocese of Rochester in the 1340s, on the other hand, contracted couples cited *ex officio* for cohabiting without proceeding to solemnization were normally ordered to solemnize their marriage immediately; in addition, they were frequently required to abjure sexual relations before they were married in church and to undergo a whipping.[91] Whether the more rigorous policy of

---

[89] Figures calculated from information in Sheehan, 'Formation and stability of marriage', pp. 257-61; Houlbrooke, *Church Courts and the People*, pp. 276-7; Ingram, 'Ecclesiastical justice in Wiltshire', pp. 124-5; and sources listed in notes 36 and 39. The figure for successful actions at Ely 1374-82 falls slightly below 50 per cent if causes originating in *ex officio* proceedings are ignored; cf. Houlbrooke, *Church Courts and the People*, p. 84.

[90] Pollock and Maitland, *History of English Law*, II, 380-4.

[91] Sheehan, 'Formation and stability of marriage', p. 250; Kelly, 'Clandestine marriage', pp. 440-2, basing his conclusion on analysis of the acts of the consistory court of Rochester, April 1347 to November 1348, printed in *Registrum Hamonis Hethe Diocesis Roffensis A.D. 1319-1352,* ed. C. Johnson (10 parts in 2 vols. consecutively paginated, Canterbury and York Society, XLVIII, XLIX, [1915-]48), 911-1043.

the Rochester court was more normal than that prevailing at Ely in the late fourteenth century is at present unclear. In any event, Helmholz thinks it likely that by the late Middle Ages most of the people who made private contracts meant to have their unions blessed by a priest at some later time, or at least to have the banns read. Houlbrooke believes that, by the early sixteenth century, the vast majority of matrimonial contracts were regarded as merely the first step towards solemnization in church; and the study of the Ely and Wiltshire material indicates that the same conclusion is unquestionably true for the late sixteenth and early seventeenth centuries.[92] In that period, the recognition of a church wedding as the only satisfactory guarantee of a socially and legally acceptable marriage was probably strengthened by a growing hostility towards bastard bearing, in part occasioned by demographic stress and the increasingly pressing problems of poverty.[93] In the late sixteenth and early seventeenth centuries, moreover, the church courts increasingly brought prosecutions for incontinence before solemnization even when the couple concerned had, before proceedings commenced, already got married in church or clearly intended to do so.[94] Such prosecutions probably did little to reduce the actual incidence of antenuptial fornication, but they may well have helped to drive home the importance of the ecclesiastical solemnization in church, which alone made sexual intercourse licit.[95] Inevitably, of course, ideas stressing the prime importance of the contract continued to exert an influence. Thus, in 1641 a certain Thomas Trepocke of Teffont Evias in Wiltshire confessed how he and Elizabeth Macy

> being ... sure together in marriage and man and wife save only the outward solemnization thereof in the church did since they were so contracted and sure the one to the other lie together. . . .

But it is notable that, even in a case like this, the couple clearly intended to marry in church when they could—Trepocke had tried to obtain a licence, but could not because some of Elizabeth's 'friends' refused their consent.[96]

The various trends which have been observed in the incidence and handling of contract litigation should be interpreted in the light of these developments. At the beginning of the period under review there probably existed some

---

[92] Helmholz, *Marriage Litigation,* pp. 29–30; Houlbrooke, *Church Courts and the People,* pp. 56–7, 66.

[93] Ingram, 'Ecclesiastical justice in Wiltshire', pp. 374–8; K. Wrightson and D. Levine, *Poverty and Piety in an English Village: Terling, 1525–1700* (New York, San Francisco and London, 1979), pp. 125–34 and ch. VII.

[94] Ingram, 'Ecclesiastical justice in Wiltshire', pp. 181–201; Marchant, *Church under the Law,* p. 137; Wrightson and Levine, *Poverty and Piety,* pp. 126–7. But cf. Houlbrooke, *Church Courts and the People,* p. 78.

[95] P. E. H. Hair, 'Bridal pregnancy in rural England in earlier centuries', *Population Studies,* XX (1966), 238–9; Ingram, 'Ecclesiastical justice in Wiltshire', pp. 200–1; Wrightson and Levine, *Poverty and Piety,* pp. 132–3. Cf. above, p. 39.

[96] Salisbury D.R., Bishop's Court Papers, Citations 5/15.

reluctance to admit the Church's claims and considerable uncertainty about what acts constituted a state of marriage. This would account for the relatively high incidence of suits at that time and the comparatively large proportion of multi-party suits with some element of implied bigamy. In these circumstances it would be appropriate for the church courts to adjudicate in favour of a relatively high proportion of disputed contracts (while nevertheless maintaining reasonably high standards of proof), and to seek as far as was administratively possible to leave few suits undetermined. At the end of the period, the widespread recognition of solemnization in church as the essential guarantee of a socially and legally acceptable marriage narrowed the possibilities for confusion, uncertainty, and deceit. At the same time, the changed conditions made it reasonable for the courts to adjudicate in favour of disputed contracts only when the issues were crystal clear. Both changing social conditions and the altered attitude of the courts probably had a part to play in reducing the incidence of contract suits to the low level observable on the eve of the Civil War. It is probable, moreover, that in these circumstances the practice of entering into binding contracts, even when it was accepted that they must be confirmed by a church wedding, tended to decline. Clearly some contracts continued to be made. But it is noticeable that, in the records of the Wiltshire church courts in the early seventeenth century, references to formal contracts involving the careful exchange of consent and the giving of a ring and gifts, with or without witnesses, are rare save in the papers actually relating to spousals suits; much more common are indications of formless *promises* to marry, clearly intended as preliminaries to a 'real' marriage in church. A similar situation may well have been prevalent in other parts of England. In 1686 the writer of the preface to Swinburne's work on spousals was constrained to admit that they were 'now in great measure worn out of use'.[97]

*   *   *

One result of the increasing difficulty of obtaining recognition of an unsolemnized union may have been to strengthen the influence of the family and other interests over the formation of marriages. The openness of solemnization (at least if the canonical requirements concerning banns, licences, places, and hours were complied with) probably made the evasion of family pressures more difficult. It also put the matrimonial opportunities of some individuals more at the mercy of the wider community. Numerous examples from the early modern period indicate that ministers, in league with more substantial parishioners, frequently refused to read the banns or

---

[97] Swinburne, *Treatise of Spousals,* sig. A2v. For earlier comments to the effect that spousals were neglected, see Gouge, *Of Domesticall Duties,* p. 202; Matthew Griffith, *Bethel: Or, a Forme for Families* (London, 1633), p. 272; Daniel Rogers, *Matrimoniall Honour* (London, 1642), p. 121; Houlbrooke, *Church Courts and the People,* p. 66.

conduct marriages between poor people who might burden the poor rates.[98] This practice was undoubtedly against the law of the Church,[99] but apparently ministers who so acted were rarely prosecuted.

However, before 1753 an escape route existed for those who accepted the need for solemnization in church yet wished to marry in secrecy. This was to procure a clandestine marriage ceremony, which as we have seen created a valid marriage with some pretence at solemnization in church, yet evaded banns, licence, or other safeguards of publicity. Little information is at present available on prosecutions for clandestine solemnization in the period before 1600.[100] But some assessment of the significance of clandestine marriage ceremonies in early seventeenth-century conditions may be made on the basis of an analysis of the relevant prosecutions found in the records for the Wiltshire portion of the diocese of Salisbury. It is clear that there were many reasons for procuring a clandestine ceremony. Some were obtained in contravention of the ban on marriages in the prohibited seasons. Others occurred when the bride was noticeably pregnant and wished for a secret marriage to avoid either prosecution or censure. Sometimes clandestine ceremonies were procured when contract litigation was in progress: the defendant hoped that speedy marriage with a third party would prejudice the issue or discourage the plaintiff from proceeding.[101] But it would seem that many clandestine marriage ceremonies were related to the evasion of social pressures against free choice. In some cases community pressures were being defied, as when poor people procured marriages despite parochial opposition; more often, secret marriages were sought when the couple could not secure the consent of their kinsfolk.[102]

To procure a clandestine marriage ceremony involved trouble, expense, and the risk of prosecution. Analysis of cases[103] indicates that principals in clandestine ceremonies convicted of planned evasion of the law were treated fairly rigorously. A few were enjoined penance, but most incurred the sentence of excommunication—though in a high proportion of cases (38 per cent), usually where there were mitigating circumstances, the judges were prepared to minimize the effects of the penalty by granting an immediate

[98] Wrightson and Levine, *Poverty and Piety,* pp. 80, 133; Salisbury D.R., Dean's Churchwardens' Presentments, 1628, no 26; Archdeacon of Salisbury's Act Bk. (Office) 11, 13 June 1612, *Office v. Fulway;* Bishop's Act Bk. (Office) 8, 2 Dec. 1617, *Office v. Hitch.*

[99] John Johnson, *The Clergy-man's Vade-Mecum* (London, 1709 edn.) pp. 185–8.

[100] But see Sheehan, 'Formation and stability of marriage', pp. 240–3, 250; *Child-Marriages, Divorces, and Ratifications,* ed. Furnivall, pp. lxii–lxiii, 140–1; Houlbrooke, *Church Courts and the People,* p. 79.

[101] For example, Salisbury D.R., Bishop's Act Bk. (Office) 10, 27 Sept. 1621, *Office v. Penn* (prohibited season); Act Bk. (Office) 11, 14 June 1628, *Office v. Amer* (pregnant); Bishop's Dep. Bk. 46, fo. 168 (*Middlecot v. Abathe,* 1631) (contract litigation).

[102] For example, Salisbury D.R., Bishop's Act Bk. (Office) 8, 2 Dec. 1617, *Office v. Hitch;* Archdeacon of Wiltshire's Act Bk. (Office) 1, 5 Feb. 1601/2, *Office v. Huntley;* Bishop's Act Bk. (Office) 5, 31 July 1605, *Office v. Bachilor;* Bishop's Act Bk (Office) 8, 14 Sept. 1616, *Office v. Aprice.*

[103] For details see Ingram, 'Ecclesiastical justice in Wiltshire', pp. 128–30.

or speedy absolution on payment of the appropriate fees. The treatment of people who had merely been present at clandestine marriage ceremonies was generally lenient. Comparatively few were prosecuted, and those decreed excommunicate stood a good chance of securing immediate absolution. Discipline over ministers who performed clandestine ceremonies posed problems. People who wanted a secret marriage often went outside the diocese or into a peculiar jurisdiction, and this made action administratively difficult. A number of beneficed Wiltshire clergymen were able to engage regularly in clandestine marriage business, mulcting their clients of substantial sums. But to inflict suspension on such men was a drastic step, for the practical result might be merely to deprive the parish of pastoral care. Nevertheless, suspensions were occasionally decreed.[104]

It is difficult to assess how serious a problem clandestine marriage actually was. Clearly the penalties were insufficient to deter a really determined couple. The number of prosecuted cases, perhaps 20 per annum for the whole county of Wiltshire in the early seventeenth century, was certainly not negligible, but small in proportion to the total number of legally performed marriages. However, it is unknown what proportion of cases escaped detection. Of the known cases, a few involved sinister or exploitative circumstances, but most can probably be interpreted as relatively innocent elopements. The impression is that in early seventeenth-century Wiltshire, clandestine ceremonies served as a useful safety valve whereby couples could evade unreasonable family or community pressures, and did not constitute a major abuse. How far clandestine marriage developed into a major social evil in the late seventeenth and early eighteenth centuries, and in particular what the effects were of the availability of easy marriage in the Fleet Prison and elsewhere, must be left to the determination of those who have studied Hardwicke's Marriage Act and its background.[105]

---

[104] For example, Salisbury D.R., Bishop's Act Bk. (Office) 8, 14 Sept. 1616, *Office v. Cole.*
[105] See R. L. Brown, 'The rise and fall of the Fleet marriages', this volume, pp. 117–36.

III

Continuity and Change in Literary Advice on Marriage[1]

KATHLEEN M. DAVIES

Whatever changes there may have been in English marriage and family life in the early modern period, there can be no doubt that at least one new kind of family developed—the legitimate family of the clergyman. For many parishioners the most obvious changes brought about by the Reformation may well have been those they saw in their parson's household. The priest's harlot became the parson's wife, and very often they were the same woman; over all the change took less than two generations, so that by the early seventeenth century a respectable, legitimate wife and family had replaced, in almost all parishes, whatever household arrangements earlier celibate priests had made. A Protestant regime had removed the legal obligation of celibacy from priests in the Act of 1549, allowing priests to marry; a developing Protestant theology denied the usefulness of voluntary chastity and other good works as a means of salvation for anyone, cleric or lay; and this combination removed any real alternatives to marriage as a vocation. This is the background to the large number of contemporary sermons, pamphlets and conduct books about family life and the management of a godly household, mostly written by clergymen and particularly by Puritan ones. But the connection between these texts and any changes which may have taken place in family life and relationships in that period is not a straightforward one. Did all this advice bring about any changes in the households of its recipients? Or, conversely, can we use this torrent of literature to show that family life was changing in any important respects in late sixteenth-century and early seventeenth-century England?

Puritan conduct books have been used to argue that the sixteenth century saw the emergence of a new ideal of family life arising specifically from Protestant teaching about the family. This new ideal form of marriage was based, for the first time, on mutual respect and love between partners who now shared a more equal responsibility for the spiritual and worldly advancement of their household. And it has been argued that these ideals represent a very different and more elevated view of family life from the ideals presented in pre-Reformation or early Protestant writings about

[1] An earlier version of this essay appeared in *Social History*, 5, May 1977. I am grateful to the editors for permission to reproduce parts of it.

marriage.[2] In recent years social historians have questioned the use of such sources as direct evidence of attitudes and behaviour, and have mounted a sustained attack on the theory that their contents can be taken at face value. Demographic studies show that literary sources have only a limited use in social history, since the patterns of behaviour which they describe may be highly unrepresentative. Church court records and popular folk customs indicate that basic attitudes to marriage and family life among the poor remained unchanged over many centuries. And even among Puritan families there seems to have been a greater diversity of structure and behaviour than the texts suggest. It would be very difficult now to maintain that the conduct books can be used on their own to show how men and women actually behaved.[3]

But the notion that these texts describe a new *ideal* of family relationships, whether that ideal was practised or not, has survived this criticism. A fairly standard list of writers tends to be quoted to support the view that there was a new ideal of mutuality in marriage, which was a direct outcome of Puritan theological principles.[4] Professor Stone has defined the general position in this way: 'Whether in Anglican or Puritan households, there was, in varying

[2] C. L. Powell, *English Domestic Relations 1487–1653* (New York, 1917); Levin L. Schücking, *The Puritan Family* (London, 1969; first edn. Leipzig, 1929); Louis B. Wright, *Middle Class Culture in Elizabethan England* (London, 1964; first edn. 1935), ch. VII; W. and M. Haller, 'The Puritan art of love', *Huntington Library Quarterly*, V (1941–42), 235–72; R. M. Frye, 'The teachings of classical Puritanism on conjugal love', *Studies in the Renaissance,* XI (1955); W. Notestein, 'The English woman 1580–1650', in J. H. Plumb (ed.), *Studies in Social History* (London, 1955). See also references in Lawrence Stone, *The Crisis of the Aristocracy 1558–1641* (Oxford, 1965), ch. XI; Carl Bridenbaugh, *Vexed and Troubled Englishmen* (Oxford, 1968), ch. I; R. B. Schlatter, *The Social Ideas of Religious Leaders 1660–88* (Oxford, 1940), where sixteenth-century writers are also mentioned. There is a discussion of the question and a list of the most relevant texts in Christopher Hill, *Society and Puritanism in Pre-Revolutionary England* (London, 1964), ch. XIII.
[3] See P. Laslett and R. Wall (eds.), *Household and Family in Past Time* (London, 1972); A. Macfarlane, *The Family Life of Ralph Josselin* (Cambridge, 1970); R. Thompson, *Women in Stuart England and America* (London, 1974); for Church courts R. A. Marchant, *The Church Under the Law: Justice, Administration and Discipline in the Diocese of York 1560–64* (Cambridge, 1969), especially ch. VI; F. G. Emmison, *Elizabethan Life and Morals; the Church Courts* (Chelmsford, 1973); Hill, *Society and Puritanism,* ch. VIII; for charivari N. Z. Davis, 'The reason of misrule: youth groups and charivaris in sixteenth-century France', *Past & Present,* L (1971), 44–75; E. P. Thompson, '"Rough music": le charivari anglais', *Annales E. S. C.,* 27ᵉ année (1972), 285–312; E. K. Chambers, *The Medieval Stage* (2 vols., Oxford, 1903), vol. I. Recent studies of the history of the family are dominated by Lawrence Stone, *The Family, Sex and Marriage in England, 1500–1800* (London, 1977). See also J.-F. Flandrin, *Families in Former Times* (trans. R. Southern, Cambridge, 1979), and Alan Macfarlane, *The Origins of English Individualism: The Family, Property and Social Transition* (Oxford, 1978).
[4] I have used the list given in Hill, *Society and Puritanism,* p. 456, most of the sources quoted by Schücking and Wright, and those listed in Stone, *Family, Sex and Marriage.* The texts most frequently cited are: Henry Smith, *A Preparative to Marriage* (1591, *STC* 22685); Robert Snawsel, *A Looking Glass for Married Folks* (1631, first edn. 1610, *STC* 22886–7); John Dod and Robert Cleaver, *A Godly Form of Household Government: For the Ordering of Private Families According to the Direction of God's Word* (1614, *STC* 5382), which was a new and expanded edition of the work of the same title by Robert Cleaver (or Cawdrey);

degrees, a new emphasis on the home and on domestic virtues, and this was perhaps the most far-reaching consequence of the Reformation in England'.[5] This is one of the reasons why he describes as a stage in his theory of family evolution what he calls the 'restricted patriarchal nuclear family'. He sees this type of family as beginning about 1530, predominating between about 1580 and 1640, and running on to at least 1700. Puritan writings are not, of course, the only evidence for his definition of this stage, but he does quote Protestant and Puritan preachers and moral theologians as evidence that there was a new ideal available for those men and women who wished to aspire to it.

Professor Stone's brief analysis of the literature has cleared away a great deal of confusion. In particular he separates very clearly the two distinct aspects of these writings—the stress on domesticity and 'affect' on the one hand, and the emphasis on patriarchy and the subjection of wives on the other. He concludes that in both these areas there is evidence that new theories were developing, theories specific to Puritanism and particularly strongly held by Puritans. First, he argues that the ideal of a harmonious and domestic family life, growing out of a close relationship between husband and wife, was a new and different approach emerging in the late sixteenth century. Second, he thinks that the stress on patriarchy was far stronger than ever before, and that the authority of husband over wife increased greatly in the same period. Unlike his Puritan authors, Professor Stone is well aware of the potential incompatibility of these two theories, but seventeenth-century writers took the paradox in their stride.

As far as printed, and therefore popularly available, works on marriage and family life are concerned, I would question whether the stress on domesticity is in fact so very new or so peculiar to Protestants. Most of the attitudes expressed in the conduct books can be found in earlier works, provided that we compare like with like, that is, if we compare Puritan sermons and works of moral instruction with earlier works about marriage and family life, also addressed to the married laity.[6] Naturally, pre-Reformation works of moral theology addressed to priests stressed the virtues of

---

William Whateley, *A Bride Bush or a Wedding Sermon* (1617, dated in the introduction 1608, *STC* 25296); William Gouge, *Of Domesticall Duties* (1622; the copy in his *Works*, 1627; *STC* 12119, 12109). I also include among this group of texts Heinrich Bullinger, *The Golden Book of Christian Matrimony* (trans. Theodore Basille, i.e. Thomas Becon, 1543, *STC* 1724) because it was so obviously a source for many of the later ones. See biographical note, pp. 79–80 for details of the authors.

[5] Stone, *Family, Sex and Marriage*, p. 141.

[6] Powell, *Domestic Relations*, deals with some early sources, but does not distinguish moral theology from domestic advice. For the early sixteenth century, i.e. pre-Reformation writers, I have used William Harrington, *Commendations of Matrimony* (1528, *STC* 12801), and Richard Whitford, *A Work for Householders* (1530, *STC* 25422), both in detail. See also Vives, *Instruction of a Christian Woman* (1529? trans. Richard Hyrde, *STC* 24856) and *Office and Duty of a Husband* (1553? trans. Thomas Paynell, *STC* 24855); Thomas Elyot, *The Book Named the Governor* (1531, *STC* 7635) and other works on education. Some

celibacy and the notion that marriage was second best, but their advice to the *laity* on domestic problems is remarkably similar to that given by Puritan writers. Unless we assume that these earlier writers were untypical of their time, or in some sense 'proto-Puritan'—an assumption which has very flimsy foundations—we must conclude that the popular Puritan authors expressed no distinctly 'Puritan' theory of domestic relations.[7]

One change of emphasis, however, is very significant indeed. In his penetrating study of domestic relations, C. L. Powell traced a change during the sixteenth century from concentration on the legal aspects of marriage to more discussion of domestic problems in general. This change of emphasis and the increased popularity of such books reflect the publishing explosion of the sixteenth century and the growth of a middle-class lay reading public, rather than changes in attitudes to marriage itself. But it makes it all the more difficult to compare like with like. Our earlier texts belong to a period when books were precious and for the specialist; by the end of the sixteenth century books were common enough to deal in generalities. There were more books printed about cookery and husbandry at the end of the sixteenth century than at the beginning, and more of them have survived, but it would be unwise to assume either that these activities were new ones or that there were new theories about them. Pre-Reformation books on marriage were written for priests, who needed to know about canon law and theological interpretation; some of them, like Harrington's *Commendations* and Whitford's *Work for Householders* also contained hints on how to help the laity with their marriage problems. In contrast, most late sixteenth-century books on marriage were written for the general market; the problems of invalid marriages or higher theology were now left to specialist works. The book market had changed so much that this must be the single most important factor in any analysis of the texts.

Most works, whether pre-Reformation, Protestant or Puritan, deal with much the same questions—the ends and purposes of marriage, and the

---

sixteenth-century works on marriage or women, like earlier ones, are either satirical or are clearly part of an elaborate courtesy ritual. (See the list in Ruth Kelso, *Doctrine for the Lady of the Renaissance* (Urbana, 1956).) Many, too, are part of the stylized controversy about the nature of woman (among these the *Treatise of the Nobility of Women* by Henry Cornelius Agrippa, trans. David Clapham (1542, *STC* 203) gives an unusually enthusiastic view); but the whole tradition of discussing the status of women, along with the courtly literature, is not really relevant to domestic matters. Agrippa's *Commendation of Matrimony* (trans. Clapham, 1540, *STC* 201) is more relevant but not very revealing. See also the 'Book of the Knight of La Tour-Landry' (1372, ed. T. Wright for *EETS,* vol XXIII, 1868); two English poems: 'How the goodwife taught her daughter' and 'How a wise man taught his son', ed. F. J. Furnivall, *A Book of Precedence* (*EETS,* extra ser., VIII, 1869), dated there as mid-fifteenth century but see the edition by Tauno F. Mustanoga, Helsinki, 1948, for earlier versions.

See biographical note, pp. 79–80 for details of the authors.

[7] Some later and more radical Puritans, of course, did. See A. L. Morton, *The World of the Ranters* (London, 1970) and Christopher Hill, *The World Turned Upside Down* (London, 1972).

ordering of the household, and they include practical advice on how to achieve the ideal form of domestic life. Their purpose is that of practical piety, they all share common sources in the Bible, particularly the Pauline Epistles, and they all express a conventional view of what their authors considered to be normal and natural in human relationships. None of the authors propounds anything startlingly unexpected in the relationships between husbands and wives, parents and children, or masters and servants. Their most obvious characteristics are a monotonous similarity of highly generalized advice, given by authors as different in other respects as a monk of Syon (Whitford) and a fashionable London Puritan preacher (Gouge), and also a considerable skill in avoiding the discussion of any really difficult problems of personal or physical relationships. Wives troubled by straying or brutal husbands are advised to try loving them more and displaying more signs of meekness by both the fourteenth-century Knight of La Tour-Landry and the Puritan Robert Snawsel; unlawful sexual behaviour is condemned before the Reformation by Harrington and long after it by Gouge, but in neither case is the unsophisticated reader enlightened about what this behaviour involves. In his early study of Puritan writers in their literary context, Professor Schücking noticed 'a complete lack of inhibition in [Puritan] readiness to theorize on the erotic side of marriage', but the texts do not bear this out.[8] Vagueness, generalization and conventionality are their chief characteristics.

The status of marriage was a question more suited to the theologians than to the general reader, but it was discussed obliquely by most authors when they dealt with the purposes of marriage. Protestant rejection of clerical celibacy and of good works, including voluntary chastity, as aids to salvation, implied that marriage had a higher theological status than it had had before the Reformation. We would expect to find this altered status reflected in a different view of the purposes of marriage, but much confusion has resulted from attempting to find logic and progression in the lists of these purposes. All our sources give the same three reasons for marriage—procreation, a remedy against fornication, and mutual comfort and help. This is the order of priorities, for example, given by Smith (1591) following Bullinger (1543), and is the reason why he disapproved of marriage by the elderly. Whateley (1617) recommended marriage principally as a means of founding a new family to store the world with people and to provide plants for God's vineyard. Cranmer had included 'mutual society, help and comfort, that the one ought to have of the other, both in prosperity and adversity' in the 1549 Prayer Book. But Tyndale and Harrington, both writing in the 1520s, also included mutual solace and help, and in the fourteenth century the Knight of La Tour-Landry praised marriage for company and protection as well as for the propagation of children. So mutuality was not in itself a new idea

[8] Schücking, *Puritan Family*, p. 38.

and there is nothing unusual or novel in the Puritan inclusion of mutual comfort as one of the ends of Christian marriage.

Trying to put the purposes in any logical order leads to even more confusion. Harrington's order of priorities is in fact exactly the same as that followed by Bullinger and a century later by Baxter: procreation first, then remedy, then mutual help. Tyndale was the first writer in English to put procreation second, but he put it second to 'a remedy', not to mutuality. Cleaver, Smith, Perkins, Niccholes and Gouge (a good 'Puritan' list) all put procreation first; Bacon, Rogers, Pritchard, Cartwright and Gataker put mutual solace and comfort first. There is no clear line of difference at all, and in this respect Puritan writers do not seem to have laid particular stress on mutuality at the expense of the older Thomist purposes of marriage. Contemporary Catholic theologians were also arguing that intercourse between husband and wife had values other than that of procreation. So whatever changes may have taken place in the behaviour of married people, this arid discussion of ends and purposes can have had little relevance to them.[9]

Professor Stone's 'paradox' is clearly visible here, since the Puritan obsession with achieving male dominance seems to argue against their theory of mutuality in marriage. The overwhelming preoccupation of the seventeenth-century writers was with the relationship which subordinated the wife to the husband. Gouge expressed the theory of male dominance in its strongest form, and it is the most important theme of his *Of Domesticall Duties:* in marriage there is a covenant of God, in which the husband 'is a priest unto his wife' (Bullinger's translator earlier called the husband a bishop) . . . 'He is the highest in the family, and has both authority over all and the charge of all is committed to his charge; he is as a king in his own house.' Whately defined the husband as God's officer and king, with the wife as his 'deputy', 'subordinate and associate', and argued that a family was 'deformed' if the husband's authority were challenged by the wife. Dod and Cleaver described the trouble which came when wives were not subject—'for God will not bless where his ordinance is not obeyed', and Smith called a wife 'an under-officer in his Commonwealth'.[10]

---

[9] James T. Johnson, 'English puritan thought on the ends of marriage', *Church History*, XXXVIII (1969), 429–36 discusses the theological significance.

[10] Gouge, p. 138. It was the husband's duty to conduct prayers and religious instruction for the household, and 'the wife may be a great help in putting her husband in mind both of the duty itself, and of the time of performing it'. She could deputize only in his absence (p. 152). See also p. 151; Gouge's views on the subjection of women were untypically strong even in this company, and it would be tedious to cite all his references to the subject. See in particular the *Third treatise: of wives particular duties* (pp. 157–201): there he describes subjection as a virtue taught to wives by the Holy Spirit, which should season their opinions, affections, speech, actions and all. The subjection should not merely be borne, but also intellectually accepted, even by the sober, religious wife of a man of lewd and beastly condition, or of a blasphemer, or an infidel, a wicked and profane man or a fool, or even an enemy of Christ (for example, pp. 160, 169, 191.) All these men must be held to be actually

There seems to be little evidence in all this to support Wright's claim that there was an 'increased emphasis upon woman's spiritual and material rights [which] paved the way towards theoretical equality' (my italics);[11] nor to support the claim of a more recent writer that 'the puritan writers generally sided with women's rights, though they carefully maintained man's superiority of station'.[12] The emphasis is all the other way.

Gouge's prayer for the use of husbands contains a long petition for aid in maintaining the stamp of authority over wives; references to shrews and froward wives in need of control abound throughout the texts; and Snawsel in particular has some interesting evidence about how social pressures were used to produce meekness in a wife through total conformity to her husband's moods and temperament, even when he was drunk, since 'it is sinful that the woman should usurp the man's authority'.[13] Male dominance was not

---

superior by their wives, not merely treated as if they were superior, and their wives must labour to bring their own judgement and will to that of their husbands (p. 195). This, of course, raises the problem of conflict of obedience, see below, pp. 68–9. Whateley, p. 16. The sentence specifically states that wives were all these things 'but not altogether equal'; ibid. p. 19, and see also p. 18, 'Now for the husbands special duties, they may fitly be referred to these two heads: The keeping of his authority, and the using of it . . . He must not suffer this order of nature to be inverted'. Dod and Cleaver, sig. F4. The passage goes on: 'This is allowable that she may in modest sort show her mind; and a wise husband will not disdain to hear her advice, and follow it also, if it be good. But when her way is not liked of, though it be the best way, she may not thereupon set all at six and seven, "with what should I labour and travail? I see my husband taketh such ways, that he will bring all to nothing". This were nothing else, but when she see-eth the house falling, to help to pull it down faster . . . she must not think herself freed from duty, because he walketh not in his duty; but hold her place . . . and so God will either bless the works of her hands . . . or give her husband more wisdom and care; or else give her a contented mind with a low estate, which is great riches'; Smith, p. 52.

[11] Wright, *Middle Class Culture*, pp. 226–7. Wright gives no source for his contrast between the Puritan insistence that a wife should be a lieutenant and a supposed earlier view that she should be 'a chattel and slave'.

[12] James T. Johnson, *A Society Ordained by God—English Puritan Marriage Doctrine in the First Half of the Seventeenth Century* (New York, 1970), p. 86.

[13] The prayers are appended to Gouge's *Treatise* in ten unnumbered pages. Snawsel, pp. 53–60. Besides the use of irrational changes of mood, and beatings (pp. 53, 60, 69, 80) very like the behaviour of Petruchio in *Taming of the Shrew*, Snawsel describes the use of neighbours—'some motherly and modest matrons', 'my loving and religious neighbour' (p. 42), 'I might much displease my husband, and hurt my neighbours' (p. 44); rejection by neighbours (p. 57); use of kin and parents (pp. 64–6); use of the fear of poverty following desertion (p. 77). All these techniques are used in his dialogues to turn a rebellious young woman into a submissive wife, and are contrasted favourably with the devices used 'to tame lions, bulls, and elephants' (p. 79); the outcome of such training is always presented as a change from a quarrelsome couple to a happy one. The 'neighbour' figure in Snawsel also advises on the appropriate way to put up with an adulterous husband—meekness, better house-keeping and hope—and there is a neighbourhood rejection of the 'bad wife' figure whose response had been: 'Here are fetters for the legs and yokes for the necks of women: must they crouch on this manner to their currish and swinish husbands: if I had such an one, as he behaved himself like a swine, so I would use him like a beast' (p. 55). The 'good' wife also encourages the other women to express from time to time a conventional disrespect for their own sex—'women most commonly are so fickle, and will find themselves so many things to do, and are so soon weary of hearing and reading any good thing' (p. 56).

peculiar to Puritanism, of course. Gouge argued that the disabilities laid upon married women by the law were a futher proof of their natural disabilities, and, like his contemporaries, he was expressing the same views as earlier writers had done. Both Vives and Whitford presented a conventional view of dominance by husbands, and Harrington counselled wives to obey because 'the husband hath the pre-eminence and is master and ruler of his wife'.[14] Puritan writers were at one with their predecessors in believing strongly in male dominance, and they seem to have experienced the same difficulties in putting it into practice.

In the same way, 'Puritan' views on free choice of marriage partner for both men and women, equality of regard and in the sharing of marriage goods, the right to follow individual conscience in religious matters, and mutual involvement in achieving both a godly household and personal salvation can all be found advocated by early writers who seem to be in no way peculiar or untypical. Harrington based the marriage contract firmly on the express consent of both partners, a consent arising from their love for each other, and there is no indication that this consent was meant to be different from that described later by Gouge or Whateley. Catholic and Puritan writers alike warned against basing marriage on beauty or wealth; and despite the theory of mutuality and constant references to freedom of choice by both partners, all their advice on what qualities to look for in a marriage partner was aimed at helping men to find the ideal wife.[15] Free choice was also limited, in both Puritan and earlier writing, by parental control.

The 'sacred condition of equality' was interpreted by the mid-seventeenth-century Puritans Rogers and Baxter as meaning similarity of social status and age in the partners, not as equality of status after marriage. Gouge also advocated equality of this kind—he approved of husbands being between five and ten years older than their wives—but he disapproved of such false indications of equality of status as affectionate nicknames between husband and wife. He discussed this matter at some length, advising that the wife should always give her husband titles of honour and should eschew words like 'brother, cousin, friend, man' because they imply equality; in the same way he advised against her use of his Christian name, particularly in any shortened form, and strongly condemned such names as 'sweet, sweeting, heart, sweetheart, love, joy, dear, etc.' or 'duck, chick, pigsnie. Common use and practice hath made the addition of the husbands surname to this title, master, more meet'. The point is also driven home in his advice to husbands: 'Wife is a mild and kind title, and least offensive of all other'; he suggested

---

[14] Vives, *Office and Duties of a Husband* (1553); Harrington, sig. d i. That is, master and ruler in all matters *other than* the right and charge of matrimony, i.e. sexual rights.

[15] Even the Knight of La Tour-Landry, who was ostensibly writing for his daughters (pp. 16–17). Bullinger, in 19 pages devoted to the subject of what to look for in a spouse, gave no advice on how to pick a good husband.

that titles such as 'woman' or 'wench' gave a wife too little respect, but those such as 'lady, mistress, dame, mother . . .' set the wife in too high a place over her husband.[16] Similarly, Whateley defined the 'reciprocal bond of duty' as a recognition by both that the husband was the wife's head.

Community of goods was also stronger in theory than in practice. Bullinger advocated 'one common purse' and later writers followed him in this. But it is clear that the spending of money other than on the basic household expenses was intended to be controlled by the husband, and both Bullinger and his followers were firm that over any particular expense or possession the husband must have the custody and government of the goods. Dod and Cleaver, for example, made this clear:

> The husband . . . must have the custody, and chief government of the goods in the house, yet may he discharge himself of the whole, or of part, as himself shall think meet and convenient . . . there are other things, in which the husband gives over his right unto his wife: as to rule and govern her maidens: to see to those things that belong unto the kitchen, and to housewifery, and to their household stuff. Other mean things, as to buy and sell certain necessary things, may be ordered after the wit, wisdom, and fidelity of the woman.[17]

The same distinction appears in our earlier texts: Harrington advocated equality in the consumption of common goods; Whitford placed responsibility for overseeing the household on both partners. The advice of the fourteenth-century Ménagier of Paris to his teenage wife deals with hiring and supervision of servants and the entire management of a large and complicated household during his long absence—all the financial arrangements were left to her discretion. In 'How the goodwife taught her daughter', married women are enjoined to keep the keys and pay the wages of workers themselves.[18] This practical equality in managing business affairs is also found in Fitzherbert's *Book of Husbandry* (1523), from which it is clear that wives commonly made many financial transactions without reference to their husbands; he described dealings with the miller and selling pigs, cows and poultry as peculiarly women's work. Financial equality of a strictly limited sort seems neither greater nor less than in the Puritan writings, and Lyly's advice: 'Let all the keys hang at her girdle but the purse at thine, so shalt thou know what thou dost spend and how she can spare', might describe

---

[16] Gouge, p. 110.

[17] Dod and Cleaver, sig. N 3; cf. Whateley, p. 32, the wife should have 'the free and plentiful use of all' his goods unless she requires more than he thinks fit, when 'his authority must sound retreat unto her lavishness'. Schücking, *Puritan Family*, p. 34, quotes Rogers on how husbands should allow their wives to choose the colour of their dresses, although they have in fact the right to obedience over this; Schücking comments that this is evidence that 'the Biblical principle of the complete subjection of the wife to the will of her husband loses the greater part of its force. However inviolate it may still appear to be, its substance has largely disappeared and the door has thus been opened to further development'. It seems a large claim.

[18] *Le Ménagier de Paris* (c.1393), ed. J. Pichon (Paris, 1856). See Eileen Power, *Medieval People* (London, 1924), ch. IV; Furnivall, *Book of Precedence,* pp. 44–51.

the financial relationship of marriage partners throughout the period.[19] It is difficult to see why Schücking thought that Puritan writers were advocating a change in the position of women in regard to property rights. He describes Baxter as 'seeing matters very differently' from other writers when he mentioned that a wife could claim a third of her husband's property in the event of death or divorce, but in fact Baxter was here merely stating the law.

The result of this partnership was a definition of mutual and complementary duties and characteristics. Dod and Cleaver, following Bullinger, listed them:

Husband	Wife
Get goods	Gather them together and save them
Travel, seek a living	Keep the house
Get money and provisions	Do not vainly spend it
Deal with many men	Talk with few
Be intermeddling	Be solitary and withdrawn
Be skilful in talk	Boast of silence
Be a giver	Be a saver
Apparel yourself as you may	Apparel yourself as it becomes you
Be lord of all	Give account of all
Dispatch all things outdoor	Oversee and give order within[20]

And a considerable part of this mutual duty was the upbringing of children in godly ways.

Advice on child-rearing is an important element in all the texts, and the mother's role is given a high value. But again there is nothing specifically 'Puritan' about this. Whitford, as well as pointing out somewhat unnecessarily that 'this word parents doth signify both the father and mother', stressed the importance of night blessings by both parents. Harrington enjoined both parents to bring up their children in the laws of God and man. Wycliffe's view that both 'father and mother ought to teach their children the belief of the Trinity and of Jesus Christ' was a description of normal medieval practice, in which the mother's role was the same as that described by Puritan authors.[21] Whatever value these later authors placed on the basic role of the family as distinct from the Church as an instrument for instilling godly beliefs and practice into children, the methods used did not seem to change. Whitford's list of daily prayers to be used by the family

---

[19] Quoted in Carrol Camden, *The Elizabethan Woman* (London, 1952), p. 192.

[20] Dod and Cleaver, sigs. L 4–5; Bullinger, ch. XVI.

[21] Whitford, sig. d iv; women could also, of course, baptize infants; Harrington, sig. d ii, 'As well is bound the husband to help the wife as the wife the husband'. He listed the most important things to teach: the creed, ten commandments, prayers such as Pater Noster and Ave, the seven deadly sins 'with their branches', the laws of man, dealing with neighbours, how to prosper 'lawfully and truly', and prudent spending; J. Wycliffe (?), 'Of wedded men and wives and of their children also', *Select English Works,* ed. Thomas Arnold (3 vols., Oxford, 1869–81), III, 188–201, esp. 195.

would have shocked Gouge by its theological content, but he would have recognized the practice, as well as the 'pretty lessons' taught to the children about basic morality—lying, backbiting, stealing, cursing, mocking, swearing, chiding, fighting, complaining. The rod, if necessary, was the answer, whatever the theology. Catholic Whitford told mothers to beat their children; Protestant Rogers told them to aid their husbands in beating them.[22]

Wife-beating was a recurrent theme, condemned in theory but often approved in practice. A strongly biblical pamphlet of 1616, quoted by Wright as evidence that Puritan writers had a horror of conjugal violence, condemned blows as 'brutish', *except when* the wife turns upon her husband 'in furious mood', when he should beat her 'for her good'. Only Gouge and Smith seem to have disapproved totally of the use of violence by husbands: Gouge allowed them to use force only in physical self-defence, and Smith made no exceptions. All the other authors found that there were some circumstances when physical correction was an unpleasant necessity; like their predecessors they believed in what they called 'moderate correction', for which, of course, there was no legal redress. There seems to be no evidence in the texts for Schücking's belief that these writers were part of 'a markedly progressive element' in this respect. The same sort of 'moderation' can be found in the earlier writers: Harrington—'the husband may moderately correct and punish his wife for a lawful cause'; Whitford—'a shrew will sooner be corrected by smiling or laughing than by a staff or strokes'; 'How a wise man taught his son':

> With love and awe thy wife thou chastise
> And let fair words be thy yard . . .
> Son, thy wife thou shalt not chide,
> Nor call her by no villein's name;
> For she that shall lie by thy side
> To call her wicked, it is thy shame.[23]

If there was any kind of move towards equality of treatment between husband and wife, it seems to have found no expression in any lessening of violent behaviour as described in the marriage manuals.

The reciprocal duty of marriage partners to care for each other's salvation and to counsel each other was a constant theme of Puritan writers. Gouge devoted a great deal of space to this, and, like other writers, he confronted the basic problem created by it—the wife's conflict between obedience to her husband and obedience to the word of God as interpreted by her own conscience. Chapter 63 of *Of Domesticall Duties* deals with the extent of a wife's obedience, and illustrates the gulf between theory and practice. Gouge

---

[22] Schücking describes this assistance as evidence of Puritan 'spiritual harmony and agreement of husband and wife' (*Puritan Family*, p. 75).

[23] Harrington, sig. c vi; Whitford, sig. h iv; Whitford also advised that' the best way to keep a woman good: is gentle entreaty and never to let her know that she is suspected and ever to be counselled and informed with loving manner' (ibid.); Furnivall, *Book of Precedence*, p. 53.

clearly stated that 'she may do nothing against God's will, but many things must she do against her own will, if her husband require her', and he maintained this position wherever he specifically discussed this conflict of obedience. Yet it is just as clear that by wifely obedience Gouge meant total subordination of her mind and judgement, not deliberately but in response to her own real belief in their actual inferiority to those of her husband, as well as simply obeying orders or appearing to be obedient. In any practical sense this makes nonsense of his theoretical view of the supremacy of her conscience. In treatise II, chapter 23, he dealt with the problem created when only one partner was called to the faith; he gave bland injunctions about seeking to draw the other to the faith, but in the case of the justified wife this must have involved some kind of belief that her own behaviour (if not her judgement) was morally superior to that of an obviously sinful husband. Gouge made no attempt to reconcile this discrepancy between theory and practice; on one page he advised a wife that she must disobey her husband's unlawful order to go to the Mass or a stage play, while on the next page he gave this advice:

Question What if a husband be an enemy of Christ: must such subjection be yielded to any enemy of Christ as to Christ himself?

Answer Yea: because in his office he is in Christ's stead, though in his heart an enemy. In this case will the wisdom, patience and obedience of a wife be best tried.[24]

And Gouge passed on immediately to eulogies of humility, sincerity, cheerfulness and constancy in wives. But how *was* it to be reconciled, particularly in view of his clear statement that the married could not separate for this kind of reason? Despite its large size and convenient index, his treatise does not seem to have offered much practical help to any Blackfriars parishioner who found herself faced with this conflict of obedience.

Whateley is just as confusing on this question. He advised husbands not to command unlawful things nor 'such also, as she upon some supposed reason, grounded on the Word of God, thinks to be unlawful', even, it is implied, if she is in fact wrong. But later in the same chapter he counselled the same kind of total obedience as Gouge: 'Mine husband is my superior, my better.' He defined it even more clearly; he advised wives to practise outward reverence, which he defined as regarding their husbands as God's deputy. The chapter ends with a description of the perfect wife 'when she submits herself with quietness, cheerfully, even as a well-broken horse turns at the least turning, stands at the least check of the riders bridle, readily going and standing as he wishes that sits upon his back'. (The metaphor of horse-breaking was a favourite one—it occurs in Bullinger, Smith, Gouge and Dod and Cleaver, but Whateley was particularly fond of it.)[25]

[24] Gouge, pp. 195–6 and 391–2.
[25] Whateley, pp. 33–4, 36, 38–42, 43.

This kind of behaviour seems to have left little room for a tender conscience. It is clear that a very real conflict existed, but no attempt to resolve it was made by any of these authors.[26] And even if we accept that these statements allowed some liberty of conscience to wives, it seems to be no greater a liberty than that described by pre-Reformation writers who discussed the same problems. Harrington stated that wives were bound to obey their husbands in lawful things, and also that neither husbands nor wives should make vows concerning spiritual matters without their partner's consent. For both partners obedience was due first to God and then to each other. The fourteenth-century Knight of La Tour-Landry advised his daughters to think carefully before giving counsel to their husbands (there is no suggestion that they were not able to give good counsel) and considered it a wife's duty to 'serve God, then her husband, to pray for him, counsel him for the wealth of his soul, and turn him from every unwise deed', waiting until husband and wife were alone to do this. But he specifically stated that no woman ought to serve her husband before God, which does not seem to be a different position from that of Puritan authors who held a different theological view of the supremacy of conscience. The lack of guidance in the Puritan texts is all the more surprising when we remember that for a Puritan a crisis of conscience such as this conflict of authority was a real practical individual problem in a way that it could never have been for a medieval Catholic woman. It is about the only real problem ever raised by the authors, and the way they turn away from it shows, I think, that they were writing conventional texts for the market rather than serious attempts to tackle novel issues. In the public relationship between husband and wife, the Puritan writers seem to present exactly the same image as Vives had done at the beginning of the sixteenth century.

A woman well brought up is fruitful and profitable unto her husband, for so shall his house be wisely governed, his children virtuously instructed, the affections less ensued and followed, so that they shall live in tranquility and virtue. Nor thou shalt not have her as a servant, or as a companion of thy prosperity and welfare only, but also as a most faithful secretary of his cares and thoughts, and in doubtful matters a wise and hearty counsellor.[27]

Over this question of the subjection of wives, Professor Stone differs from earlier commentators in his views that patriarchy in general and the domi-

---

[26] Some radical Puritans did produce genuine solutions to the problem. See K. V. Thomas, 'Women and the civil war sects', *Past & Present*, XIII (1958), 42–62. And such a situation happened in Dedham in 1637 and in other American communities, where it was not uncommon for wives to be admitted to church membership before their husbands, and could therefore vote for or against their admittance. (See R. Thompson, *Women in Stuart England and America* (London, 1974), ch. 4.) But most of our authors, none of whom was radical in this sense, simply did not discuss it.

[27] Quoted in Foster Watson, *Vives and the Renascence Education of Women* (London, 1912), p. 209. Compare this definition with the Puritan pamphleteer Philip Stubbes's eulogy of his young wife, who was married at 15 and died at 20; she was silent, learnt at home from her husband, never contradicted him, and always suited her mood to his: Philip Stubbes, *A Cristal Glass For Christian Women* (1591, *STC* 23381).

nance of husbands over wives was on the increase in the sixteenth century, and that both the status and the legal rights of women positively declined. He links this tendency too with the Reformation; the end of Catholicism eliminated the cult of the Virgin, the supportive celibate priests, and the alternative option of the convent. He argues that along with the decline of protective kinship and the emphasis placed by state and law on subordination of wives as a guarantee of general law and order, the new sanctification of marriage itself facilitated subordination. 'By a paradoxical twist, one of the first results of the doctrine of holy matrimony was a strengthening of the authority of the husband over the wife, and an *increased* readiness of the latter to submit herself to the dictates of the former' (my italics).[28] Puritan writers do certainly emphasize subjection, and there are more of them, but whether the subjection they advocated was more intense or far-reaching than that advocated by earlier writers can only be a speculation. Certainly none of the earlier writers of marriage-books argued against the subjection of wives. The tradition of courtly writing in praise of women, like the tradition of conventionally disrespectful and bawdy works about women, continued in the sixteenth and seventeenth centuries, but their stylized generalizations and stereotypes are not very revealing about real attitudes to domestic relationships or the status of women.

Among more serious earlier works about women, Thomas More's authoritarian view of the subjection of wives in *Utopia* (or indeed in his own home) is no different from other humanist writing on the subject. When Vives described the education and characteristics of an ideal wife in the *Instruction of a Christian Woman* he did not in any way connect a smattering of classical education with a higher status for women or more equality between husband and wife. The classical humanist education which was briefly fashionable in the early sixteenth century was intended by its advocates to increase the quiet domestic virtues of women; they specifically argued against any public role for women or any aggressive behaviour towards husbands. More wrote to his scholarly married daughter Margaret Roper, 'in your modesty do not seek for the praise of the public, nor value it . . . but because of the great love you bear us, you regard us—your husband and myself—as a sufficiently large circle of readers for all that you write'.[29] If we find a discrepancy between humanists' theories about the education of women and their views on the status of wives, we may be assuming a connection which they would not themselves have made. Humanists, like other writers of pre-Reformation works on marriage, seem to have approved of husbands' superiority and wives' subjection as much as Puritan writers did.

In the more private relationship too there are many similarities between Puritan texts and pre-Reformation ones. Schücking contrasted the Puritan

[28] Stone, *Family, Sex and Marriage*, p. 202.
[29] Quoted in P. Hogrefe, *The Sir Thomas More Circle* (Urbana, 1959), p. 218.

attitude towards the sexual side of marriage, 'Puritanism's greatest and most admirable cultural achievement', with earlier contempt and what he calls 'a rather repulsive Jesuit output'. But these latter handbooks for use in confession by celibate priests following the recommendations of Canisius and Bellarmine are not strictly comparable with general works on marriage for the laity, and where books addressed to the same kind of reader are compared the discussion of sex within marriage is not very different.[30]

Pre-Reformation preachers certainly gave celibacy, widowhood and virginity a higher theological value than marriage, but the vices they condemned were the same as those condemned by Puritans: adultery and fornication by either partner, and shrewishness, disobedience and over-adornment in wives. From time to time they let fly about the sexual snares of women, but they do not seem to have included modest and humble wives in that category. Like the Puritan preachers, they attacked painted harlots and rowdy, flamboyant women who roistered in taverns or flaunted their sexuality—a stock target not at all peculiar to the pre-Reformation pulpit. They condemned gluttony and drunkenness with equal vigour, but it would be unreasonable to assume that they included all lawful eating and drinking among those vices. Medieval sermons frequently condemned adultery and fornication, and any behaviour which might lead to them. But it is not clear that a preacher, who used King David as an example for how 'clipping and kissing' were sinful, was also condemning 'kissing and gripping and beholding *of the apparently harmless sort*' (my italics). David was, after all, a famous adulterer, not a respectable married bourgeois. It is unreasonable to compare Puritan discussion of *marital* sex with pre-Reformation condemnation of *extra-marital* sex as many have done, and to conclude that pre-Reformation writers therefore condemned all forms of sexual activity. Preachers who thundered against 'wooings, kissings, secret singings, gay array, nice cheer', and even 'songs of love paramour and letters of love' and all such 'things that be forbidden as dancing of women and other open sights that draw men to sin' also preached marriage sermons, in which they extolled 'stillness in bearing, honesty in clothing, abstinence in meat and drink, shame in appearance and countenance' as qualities of the ideal wife. They do not seem to be talking about the same women; good wives were to use their fine clothes to 'adorn and prepare themselves to please their husbands', and so presumably to enable both partners to avoid the temptations of adultery.[31]

Harrington condemned adultery and also 'every spending of mans or womans nature otherwise than in lawful matrimony ordinately and naturally'

---

[30] 'Moral theology in the vein of Bishop Burchard, or St. Raymond, or Sanchez, does not set out desirable aspirations; it provides minima of conduct for the instruction of the confessor judging sins'; John T. Noonan, *Contraception, A History of its Treatment by the Catholic Theologians and Canonists* (New York, 1956), ch. XI, which has a discussion of sixteenth- and seventeenth-century Jesuit works of this kind; Schüking, *Puritan Family*, pp. 37–8.

[31] G. R. Owst, *Literature and Pulpit in Mediaeval England* (Oxford, 1933; 2nd edn. 1966), pp. 383, 384–91.

as being 'deadly and some way most abominable sin'. His advocacy of honest temperance and moderation, which seems to include abstaining from sexual activity during the forbidden times of menstruation and pregnancy 'nigh the time of the birth', is very similar to that found in Puritan writers. Whately has a long description of menstruation (which includes an apology to those readers who might find discussion of such a subject offensive), because this was a forbidden time for sexual intercourse; like his contemporary William Gouge he counselled abstinence at the same time as their predecessors had done: menstruation, late pregnancy, and the period after childbirth, though Puritan writers did not, of course, end that period at the woman's churching. Some Puritan writers also enjoined abstinence at times of fasting, as their predecessors had done for rogation days and other ecclesiastical occasions. Such temperance and moderation, along with cheerfulness in sexual behaviour, are advocated by all the writers. It is not clear where their 'lack of inhibition' is to be found. Apart from the occasional mention of menstruation and some discussion of barrenness in women, there is no explicit advice about either conjugal activity or sexual problems. There are long passages by most of the authors about the advantages of breast-feeding, but apart from the rather vague advice offered by one pamphlet that neglected wives should invite their husbands to try 'walking with you into this temple of Eroto', these texts, like the earlier ones, are a disappointingly vague source of information.[32]

It is clear that sexual activity was meant to be regular. All the writers condemn the separation of husband and wife because it interfered with their conjugal relationship—Gouge is particularly strong on this—and also any refusal by either partner of conjugal rights. Absence was allowable for the good of the state or for business but not for pleasure, and it was not right for husbands and wives to occupy separate parts of the same house. But this view, too, is common in earlier writers. Harrington warned husbands and wives not to make vows 'in any part prejudicial to the duty of matrimony', such as vows of chastity, and disapproved of refusal to take part in sexual behaviour even of a sinful kind.[33] There does seem to be one sharp difference, however. Many Puritan preachers were convinced that when they rejected abstinence by the married they were differing from Romish beliefs, and there is some evidence that they were right; none of the early sixteenth-century

---

[32] Menstruation gave rise to some coyness. Dod and Cleaver refer to the time 'when it is with the wife (as is common to women Ezech. 18.6)' (sig. M 2); Gouge is slightly more forthright: 'that time which under the Law was called *the time of a wives separation for her disease*' (p. 131). The pamphlet is Anon., *The Great Advocate and Oratour for Women* (1682), p. 7; cf. Harrington's advice (sig. d iii) that those with problems should consult 'such as have further learning and experience in that behalf'.

[33] Harrington, sigs. c vi, d ii, 'In these times and seasons man and wife ought not to meddle fleshly together and if they do he or she which is occasion and the provoker thereof doth sin greatly. But the other which doth obey doth not sin. For the one must answer the other in that behalf at all seasons when he or she doth require.'

conduct books actually advocates virtuous abstinence, but a hint of it is present in a story told by the Knight of La Tour-Landry about a cold bath, and other stories abound in which virtuous couples make great efforts to overcome conjugal desire.[34] The change seems to have been gradual; Bullinger allowed abstinence, provide it was 'with consent' and not 'always or long but only for a time' but his later plagiarists did not follow him in this respect. Instead they condemned voluntary abstinence as positively harmful.

Adultery was the only acceptable reason for separation, and several late sixteenth- and early seventeenth-century writers shared some common ground on this with those later more radical Puritans who advocated divorce as a remedy. Censorship may have exercised a restraint over open approval of divorce; Whateley appeared before High Commission for his approval of remarriage by a deserted spouse, and in *A Care Cloth* (1624) he retracted the views he had expressed in *A Bride Bush* seven years earlier.[35] Approval of divorce on the grounds of adultery expressed in texts published after the removal of censorship may not indicate development of ideas so much as freedom to express some ideas which earlier Puritan writers may well have shared. It is in this area that we do see a different point of view from that of pre-Reformation writers. If matrimony was a covenant, and not a sacrament, then adultery destroyed the basis of the contract, and it was therefore dissoluble. But the different positions over the indissolubility of marriage arose from different theological positions, not necessarily from different views of domestic relationships or of the importance of conjugal affection. And they were not differences which arose from the Reformation, but within Protestant theology; the Anglican Church maintained continuity over this question. Milton was quite exceptional in arguing that incompatibility and lack of mutual affection should be grounds for divorce; some other Puritan authors required a fundamental breach of the central mutual obligation to dissolve the contract; but mainstream Protestantism retained the Thomist view of marriage as an indissoluble bond. This divorce controversy did not arise from a different belief about the intensity of married love but from different views about the relationship between God and mankind. It is an

[34] Harrington describes as the conventional view (sig. a vi) that it was a good custom for the newly-married to abstain 'the first three days and nights from fleshly meddling together and give themselves in that space to prayer ... [Or at least one night] ... in reverence of the sacrament'. He states specifically that this was 'good counsel and no commandment', and that non-observance did not create sin, but it was a means to 'great merit with good fortune and gracious fruit and the better prosperity in all their works'. In opposing this, Puritan writers were, of course, opposing the notion of good works contained in it at least as much as any low value placed on physical love.

[35] See W. and M. Haller, 'The Puritan art of love', pp. 267–72. The offensive passage ran: 'And if it so fall out, that either party do frowardly and perversely withdraw him or herself from this matrimonial society (which fault is termed desertion) the man or woman thus offending, doth so far violate the covenant of marriage, that (the thing being found incurable, through the obstinacy of that party, after just care had to redress it) the other is loosed from the former bond, and may lawfully (after an orderly proceeding with the church or magistrate in that behalf) join him or her self to another' (Whateley, pp. 3–4).

important controversy for our understanding of the development of Puritan theology, but it does not reveal much about attitudes towards conjugal relationships.

Many of the Puritan writers had the same masculine bias about adultery as they had about choice of marriage partner. Although both partners are mentioned, all the actual examples of separation for adultery are described as arising out of adultery by the wife, not by the husband, which might lead the reader to conclude that it was the more serious offence. Smith, for example, defended separation because it was a means of identifying bastards, and Whateley, while mentioning women, thought that it was necessary for the innocent partner to separate *him*self from the sinful partner, though in other matters he was most careful in his use of pronouns. There is predictable agreement on the double standard: Bullinger gave a long list of reasons why adultery was worse by women than by men. He argued that it altered the inheritance, gave honest poor husbands great shame, travail, sorrow and pain, dishonoured fathers, mothers, and husbands, made children ashamed of the mothers and doubtful of their own legitimacy, and made husbands despised and of no reputation.[36] There is rather an odd contrast here with Harrington, who thought that the penalty in civil law for male adultery should be death, but women should be beaten naked and kept in a convent for two years, then, if not reconciled with their husbands, for life. However, apart from Harrington, who specifically mentioned adultery as the only grounds for separation—'but that must be done by authority of their ordinary'—there is no evidence that the earlier writers shared Puritan beliefs about separation on these grounds.

Many of the more peripheral characteristics assumed to be peculiar to Puritan writings on marriage are also to be found in earlier works. Careful prudence and foresight are constant features of both; Whitford's advice to householders to keep a year's rent or a year's income in store 'for chances' is an example of capitalistic caution, and his remedy for times of poverty—to spend less—is typical of the rather banal quality of the advice offered by all these conduct book writers. He also advised a careful watch on servants, in case they wasted their master's goods, and a plain but sufficient diet. Vives, too, was much exercised about the prudent governing of the household, as were the Knight and the Ménagier in the fourteenth century. The sobriety and prudence described in Roper's life of More are very like the characteristics advised by Bullinger as a means to material prosperity; Whateley reversed this combination by condemning unthriftiness as an enemy to authority in the home.[37]

---

[36] See also K. V. Thomas, 'The double standard', *Journal of the History of Ideas*, XX (1959), 195–216. Gouge pointed out that more *inconveniences* may follow upon a wife's adultery, but not more sin. The sin was the same for either partner.

[37] Whitford also recommended his readers (sig. H iii) to 'make your testament every year new and surely sealed by witness. Lay it where (when need is) it may be found'; and he discussed

This common characteristic may provide an explanation of the similarity of view expressed by men writing from very different theological positions. It is clear that the recipients of the advice belong to what Christopher Hill has called households 'of the industrious sort'. Servants are mentioned in all the texts, and both husbands and wives are involved in the day-to-day management of these households. Vives' work *Of Wives* implies that he was writing about a very different life style from that described in his *Plan of Studies for Queen Catherine;* he dealt at length in the former with a wife's need to know medicines for cough, murr, stomach-ache, diarrhoea, constipation, worms, headache, eye-pains, ague and bones out of joint, rather than with the learned accomplishments of the great lady. Both Whitford and Harrington described child-rearing by mothers unaided by nurses or by separate accommodation for children of the kind which was usual in aristocratic houses.[38] Similarly, the advice in Bullinger or Dod and Cleaver about how husbands should beat the men-servants and wives beat the maids implies personal control of a small, comfortably-off household, not a great aristocratic estate. It is in fact a picture of a household built on the firm economic base of bourgeois endeavour, whether of the fourteenth or of the seventeenth century.[39] There are urban overtones in all the works: Snawsel's conventional literary device of a dialogue between women chatting in the street with passers-by intervening has the same setting as Whitford's injunction to parents that children found stealing should be dealt with by shaming them 'through the open streets'. All the authors seem to have the same group in mind—the urban bourgeoisie.

It may be, therefore, that what we are seeing in the early seventeenth

---

the value of industry as a remedy against sin as well as a means to prosperity. Compare his commendation of 'an old proverb':

Who so do spend beyond their faculty
no marvel though with need they grieved be

with the equally pointless advice given by Dod and Cleaver a century later, 'so to cut his coat according to his cloth, and to eat within his own tether'.

These characteristics of domesticity and prudence are well combined in one of the Knight's stories, in which a knight, coming back from a long voyage with a gown for each of his nieces, was greeted by one of them who ran out with her hands covered in flour from baking. She got both gowns as a reward for her virtues and domesticity.

[38] Harrington advised mothers against putting babies in the parent's bed, or leaving young children alone near fire or water. It does not accord with what seem to have been aristocratic habits of child-rearing in a separate part of the household (cf. Philippe Ariès, *Centuries of Childhood* (London, 1962) and also Stone, *Crisis of Aristocracy*, ch. XI; the entries concerned with the nursery in the *Northumberland Household Book* (*c.* 1512), ed. Thomas Percy (London, 1770), also imply a separate establishment). But it does fit a bourgeois life style.

[39] Both Whitford and Bullinger specifically contrasted the life of their ideal Christian man with that of princes and lords (Whitford, sig. H ii), and Bullinger dismissed any notion that he was addressing himself to 'gentle women and such as are of noble birth' (sig. f. lxxv). Instead he advocated spinning, sewing and weaving: 'It becometh her better to have a pair of rough and hard hands, than to be fair and soft glistening with rings or covered continually with smooth gloves' (f. lxxviii v).

century is a collection of descriptive, rather than prescriptive texts, written by authors who were not advocating new ideals for marriage but were describing the best form of bourgeois marriage as they knew it. They were describing behaviour by husbands and wives which had in fact changed very little, in spite of considerable changes in theological views about the status of marriage itself.

We know that domestic life changed in certain important respects for many aristocratic families during the sixteenth century; but it is difficult to see what direct effect these texts could have had on the process. Could many great ladies in fact identify with the shrewish chatterboxes or the meek and busy housewives described in them?[40] These ladies seem to have been unaffected by the literary stereotypes even when they were confronted by them; it is almost as though everyone assumed that rank conferred exemption from the natural weaknesses of femininity. There seems no other explanation for Bishop Aylmer's temerity in standing before Queen Elizabeth, and preaching the following:

> Women are of two sorts; some of them are wiser, better learned, discreeter, and more constant than a number of men; but another and worse sort of them are fond, foolish, wanton, flibbergibs, tattlers, triflers, wavering, witless, without counsel, feeble, careless, rash, proud, dainty, tale-bearers, eavesdroppers, rumour-raisers, eviltongued, worse-minded, and in every way doltified with the dregs of the devil's dunghill.[41]

Perhaps, like modern mothers-in-law, the great ladies smiled at the stereotype, without seeing any application to themselves.

The amount of space devoted in these texts to wife-beating seems to imply a different life style from that experienced by the daughter of a great house entering marriage under the protection of dower or jointure, or surrounded by a protective kinship network. It is difficult, too, to find much in common between the day-to-day governing of the busy, prudent, small household of these texts and the bureaucratically-organized estate with its complicated investments and large intermediate management.[42] If there was any dissemination of ideas through the medium of these books and sermons it would hardly have been because of the relevance of their practical advice. Professor Stone has detailed the changes which many aristocratic families made in the financial and legal arrangements for their marriages; these were fundamental to any change in aristocratic behaviour. Puritan divines must have played

---

[40] For example, Gouge, p. 14: 'As when tattling gossips meet, their usual prate is about their husbands, complaining of some vice or other in them.' Cf. Eileen Power on the incompatibility of the standard image of women presented by medieval satiric preachers, and the evidence of real women's lives in that period, 'The position of women', in C. G. Crump and E. F. Jacob (eds.), *The Legacy of the Middle Ages* (Oxford, 1926).

[41] Quoted in Stone, *Family, Sex and Marriage,* p. 196.

[42] Cf. Whateley, pp. 14–15: both partners must be laborious and industrious in their calling; he described his ideal couple as 'a good housewife . . . [and] a good diligent hand, for the man's part'.

at most a peripheral part in the process, and if they had any effect at all, it was, I suggest, not because they were preaching any new ideas, but because they were disseminating more widely a rather unchanging style of successful bourgeois family life, at a time when the thrifty and prudent habits of such a life may have appealed to some of their social superiors.

It seems unlikely that the urban bourgeoisie would have found a great deal that was new or unusual in the writings of Gouge or Whateley; their popularity may have had more to do with the very familiarity and acceptability of what they contained. People who listen to sermons are very often exhorted to do exactly what they think they are doing already, and a taste for reading analyses of one's own life style is not peculiar to the bourgeoisie of the seventeenth century. What is interesting about the Puritan conduct books is in fact their very continuity; the likelihood is that despite all the religious, economic and social changes which transformed the political history of the nation, the bourgeoisie went on quietly and prudently endeavouring to form partnerships in the ways which worldly experience showed had the greatest chance of success.

There is enough continuity in the advice to the laity about the purposes of marriage and about the relationship between husband and wife in all its behavioural aspects—choice of partner, dominance of husband, mutual affection and respect, sexual activity, and sharing of work—to indicate that Puritan conduct books do not show any *change* to domesticity and affection as ideals of marriage. There was nothing new in such ideals. And whether they show anything about how people actually behaved, for example whether there was an *increase* in patriarchy, seems highly questionable.

The advice they gave differed from earlier advice in only two respects—rejection of the theory that voluntary sexual abstinence by married couples was a means of obtaining grace, and a suggestion that divorce and remarriage might be permissible in some circumstances. However significant these theories, and they seem to relate more to a different view of the sacraments than to a different view of society, they are far outweighed by the similarities. I am not suggesting that Puritanism could not be a source of revolutionary ideas about marriage and family life; for some radical groups in both England and America it clearly was. But these were groups of the untypical, far left of Puritanism. The word 'Puritan' has been used very loosely in this context. We have become accustomed to distinguishing between different kinds of Puritanism when we discuss the development of science or of political thought, and such a distinction seems just as relevant when we are considering their teachings about family relationships. As far as mainstream Puritanism is concerned—and the popularity of these books must indicate a readership far wider than radical groups—the most commonly cited texts seem to be of a very conventional nature. The godly Puritan and the pious pre-Reformation bourgeois may well have lived very similar lives, at least if they practised what their clergy preached.

APPENDIX: BIOGRAPHICAL NOTES

HARRINGTON's *Commendations* (*STC* 12799, first edn. 1528) was printed posthumously at the instance of Polydore Vergil but may have circulated earlier. It consists of advice to curates on how to give general instruction to their parishioners. Signs of orthodoxy include: references to seven sacraments, 'our most blessed lady', holy days appointed by holy mother church, and the proper way of keeping Advent and rogation days. Harrington discussed whether the sacrament of marriage could be received in deadly sin, and whether the offspring of a doubtful marriage was legitimate enough to take holy orders—his manner of discussing them seems distinctly non-Protestant. There are orthodox descriptions of the rites of baptism and confirmation, he gives the full orders of the clergy, and refers constantly to bishops. The Bodleian edition (*STC* 12801) has the word 'Pope' scratched from the printed page where Harrington was discussing dispensations. The book is conventional in tone; there is no hint that the writer thought he was expressing new ideas. It was a popular work—there was more than one edition within a few years and it was also re-issued.

RICHARD WHITFORD (1495–1555) was a far greater figure in the intellectual world. He was a friend of More and Erasmus and well connected—he had been Mountjoy's tutor and chaplain to Bishop Foxe of Winchester. A Brigettine monk since 1506, he resisted the dissolution of Syon—Bedyll described him as very obstinate in a letter to Cromwell—but took a pension and found asylum with the son of his former pupil. (For details of his life see Glanmor Williams, 'Two neglected London Welsh clerics', *Transactions of the Honourable Society of Cymrodorion*, 1961, 23.) His books all express emphatically conservative ideas; they include a translation of the *Mirror of our Lady* for the abbess of Syon and a treatise against the Lutherans with special warnings against their heretical views on the sacrament of penance. *A Work for Householders* seems to be a compilation, the last seven pages being taken from 'an epistle of a great learned man called Bernard Sylvestre and put among the works of Saint Bernard for because that many do judge and think it was his own work'. The first edition was printed by Wynkyn de Worde in 1530 and there were at least five other editions by 1537 (*STC* 25422–26). There are no indications of unorthodox religious views: the book includes a form of private confession and several edifying stories of miracles, usually punitive in effect. Whitford urged his readers to be constant in their devotion to 'such saints as you have special devotion unto . . . and all holy virgins'.

HENRY SMITH (1550?–1591) was a pupil of Greenham, and was suspended by Bishop Aylmer in 1588 for preaching against the Book of Common Prayer and for not subscribing the Articles.

WILLIAM WHATELEY (1583–1639), the 'Roaring Boy of Banbury', appeared before the Court of High Commission in 1621 for his views on divorce, which he later retracted.

JOHN DOD (1549?–1645) was a lecturer at Banbury; he was silenced by Abbott in 1611. RICHARD CLEAVER wrote sermons on the proper keeping of the Sabbath.

WILLIAM GOUGE (1578–1653) was vicar of Blackfriars and a fashionable Puritan preacher. He described himself in his treatise as 'the watchman of your souls'. In 1626 he was involved as one of 12 trustees in buying up impropriations to foster a Puritan ministry later threatened with prosecution by Laud. He refused to read the Book of Sports in 1618 and in 1633. In 1643 he was a member of the Westminster Assembly and on the committees for the examination of ministers and for drafting a confession of faith.

ROBERT SNAWSEL was perhaps the least definitely Puritan of these latter authors. His *Looking Glass,* dated 1631 (*STC* 22886), is in the form of a dialogue between women, some godly and some wicked, and is very close in both style and content to Erasmus's *Coniugium.* But many passages have been given a Calvinistic gloss by Snawsel. (A. M. McLean, 'Robert Snawsel, Translator of Erasmus's Coniugium', *Moreana,* XI (1974), pp. 55–64, discusses their relationship.)

There were many editions of all their works, and Gouge was a distinct best-seller. *Of Domesticall Duties* was reprinted three times in ten years, and his *Catechism* (1615) had seven editions by 1635. *STC* lists at least three issues of his complete works in three years.

BULLINGER had had five editions and many re-issues by 1575, and was clearly the source for much of the later writing. Most of his metaphors crop up again and again, and Dod and Cleaver used whole paragraphs at a time. Smith simply re-issued it under his own name with a dedication to Lord Burghley and no acknowledgment.

IV

Single Women in the London Marriage Market: Age, Status and Mobility, 1598–1619

VIVIEN BRODSKY ELLIOTT

.

The demography and social structure of early seventeenth-century London have remained only partially explored territory in English social history. The study of marriage in London is particularly neglected. While family reconstitution techniques can add greatly to our knowledge of the marriage patterns of village populations, the same technique applied to London parish registers (at a time of rapid population increase resulting from heavy migration to the capital) will inform us only about the very small minority born in London and residing, at the time of marriage, in their parish of birth. A more representative source for the study of marriage in London, representative in the sense of including both the native born and migrant population, are the intentions of marriage or applications for a licence to marry in the diocese of London between the years 1598 and 1619.[1] Not only do these marriage allegations disclose the age, residence and marital status of both parties, but in their patriarchal concern for the safeguarding of single women in particular, they also furnish many details of residence, parental consent, the situation of the woman at the time of her marriage, and geographical and social origins which enable the historian to reconstruct an intimate, many-faceted picture of the marriage process for single women within London, albeit for a short 20-year period. After 1620 the rising volume of entries and the adoption of a standardized, schematic form banish such detailed entries as the following:

16 August 1598.
This day appeared personally before me, the said Doctor Stanhope, William Giddy of the parish of Stepney in the county of Middlesex, mariner, being a widower and aged about 36 years and he alleges he intends to marry one Marion Lawrence of the same parish, spinster, aged about 32 years, the natural daughter of Richard Lawrence of Huelfield [*sic*] in the county of Gloucester, yeoman. Then likewise appeared personally, Catherine Pinnock, the wife of Thomas Pinnock of the same parish, being the cousin germane of the said Marion Lawrence and she alleges that she (has spoken with Thomas Lawrence, the said Marion Lawrence's own brother and that he told her that his father, Richard Lawrence, was well content with this foresaid intended marriage). The said Marion Lawrence has dwelt with her these two years and her father, being living in Gloucestershire, a very old man and of mean estate, has placed her in London where she has lived

[1] Guildhall Library (henceforward GL), MS 10, 091/1–7.

these seven years and is now willing to prefer her in marriage, leaving her to her own choice. And they desire to be married in the parish church of Stepney aforesaid, where both the abovenamed parties are dwelling.
William Gidde [signs]
The mark of Marion Lawrence. The mark of Catherine Pinnock.[2]

Marriage allegations cannot claim to be a socially representative source for the study of marriage. They are biased to the higher status groups in the London diocese. The gentry, clergy and high status tradesmen are all numerically over-represented, while craftsmen, husbandmen and labourers are under-represented. The expense of a licence was a deterrent for most persons of low socio-economic standing and they accordingly married by banns.[3] Licence marriages form about one-sixth of all marriages celebrated in the diocese during the years 1598–1619.[4] Exclusion of the lower status groups limits the generalizations that can be made about social mobility. There is, however, no reason to regard the ages reported in these allegations as being particularly unrepresentative of all single women marrying at the time.[5]

While the focus of this study is female marriage patterns, it is relevant to outline briefly the characteristics of the male population marrying by licence. Comparison of the rural parts of the diocese with the city itself establishes a marginally later average marriage age for London city dwellers than for men residing in Essex, Hertfordshire and Middlesex. The difference is slight and both rural and urban inhabitants shared a late age at first marriage, as is shown in Table I. London conformed to the western European pattern of a late age at first marriage, and the ages given in Table I are identical with those usually offered for average male age at first marriage in village populations.[6] Moreover, where there was variation in age at marriage for different occupational groups, in London it was confined to average differences of no more than two years between occupations. City and country dwellers alike, therefore, tended in the main to marry for the first time between the ages 26 and 30.

---

[2] GL, MS 10, 091/1: 16/8/1598: Giddy-Lawrence. The bracketed section is crossed out in the manuscript. Note that spelling in this and subsequent quotations has been modernized and punctuation added.

[3] Vivien Brodsky Elliott, 'Mobility and marriage in pre-industrial England' (unpublished Ph.D. dissertation, University of Cambridge, 1979), p. 14.

[4] Elliott, 'Mobility and marriage', pp. 12–13.

[5] Analysis of marriage ages has been restricted to first marriage only, since the age-statements of widows and widowers are usually distorted. On the accuracy of age-statements in marriage licences see Elliott, 'Mobility and marriage', appendix B, pp. 374–86.

[6] For example, in Colyton, Devonshire, the mean age at first marriage for men was 28.1 years, 1560–99, 27.4 years, 1600–29. E. A. Wrigley, 'Family limitation in pre-industrial England', *Economic History Review*, 2nd. ser., XIX, 1 (1966), 86–7. In Bottesford, Leicestershire: 29.2 years, 1600–49, and in Shepshed, Leicestershire, 1600–99, 29.4 years. D. C. Levine, 'The demographic implications of rural industrialization' (unpublished Ph.D. dissertation, University of Cambridge, 1975), pp. 105, 150.

Table I: Age at first marriage of London-resident and rural bachelors marrying spinsters and widows and spinsters only

Category	No.	Mean age at marriage	Median	Standard deviation	Significance
Rural bachelors marrying spinsters and widows	499	28.2	27.7	7.8	Rural bachelors significantly younger than London bachelors at the 0.02 level.
London bachelors marrying spinsters and widows	1,402	28.4	28.1	9.2	
Rural bachelors marrying spinsters only	380	27.1	26.9	3.3	Rural bachelors marrying spinsters significantly younger than London bachelors at the 0.01 level.
London bachelors marrying spinsters only	1,037	27.6	27.2	4.7	

The assumption of an inverse correlation between status and marriage age, that is, the higher the status the earlier the marriage age, does not hold for London. While other studies suggest that the more privileged members of society could afford to marry early, whereas those of low socio-economic standing had to delay marriage, the reverse is true of London.[7] The average age at first marriage for gentlemen was as high as 28.6 years; for high status London tradesmen, such as grocers, haberdashers, goldsmiths and drapers, it was 27.5 years; and for low status craftsmen, such as blacksmiths, weavers, butchers, carpenters, cordwainers, tailors and mariners, the average marriage age was one year younger at 26.5 years.[8]

Ages at first marriage for members of all these occupational groups would be higher if the numerous marriages of London bachelors with widows are taken into account. Nearly 30 per cent of all low status craftsmen marrying by licence for the first time married widows as against 22 per cent of high status tradesmen. Both proportions are high and this is in part attributable to London's mortality rates in the early seventeenth century, since many marriages were interrupted by the death of the husband especially when, as often happened among high status tradesmen and gentlemen, the wife was several years younger. Widows were at a high premium in the London marriage market, and for many a young journeyman without capital,

[7] For example, Peter Laslett, *The World We Have Lost* (London, revised edn. 1972), p. 86. The mean age of all male applicants for marriage licences was 26.7 years, for gentry applicants only 26.2 years.

[8] See Elliott, 'Mobility and marriage', part III, ch. 1, 'Age at first marriage for men in London diocese, 1597–1619', pp. 253–88 for a full discussion of occupational variation in male marriage age.

marriage with a widow was a tempting means of gaining economic independence and freeing himself from subordinate status under a master.

The London apprenticeship system institutionalized the migration of youths from all over provincial England: some 85 per cent of London apprentices were migrants.[9] Apprenticeship was an effective restraint on early marriage for London craftsmen and tradesmen, given the late age at which apprentices took out their seven- to eight-year indentures. Carpenters' apprentices began their training at an average age of 19.5 years and were thereby unable to marry until at least the age of 26.[10] The narrow range of ages at first marriage for London craftsmen and tradesmen, concentrated around the ages 26, 27, 28, 29, 30, was an artefact both of the apprenticeship system and of tradition which demarcated the ages at which men should customarily marry for the first time. In this respect the male population differs considerably from the single women marrying at the same time. For women, more complex variables such as migratory status, socio-economic background, paternal mortality and the presence or absence of London kin affected the timing of their marriages, and created considerable variation in their ages at first marriage.

While a relatively slight factor in male marriage age variations, status was of decided significance in the patterns of age-difference between husband and wife. In Table II occupations are arranged according to the age-difference between partners. The social ordering which emerges quite independently replicates the London occupational hierarchy recovered from other sources.[11] Average age-difference at marriage provides a telling indicator of social status. The first ten occupations, for which age-difference ranges from 7.8 years for the drapers to 4.2 years for the fishmongers, are trades from the high status London Livery Companies while the remaining 12 are dominated by craft occupations.

From Table II it is apparent that there were two main marriage patterns. One was where the husband was several years older than his wife. Here the marriage was in all likelihood arranged, and, as will be apparent later, the bride usually born in London and the daughter of a wealthy London tradesman, clergyman or gentleman. Lower down the occupational hierarchy, we encounter the second pattern. Here age-difference was much smaller and such marriages were less likely to be arranged and more likely to be egalitarian in character, since these London craftsmen and sailors tended to marry migrant single women who were free from parental authority. Only the nobility, gentry, wealthy merchants and tradesmen would have followed

---

[9] Elliott, 'Mobility and marriage', part II, 'Migration to London and demographic changes in seventeenth century England', pp. 162, 214–15.

[10] Elliott, 'Mobility and marriage', p. 199.

[11] On the subject of the London social hierarchy and the social status of occupations see Elliott, 'Mobility and marriage', part I, 'The social status of occupations in seventeenth century England', especially p. 74, figure 5, p. 704, figure 10, and p. 107, figure 11.

Table II: Age of bachelors at first marriage, age of brides (spinsters only) arranged by positive age-difference

Occupation	Bachelor husbands no.	Mean age at first marriage	Spinster brides no.	Mean age at first marriage	No.*	Age-difference: no. of years by which husbands older
Mercers	20	28.9	20	21.3	20	7.6
Drapers	31	27.8	31	20.0	31	7.8
London-resident gentry	175	28.6	168	22.0	168	6.5
Grocers	56	27.8	54	22.4	54	5.3
Merchants	28	28.8	25	23.3	25	5.0
Haberdashers	43	27.3	44	22.6	43	4.7
Goldsmiths	19	28.6	16	23.9	16	4.7
Yeomen-servants	88	28.2	78	24.1	78	4.5
Vintners	35	27.1	32	22.8	30	4.3
Fishmongers	12	27.0	11	23.8	11	4.2
Carpenters	11	27.5	11	24.0	11	3.5
Merchant-Taylors	66	26.7	66	24.2	65	3.5
Clothworkers	26	27.9	25	24.6	25	3.3
Sailors	60	26.9	59	23.1	59	3.1
Tailors	52	26.1	48	23.6	48	2.8
Barber-surgeons	21	26.8	20	24.1	20	2.7
Bakers	17	28.8	17	26.6	17	2.6
Skinners	14	27.6	12	25.6	12	2.1
Weavers	15	24.1	14	23.5	14	0.6
Brewers	9	24.0	10	23.5	9	0.5
Blacksmiths	13	25.5	13	25.3	13	0.5
Cutlers	10	25.8	9	25.4	9	0.4

* This is the number of cases in which both parties' ages are given. The age-difference in the final column is based on these cases.

the advice of the Puritan divine, William Gouge, who advocated a disparity of:

> five or ten or somewhat more years: especially if the excess of years be on the husband's part ... it is very meet that the husband should be somewhat older than his wife because he is a head, a governor, a protector of his wife.[12]

The difference between the two styles of marriage might be illustrated by contrast. In 1610, John Pemberton, a grocer aged 27, the son of a Hertfordshire gentleman, alleged marriage with London-born, 17-year-old Katherine Angell, the daughter of Mr. William Angell, citizen and fishmonger who 'appeared and gave his express consent'.[13] When Jonas Butler, a butcher of St. Sepulchre's parish, applied for a licence to marry, he was aged 26, 'a free man and out of his apprenticeship and so has been this half year'. His bride,

[12] William Gouge, *Of Domesticall Duties* (London, 1619), p. 119.
[13] GL, MS 10, 091/4: 19/1/1610: Pemberton-Angell.

Margaret Phillips, was one year younger than him, the orphaned daughter of a Somerset clothier. In 1604 she was 'now servant unto Robert Lewis, of St. Sepulchres, a butcher with whom she has dwelt about half a year and before that time with one Arnold, of Ludgate Hill in St. Martin's parish, for a year's service. And at her first coming forth of the country, which was some three years past, with one Andrew Wise of St. Faith's, Warwick Lane, Stationer.'[14] For the unattached migrant servant, the issues of personal choice, mutual liking and love were equally as important as the small dowry saved from her independent earnings. Parental involvement in her marriage in the form of financial provision, introduction of suitable partners, supervision of the courtship and the wedding celebrations was negligible. Parental consent, recorded in the documents of such marriages, was often merely a formal device used to satisfy the granters of the licence. In short, such marriages were individualistic and closer to modern marriages than the traditional, arranged marriages of the London-born.

There are many ways of analysing the ages at first marriage of single women but for the present study the most meaningful division is between the London born and the migrant population. For London-born daughters the status of their fathers had little effect on marriage ages: the gentleman's daughter and the carpenter's daughter were both very young at marriage. The over-all mean age at first marriage for 496 London-born single women was 20.5 years. Perhaps literary evidence is not so deceptive after all. Shakespeare's Juliet had many counterparts in London with 16-, 17- and 18-year-old brides. In contrast, migrant brides married some 3.7 years later on average than the London brides: their mean age at marriage was 24.2 years. In Table III the remarkable uniformity of London-born daughters' ages at marriage is revealed. Apart from migrant gentry daughters, the migrant daughters of provincial husbandmen, yeomen, tradesmen and craftsmen tended to marry at closely similar ages. Migration was far more important a factor in determining marriage age than status in early seventeenth-century London.

In addition to these two groups of single women marrying bachelors were those single women, London-born and migrant, who married widowers. Their different social origins notwithstanding, the age at marriage of London-born daughters marrying widowers was uniformly early: an average of 22.5 years. Their widower husbands were some 14 years older on average. In Table IV the ages for each status group are presented.

This lack of variation in marriage age for all women marrying widowers illustrates the unique pattern of early marriage age for all London-born women. The difference from migrant women marrying widowers is particularly striking when their respective ages at marriage are compared: migrant women marrying widowers were, at 28.5 years, some six years older.

[14] GL, MS 10, 091/2: 24/3/1603/4: Butler:Phillipps.

Table III: Mean age at first marriage of single women

Occupation or status group of fathers	LONDON-BORN		MIGRANT		Difference between the two
	No.	Age	No.	Age	
Knights, esquires, gentry	77	20.1	136	22.7	2.6 years
High status tradesmen, clergymen	212	20.1	54	24.0	3.1 years
Yeomen	14	22.9	141	25.2	2.3 years
Craftsmen	159	20.9	72	23.9	3.0 years
Husbandmen and labourers	—	—	64	25.4	—
Unknowns	34	21.1	33	26.4	5.3 years
All	496	20.5	500	24.2	3.7 years

Migrant brides significantly older than London-born brides at .001 level ($x^2 = 44$)

Most London widowers remarried soon after the death of their wives and the speed with which they found a new partner was in many cases precipitated by the family's need for a mother surrogate. Thomas Ivie, for example, a blacksmith of St. Mary Somerset parish, lost his first wife, Marie, in December 1604. Of the five children born to their marriage, only the youngest, Marie, a baby of seven days old at his wife's death, was still living when he married, six weeks later, the 21-year-old daughter of a London haberdasher.[15] Thomas Makyn, a London barber-surgeon, had two small daughters living when he married, four months after his first wife's death,

Table IV: Mean age at first marriage of London-born brides marrying widowers, age of husband and age-difference

Occupation or status of fathers	Mean age of single women marrying widowers	Mean age of widowers	Mean age difference	Ratio of single women marrying widowers to single women marrying bachelors*	% of first marriages with widowers
Esquires and gentry	21.7 (n = 13)	36.5 (n = 13)	14.8 (n = 13)	13:90	12.6
High status tradesmen	22.2 (n = 44)	36.9 (n = 42)	14.3 (n = 42)	44:158	21.8
Low status craftsmen	22.3 (n = 24)	34.7 (n = 24)	12.4 (n = 24)	24:183	11.6
Others: yeomen, unknowns	28.3 (n = 4)	40.8 (n = 4)	12.5 (n = 4)	4:60	6.2
All	22.5 (n = 85)	36.4 (n = 83)	14.1 (n = 81)	85:491	14.8

*Includes all cases with or without ages.

[15] Cambridge Population Group, 'London Reconstitution: FRF 55': Thomas Ivie-Elizabeth Hills.

the 20-year-old daughter of a London vintner.[16] Anthony Ollerenshaw, a cloth-worker, had three young sons aged six, five, and three, when he remarried nine months after the death of his wife.[17] Widowers would have appeared as particularly acceptable suitors to London tradesmen and craftsmen fathers, since they were usually in command of their own businesses or shops and may have been less demanding of dowries than the lately freed apprentice anxious to establish himself with capital.

In Table V the ages of migrant brides marrying widowers, their husbands' ages and the age-difference between partners are set out. Status appears to have some effect on marriage age: higher status daughters married widowers three to four years younger than the migrant daughters of yeomen, craftsmen and husbandmen. The over-all age-difference of 12.9 years was marginally smaller than that of London daughters marrying widowers. Nearly 40 per cent of the migrant women who married widowers were servants, including some who were servants to their future husbands. As servants they could have accumulated considerable experience in caring for children and in household affairs. They also occupied well-defined subordinate positions

Table V: Mean age at first marriage of migrant brides marrying widowers, age of husbands and age-difference

Occupation or status of fathers	Mean age of single women marrying widowers	Mean age of widowers	Mean age difference	Ratio of single women marrying widowers to single women marrying bachelors*	% of migrants marrying widowers
Gentry	26.2 (n = 23)	40.0 (n = 23)	13.8 (n = 23)	23:136	14.5
High status tradesmen	26.3 (n = 9)	41.3 (n = 9)	15.0 (n = 9)	9:54	14.3
Yeomen	29.4 (n = 25)	41.4 (n = 24)	11.1 (n = 22)	25:186	11.8
Low status craftsmen	30.9 (n = 13)	43.0 (n = 13)	21.1 (n = 13)	13:72	15.3
Husbandmen	29.7 (n = 18)	44.2 (n = 18)	14.5 (n = 18)	18:64	21.9
Unknowns	28.3 (n = 8)	34.1 (n = 9)	5 (n = 8)	8:155	4.9
All	28.5 (n = 96)	40.8 (n = 96)	12.9 (n = 93)	97:667	12.6

*Includes all cases with or without ages.

[16] 'London Reconstitution: FRF 28': Thomas Makyn-Ann Swister. GL, MS 10, 091/3: 20/2/1608/9: Makyn-Swister.
[17] 'London Reconstitution: FRF 36': Anthony Ollerenshaw-Mary White. 'London Reconstitution: FRF 37': Anthony Ollerenshaw-Ann Smith. GL, MS 10, 091/3: 8/8/1609; MS 10, 091/6: 25/4/1618.

within the household and in marrying their masters were moving upwards socially, anticipating a change in fortune as the wives of tradesmen or craftsmen and perhaps subsequently as wealthy widows.

In some cases it is clear that a long-term relationship as servant and master preceded that of husband and wife. Margery Cooke, originally from Lichfield, Staffordshire, at the age of 27 had been a servant to her master, Thomas Flint, a goldsmith, for over seven years. They married four months after the death of his wife.[18] Elizabeth Jackson, a single woman of 26 from Kent, the daughter of a deceased husbandman, was a servant for three years to Leonard Harwood, a merchant and widower aged 50.[19] In terms of their social origins, the marriage of a husbandman's daughter with a merchant was a rare crossing of two opposite poles of the social spectrum. Doubtless, 'both she and all her friends will not only be willing but very glad of her preferment in this marriage' as the groom testified. Similarly, Katherine Clerke, a 26-year-old husbandman's daughter, married her widower master, William Clibbery, a haberdasher, after two years in his service.[20] Joan Scott, the 28-year-old daughter of a Banbury innholder, servant to Thomas Ellis, a London upholster, was six months pregnant when she married her master.[21] Pre-nuptial pregnancy rates of servant brides in this category may have been high, given the context in which they were living.

The two age-patterns of marriage for London-born and migrant brides have broader social and demographic implications. The migrant bride pattern of a later age at first marriage and a small age-difference between partners implies greater freedom of choice of spouse and a more active role for women in the courtship and marriage process. Demographically, the consequences of this type of marriage were decreased fertility but a closer joint expectancy of life. This may have offset decreased fertility since there was a correspondingly lower chance of the marriage being interrupted by the death of the male partner during the woman's fertile years. In contrast, the pattern of early marriage for London daughters implied arranged marriage and greater patriarchalism within marriage occasioned by a husband several years older. Demographically it implied higher net fertility and a greater life expectation than that of the husband. Brides of this type would show a greater propensity to be widowed.

Early seventeenth-century marital fertility rates of London-born women, recovered by Dr. Finlay from the reconstituted families of London-born women from selected city parishes, were as high as 500 per 1,000.[22] The current finding of an early marriage age for all London-born single women

[18] GL, MS 10, 091/1: 18/1/1597/8: Flint-Cooke.
[19] GL, MS 10, 091/3: 11/9/1606: 23/10/1606: Harwood-Jackson.
[20] GL, MS 10, 091/3: 14/8/1605: Clibbery-Clerke.
[21] 'London Reconstitution: FRF 49': Thomas Ellis-Joan Scott. GL, MS 10, 091/2: Ellis-Scott.
[22] R. A. P. Finlay, 'Population and fertility in London, 1580–1650', *Journal of Family History*, 4,1 (1979), 30.

marrying by licence might be extended to the general female population born in London marrying by both banns and licences.

*   *   *

In 88 of the 604 marriage allegations of migrant brides it was possible to estimate an average age at migration by subtracting from the stated age at first marriage, the period of stated residence in London. The mean age at migration was 17.1 years, median 18.4. It would seem that women migrated at ages similar to apprentice migrants, in their late teens—17, 18 and 19.

Calculated from independent sources, life expectancy in early seventeenth-century London was drastically low: 22.3 years on average. For most of provincial England, average life expectancies ranged from 36.4 years for the north-easterly provinces to 49 years for the north midlands.[23] Given the low figure for London, it is unsurprising that as many as 47 per cent of daughters had lost their fathers by age 20. Such a high figure could not be expected for migrant brides, however, who had much better probabilities of having their fathers alive when they married. Nevertheless, the finding that some 64 per cent of all women migrants—over two-thirds of the sample—had in fact lost their fathers suggests that the death of a father was bound up with the original decision to migrate. The loss of a father's economic support could have prompted the finding of an alternative means of subsistence. This inference is supported by the case of migrant women who were known to be servants: 74 per cent of servants' fathers were dead when they married. Without evidence of the ages of daughters at orphanhood and migration it might, however, be argued that the loss of a father was independent of the decision to migrate. The over-all age at orphanhood for 109 migrant daughters was a median of 15 years and a mean of 17.6 years. As the median age at migration was 18.4 years, mean 17.2, it can be seen that in the majority of the cases, the pattern was one of the death of the father before migration.

In a patriarchal society in which the nuclear family was the normal, most commonly occurring form of family structure, fathers were decisive figures in the business of daughters' marriages, introducing appropriate suitors and negotiating and providing dowries in the form of land, goods or capital. Daughters were relatively passive agents in the marriage process. Though admittedly an example from rural Yorkshire, Henry Best's description of a marriage in the 1640s could well be extended to those of high status London tradesmen's sons and daughters:

> then the father of the maid carries her over to the young man's house to see how they like of all and there does the young man's father meet them to treat of a dower and likewise of a jointure and feoffment for the woman.[24]

[23] Elliott, 'Mobility and marriage', part II, ch. 2, 'Migration, demographic change and life expectancy in seventeenth century England', p. 193.

[24] Henry Best, 'Concerning our fashions of our country weddings', in C. B. Robinson (ed.), *Surtees Society*, XXXIII (1857), 116–17.

Such paternal influence depended on having a daughter resident at home. Control could of course be extended, even if the daughter was absent, by kin supervision, less effectively if the daughter was in service. Yet generally the high figure of 64 per cent of paternal deaths, combined with residence away from home, suggests some transference of control to the daughter herself. For this reason, migrant brides differ radically from London-born daughters, some 70 per cent of whom were living with families, including step-parents and widowed mothers, at the time of their marriages.

Of the 604 migrant brides, 35 per cent were explicitly stated to be servants. Nearly 23 per cent were residing with kin in London and a further 4 per cent had migrated to London with their widowed mothers. Of the remaining 38 per cent there is not enough information given to illuminate their situations. Discussion will focus on those who were definitely known to be in service or to be residing with kin.

Employment opportunities for single women in London in this period were severely limited. The apprenticeship registers for 15 London companies disclose over 8,000 entries but fail to reveal a single woman apprentice between 1580 and 1640. A minuscule percentage of migrant women were known to have been self-employed. Anne Porter, a single woman of 30, the daughter of a Wiltshire yeoman and residing in the parish of St. Katherine Creechurch, was obviously exceptional. She was 'at her own government and keeps a flax shop for herself and hires servants and so has done these 4 years or so'.[25] Elizabeth Chauncey, the daughter of a Leicestershire gentleman, at the age of 24 'keeps shop for herself'.[26] Elizabeth Lloyd, a migrant from Oswestry, Salop, was 'a sempster and boards at a sexton's house . . . maintains herself with her needle'.[27] Christian Benson, a migrant from nearby rural Surrey, had the unusual occupation of 'a scrivener in the house of a butcher' and before that had been in attendance upon an esquire for two years.[28] She had the rare distinction of being able to read and write, unlike the majority of women migrants who made marks on the occasions when they were present at the alleging of their marriages.[29] Susan Carnell, the orphan of a Kentish tailor, had lost both her parents many years before and 'lives at her own hands knitting stockings'.[30] Margaret Jones, at 26, originally from Woodford, Essex, less specifically 'lives of her industries and painstakings'.[31] 'Sempsters' or seamstresses were usually women, and some migrants supported themselves by this means. Eleanor Reade, the daughter

---

[25] GL, MS 10, 091/2: 10/5/1602: Greenfynne-Porter.
[26] GL, MS 10, 091/5: 22/4/1614: Bushe-Chauncey.
[27] GL, MS 10, 091/2: 15/12/1602: Tayler-Lloyd.
[28] GL, MS 10, 091/2: 30/6/1604: Stanford-Benson.
[29] In only a limited number of cases could this information be gleaned since the general practice was for the groom to apply for the licence. From the Commissary Court depositions, in 51 cases, 49 single women deponents were unable to sign their names. GL, MS 9065 A/1–3.
[30] GL, MS 10, 091/1: 24/8/1598: Cocker-Carnell.
[31] GL, MS 10, 091/4: 15/10/1612: Owen-Jones.

of a Gloucestershire gentleman, was 'a sempster keeping shop for herself and at her own government and maintenance'.[32]

Statistically the probabilities of a migrant woman supporting herself in these ways were extremely low. She was far more likely to have been a servant or living as an economic dependant on her London kin. Domestic service provided a means of subsistence for a large number of single migrant women. Compared with keeping a shop or being a seamstress it was, like apprenticeship, a subordinate position within a household. Yet service held out few of the future opportunities of apprenticeship and, unlike the apprentice, the servant maid was usually of lower socio-economic status than her master and mistress. With extended periods of service, more familial relationships might have developed. The average length of service within the one household was in fact over four years. Only 12 servants from a sample of 88 had served the one master and mistress for periods less than 12 months. One had been in service for only eight weeks, another for ten, a third for twelve weeks, and six for six months when they left service to marry. In contrast nearly one-third of migrant servants had worked for the same master and mistress for six years or more. Agnes Sherwood, originally from Alburton, Shropshire, marrying in London at the age of 32, had been the servant of Mistress Anne Shacklieffe, a widow, for sixteen years.[33] In such cases, the long period of service brought its material rewards, as is clear in the case of Katherine Gandy, a spinster of 24, originally from Walkerton, Cheshire, 'servant to one Mr. Francis Lodge, haberdasher, and has dwelt with him 6 or 7 years. And is to have her only preferment of and from him, the same Mr. Lodge'.[34]

For many migrant servants the relationships they formed with their masters, mistresses and other members of the household may have been of critical importance especially as they had no kin to turn to in times of difficulty or for assistance in matrimonial affairs. Margaret Potter, for example, servant to a London virginal-maker, was the orphan of a Staffordshire blacksmith. Her only live relative, it was pathetically noted, was her 'cousin german of Brainford, Middlesex'.[35] Margery Cooke, an orphan and migrant servant, originally from Lichfield, Staffordshire, described her master as 'he is and hath been her sole governor for many years'.[36] Dorothy Elliott, the orphan of a Warwickshire yeoman, dwelling with Mr. Garret, merchant, 'has no other friends here in the city'.[37]

---

[32] GL, MS 10, 091/3: 2/2/1609/10: Rooke-Reade.
[33] GL, MS 10, 091/3: 4/3/1607/8: Hone-Sherwood.
[34] GL, MS 10, 091/2: 2/12/1602: Plomer-Gandy. 'Preferment' may be defined here as an act of advancement and promotion in one's condition or status—in this case, the master's promotion of his servant's marriage by his financial provision for her.
[35] GL, MS 10, 091/1: 15/5/1659: Rose-Potter.
[36] GL, MS 10, 091/3: 8/9/1605: Goode-Cooke.
[37] GL, MS 10, 091/3: 17/12/1603: Gawen-Elliott.

The migrant servant was not of course always alone or without family in London. Two hundred and twenty-six of the 604 migrants mentioned kin living in the city. One hundred and thirty-five migrants were known to be living with such kin and as many as 85 per cent of these women had lost their fathers. In Table VI the range of kin relationships and the numbers living with kin are set out.

Table VI: Range of kin of migrant women resident in London and numbers of migrant women who lived with kin

Kin	Number present in London	Number of women who lived with kin
Brother	57	16
Uncle	37	23
Sister and brother-in-law	36	30
Kinsman	25	16
Aunt	17	17
Widowed mother	15	10
Mother and stepfather	8	7
Cousin	8	2
Kinswomen and husbands	6	6
'Friends' of father	6	3
Father	4	1
Grandmother	2	2
Widowed sister	2	2
Others	3	1
Total	226	135
	37 % of all migrant women	22 % of all migrant women

In a few cases, migrant women had the dual role of being servants to their near kin. Agnes Brown, an orphan of 22, the daughter of a yeoman of Bridgnorth, Shropshire, was 'servant to her brother-in-law, a merchant-tailor'.[38] Mary Evans, aged 30, also from Shropshire, was 'dwelling with her kinswoman, Margaret Hughes, the wife of Robert Hughes as their servant'.[39] Such cases appear to have been confined to those instances where a migrant woman lived with her married sister and brother-in-law or with a 'kinswoman' and her husband. There were no cases of a migrant woman living with her brother and sister-in-law in the capacity of a servant and it may be of relevance to recall the statement of Ralph Josselin, the Puritan diarist of Earls Colne in Essex, who wrote in 1644, 'my sister Mary is come under my roof a servant', qualifying this statement with 'my respect is and shall be towards her as a sister', implying the different ways in which family and servants were commonly regarded.[40]

[38] GL, MS 10, 091/1: 15/4/1598: Ramsey-Brown.
[39] GL, MS 10, 091/3: 7/9/1601: Gybbins-Evans.
[40] Quoted in Alan Macfarlane, *The Family Life of Ralph Josselin* (Cambridge, 1970), p. 129.

From Table VI we can reconstruct a possible connection between apprenticeship and female migration. Fifty-seven migrant women had brothers living in London, nearly all of whom were following trade and craft occupations. Joan Burrough, for example, the daughter of a Gloucestershire blacksmith, was servant to a London alderman. Her brother lived in the same parish and was described as a gunmaker.[41] Similarly Katherine Simpson, servant to a London skinner but originally from distant Cumberland, had a brother who lived in an adjacent parish and was a silkweaver by occupation.[42] Many women may have followed their brothers to London after those brothers had secured an apprenticeship and then a position of service for their sisters. Amy Slater from Towcester, Northamptonshire, a yeoman's daughter, was a servant to a London vintner. She had met her husband, a vintner, when he was apprenticed to her master. Her brother was also described as a vintner, although his parish of residence was different.[43] We can surmise that her brother came from Towcester to serve an apprenticeship with a member of the Vintners Company and then arranged a place for his sister. The low proportion of women actually living with their brothers, compared with the proportion living with their married sisters and brothers-in-law, suggests that many such brothers were probably too young to have set up their own households and were still serving out their terms of apprenticeship or working as journeymen.

London kin were important intermediaries in the London marriage market and provincial daughters who came to reside with such kin tended to be of higher social status and to marry earlier than other migrant servants. In Table VII the social origins of kin-resident and servant migrants are compared. Over a third of migrant women residing with London kin came from the highest social status group and it may well have been a common practice to send noble and gentle daughters to London families to acquire not only social graces but more importantly to ensure a range of suitable

Table VII: Social origins of kin-resident and servant migrants

Occupation of fathers	Migrant women resident with kin no. = 141	Migrant servant women no. = 212
Knights, esquires, gentry	34.7%	11.1%
Provincial high status tradesmen, clergymen	10.4%	8.5%
Yeomen	27.8%	40.2%
Low status craftsmen	17.3%	15.8%
Husbandmen and labourers	9.8%	24.4%
Total	100.0%	100.0%
Mean age at marriage	23.7	26.5

[41] GL, MS 10, 091/1: 13/5/1598: Alexander-Burrough.
[42] GL, MS 10, 091/2: 4/9/1601: Brown-Simpson.
[43] GL, MS 10, 091/3: 7/7/1605: Hamye-Slater.

marriage partners. In such cases paternal control was transferred to London uncles, grandfathers or brothers, and personal choice of marriage partner for such daughters may have been circumscribed. The passivity of daughters was implied in the often repeated phrase 'she being sent up to London by her father for that purpose', that is, to marry.

There was a difference of three years in the average ages at which migrant women residing with kin and migrant servants married. Migration, coupled with service, pushed up marriage age. (It is likely too that migrant servants marrying by banns also married late: around the ages of 26, 27 and 28.) It could be argued that such women did not experience any great sense of delay in marrying when they did, since an average of 26.5 years is close to the customary marriage age for women in village populations. While it is impossible to recover the original subjective perceptions of individuals on these issues, the force of rural cultural norms should not be ignored.

Added to social norms were also the delaying features of the initial migration and the need to acquire some sort of dowry to bring to marriage. While it is impossible to accept the notion that all marriages in traditional society were motivated by wholly economic concerns, one cannot, given the difficulties and precariousness of life in London, ignore the importance of the economic dimension for women who had no families and often no kin to fall back on. Women at all levels of the social hierarchy may have found it essential to bring a dowry to marriage even if it consisted solely of household goods. Service provided the means of accumulating the necessary capital, yet it was a drawn-out process since wages were rarely more than £3 per annum.

Long periods of courtship may have been common in those situations where the husband and wife were both in positions of dependence and required capital to establish themselves in a craft, inn or shop. Dorothy Ireland, originally from Newark upon Trent in Nottinghamshire, married at the very late age of 36. She was a servant and her husband-to-be a 40-year-old ostler. A witness testified 'that they, the said parties, have been sure together these 8 years'.[44] Margery Bayley, a 30-year-old minister's daughter from Liverpool, was servant to an esquire of Brainford, Middlesex, and intended marriage with Humphrey Bedcake, a waterman and bachelor of 32. Her master, Mr. Edward Varnham, testified

> his free consent to the said marriage between the said Humphrey Bedcake and his said servant Margery Bayley for that, as his letter testifies, the said Humphrey Bedcake has been a suitor unto his said servant these two whole years and more.[45]

Until more is known about the social networks of London servants and apprentices and the extent of freedom allowed to them, we can only conjecture that the most common meeting ground for potential spouses was in the

[44] GL, MS 10, 091/4: 30/10/1610: Seton-Ireland.
[45] GL, MS 10, 091/1: 8/12/1598: Bedcake-Bayley.

households which brought together unmarried men as apprentices and women as servants. Given the universality of the apprenticeship system in London and the high percentage of young men in the age groups 15–19 and 19–26 who were in apprenticeship, most London craft and trade households would have provided opportunities for prolonged relationships between unmarried male and female dependants. Women servants in such positions would have delayed marriage until their future husbands had completed their training. This was obvious in the marriage of Margaret Lawe, a 28-year-old spinster, originally from Edgware, Middlesex, and William Fellowe. She was servant to John Greene, scrivener, and William Fellowe was described as a scrivener and bachelor aged 26, 'a freeman and so has been ever since Midsummer last, dwelling with John Green, scrivener'.[46] The courtship of Margaret Lawe and William Fellowe began when she was a servant and he an apprentice in the same household. Until he had completed his training, they were not free to marry.

A number of migrant women servants preferred to terminate their period of service a little before they married. It might be inferred from the cases cited that servants had to elicit their masters' and mistresses' consent before they were free to marry. Leaving service was an effective means of dispensing with such approval, and a number of migrant servants stayed temporarily with their London kin who helped them in the preparations for the wedding. When Margery Richardson from Cheshire married, she was currently staying in the parish of St. Sepulchre's without Newgate but she had been a servant,

> remaining 10 years with one Peacocke and his wife, an apothecary in Little Old Bailey from whom she came within this fortnight . . . at her own government and remaining with one William Evans, merchant-tailor, her kinsman, and his wife, Ellen Evans, who gave their consent to this intended marriage.[47]

Other migrant women terminated their service and went to live with their husbands-to-be, a custom which may have had a significant bearing on nuptial pregnancy rates. Susan Kinge was described as living

> of herself, not servant to any—she dwelt a year as a servant to a linendraper. Since her coming from the same Hopward [her master] she remains about with the same Francis [her future husband] as a lodger.[48]

In 1602 the marriage was alleged of 28-year-old Edward Hawke, a skinner of St. Andrew's in Holborn parish, and Avis Bishop aged 24. She was 'late servant with Mr. Harrison, shoemaker in Fenchurch St. and has dwelt with the aforesaid Edward Hawke this three weeks'.[49]

[46] GL, MS 10, 091/2: 3/8/1604: Fellowe-Lawe.
[47] GL, MS 10, 091/2: 8/3/1603/4: Roades-Richardson.
[48] GL, MS 10, 091/5: 5/1/1613/14: Speare-Kinge.
[49] GL, MS 10, 091/2: 6/2/1601/2: Hawke-Bishop.

In their marriage characteristics, migrant servant women in particular and migrant women in general enjoyed greater freedom in the choice of a spouse, and without the control or influence of their parents the marriage process for them was one in which they had an active role in initiating their own relationships, in finding suitable partners, and in conducting courtships. To stress wholly economic motivations or to ascribe to them desires for upward mobility would be to ignore important contemporary considerations such as the astrological compatibility between partners. London astrologers such as Simon Forman and William Lilley were often frequented by maidservants requiring advice and counsel in their love affairs and courtships. The 'freedom' and self-government of migrant women must, of course, be placed in the wider context of patriarchalism and the generally subordinate position of women within both service and marriage. These constraints are apparent in the life of one migrant, Sybil Powell, the daughter of a deceased Worcestershire husbandman. Her father had died five years earlier when she was only 15. A gentleman of the parish of St. Martin's Ludgate testified that

> the mother of the said Sybil Powell is a poor woman and not able to bestow any portion upon her and therefore has left her to her own disposition. And that the said Sybil has inhabited in and about London for the most part, these seven years, or thereabouts, and was servant to him, the said Edward Pye, about four years last past and is now out of service, remaining at the house of one Henry Lackeland of St. Sepulchre, turner, brother of the said Richard [the groom] who placed her there about 3 weeks since and maintains her at his own cost until such time as they shall be married conveniently.[50]

Sybil Powell was clearly very much under the paternalistic protection of her future husband although she had been left 'to her own disposition'.

*　　*　　*

Although nearly half of the fathers of London-born women were dead when their daughters married, the majority of London daughters (73 per cent) were living in familial situations at marriage. These families were necessarily mixed in composition, consisting of half-brothers, half-sisters and step-siblings. Very few London-born daughters were living away from their families in positions of service or with kin. The extremely high percentage living with their families at the time of marriage suggests that most London daughters' marriages were arranged. Associated with their early age at marriage was a large positive age-difference between partners. Such a pattern in more exaggerated form has been found in fifteenth-century Florence, where the mean age at first marriage of women was 18 years and the age-difference 12 years.[51] Sjoberg has argued that arranged marriage was a general structural characteristic of the pre-industrial city, but it is now clear,

---

[50] GL, MS 10, 091/3: 24/8/1607: Lakeland-Powell.
[51] Kindly communicated by Professor David Herlihy of Harvard University.

Table VIII: Situation of London-born, London-resident single women at marriage, by occupation or status of fathers

Occupation or status of father	No.	% living with fathers and mothers	% living with stepfathers and step-mothers	% living with widowed mothers	Total in familial context	% living with kin	% of known servants	% of presumed servants or with kin
Esquires, knights, gentry	90	48.8	6.6	11.1	66.5	5.5	6.6	21.4
High status tradesmen	158	53.7	10.1	14.5	78.3	5.6	3.2	12.9
Yeomen	20	4.2	2.2	3.2	9.2	3.2	3.2	5.2
Low status craftsmen	183	48.0	15.3	10.3	73.6	6.5	6.5	9.2
Unknown origins	40	17.5	10.0	40.0	67.5	10.0	7.5	7.5
All	491	46.8	11.6	14.4	72.8	6.7	5.9	14.6

for London at least, that this generalization can apply only to those daughters living in London with their fathers, stepfathers and mothers, or widowed mothers, and to migrant brides living with kin.[52] In Table VIII the situation of London-born single women at the time of their marriage is analysed according to the status of their fathers.

Mean age at orphanhood in all status groups was much lower for the London-born daughters living with their mothers and stepfathers or with their widowed mothers. An average of 12.9 years implied that for orphaned daughters an interval of seven to eight years was spent in a family consisting of a mother and stepfather or with one parent only. There is insufficient detail in the records to estimate the probability of living with *both* biological parents. In many instances daughters whose fathers were alive, may have been living with fathers and stepmothers. A minimum of 20 per cent of London daughters would have been living with a parent and stepparent.

In a demographic context of severe plague mortalities and low life expectancies, London parents may have been anxious to see their daughters settled in marriage before they died. This would encourage both arranged and early marriages. It was, for example, poignantly related in the marriage of 17-year-old Sybil Hunt of St. Bride's parish with Thomas Harrad, a 25-year-old cordwainer of St. Sepulchre's parish, 'that the late deceased mother of the said Sybil Hunt did testify on her death bed to this intended marriage and did also desire that the said Thomas Harrad and Sybil Hunt might be joined together in matrimony'.[53]

[52] Gideon Sjoberg, 'The nature of the pre-industrial city', in P. Clark (ed.), *The Early Modern Town* (London, 1976), p. 45.
[53] GL, MS 10, 091/6/: 9/3/1617/18: Harrad-Hunt.

When we consider the mixed composition of most London households—parents, stepparents, sons and daughters, apprentices and servants—it is not difficult to appreciate the natural advantages of London-born daughters in the marriage market. The magnitude of male apprenticeship migration suggests that in early seventeenth-century London men outnumbered women, a further factor favouring the native-born in the marriage stakes. Within each household the master's daughter was well positioned to make a more socially advantageous marriage than the migrant servant. Consequently most London daughters either married into their own status group or into the one above them. Luke Walthall, a merchant of the City of London, a bachelor aged 24, was 'at the government of his Master, Mr. Humphrey Basse, merchant of the same place whose consent he has'. He was to marry his master's daughter, Mary Basse, living at home with her father.[54] Poel Blomefield, a fishmonger aged 22 of the parish of St. Magnus the Martyr, alleged marriage with Alice Drewe, spinster of the same parish, aged 25. He was 'servant to Richard Knight, fishmonger, who testified the consent of his wife, Jane Drewe alias Knight, mother of Alice Drewe'.[55]

*   *   *

A detailed discussion of social mobility is not possible here since it requires a breakdown of the marriage choices of single women from all occupational backgrounds. Instead we can simply summarize the general findings which relate to migrants and native-born daughters.[56] For male apprentices in early seventeenth-century London, it was certainly true that geographical mobility promoted upward social mobility. The same could not be said of the migrant daughters of gentlemen, high status provincial tradesmen and craftsmen: the only migrant group who succeeded in making upward mobile marriages were yeomen's daughters. Forty per cent of migrant daughters of yeomen married gentry and high status tradesmen husbands in London, compared to only 28 per cent of yeomen's non-migrant daughters in the rural parts of the diocese. Yet even for these migrant women there were wide variations, depending on whether they were living with kin or in service: 53 per cent of yeomen's daughters in service married low status craftsmen, porters and labourers, as against 13 per cent of yeomen's daughters living with kin.

As a general finding we can conclude that the concomitant of service was downward social mobility: social origins became of negligible importance upon entry into this apparently low status female occupation. In sharp contrast, migrant women who resided with kin almost invariably made upwardly mobile marriages. Thus London kinship networks were a highly

---

[54] GL, MS 10, 091/4: 12/2/1610/11: Walthall-Basse.
[55] GL, MS 10, 091/4: 16/2/1610/11: Blomefield-Drewe.
[56] For a detailed analysis of social mobility in London in this period see Elliott, 'Mobility and marriage', part III, ch. 3, 'Social mobility through migration, apprenticeship and marriage'.

effective medium for promoting the marriages of provincial daughters. Direct comparison of all migrant daughters with the London-born, however, establishes how very favourably placed the latter were in the marriage market; for all status groups they had consistently higher levels of endogamous and upwardly mobile marriages than did migrant brides.

V

Marriage Settlements, 1660–1740:
The Adoption of the Strict Settlement in Kent and Northamptonshire[1]

LLOYD BONFIELD

The development of the strict family settlement in the mid-seventeenth century is of interest to both legal and economic historians. To the former, the strict settlement is intrinsically important; and the innovation of trustees to preserve contingent remainders, the keystone of the strict settlement, has been described as the 'most notable achievement of the conveyancers'.[2] Such a conclusion is not unwarranted since strict settlements were subsequently employed by the upper strata of English landed society to effect the inter-generational transfer of land for over two centuries. But its significance to the legal historian does not lie solely with the ingenuity of its mechanics, for the strict settlement also had a profound effect on the complex law regarding real property. Accordingly, it has been suggested that the strict settlement helped to simplify 'that ungodly jumble' which was the land law.[3]

Economic historians, on the other hand, consider the advent of the strict settlement to be a crucial factor in establishing the more stable pattern of landownership which they claim characterized post-Restoration England.[4] More specifically, it has been argued that the strict settlement promoted the drift of landed property towards the greater landowner by assisting in the acquisition and preservation of estates. During the period 1680–1740, the era of the 'rise of great estates', the acquisition of land through marriage and inheritance, long considered instrumental in the rise of certain landed families, came to operate in part due to the operation of the strict settlement according to a fixed pattern. Although other factors such as office and the land tax contributed to this trend, it was the strict settlement which preserved the acquisitions of landowners with rising economic fortunes. By employing

---

[1] Mr. D. E. C. Yale of Christ's College, Cambridge read an earlier draft of this paper. I am grateful for his comments, and for his constant assistance with regard to my research into marriage settlements.

[2] A. W. B. Simpson, *An Introduction to the History of the Land Law* (Oxford, 1961), p. 220.

[3] J. H. Baker, *An Introduction to English Legal History* (London, 1971), p. 156.

[4] The prevailing view remains the one established by Sir John Habakkuk in H. J. Habakkuk, 'English landownership 1680–1740', *Economic History Review*, X (1940). It has, however, come under some criticism: C. Clay, 'Marriage, inheritance and the rise of large estates in England, 1660–1815', *Economic History Review*, 2nd ser., XVIII (1968); B. A. Holderness, 'The English land market in the eighteenth century', *Economic History Review*, 2nd ser., XXVII (1974); J. V. Beckett, 'English landownership in the later seventeenth and eighteenth centuries', *Economic History Review*, 2nd ser., XXX (1977).

the strict settlement earlier than their lesser neighbours, and by placing more of their land under settlement, the greater landowners 'increased the stability of the large estate relative to the small'.[5] The result was the concentration of land in fewer hands. Yet the move towards the employment of the strict settlement was gradual, and it has been asserted that it did not become the 'stock recommendation of the conveyancer' until the beginning of the eighteenth century.[6]

It is not my intention in this chapter to discuss in depth the developments in legal mechanics which led to the formulation of the strict settlement, important as they no doubt are. Rather, I propose to test the suppositions of economic historians regarding the dissemination and effect of the strict settlement by employing hitherto unused family muniments.[7] By charting the adoption of the strict settlement in a finite group of landowners in post-Restoration England, two points may be determined. The first is whether there was indeed a lapse of nearly half a century between the innovation and the widespread employment of the device. Secondly, we may consider whether those segments of landed society which are said to have been building and consolidating their estates actually employed strict settlements more actively. Before doing so, it is appropriate to consider both the mechanics of the strict settlement, and the over-all role of marriage settlements in early modern England.

*   *   *

It has been suggested that the development of the strict settlement should not be seen as the result of the turmoil of the Civil War, but as the culmination of efforts by conveyancers to devise a precedent which would allow landed families to transmit their estates intact.[8] Such an hypothesis perforce considers the development of the strict settlement as a response to the refusal in the early seventeenth century of the common law courts to sanction the use of

---

[5] Habakkuk, 'English landownership', p. 7.

[6] H. J. Habakkuk, 'The English land market in the eighteenth century', in J. S. Bromley and E. H. Kossman, eds., *Britain and the Netherlands* (London, 1960).

[7] I am preparing a monograph on *Marriage Settlements 1600–1740*. This paper is therefore a preliminary one. My conclusions are based on a study of settlement practice in Kent and Northamptonshire. The data set is a body of 143 settlements—all those executed during the period 1660–1740 which are on deposit in the respective county archives in Maidstone and Northampton. I am aware that I am not working with a random sample of marriage settlements executed by the peerage and gentry. Implicit in all my conclusions is a recognition of the limits of my data set. A more detailed discussion of the data can be found in L. Bonfield, 'Marriage settlements, 1601–1740: the development and adoption of the strict settlement' (unpublished Cambridge Ph.D. thesis, 1978), Introduction. The settlements were analysed by computer with the assistance of Dr. John Dawson, Director of the Literary & Linguistics Computer Centre, at Cambridge. I am grateful for his assistance. Because of the nature of the data, I have omitted direct references to the settlements, but they can be found in the bibliography of my thesis. The data remain on magnetic tape at the Computer Centre.

[8] M. E. Finch, *Five Northamptonshire Families* (Northampton, 1956), Introduction by H. J. Habakkuk, p. xv.

unbarrable entails and perpetuities, since those ingenious forms of settlement had similar aims. Certainly the relatively short period between the judicial exclusion of any form of settlement which unduly restrained the alienation of land and the development of the strict settlement lends support to this theory.[9]

Regardless of this connection, the similarities between the strict settlement and perpetuities are rather limited. Indeed, what is striking about the two forms is their differences, the most significant being the period during which an individual settlement restrained alienation. Unlike the perpetuity which sought to prevent future generations from alienating the patrimony, a strict settlement looked only to the next generation: that is to say, it merely prevented the present or next life tenant in possession from defeating the entail assured to his unborn son. An individual strict settlement, therefore, merely passed the patrimony from one generation to the next, and if it was designed as an alternative to unbarrable entails and perpetuities, then mid-seventeenth-century landowners had far more circumscribed designs for their patrimonies than their ancestors.

The duration of an individual strict settlement can best be illustrated by considering its mechanics and operation. Generally strict settlements were executed upon the marriage of a landowner's eldest son. In the form most commonly employed, a settlor limited a life estate to his own use, followed by a life interest in his eldest son, the prospective groom. A contingent entail in remainder was limited to the eldest son produced by the marriage, but it was preceded by a limitation in trustees to preserve this contingent remainder. Additional remainders over followed the contingent entail to take effect if the marriage produced no male heir. Thus an individual strict settlement did not operate far into the future. The estate in the trustees merely protected the contingent interest in the next generation; and that remainderman came into possession seised of an entail: an alienable interest. The mechanics of the strict settlement therefore suggest that it was intended to effect the intergenerational transfer of land rather than to insure the continuation of the patrimony in the settlor's descendants for an indefinite period of time.

Now it has been suggested that the strict settlement created the possibility in the later seventeenth century of making entails permanent.[10] While the use of the term permanent entails is unfortunate, since the common law courts had already clearly indicated that one of the inherent properties of

---

[9] The century following the enactment of the Statute of Uses of 1536 (27 Hen. VIII, c. 10) witnessed considerable innovation in forms of settlement. Many of these attempted to restrain the power of the tenant in possession to alienate. The courts of common law and equity had difficulty in reconciling these forms to the common law system of future interests in real property. By the beginning of the seventeenth century it was becoming apparent that restraints upon alienation were not favoured, and in *Mary Portington's Case*, 10 Co. Rep. 35b (1614) the Court of Common Pleas made it clear that any settlement which tended towards a perpetuity was invalid. The strict settlement was developed in the 1640s: Bonfield, 'Marriage settlements', pp. 140–54.

[10] Habakkuk, 'English landownership', p. 7.

an entail was its liability to be barred, the rationale which supports this suggestion relies upon the concept of estate resettlement. Upon the marriage of the eldest son in each generation it is argued that the estate is resettled, thereby leaving it in the possession of a series of life tenants with limited powers of disposition.

Such a situation is not beyond the bounds of possibility; but it would only come to pass if *each* successive father lived to the marriage of his eldest son in *each* generation. This pattern of estate resettlement is said to have operated in the following fashion. Upon the marriage of the eldest son, father and son join to break the existing settlement, and execute a further settlement. In return for a present income to support his prospective family, the eldest son consents to relinquish his contingent entail, and accepts instead a life tenancy to commence on the termination of his father's life tenancy. The enjoyment of the entail, and therefore the ability to alienate in fee, is postponed until the next generation because it is settled in the eldest son as yet unborn produced by the impending marriage. Consequently, the estate must pass to the next generation intact.

Assuming that no land sales were undertaken jointly at the time of resettlement, such a process repeated in each generation might secure the patrimony from dispersion in perpetuity. Yet the viability of this theory rests on a single demographic assumption: that fathers in the late seventeenth century and early eighteenth century lived to the marriage of their eldest sons. Obviously some did; but for the theory of estate settlement to be broadly applicable to the landed class, a large proportion of fathers must have done so in *each* generation over the *entire* period. One break in this pattern of resettlement would leave the estate in the hands of a tenant in tail and therefore vulnerable.

Although our knowledge of the demography of the period is limited, what we do know suggests that we should approach this demographic assumption with scepticism. This question has been dealt with in detail elsewhere by constructing a model of intergenerational succession.[11] By employing the vital statistics ascertained by historical demographers, it has been demonstrated that fathers lived to the marriage of their eldest sons infrequently; only about one in three did so in each generation. Due to a combination of high mortality (and thus limited life expectancy), late age at marriage and the failure to produce a surviving male child, successive estate resettlement over an extended period must have been uncommon.

Unlike the perpetuity and unbarrable entail then, the strict settlement by its mechanics did not seek to render estates inalienable for more than a generation. Moreover, its operation did not lead to a succession of life tenants in most families. With each succession, therefore, it was likely that an heir

[11] L. Bonfield, 'Marriage settlements and "the rise of great estates": the demographic aspect', *Economic History Review,* 2nd ser., XXXII (1979), 483–93.

would come into possession of his inheritance seised of an entail with plenary powers of alienation. There is no reason to suspect that contemporaries were unaware of their dilemma. Nevertheless they generally settled the patrimony upon marriage, and it is appropriate to consider why strict settlements were actually executed, even though the documents themselves do not allow us to make more than inferences regarding the motives of settlors.

Recent research has confirmed that the execution of marriage settlements preceded the development of forms of settlements which restrained alienation.[12] Bearing in mind that strict settlements were most often executed upon marriage, it is not inappropriate to look for the origins of the strict settlement in earlier forms of marriage settlements, in particular those executed in the first half of the seventeenth century. Such a search is not fruitless since it appears that the previous 200 years witnessed a considerable evolution in the forms of marriage settlements. In particular, settlement practice in the early seventeenth century differed substantially from that of the previous century. In the sixteenth century the most common form of marriage settlement was the grant of an entail to the prospective bride and groom.[13] Around the turn of the century, however, one can detect a dramatic shift in form. Instead of the grant of an entail to a living person, the most common form was a limitation of a joint life estate in the bride and groom, with a remainder in tail to their male heir.[14] With the exception of the limitation of trustees to preserve contingent remainders, this new form of marriage settlement was strikingly similar to the strict settlement.

Given the similarity in form between the strict settlement and the 'life estate-entail mode', one may assert with some confidence that the strict settlement was merely a refinement of this pre-existing form. Moreoover, the need for some type of mechanism like the trustees to preserve contingent remainders is apparent, since the early seventeenth-century settlement was rather vulnerable: the life tenant was free to enlarge his interest into a fee, thereby destroying the contingent entail.

In suggesting that the origins of the strict settlement are to be found in the prevailing mode of marriage settlement in the early seventeenth century and not in the perpetuity, I do not mean to imply that perpetuities were never employed in marriage settlements, nor that no settlors were bent upon fettering their patrimony.[15] Rather, I would suggest that the strict settlement may not have been *intended* as a restrictive disposition, and also may not have been considered unduly burdensome by landowners. It was merely a

---

[12] Bonfield, 'Marriage settlements 1601–1740', chs. 3 and 4. J. P. Cooper, 'Patterns of inheritance & settlement by great landowners from the fifteenth to the eighteenth centuries' in J. Goody, J. Thirsk, and E. P. Thompson, eds., *Family and Inheritance* (Cambridge, 1976), pp. 192–233.

[13] This conclusion is based on a study of settlements involved in litigation, and noted in printed law reports of the period.

[14] Bonfield, 'Marriage settlements 1601–1740', pp. 120–8.

[15] No marriage settlement in my data set contains a clause of perpetuity.

refinement of a pre-existing form whose goal it was to pass the patrimony from one generation to the next upon the marriage of the male heir.

To some extent, the focus upon restrictive elements has overshadowed what may well have been a primary consideration in the execution of marriage settlements: fixing the bride's jointure. Provisions for widows were secured at common law by the right of dower, a life interest in one-third of the land and hereditaments of which her husband stood seised at any time during coverture.[16] To the heir, dower claims were often a nuisance, preventing him from consolidating his estate, and sometimes interfering with his freedom to alienate. Because a jointure specified the land from which the widow was to enjoy the profits for her maintenance, these problems were avoided. Moreover, there were advantages in jointure for the bride as well; upon marriage she became seised of an immediate life estate, and upon the death of her husband she did not need to sue out a writ.[17] By the reign of Elizabeth, the settling of jointures was becoming increasingly popular.[18]

Consequently, there was a somewhat pressing need to execute marriage settlements, and it was preferable to do so prior to the union. Due to a legal technicality with regard to the law of jointure, post-nuptial settlements were rendered less acceptable to the groom's family. Although a widow was bound to accept the jointure provided in a pre-nuptial settlement, she could renounce one provided by a post-nuptial settlement in favour of her common law right of dower, even if she joined in the execution of the settlement.[19] Often it was to her pecuniary advantage to do so, because by electing to receive her dower the widow could take advantage of any increase in the size of the patrimony during coverture. And since she was entitled to one-third of all lands and hereditaments of which her husband stood seised at any time during the marriage, a transfer or exchange of land would also increase the amount of her dower even if there was little net increase in the value of the estate.[20]

Finally, there was another practical advantage to the pre-nuptial settling of a jointure; by specifying the lands which were to comprise the widow's jointure, the groom's family avoided the often arduous task of sorting out her thirds after her husband's death. In the absence of a pre-nuptial agreement, both the amount and the form of the maintenance was subject to negotiation. If the marriage had produced a male heir it might be less difficult to reach a compromise because there was some community of interest between a mother and her son. But if her husband's heir was a brother or more remote relation, the negotiations might be less amicable; and the widow

---

[16] *The First Part of the Institutes of the Laws of England, or a Commentary on Littleton,* F. Hargrave and C. Butler, eds., 18th edn. (London, 1843), §31a *et seq.*

[17] Land set aside as jointure was held in a form of joint tenancy. Ibid.

[18] M. L. Cioni, 'Woman and law in Elizabethan England' (unpublished Cambridge Ph.D. thesis, 1974), p. 198.

[19] 27 Hen. VIII, c. 10 (1536); Hargrave and Butler, eds., *First Part of the Institutes,* §41.

[20] Ibid., § 38.

had every reason to be rapacious since the size of her dower often bore heavily upon her prospects for remarriage.

By way of example, the notebook of Sir Walter Calverley of Esholt, baronet, provides an account, albeit an incomplete one, of the complexity of negotiations carried out to secure maintenance in the absence of a marriage settlement.[21] Married to John Ramsden in February of 1689, Sir Walter's sister, Bridget, was widowed the following July.[22] No marriage settlement was executed, and the scattered notes penned by Sir Walter attest to the difficulty experienced in securing maintenance for his sister. Although initially a preliminary agreement was reached between Thomas Ramsden, the husband's brother and the next heir, and the Calverleys to enable him to take up administration of his brother's goods,[23] a dispute arose over the amount and the method of payment, and over two years later Sir Walter 'went to Crowstone to make an end with Mr. Ramsden about my sister's thirds'.[24] No satisfactory accord was apparently reached, although some payments were made. The negotiations became more complex with Bridget's remarriage to William Neville, Esquire, in 1696, [25] and with the death of Thomas Ramsden in January 1697.[26] A preliminary agreement to accept a rent charge was reached between Ramsden's executors and Sir Walter and Neville.[27] Yet Sir Walter's troubles were not over, because the rent charge was in arrears.[28] Moreover, the family attorney advised the creation of a trust to recover Bridget's dower and 'receive them to her own use without the disturbance of Mr. Neville'.[29] It was not until January 1703, 13½ years after the death of Mr. John Ramsden, that the dispute was finally settled; a mortgage was accepted in lieu of the arrears, and a formal written agreement was executed.[30] Not only must the negotiations have been irksome for Sir Walter, but given the number of lawyers involved they must have been expensive as well.[31]

Thus postponing settlement until after marriage could prove to be both tiresome and costly, and perhaps a greater risk to the patrimony than a profligate heir. By focusing on the desire to restrain freedom of alienation as the primary motive for marriage settlements, historians have virtually ignored a more practical consideration: ensuring that maintenance for the

---

[21] *Publications of the Surtees Society,* LXXVII (1883), 43–148.

[22] Ibid., p. 46.

[23] Ibid., p. 47.

[24] Ibid., p. 63.

[25] Ibid., p. 71.

[26] Ibid., p. 73.

[27] Ibid., p. 78.

[28] Ibid.

[29] Ibid., p. 84.

[30] Ibid., pp. 99–100.

[31] The Calverleys consulted Mr. Witton of Wakefield, Mr. Lawrence Breases of Leeds, Thomas Barker, Esq., of York. At least seven other men take part in the negotiations, but it is impossible to determine who they are.

bride in the form of land or an annuity be specified and incontrovertible should she survive her husband. Consequently, the widespread employment of pre-nuptial marriage settlements preceded the development of forms of settlement which restrict the freedom of alienation of the tenant in possession.

In addition to the need to fix jointures, another suggestion may be offered to explain the widespread use of marriage settlements. Again it concerns the orderly transmission of the patrimony. After the Statute of Wills,[32] a large proportion of freehold land could be disposed of by testament. Wills, however, were most often executed on one's death-bed, and without the assistance of a lawyer. Enumerating all the various parcels of land which comprised the patrimony would have been awkward. Without the assistance of counsel a complex disposition might have been impossible. Admittedly, a testator could will all his lands and tenements to his male heir in the 'life estate-entail' mode, but marriage settlements often went further. One could provide portions for younger sons and daughters or grant powers to the next tenant which exceeded those provided at common law. Although a will might include similar provisions, the death-bed was not the most appropriate place for prudent estate planning. Moreover, sloppy draftsmanship by a non-lawyer might pave the way to an expensive law suit regarding matters of interpretation.

Thus it is likely that the use of marriage settlements arose from the desire to secure an orderly transmission of the patrimony and the need to fix jointures. Although other legal instruments might achieve similar goals, only the pre-nuptial marriage settlement could do both. While the desire to assure the patrimony in the 'name and blood of the settlor for so long as it pleaseth Almighty God' may have in part motivated some settlors, the landowner in the seventeenth century also had other more immediate concerns.

*   *   *

Having described the workings of the strict settlement and considered the role of the marriage settlement in early modern England, we may now begin to chart the dissemination of the strict settlement in order to ascertain how actively it was employed, and whether its use may have contributed to the emerging pattern of landownership. In particular, it is important to recall that Professor Habakkuk has suggested that it was not until the turn of the eighteenth century that the strict settlement achieved prominence, and that its use by the greater landowners contributed to their rising economic fortunes.[33]

Two considerations would appear to support Professor Habakkuk's view. First, the mechanics of the strict settlement were not sanctioned by a court of common law until 1697.[34] Given the common law courts' abhorrence of

---

[32] 32 Hen. VIII, c. 1. (1540).
[33] See above, pp. 101-2.
[34] *Duncomb v. Duncomb,* 3 Lev. 437 (1697).

innovation, cautious settlors might have been reluctant to experiment with a conveyance of dubious validity. Secondly, some settlors may have felt that the strict settlement unduly circumscribed the powers of the life tenant to deal with his estate.

Contemporary reservations regarding the use of the strict settlement may best be summarized by reference to a letter from Heneage Lord Finch to the Earl of Orrery.[35] It would appear from the contents of the letter that Orrery was discussing financial arrangements with the Countess of Warwick regarding a proposed match between her daughter, Anne, and Lord Finch's heir, Daniel. Apparently, the Countess favoured the execution of a strict settlement of the Finch patrimony. Although he acknowledged the reasonableness of such a demand, Lord Finch was adamant in his refusal. The objections he put forward offer insight into contemporary misgivings regarding the strict settlement.

Lord Finch cited three. The first concerned the restriction that the strict settlement imposed on the tenant in possession preventing him from providing a more generous endowment for his wife and their offspring than the one specified in the marriage settlement should the husband predecease his wife. Lord Finch wrote, 'As concerns my Lady Essex, if my son die before her, he could not add a shilling to her jointure or to his daughter's portions, whereas in the way I propose he could give what increase he pleaseth.'[36] Yet to the bride's family, this rigidity conferred some advantages: without a secure disposition the surviving children might find themselves in a rather tenuous position if their father outlived their mother and remarried. Even the heir male might be disinherited in favour of the eldest son produced by the second match. In the peerage, however, Lord Finch contended that such a 'scruple' was unfounded: 'Tis true he may live to marry again, but tis true the barony must descend upon his sons by the first wife, and that alone carries with it the necessity of leaving an estate to it . . .'.[37]

There was, however, another contention, for it was believed that a strict settlement was far too inflexible a device to assure the patrimony, given the uncertain economic and political climate which followed the Restoration. In particular, family circumstances might necessitate land sales. But, as Lord Finch conceded, this flaw might be remedied by the inclusion of a power of revocation which would allow the tenant in possession to 'remain master of his estate'.[38] To some extent this course would be somewhat anomalous, since it would in effect nullify even the limited restraint upon alienation which a strict settlement conferred.

Finally, with the contention that was perhaps uppermost in his mind, Lord Finch argued:

[35] Historical Manuscripts Commission, *Finch MSS*, II, 17–18.
[36] Ibid., p. 18.
[37] Ibid.
[38] Ibid.

It is against nature to make the father subject to his child ... It is against experience, and a bitter one in my family; for I have known the son of such a settlement cast away himself in marriage and then offer to disinherit his father by treating to sell the inheritance for a song while his father lived.[39]

Consequently, according to Lord Finch, employing a strict settlement considerably diminished parental authority. Indeed, the situation was reversed with the father financially at the mercy of his son.

Yet in the end, the landed class overcame their objections to the strict settlement, and our task is to determine when. We may do so by analysing the form employed in those settlements which comprise our data set. For establishing the frequency with which the strict settlement appears, the period under consideration (1660–1740) has been divided into equal segments. Since we are to test Professor Habakkuk's assertion that it is not until the 'turn of the century' that the employment of the strict settlement became widespread, using 20-year periods conveniently provides a break at 1700.

Table I is a frequency distribution of the dissemination of the strict settlement in Kent and Northamptonshire. During the first period, limitations in trustees to preserve contingent remainders appeared in slightly less than two-thirds of the marriage settlements in the data set. However, in the second period, and therefore before the turn of the century, the ratio rises to nearly four out of every five (78.4 per cent). Thereafter, during the first 40 years of the eighteenth century, the percentage fluctuates slightly, but is not significant statistically given the size of the data set. Consequently, it was the last 20 years of the seventeenth century rather than the early eighteenth century which witnessed the transformation in the settlement habits of these landowners.

What is perhaps more striking is how early on the strict settlement was adopted. It was employed by a considerable majority of settlors in the first generation after it was 'invented'. During the final two decades it reached the same relative pre-eminence it was to enjoy during the eighteenth century.

Table I: Frequency distribution of the employment of the strict settlement

| | SETTLEMENT FORM | | | |
| | Strict settlement | | Other forms | |
Time span	No.	%	No.	%
1660–1680	26	63.4	15	36.6
1681–1700	29	78.4	8	21.6
1701–1720	25	80.6	6	19.4
1721–1740	25	75.8	8	24.2
Totals	·105	73.9	37	26.1

[39] Ibid.

Settlors were therefore willing to experiment with a conveyance which had not yet received judicial sanction. Indeed, contemporary juristic opinion would appear to confirm the conclusion derived from our settlements. As early as 1672, Peyton Ventris (later Justice of the Court of Common Pleas) reported:

> It hath been the most common way of conveyancing to prevent the disappointing of contingent Estates to make Feoffment etc., to the use of the Husband etc., for Life, Remainder to the use of Feoffees for the Life of the Husband, and so on to contingent Remainders ... he which hath the first Estate cannot destroy the remainder.[40]

Having determined that the strict settlement was rather rapidly adopted by landed families in Kent and Northamptonshire, we may now consider the distribution of its employment by the three segments of landed society defined by Professor Habakkuk.[41] If the segment that was building and consolidating its estates, the 'great magnates', tended to use the strict settlement more actively than their lesser neighbours, then its employment may well explain in part the 'rise of great estates'. If, however, the reverse is the case, or if all segments of landed society employed the strict settlement with equal frequency, then the strict settlement may well be a neutral factor in explaining the apparent trend in landownership.

Table II illustrates the employment of the strict settlement by Professor Habakkuk's three segments of landed society: the 'great magnates' reckoned to have estates with a rental value in excess of £2,000 per annum; the 'substantial squirearchy' with estates returning £800 to £2,000; and the

Table II: Frequency distribution of the employment of the strict settlement by social classification 1660–1740

Social classification	TIME SPANS									
	1660–1680		1681–1700		1701–1720		1721–1740		TOTALS	
	Strict settle-ment	Other forms	Strict settle-ment	Other forms	Strict settle-ment	Other forms	Strict settle-ment	Other forms	Strict settle-ment	Other forms
	%	%	%	%	%	%	%	%	%	%
Great magnates	100	—	100	—	100	—	100	—	100	—
Substantial squires	70	30	88.9	11.1	80	20	100	—	82.1	17.9
Lesser gentry	50	50	69.6	30.4	76.5	23.5	63.6	36.9	64.6	35.4

[40] *Lloyd v. Brooking,* 1 Vent. 188, 189 (1672). Cf. *Hales v. Risley,* Pollex. 369, 383 (1674).
[41] Habakkuk, 'English landownership', p. 3.

'lesser gentry' with rent rolls of under £800 per annum.[42] The settlements which comprise the data set tend to confirm Professor Habakkuk's assertion that the 'great magnates' uniformly adopted the strict settlement immediately after its invention. Yet the data also indicate that a rather large segment of the 'substantial squirearchy'—that segment of landed society which was supposedly 'stable'—also adopted the strict settlement rapidly; and in the period of the 'rise of great estates' after 1680, nearly nine out of ten 'substantial squires' (88.9 per cent) employed strict settlements. Consequently, it is difficult to attribute the differing economic fortunes of these two segments of landed society to the employment of this device.

But what about the lower strata of landed society? According to Professor Habakkuk, it was the 'lesser gentry' who fared worst during the period 1680–1740; and it was at their expense that the hegemony of the 'great magnates' was fashioned.[43] Table II illustrates that the 'lesser gentry' adopted the strict settlement less quickly, and employed it far less frequently after 1680 than the other two segments of landed society.

A closer look at the settlements of the 'lesser gentry' is revealing. If these settlements are sorted by quantity of land conveyed, two distinct patterns emerge. Many of the 'lesser gentry' continued the practice, somewhat common in the sixteenth century, of settling upon marriage only that portion of the estate which was to comprise the bride's jointure. Thus in a number of settlements of the 'lesser gentry' we often find the conveyance of a messuage, usually the capital messuage, and a few acres, an amount clearly insufficient to support a gentleman, but one which would provide a competent jointure. For the most part these settlements are not 'strict', that is to say, the entail in remainder to the eldest son is not preceded by trustees to preserve contingent remainders. If we eliminate these partial settlements and include only those conveying at least a manor and appurtenances a far different picture emerges (see Table III).

A comparison between the percentages in Table III and those in Table II indicates that a large proportion of those 'lesser gentry' settling at least a manor and appurtenances employed the strict settlement. Moreover, during the period of the 'rise of great estates', 92.1 per cent (35 out of 38) settled their patrimonies in this manner. Indeed, this segment of the 'lesser gentry' adopted the strict settlement as quickly as the 'substantial squires', and employed it as frequently. The differential in employment of the strict

---

[42] Ibid. In placing my settlors in Habakkuk's social classifications I considered all baronets and knights as 'substantial squires' and all squires and gentlemen as 'lesser gentry'. I believe such a course to be justified because in those cases where rental value is set out in the settlement, I found that the social degree conformed to Habakkuk's income brackets. However, this was only a presumption. Where the amount of land settled appeared to be greater or lesser than the income bracket, I made the appropriate change in social classification.

[43] Habakkuk, 'English landownership', p. 3.

Table III: Frequency distribution of the employment of the strict settlement by the 'lesser gentry' settling at least a manor

| | SETTLEMENT FORM | | | |
| | Strict settlement | | Other forms | |
Time span	No.	%	No.	%
1660–1680	10	71.4	4	28.6
1681–1700	12	92.3	1	7.7
1701–1720	10	83.3	2	16.7
1721–1740	13	100	0	—
Totals	45	86.5	7	13.5

settlement in these three groups is so minimal that it is unlikely that it was a significant factor in their allegedly differing economic fortunes.

Isolating this segment of the 'lesser gentry' requires some defence. Admittedly, Professor Habakkuk has never argued that the 'lesser gentry' disappeared altogether; but he does create a distinction between surviving but stagnating 'substantial squires', and disappearing 'lesser gentry'.[44] Furthermore he has contended that the success of the 'great magnates' may be attributed in part to their settlement habits: they adopted the strict settlement sooner and entailed more of their estate.[45] However, the settlements which comprise our data set do not appear to confirm this. For example, in two peerage settlements, the settlor retained an interest in fee in a portion of the patrimony.[46] But what is most significant is that a large segment of the 'lesser gentry' settled their estates in the same manner as the 'great magnates' during the period 1680–1740, and employed strict settlements as often as their counterparts in the 'substantial squirearchy'. If, other things being equal, the strict settlement was the principal factor in establishing the primacy of the 'great magnates' and the survival of the 'substantial squirearchy', one should expect it to have assisted also those members of the 'lesser gentry' who employed it. Consequently, the period 1680–1740 should also have witnessed the emergence of a reasonably healthy, though perhaps diminished, 'lesser gentry'.

But rarely are all other economic factors equal. In dispelling the theory of continuity in landownership fostered by successive resettlements, I suggested that the 'rise of great estates', if the phenomenon did occur, should be attributed to other demographic or economic factors rather than to the emergence of the strict settlement.[47] Similarly, it would appear that the

[44] Ibid., p. 8.
[45] Ibid., pp. 6–8.
[46] Lord Teynham (Kent Archives Office, U4981/T11). Viscount Falkland (Kent Archives Office, U1236/T26).
[47] Bonfield, 'Marriage settlements and the "rise of great estates"', pp. 492–3.

relatively rapid adoption, and the rather widespread employment of the strict settlement by all segments of landed gentry corroborates this assertion.

*   *   *

In discussing the role of the marriage settlement in early modern England, I suggested that the motives of landowners in executing marriage settlements, strict or otherwise, may be attributed to factors other than the desire to restrain the power of alienation of the tenant in possession. Moreover, I have questioned whether contemporaries considered the strict settlement to be unduly restrictive. The harsh demographic climate of the late seventeenth and early eighteenth centuries left most patrimonies in the hands of tenants in tail with each succession; for, as we have seen, unless a father survived to the marriage of his eldest son, that son was likely to succeed to the patrimony as a tenant in tail under the terms of the existing settlement. Most of these landowners were destined to marry, and the form of marriage settlement they employed is telling. If the tenants in possession considered the strict settlement to be unduly burdensome, then they might have been reluctant to employ it. By comparing forms employed by 'father settlors'—landowners resettling the patrimony upon the marriage of their eldest sons, with those of 'groom-settlors'—tenants in tail executing a settlement on their own marriage, some light may be shed on the question of whether contemporaries really did consider the strict settlement to be restrictive.

Table IV is a frequency distribution of the employment of the strict settlement by each of these two groups of settlors. The relative percentages in Table IV suggest that grooms were not reluctant to employ strict settlements. Tenants in tail in possession of their patrimonies were therefore in the main not unwilling to circumscribe their powers of disposition. Admittedly, these landowners could have alienated parcels of their estates before marriage, or they may have placed less land under settlement. Alternatively, perhaps, other brides' families were as insistent as the Countess of Warwick, and were able to prevail. Regardless of the reasons, the fact remains that the 'groom settlor' was willing to circumscribe his future power of disposition

Table IV: Frequency distribution of marriage settlements: settlement form by settlor

| | SETTLEMENT FORM | | | |
| | Strict settlement | | Other forms | |
Settlor	No.	%	No.	%
Groom settlor	59	73.8	21	26.3
Father settlor	44	75.9	14	24.1
Totals	103	74.6	35	25.4

Table V: Frequency distribution of marriage settlements:
propensity to employ the strict settlement by settlor

Propensity	GROOM SETTLOR		FATHER SETTLOR	
	No.	%	No.	%
Most likely to employ strict settlement	26	32.5	25	43.1
Least likely to employ strict settlement	54	67.5	33	56.9
Totals	80	58.0	58	42.0

over the bulk of the patrimony, and it is unlikely that he would undertake to do so if he considered a strict settlement to be unduly burdensome.

Since we have determined that certain segments of landed society were somewhat more inclined to execute strict settlements than others, it may be argued that the percentages illustrated in Table IV are biased due to the social distribution of settlements in each class of settlor. To be more precise, if we are to isolate a given variable—the propensity of each group of settlors to employ strict settlements—we must control the variable of social classification. Thus we must separate the 'great magnates' and the 'substantial squires' from those 'lesser gentry' whom we have determined to be in the main less likely to employ strict settlements.

Table V is designed to illustrate any bias due to the social distribution of our data set. It indicates that there is a slight tendency for 'groom settlors' to be in the 'lesser gentry', the social division less likely to employ strict settlements. Therefore, the propensity of 'groom settlors' to employ strict settlements is somewhat understated in Table IV. We may conclude with some confidence, then, that tenants in tail were not less likely to employ strict settlements than their fathers

*   *   *

In this chapter I have argued that the strict settlement was a conveyance of limited duration designed primarily to facilitate the transmission of the patrimony between the generations, and to fix the bride's jointure. These Kentish and Northamptonshire settlements indicate that the adoption of the device was rather swift. The strict settlement, even by the 1680s, was by far the most common form of marriage settlement for all segments of landed society, save for a minority of 'lesser gentry' who settled only prospective jointure land. That such a large proportion of each segment of landed society employed the device in an era when the various groups were allegedly experiencing differing economic fortunes tends to indicate that the strict settlement was rather a neutral factor in determining their fate. No doubt it could preserve the patrimony of those members of landed society whose economic state was sound, but one must wonder whether the estates of the economically healthy actually required such protection.

Moreover, the marriage settlements which comprise the data set tend to indicate that grooms in possession of the patrimony as tenants in tail were not in the main reluctant to circumscribe their future powers of disposition by executing strict settlements upon their marriage. In part, then, it was their decision which accounted for such a high proportion of the land in England being held under such terms. Admittedly, the voluntary adoption of the device does not prove that contemporaries did not regard this assurance as restrictive. Perhaps 'groom settlors' succumbed to the demands of their prospective fathers-in-law. Yet we cannot detect a reluctance on the part of tenants in tail to circumscribe their powers of disposition, and we must therefore question whether landowners indeed considered the strict settlement to be unduly restrictive.

VI

The Rise and Fall of the Fleet Marriages[1]

ROGER LEE BROWN

Lord Hardwicke's Marriage Act of 1753, correctly entitled 'an act for the better preventing of clandestine marriages',[2] was accepted by most contemporary observers as being designed primarily to prevent the clandestine marriages performed in the 'rules' of the Fleet Prison, and at various other centres in London, even though the specific cause of the act was a case which had come to the House of Lords on appeal from the Scottish courts. Although the original draft of the bill expressly referred to 'marriages within any Prison or the Rules thereof', in the debates on it the only instances of clandestine marriage recorded were those performed at the Fleet.

Between 1694 and the year 1754, when Hardwicke's Act became effective and such clandestine marriages were ended, between two and three hundred thousand marriages were solemnized within the Fleet Prison and its rules.[3] Other but lesser marriage centres in London included such places as Alexander Keith's May-Fair Chapel, the Southwark Mint, and the area within the rules of the King's Bench Prison. In the provinces there were centres at Dale Abbey and Peak Forest Chapel in Derbyshire,[4] and Tetbury in Gloucestershire.[5] There is also considerable evidence that clandestine marriages were solemnized by many parochial clergy throughout the country.[6]

---

[1] J. S. Burn, *The Fleet Registers* (London, 1833) and John Ashton, *The Fleet, its River, Prison and Marriages* (London, 1889) represent the principal printed works relating to these marriages. An unpublished London University M.A. thesis by R. L. Brown, 'Clandestine marriages in London, especially within the Fleet Prison, and their effects on Hardwicke's Act, 1753' (1973) is the only modern study. The 800 or so Fleet registers which survive are contained at the Public Record Office and classified under the press mark R.G.7. An article relating to these registers and their use may be found in D. J. Steel's *National Index of Parish Registers* (London, 1968), I, 292–321.

[2] 26 Geo. II c. 33.

[3] The 'rules' was an area around the prison house in which debt prisoners, for a substantial fee and after the giving of such collateral security as would clear their debts if they escaped, were able to live and to continue working at their normal occupations if that were possible. The rules covered that area which lay alongside the prison in Farringdon Street, up the north side of Ludgate Hill, to the Old Bailey, along that street as far as Fleet Lane, and down Fleet Lane until the prison house was again reached.

[4] R. Haw, *The State of Matrimony* (London, 1952), p. 145.

[5] E. A. Wrigley, 'Clandestine marriage in Tetbury in the late 17th century', *Local Population Studies*, X (1973), 15–21.

[6] R. Brown, 'Clandestine marriages in Wales', *Journal of the Historical Society of the Church in Wales*, XXV (1976), 66–71. Compare *A Representation of the Prejudices from an*

Dean Prideaux complained in the late seventeenth century about serious illegalities in the issuing of licences, stating that some surrogates even held weekly marriage 'markets'.[7]

The canons of the Church required that marriage needed the free consent of the parties to it, and that there should be no legal impediments to prevent that marriage. Impediments were created by the prescribed degrees of consanguinity and affinity, and by the age of consent, which was fixed at 14 years for males and 12 for females. The second main requirement was that the performance of the ceremony, and the steps leading to it, should be accompanied by publicity to ensure that all was in order, and to remove any doubt as to its actual performance. Publicity was acquired by the calling of banns or by the issuing of an ecclesiastical licence. The marriage had also to take place in as public a manner as possible in the parish church of one of the parties between the hours of eight a.m. and noon, and in accordance with the service prescribed in the Book of Common Prayer. Any marriage which failed to observe one, or more, of these latter requirements was regarded as clandestine, yet so long as a marriage was free of impediments and met the demands of free consent, it would be upheld by the Church as a valid and indissoluble union, as all other ecclesiastical requirements were directory and not negatory in the sense that their absence could void a union. However, the ecclesiastical authorities insisted that before they could allow the civil rights of marriage to an irregularly married couple their union had to be solemnized *in facie ecclesiae*, and they also imposed various ecclesiastical penalties on those so married and on the clergy who officiated at their earlier union.

By the late seventeenth century the common law lawyers were adopting the attitude that a marriage performed without the presence of a priest or deacon was neither good nor effectual, so adopting the old notion that where the priest was, there was the Church. The reason for this was that these men were increasingly dealing with cases relating to legal succession to property in which the legitimacy of a marriage was concerned, and as a result began to insist on better evidence of marriage being produced than the word of the parties to it or the testimony of a witness. They laid down that a marriage conducted by a priest was the standard of proof they required.[8] The lawyers had replaced, therefore, the Church's doctrine of consent alone by a doctrine of consent with ministerial intervention. Thus clandestine marriages, if performed before a priest, came into a middle position between those marriages *in facie ecclesiae*, celebrated according to the Church's full

---

Intended Act Concerning Marriages (London, 1692), pp. 14–15, which notes the pressures put upon clergy to marry couples clandestinely.

[7] H. Prideaux, 'The case of clandestine marriages stated' (1691), in the *Harleian Miscellany*, I (1743), 364 ff.

[8] Salmon, *A Critical Essay Concerning Marriage* (by a 'gentleman') (London, 1724), pp. 206 ff. This view is seen in such legislation as 7 & 8 William III c. 35.

requirements, and those marriages performed without any ministerial intervention. This 'middle' type of union lacked the full ecclesiastical privileges of the former, yet possessed the legal completeness determined by the common law lawyers, which was wanting in the latter, and while punishable in canon law for the manner of its celebration, was regarded by the common law lawyers as a complete union with the full legal rights of matrimony. This is the reason why these clandestine marriages were able to continue in the face of substantial ecclesiastical opposition, for the common law lawyers, having found for themselves a theory for distinguishing between those marriages which the common law was prepared to recognize and those which it declined to protect, discovered that by its implications they could not exclude from recognition the clandestine marriages performed at the Fleet and other such places.

The Fleet was not the first centre for clandestine marriages in London. The chaplains of the Tower of London had conducted a trade in irregular unions by 1546, if not before. They claimed as early as the reign of Edward VI that its status as a royal peculiar enabled them to marry couples without banns being called or licenses previously being obtained.[9] Archbishop Laud ended this practice. However, business switched to other centres, eventually centring upon two particular churches in the City of London, St. James', Duke's Place, and Holy Trinity, Minories. Each claimed to be a privileged place, not only exempt from ecclesiastical jurisdiction but also having the right to issue its own marriage licences. The boom in marriages at Holy Trinity appears to have begun in 1644, and Tomlinson has established that between that date and 1695 over 32,000 marriages took place there,[10] while at St. James', a parish of around 160 houses, in two periods 1664–8 and 1676–92 over 40,000 marriages were celebrated.[11] James II's commissioners for ecclesiastical causes endeavoured with little success to close these centres in 1686,[12] and a further commission of 1690–1 was revoked because of episcopal protests at the powers given to the commissioner and his abuse of them.[13] The demise of these two centres came eventually from an entirely different direction, namely the attempt by the Crown to increase the revenue 'in order to continue the war with France' by taxing marriages according to a specific rate, and by imposing a stamp duty on every licence or certificate of marriage issued. By these measures of 1694–6 the Crown was given a vested interest in regular unions. Clauses in the various acts relating to these measures contained provisions to prevent marriages taking place in any pretended 'exempt place' without banns being first published or licences

[9] E. M. Tomlinson, *A History of the Minories, London* (London, 1907), pp. 228 ff.
[10] Ibid., p. 239.
[11] W. P. R. Phillimore and G. E. Cokayne, *The Registers of St. James' Duke's Place* (London, 1900), I, v.
[12] Greenwich Newsletter, Public Record Office, Adm. 77 iii, items 32–7.
[13] State papers, P.R.O., SP 44/150, p. 75 and 44/274, p. 59: Rawlinson Manuscripts, Bodleian Library, Oxford, C 983, fo. 7.

being obtained. Severe penalties were imposed on the offending clergy: a fine of £100 upon conviction and for a second offence suspension of office for three years. A further act placed a penalty of £10 on the bridegroom.[14] Though a suspicion remained that clandestine marriages were still being performed at these churches until the early eighteenth century, these acts dealt a death blow to their position as major centres of clandestine marriage.

The Fleet Prison had been regarded from at least 1674 as a centre for clandestine marriages, but it was not until the legislation of 1694–6 that it achieved notoriety. Paradoxically this legislation drew attention to the advantages of the prison, and by partially eliminating other competition, gave it an almost total monopoly of this matrimonial trade, especially in the all-important metropolitan area. The prison itself, which stood on the Ludgate side of Farringdon Street, was regarded as a commercial enterprise by its wardens, several of whom maintained that the prison house was their own private property. There was also a parallel claim that the prison chapel was an exempt place, over which the bishop had no rights of jurisdiction or visitation. There was, furthermore, unrestricted access to the prison house. Indeed in 1742 it was estimated by an irate warden that sometimes up to 3,000 people a day visited the prison, many of whom entered it not merely to see those imprisoned there for debt, but to make use of its facilities, which included a coffee house, a tap room, rackets courts, and a public eating room known as 'Bartholomew Fair' situated in the basement alongside the public kitchen.[15]

It is clear that the prison authorities encouraged marriages there for reasons of profit. A committee of the House of Commons which investigated in 1705 the prison and its marriages alleged that some of the prison officers were given a share of the resulting fees.[16] The prison chaplain, one Elborrow, seems to have officiated at several of these marriages, though it was said of him that 'under a colour [he] doth allow his clerk to do what he pleases'; his clerk being Bartholomew Bassett, who leased the kitchen of the prison and the eating house named after him. Although it is often alleged that Elborrow was joined in this business by several clergymen who were themselves prisoners in the Fleet, it is more probable that clergy entered the prison on a voluntary basis, possibly through the use of 'friendly actions', in order to obtain some pretended immunity from legal and ecclesiastical proceedings. It is significant that Nehemiah Rogers, who was active as a Fleet parson from 1697, only entered the Fleet as a prisoner in the January of 1700–1, and was still able to proceed at large to his living at Ashington in Essex until deprived of it in 1706. Other Fleet clergy, such as John Draper and

---

[14] The legislation was as follows: 5 & 6 William and Mary c. 21; 6 & 7 William III c. 6; and 7 & 8 William III c. 35.

[15] Simon Wood, *Remarks on the Fleet Prison* (London, 1733), p. 17 and W. Paget, *The Humours of the Fleet* (London, 1749), pp. 13 ff.

[16] Journal of the House of Commons, XV, 188.

James Coulton, were admitted as debt prisoners long after they had commenced their activities as Fleet parsons.

The prison chapel was generally used on these occasions, and the officiating clergy appear to have paid the chaplain or his clerk a fee, generally a shilling, for its use. However at least one marriage is recorded as having taken place in one of the prison chambers, 'a darkish room [which] had two candle [*sic*] alight in it', and where there was 'a man in a morning gown and cap, another person in the habit of a minister of the Church of England . . . and the Defendant observed that the said minister was just beginning to solemnize a marriage . . .'.[17]

After allegations that the collectors of the queen's taxes were bribed not to enquire into this business, an ecclesiastical visitation of the Fleet took place in 1702. Its aim appears to have been more to regularize the position than to end the marriages there, for Thomas Bassett swore not to marry any persons without banns or a licence, unless they had been recommended by a justice in the case of a 'big belly'.[18] It had little effect, for three years later a committee of the House of Commons noted that evasion of the various duties and taxes at these marriages was defrauding the Crown to the extent of £1,000 a year. The committee noted many other abuses, but did nothing whatsoever to remedy the situation.[19] This had to wait for the House of Convocation, which, prompted by the queen's licence, discussed measures for the prevention of clandestine marriages in 1710. That House finally agreed that all those clergy who officiated at such marriages in prisons should be fined and committed to the *county* gaol for one year (which for Middlesex meant Newgate Prison), together with the couples who were so married, while the prison keepers who allowed such marriages to occur in their prison were to be fined.[20] Though these measures, save for the penalty on the couple so married, were implemented by parliamentary legislation (10 Anne c. 19) the Act remained a dead letter, partly because the clergy could be proceeded against only if they had been successfully prosecuted beforehand. This required a private prosecution, and few were willing to risk their money in this way.

Instead, the Act speeded up one important process which was noticeable long before its enactment. In the ecclesiastical visitation of 1702 Coulton was described as marrying couples 'in and around the Fleet gate and all the Rules over . . .' and by 1710 two particular houses in the rules, those run by Tuftin and King, can be identified as marriage houses, each possessing its own register book. After 10 Anne c. 19, which became operative in June 1712, the prison authorities took great care to ensure that no marriages took place within the prison house. Immediately before this act, however, John

---

[17] Guildhall Library, London, MS 9657, box 2, bundle 3.
[18] Rawlinson Manuscripts, B382, fos. 445 ff.
[19] Journal of the House of Commons, XV, 108, 169, 188.
[20] Tanner Manuscripts, Bodleian Library, Oxford, 282, fos. 159 ff.

Lilley, a turnkey of the prison, had established his own chapel at the Bull and Garter alehouse which lay alongside the prison, and Thomas Hodgkins, who appears to have succeeded to the position of clerk of the prison chapel, established himself in a similar way in a house in Fleet Lane. Having been driven into the rules, the clergy found that the area possessed facilities far greater than those which the prison afforded. It was not only a far larger and more prominent area, it was also free of the stigma of being within the walls of the prison itself. Moreover the problems of too many clergy using one prison chapel and being dominated by the apparent tyranny of its clerk were overcome, though these were eventually replaced by the problems of too many marriage houses and too few clergy to service them. There can be little doubt, however, that this legislation proved a great blessing to the Fleet parsons and inaugurated the era of their greatest prosperity.

As it developed the Fleet matrimonial trade required clergy, customers, 'middle men' to tout for them, and marriage-house keepers who supplied appropriate premises. The clergy, by and large, were the relics of that situation of the eighteenth-century Church in which there were too many clergy and too few adequate livings for them. Several had had small livings, from which two at least had been suspended for marrying couples clandestinely; others, such as Peter Symson, argued that they 'have had but little petty curacies twenty or thirty pounds per year'. Another parson, the notorious Gaynam, argued that he was 'old and infirm and not able to get any Preferment'.[21] Several others had supplemented a meagre income by schoolmastering; or had served as naval chaplains, a fact which James Lando frequently noted in his advertisements; or had been admitted, like Edward Marston, into 'the ministerial function in Carolina' or some other colony. Thus, although the popular press of the day frequently suggested otherwise, most of the Fleet clergy were lawfully ordained, although one, Jerome Alley, did disappear when told to produce his letters testimonial in the 1702 visitation, and a letter relating to another, Edward Ashwell, suggested 'he is in no orders tho' the Audacious Villain preaches where he can get a Pulpit'.[22] But these were noteworthy exceptions. Another allegation which was frequently made was that the clergy were prisoners at the Fleet. Though Daniel Wigmore, Michael Bassett and Edward Ashwell were all imprisoned there for short periods for contempt of court because of their participation in clandestine marriages involving minors, there is no evidence to suggest that any clerical prisoner, after the legislation of 10 Anne c. 19, was able to solemnize marriages during the period of his imprisonment in the Fleet. Indeed, at the various trials at which this assertion was made, it was indignantly denied by the Fleet parsons, while the prisoners themselves, in a petition for an extension of the limits of the rules, replied to one objection by stating:

[21] *The London Sessions Papers*, 1752, p. 140; 1735, p. 208.
[22] Lansdowne Manuscripts, British Library, 841, fo. 123.

not one of the parsons who marry uncanonically in or about the Rules of the Fleet Prison or of the pretended clerks who assist those parsons at such marriages or of the pliers for weddings that infest the streets as setters for these parsons and clerks are prisoners, but on the contrary these parsons, clerks and pliers live and marry at houses out of the Rules, as well as in several of the Rules not occupied by Prisoners, which Evil neither the Warden nor the Prisoners can prevent.[23]

It is difficult to give any precise figures as to the number of marriages solemnized at the Fleet for any given year, for the marriages are recorded in numerous registers and notebooks, belonging to individual parsons, marriage-house keepers and registrars, and many marriages are recorded in three or four different books. In all probability many of the registers have been lost, while there are gaps in many of the known register sequences caused by the disappearance of a particular book. It is possible, however, to form an estimate of the total number of marriages based on the surviving registers, making allowances for known gaps in their sequence, and this has been done for specific years. Table I provides such figures.

Table I: The number of marriages solemnized at the Fleet in specific years

Year	Total number of marriages recorded	Estimated number
1700	1,989	2,251
1710	2,912	3,679
1711	3,109	4,919
1712	2,683	2,799
1713	2,021	2,228
1720	3,547	4,021
1740	5,551	6,609

The numbers of marriages actually occurring probably exceeded even the estimated numbers given here. The 1702 visitation suggested that there were between 50 and 60 marriages each week, or 2,600 to 3,100 per annum.[24] The register of King's marriage house for 1709 records 1,162 marriages.[25] In 1730 Parson Gaynam married 1,349 couples,[26] and in 1740 Parson Wyatt solemnized over 1,500 marriages, while Parson Dare recorded 1,627 marriages in his notebooks for 1744.[27] Such figures suggest that the number of marriages was more substantial than the surviving records allow us to attest.

It may be that by the 1720s it had become the social habit of the working classes of London to resort to the Fleet for their marriages, particularly of

[23] City of London Record Office, MS 84.21, fos. 5 ff.
[24] Guildhall Library, London, MS 9657, box 2, bundle 3.
[25] Fleet register, P.R.O., R.G. 7/18, fos. 68 ff.
[26] Ibid., 604–10.
[27] Ibid., 507–17.

those who had little or no religious affiliation. The costs of a Fleet marriage were variable but the average total cost, about 7s 6d, was not dissimilar to the cost of a marriage at some of the City churches, though the expenses of a full-scale entertainment, the stamp duty on the marriage certificate, and the cost of calling the banns might all be spared. Two additional factors, however, may have contributed to the attractiveness of these Fleet marriages, the first being that they could be had, as one commentator declared, 'without loss of time, hindrance of business, and the knowledge of friends',[28] and the second was the fact, noted again and again in the debates on the Hardwicke Marriage Act, that the calling of banns was bitterly resented.[29]

It is clear from even a casual glance at the Fleet registers that the clientele for these marriages was drawn from all over London and beyond, although a reasonable doubt must remain as to whether the registers record the place of origin rather than the place of settlement in London. Table II records the places of settlement of those married at the Fleet.

Table II: The places of settlement of persons married in the Fleet expressed as a percentage of the whole

		Nos.						Percentages		
1700	1710	1720	1740	1750*		1700	1710	1720	1740	1750*
17	11	25	30	10	Savoy & St. Mary-Le-Strand	0.4	0.2	0.4	0.3	0.5
25	36	58	91	18	Covent Garden	0.7	0.7	0.9	0.8	0.8
73	87	108	179	38	St. Clement Danes	2.0	1.7	1.8	1.7	1.8
32	36	12	52	6	St. Dunstan-in-the-West	0.9	0.7	0.3	0.5	0.3
113	98	44	117	38	St. Bride's	3.1	2.0	0.7	1.1	1.8
10	9	4	8	4	St. Martin, Ludgate	0.2	0.1	0.06	0.07	0.2
140	119	128	198	57	St. Sepulchre	3.8	2.4	2.1	1.9	2.7
256	391	365	524	160	City	7.0	7.9	6.1	5.0	7.8
262	411	426	676	119	Stepney, including St. George in the East, Spitalfields and Bethnal Green	7.2	8.3	7.2	6.5	5.8
70	97	67	177	20	Wapping	1.9	1.9	1.1	1.7	0.9
74	100	109	141	13	Shadwell	2.0	2.0	1.8	1.3	0.6
99	151	193	313	71	Whitechapel	2.4	3.0	3.2	3.0	3.4
89	90	128	258	59	Shoreditch	2.4	1.8	2.1	2.5	2.8
122	125	102	177	57	Aldgate	3.3	2.5	1.7	1.7	2.7
78	50	74	93	26	Bishopsgate	2.1	1.0	1.2	0.9	1.2
221	172	271	470	103	Cripplegate, including St. Luke, Old Street	6.1	3.5	4.5	4.5	5.0
29	36	15	49	16	Aldersgate	0.8	0.7	0.2	0.4	0.8

[28] *A Letter to the Public . . . upon the Subject of the Late Act of Parliament for the Better Preventing of Clandestine Marriages* (London, 1753), p. 6.

[29] Cobbett's *Parliamentary History*, XV, pp. 19–20, 39, 60; cf. M. Misson, *Memoirs and Observations in his Travels over England* (London, 1719), p. 183.

Table II: continued

Nos.						Percentages				
1700	1710	1720	1740	1750*		1700	1710	1720	1740	1750*
96	97	72	138	36	Clerkenwell	2.6	1.9	1.2	1.3	1.7
					St. Andrew, Holborn, including St. George,					
200	238	244	407	84	Queen Square	5.5	4.8	4.1	3.9	4.1
					St. Giles-in-the-Fields, including St. George,					
265	299	418	651	109	Bloomsbury	7.3	6.0	7.0	6.3	5.3
47	61	97	162	34	St. Anne, Soho	1.3	1.2	1.6	1.6	1.6
					St. Martin-in-the-Fields, including St. George,					
184	244	334	592	119	Hanover Square	5.0	4.9	5.6	5.7	5.8
					St. Margaret, Westminster,					
108	151	275	295	57	including St. John	2.9	3.0	4.6	2.8	2.7
164	222	285	419	70	St. James, Piccadilly	4.5	4.5	4.8	4.0	3.4
42	111	91	64	16	Chelsea and Kensington	1.1	2.2	1.5	0.6	0.8
25	29	36	89	30	Islington and St. Pancras	0.7	0.6	0.6	0.8	1.4
17	15	18	38	8	Hampstead and Finchley	0.4	0.3	0.3	0.3	0.4
212	268	320	555	122	Southwark	5.0	5.3	5.2	5.2	5.8
22	69	42	114	20	Lambeth and Battersea	0.6	1.4	0.7	1.1	0.9
33	50	21	119	15	Bermondsey	0.9	1.0	0.3	1.1	0.7
9	40	22	130	20	Rotherhithe	0.2	0.8	0.3	1.2	0.9
111	236	401	592	72	Middlesex‡	3.0	4.7	6.7	5.7	3.5
120	200	210	542	77	Surrey‡	3.3	4.0	3.5	5.2	3.7
33	109	208	377	57	Kent‡	0.9	2.2	3.5	3.6	2.7
4	40	19	71	15	Greenwich	0.1	0.8	0.3	0.6	0.7
34	37	62	100	16	Deptford	0.9	0.7	1.0	0.9	0.8
44	163	243	522	72	Essex	1.2	3.3	4.1	5.0	3.5
9	25	27	87	19	Berkshire	0.2	0.5	0.4	0.8	0.9
8	25	15	87	15	Buckinghamshire	0.2	0.5	0.2	0.8	0.7
42	62	113	235	34	Hertfordshire	1.1	1.2	1.9	2.3	1.6
14	16	16	46	11	Sussex and Hampshire	0.4	0.3	0.2	0.4	0.5
66	100	182	301	88	elsewhere in England	1.7	1.9	2.9	2.8	3.9
					Wales, Scotland, Ireland					
4	7	15	23	12	and overseas	0.1	0.1	0.2	0.2	0.5
					total number of persons for whom a place of					
3,623	4,933	5,913	10,319	2,043	settlement is recorded†					
					total number of persons					
3,978	5,824	7,094	11,102	2,184	recorded					

*A sample only was taken for this year.
†The percentages on the right-hand side of the table have been worked from these totals.
‡This number excludes those parishes and areas already recorded in this table.

One notes in particular the substantial number who came from such populous parishes as Stepney, Whitechapel, Cripplegate, Aldgate and St. Giles-in-the-Fields, while the large number who travelled in from the counties of

Middlesex, Surrey, Essex, Kent and Hertfordshire indicates the drawing power of the Fleet as a matrimonial centre.

The Fleet marriages catered mainly for the artisan sections of society, as the better organized and more genteel establishment of Parson Keith of May-Fair attracted the professional and aristocratic ranks of society. Table III records the occupations of the bridegrooms married at the Fleet, when such information is recorded in the registers.

Table III: Occupation of the bridegrooms

	Nos.						Percentages			
1700	1710	1720	1740	1750*		1700	1710	1720	1740	1750*
7	39	39	61	10	professional & clerical	1.0	1.4	1.4	1.2	0.9
8	44	114	197	20	'gentlemen'	1.1	1.6	4.1	4.0	1.9
299	882	1,058	1,914	445	craftsmen	43.2	32.8	38.1	39.5	43.8
57	210	248	581	104	tradesmen & innkeepers	8.2	7.7	8.9	11.8	10.2
22	130	138	211	41	servants	3.1	4.8	4.9	4.3	4.0
26	109	182	280	75	coachmen & watermen	3.6	4.0	6.5	5.7	7.3
	10	13	17	7	fishermen		0.4	0.4	0.3	0.6
					agricultural workers, farmers, husbandmen					
66	250	196	566	75	& gardeners	9.5	9.3	7.0	11.6	7.4
4	76	36	10	1	pensioners	0.6	2.8	1.3	0.2	0.1
57	166	196	265	50	soldiers	8.2	6.1	7.0	5.4	4.9
113	684	385	371	88	sailors	16.3	25.4	13.8	7.6	8.6
32	68	145	341	93	labourers	4.6	2.5	5.2	7.0	9.1
					itinerants (drovers,					
4	9	17	40	2	pedlars, travellers)	0.6	0.3	0.6	0.8	0.2
	11	10	14	2	others		0.4	0.3	0.3	0.2
695	2,688	2,777	4,865	1,013	total number of entries recording occupation					
35.0	92.0	78.3	87.5	92.7	expressed as a percentage of the total number of marriages recorded					

*A sample only was taken for this year.

One significant feature indicated in Table III is the number of seafaring men married at the Fleet: 16.3 per cent in 1700 and 25.4 per cent in 1710. Such men may not have had time to wait for the legal formalities of banns, nor the ability to obtain a licence, and thus the speed and informality of a Fleet marriage would attract them, a situation which repeated itself for soldiers in Scotland during the First World War.[30] Thus Alexander Keith noted, 'from experience . . . that a young man, a mariner, comes ashore, receives his wages, is recommended by his friends and acquaintances to marry the daughter of a neighbour, comes acquainted with her one day, is married the next, and gets his wife with child, and is again on shipboard . . . before the week is out . . .'.[31]

[30] *The Scotsman*, 21 Jan. 1916.
[31] Alexander Keith, *Observations on the Act for Preventing Clandestine Marriages* (London, 1753), p. 21.

As for the marriage houses at which the marriages took place, their matrimonial trade was often supplementary to their real business as alehouses or taverns; their real concern and profit in this business lay in the provision of refreshments after the ceremony itself, and in the provision of a special room often designated as 'the chapel'. Some of these houses even possessed their own register book of marriages. The marriage business was widespread, however, and it was held in 1755 that every second or third house in the rules had been used for the purposes of the marriage trade, though many of these would have been used on a very casual basis. Another group of houses, though not within the rules, was concentrated along the direct routes into the Fleet, and for those unable or unwilling to journey to this area the parsons advertised their own willingness to travel to houses all over London in order to conduct matrimony. Their pocket books are full of addresses, and directions to them, while Lilley, one of the leading marriage-house keepers, let it be known in the public prints that his parsons were 'ready to wait on any person in town or country', and marriages are recorded in the registers as having taken place in such places as Greenwich, Plumstead, Guildford, and Up Park in Sussex.

Several of the marriage-house keepers either kept a parson as a regular member of their establishment, or made some agreement with one or several of the Fleet clergy to serve them as required. In 1723 the *British Gazetteer* stated that 'several of the brandy shop men and victuallers keep clergymen in their houses at twenty shillings per week each, hit or miss',[32] while John Lilley advertised that 'at the *Hand and Pen* next door to the china shop, Fleet Bridge, London, will be performed the solemnization of matrimony by a Gentleman regularly bred at one of our Universities and lawfully ordained according to the Institutions of the Church of England.'[33] James Starkey, declared Mrs. Hodgkins, another prominent keeper, 'was a minister that lodg'd with me nine years but was not a Prisoner'.[34] In fact Starkey appears to have received a third share in the marriage fees obtained at that house. Other clergy entered into an agreement to marry at a particular house whenever called upon to do so, though this did not prevent them marrying elsewhere, even at their own homes. Nor did it prevent the marriage-house keeper from employing other parsons. By the 1730s the number of marriage houses had increased while the number of available clergy had decreased, and so the clerics were able to make more satisfactory agreements for themselves. Thus Walter Wyatt, one of the more prominent parsons, was involved mainly at the houses of Wheeler and Harling in 1737, while in 1745 he was concerned with the houses of Mrs. Crook, Gillet and Lilley, besides marrying couples at many other houses. For such 'divinity jobs' he obtained an income of over £500 per annum.[35]

[32] Issue of 29 June 1723. [33] Fleet register 219, fo. 2.
[34] *Session Papers*, 1731, p. 21.
[35] From accounts given in his notebooks, Fleet registers 795–6.

The whole business was as highly competitive as it was highly organized. Advertisements were placed in newspapers in order to attract people to particular houses, although the majority of clients may have been drawn to particular houses through the agency of the pliers, men who touted for particular keepers for a small gratuity of 6d or so. Many such touts were watermen, coachmen or chairmen. Other pliers would gather around the Fleet Bridge, awaiting the arrival of customers by foot or by coach and greeting them with the then time-honoured cry, 'Do you want a parson? Will you be married?' The *Grub Street Journal* for 27 February 1735 describes how a coach was stopped near Fleet Bridge:

> One said, 'Madam, you want a parson?' 'Who are you?' says I. 'I am the Clerk and Register of the Fleet', at which comes a second, desiring me to go along with him. Says he, 'That fellow will carry you to a peddling alehouse'. Says a third, 'Go with me, he will carry you to a brandy shop'. In the interim comes the Doctor, 'Madam', says he, 'I'll do your job for you presently'.

There was some attempt on the part of all those concerned in the Fleet marriages to make their ceremonies appear as legal and as solemn as they possibly could. The royal arms were printed on some certificates. Lilley let it be known not only that he had been appointed 'Clerk of the Fleet' by the Lord Chancellor, and that his chapel was tolerated by the Bishop of London, but also that his certificates, termed 'my Lord Mayor's certificates', were approved by the Lord Mayor of London. Mottram, another of the parsons, had the city arms displayed on his certificates, and he, like the majority of the Fleet operators, described his place of marriage on the certificate with the name of one of the three parishes in which the rules were situated: St. Bride's Fleet Street, St. Martin Ludgate, or St. Sepulchre. The ceremony often took place in a specifically fitted room, frequently designated a 'chapel', of which the 'St. John Chapel' of Parson Lando forms one example. Yet the ceremony itself was conducted as quickly as possible, and while the service of the Book of Common Prayer was used, it seems clear that all save its essentials was omitted, even though the term 'according to the Rites and Ceremonies of the Church of England' frequently appeared on the marriage certificate. In order to circumvent the canonical requirement that marriages should be celebrated only between the hours of eight and twelve in the morning, one writer suggested that they left 'the clocks at their offices ... still standing at the canonical hour, though perhaps the time of the day be six or seven in the afternoon'.[36] Indeed many marriages were conducted late into the night or in the early hours of the morning, and on many occasions it is recorded that the parson was summoned out of bed in order to oblige a couple.

The cost of these marriages varied considerably, for it depended mainly on what the keeper or the parson considered the bridegroom could afford,

[36] J. P. Malcolm, *Anecdotes of the Manners and Customs of London during the Eighteenth Century* (London, 1810), I, 272.

and in addition charges were sometimes made for the clerk's fee and for the registering of the marriage.[37] Some, like Valentine Carlisle, made a 'bargain' with the marriage-house keeper before the marriage took place, and at least one couple went round the various houses to establish prices, but others tried various expedients, as one parson sadly noted in his register book, 'in order to prevail with me to give my fees away'. In the majority of cases the fees were first demanded, and perhaps even specified, during the actual ceremony, following the requirement of the rubric that the fee be laid on the book together with the marriage ring. It was at this point, therefore, that many started to argue, or caused a 'great uproar', or behaved like a certain 'gentleman' who 'would not pay but in a mean and scandalous manner, he offered five shillings and went down stairs and down the court, came back again and paid three shillings for all'. Some underestimated the amount required, and were either turned away for want of sufficient money, or were allowed to promise 'to come and make it better another time', a not infrequent note. Others pawned such items as the wedding ring or other valuables in order to make up the required sum. But many left the premises 'half married', as the registers delicately described their position, and often only their Christian names, required for the ceremony itself, were recorded. A few, at this point, assumed that they had been 'married enough' and so left. As many of these marriage houses were also public houses an entertainment could follow. Many sold 'bride cakes' at 6d each. Scenes of drinking, singing and dancing are depicted in one of the few prints relating to the Fleet marriages, *The Sailor's Fleet Wedding Entertainment,* and the guests in a popular broadside called *The Bunter's Wedding* are described as 'making the house ring'.[38] Matters could get out of hand. One group 'had the assurance to stay from about 7 to 11 at night making a noise till the watch came', and another group of 'vile people continued mobbing for three hours till 1 o'clock in the morning till the constable came to disperse [them]'.

It is hardly surprising, therefore, that many of the customers earned the condemnation of the more upright Fleet parsons: Dr. Ashwell adds in liberal measure such terms as 'rude', 'quarrelsome', 'wicked', 'scandalous', 'saucy', 'troublesome', 'very abusive' to the entries in his private notebooks. An indication of what may be behind such words of parsonical rebuke may be found in Burnford's account of the circumstances surrounding the marriage of one Alexander Bunt of Deptford in 1742. This Alexander arrived with his friends, but became

> very wicked and abusive and raised a mob . . . beate my daughter Kitty, swore violently that if the parson or I ever dare to come out they would have our hart's bloods, and a woman whoe was with them . . . swore many times yt she would

---

[37] Marriage fees at the Fleet varied enormously; in some cases the fee was as low as 2s 6d. The average fee for both Burnford and Lilley in 1740 was 7s 6d.

[38] *The Humours of the Fleet,* a scrapbook at the British Library (press mark 11633 h 2), pp. 85, 88b.

come and bring her giant who should brake every bone in our skins or if we dare come to Deptford wee should not be suffer'd to [come] alive away . . . they locked the door and would not lett Mr. Ashwell nor me out a great while, struck Mr. Ashwell, and Bunt struck me.[39]

The registers make it quite clear that this was not an isolated incident.

As no marriage would be supported in English law until proof of its existence had been established, it was politic for those concerned in the Fleet marriages to provide some means of registration. The prison chapel had always maintained its own register, and this practice was continued by all the leading marriage houses, several of whose keepers also entered into their registers the marriages performed at other houses by their own 'ministers'. In this way Burnford was able to describe himself as the 'clerk and register keeper of the marriages in the Fleet'. Not all customers were prepared to pay the additional charge demanded for registering the marriage, with the result that in many cases only their Christian names are recorded.

'Would you trust a Fleet parson with keeping a Register?' asked Lord Hillsborough in the debates on the 1753 Marriage Act, and he answered himself, 'no one can suppose you would'. This was true, for it was well known that not only were the register books unsystematically kept, but they were often kept in such a way that entries, including forged ones, could be fitted in at will, or alternatively be removed.[40] This could be done with impunity, for the registers possessed no legal status whatsoever. A witness at John Miller's trial for bigamy asserted, 'I went with her to prove her marriage at Mrs. Hodgkins, and Mrs Hodgkins said, for half a guinea, she'd enter her name in the register; for a certificate would not do if the marriage was not registered; her name was not in the Book, and I saw Starkey, the parson, interline her name in the Books five years backwards.'[41] At another trial, the same Ann Hodgkins, accused of a similar practice, justified her action by stating that Ann Inott 'begg'd, pray'd, and cry'd . . . I am sure you would have had some compassion for the poor creature'.[42] On the other hand good entries could be erased, although the evidence for this is slight, and it does appear that the practice was resisted by the clergy. When one Mrs. Wells, in matrimonial troubles with her husband, desired to be 'more esteemed his whore' than his wife, and requested the erasure of their marriage entry, Floyd recorded, 'I made her believe I did so for which I had half a guinea'.[43]

Antedating a marriage entry became such a well-known practice that few clients felt any inhibition about requesting its application in their favour. Thus Barry Richards obtained 'an antedate to March the 11th in the same

---

[39] Fleet register 451.
[40] *Session Papers*, 1736, p. 39.
[41] Ibid., 1736, p. 22.
[42] Ibid., 1736, p. 147.
[43] Fleet register 90, fo. 14.

year, which Lilley comply'd wth and put 'em in his book accordingly there being a vacency in the book suitable to the time'.[44] In the majority of cases the reason was either to legitimize an existing pregnancy or to regularize an already existing situation.

Certificates were also issued, often with the royal arms placed upon them, but however impressive they may have been they had no legal validity, for they were neither issued by a legal authority nor were they stamped with the required 5s stamp duty, although such 'stampt certificates' could be had if required. Similar abuses took place with these certificates as with the registers, but upon a much larger scale, for the certificates were easier to abuse than a register entry, and were often given on the most casual information. It thus became a standard part of the defence at any bigamy trial in which a Fleet marriage was implicated to insinuate that such certificates could be obtained without any marriage having taken place. Hence William Morris testified in 1737: 'here is a certificate I had from the Fleet last Tuesday: this is a certificate of my being marry'd to one I never saw in my life. They'll give certificates to anybody'.[45] With such entries in the registers as 'this was a certificate . . . granted without a marriage'[46] it is not surprising that such testimonies were forthcoming.

Such abuses caused a deep suspicion to remain about the validity of any Fleet marriage when evidence in its favour was produced to the courts, for, as Dr. Gally pointed out, the entries of such marriages were,

> as in the case of Miss Scrope, ready to be produc'd or conceal'd, as a marriage is to be prov'd or disprov'd, which management is at the command of the person that pays best . . . There never was a Tryal concerning a clandestine marriage, but that was attended with many oaths on both sides. In which case there must be perjury. There are persons prepar'd for this purpose at the Fleet. They can prove or disprove a marriage, as they are paid for it, by making erasements of marriages which have been solemniz'd, which erasements and entries cannot be deem'd forgeries in law, because their books are only private books.[47]

The records of the bigamy and other trials in which a Fleet marriage was implicated reveal many of the other irregularities and abuses practised at the Fleet. While some claimed, as noted above, that Fleet certificates were readily available, others like Robert Wilson alleged:

> When I was a little out of the way, a little in liquor . . . they got me to an Alehouse, but whether I was married or not I cannot tell, indeed she told me we were married, and we liv'd together afterwards.

He doubted whether the necessary words of the ceremony were said, and he claimed, as did many, that his first wife had deserted him and that he had no means of knowing whether she was alive or dead.[48] Others made use of

---

[44] Ibid., 382, fos. 21–22.
[45] *Session Papers*, 1737, p. 120.
[46] Fleet register 79, fo. 75.
[47] Henry Gally, *Some Considerations upon Clandestine Marriages* (London, 1750), pp. 19 ff.
[48] *Session Papers*, 1736, p. 139.

these marriages as a means of seducing into marriage a wealthy woman or an heir to an estate. Dr. Gally suggested that the Fleet had become a market for this kind of marriage, while l'Abbé Le Blanc commented on this state of affairs,

> a girl that deigns to be the wife of a man, who would blush to own her for his mistress, works him up to such a pitch by her dangerous caresses, that she makes him declare, before witnesses provided for that purpose, that he takes her to be his wedded wife. Nay, it frequently happens that he has no other intent in giving his consent, but to carry on a joke, but to her all joking in this subject becomes serious, the *I will* is taken literally, and she takes care to have a chaplain ready.[49]

Such an incident occurred, for example, when a youth by the name of Hill was persuaded to drink himself into a state of intoxication at an alehouse near the Fleet Prison, and was then drawn into a marriage with a woman 'in mean circumstances and of a bad character'.[50]

Sham marriages were also practised at the Fleet; these being marriages in name only which were used by one partner to obtain some favour from the other. The most common of these sham marriages were those in which a woman in debt professed a willingness to marry any man in order to obtain her financial freedom, for the husband then possessed a legal liability for the debts contracted by his wife before their marriage. Another traveller to England, César de Saussure, noted that 'it is well known to be a common practice at the *Fleet,* and that there are men provided *there* who have each of them, within the compass of a year, married several women for this wicked purpose'.[51] One of these men was Josiah Welch. He is recorded in the registers as one who 'marries in common', and it is known that within the space of 14 months, under three different names, he married three different women, all presumably for this purpose.[52]

A further abuse, but one far more serious for family life, was that in which a supposed partner came forward with the alleged proof of a matrimonial alliance, often in order to gain by it some financial reward. This may best be illustrated from the life of the father of Francis Place. A woman claimed him by virtue of an alleged precontract made at the Fleet 40 years earlier. His son wrote that though he was advised to make a small weekly allowance for the woman, he refused, and so 'saved 4.6d a week at the expense of a thousand pounds' spent on his defence.[53] In the case of *Phillips v. Delafield* two wives came forward to claim the estate of a deceased man, both on the grounds of a precontract with him many years earlier, while in another instance one Hannah Green, calling herself Luff, attempted to claim

[49] L'Abbé Le Blanc, *Letters on the English and the French Nations* (London, 1747), p. 62.
[50] J. T. Atkyns, *Reports of Cases in Chancery* (London, 1794), pp. 515 ff.
[51] César de Saussure, *A Foreign View of England in the Reigns of George I and George II* (London, 1902), p. 343.
[52] Fleet register 90, fos. 3, 8.
[53] The autobiography of Francis Place, British Library Additional Manuscript, 35,142, fos. 157 ff.

the estate of James Luff, a deceased brewer, basing her claim upon the evidence of a Fleet parson and of an entry in a Fleet register.[54]

Secret marriage was a great curse in eighteenth-century society, for such marriage was almost impossible to prove and establish at law, and it was easy also for one of the partners to repudiate it. Many such 'secret' marriages are recorded in the Fleet registers. In some cases this was because the couple concerned declined to provide particulars, in others it was because payment was made for the entry to be placed in a 'private' book. Several offered their reasons: 'the lady having a jointure during the time she continued widow'; or because the bridegroom was still under articles of apprenticeship which forbade any matrimonial assignment during that period; others because one or both of the partners were under age, and possibly wished to marry in defiance of parental wishes, in an age when the right of parents to decide the future partners of their children was, though slowly challenged, still widely upheld.[55]

These abuses, accepted and tolerated by the Fleet operators, threatened the whole fabric and security of family life, for however irregular the marriages may have been, the ecclesiastical courts regarded them as valid unions. Despite this, marriages lightly entered into could be just as irresponsibly left, leaving a young family to depend precariously upon parochial charity. Marriages once regarded as a joke, or as a drunken delusion, became serious when they affected a later marriage by reason of precontract, or became the basis of proceedings for bigamy. The facilities by which sham marriages or certificates could be obtained endangered unions regarded as legal and valid in every sense, and which had been established over a long period of time. Such fears, added to parental concern for the wellbeing of their children, and clerical concern at their deprivation of the fees arising from matrimony—not for nothing was the leading clerical agitator against the Fleet marriages, Dr. Gally, vicar of one of the parishes most directly affected by these marriages—together with a real concern on the part of some for the dignity and honour of the 'holy estate of matrimony', led to such a climate of opinion against the existence of this matrimonial business that many looked to parliamentary and legal circles for a lead which would end this kind of clandestine marriage once and for all.

Yet such a lead was not readily forthcoming. The ecclesiastical authorities found themselves in a delicate position, for however irregular the marriages may have been, canon law was bound to recognize their validity. It was true that the offending clergy could be deprived of their benefices, or suspended from their ministerial functions, and there was always the final threat of excommunication, but proof was difficult to obtain, and even if the clerical offenders publicly admitted their guilt at various court cases, it appeared

[54] Guildhall Library MS 9184.
[55] Lawrence Stone, *The Family, Sex and Marriage in England* (London, 1977), pp. 185–6; cf. p. 275.

that the church authorities were reluctant to act. Indeed, many believed that the Church seemed more concerned with the abstract and theoretical side of marriage than with the practical and moral results arising from the practice of clandestine marriage. The case of *Hill v. Turner,* heard in 1737, provides a good illustration of this attitude. A youth had been abducted into a marriage at the Fleet, and was sent by his mother to Holland, but the abductor, now his wife, instituted a suit in the ecclesiastical courts for the restitution of her conjugal rights and for alimony, and, in spite of the injustice of her claim, she was successful.[56] It seemed also that Parliament was more concerned about the financial implications of these clandestine marriages than about the remedying of abuses caused by them, for clandestine marriages meant revenues lost through the evasion of the various stamp duties imposed on marriage licences and certificates. To remedy this the State endeavoured, unsuccessfully, to bring in legislation to end these marriages in 1718 and 1735,[57] but public opinion was not ready at that time to support the idea of voiding clandestine marriages as these bills proposed.

In the absence of any real legislative or ecclesiastical interference the attempt to regulate these marriages was left to the common law courts, although because of the 'rule of thumb' accepted by the lawyers, by which such marriages were accepted as valid because of the presence at them of a duly ordained priest, the courts' function was rather a negative one, namely to punish those who had committed malpractices against the legal form of marriage, and to make appropriate judicial noises of distaste. However, it is clear that by the 1730s the courts were deeply concerned about this matter, and refused to recognize such marriages unless the clearest possible evidence was presented in their favour. Thus, in the case of *Green v. Luff* of 1732 the court refused to intervene in an alleged case of precontract stating that 'it did not think it proper to give any credit to the proofs of the marriage', and adding that 'such marriages ought never to be supported by law, but upon the most clear and common proofs'.[58] Following this judgment many other courts declined to accept the Fleet registers as offering any weight of evidence,[59] while a tradition lingered at Westminster Hall that Lord Chancellor Hardwicke had torn up on one occasion a Fleet register presented to him as evidence.[60] Furthermore in the case of *Hill v. Turner* of 1737 Hardwicke had adopted the principle, 'it is incumbent on this court to prevent as far as they can persons from profiting themselves by such infamous methods',[61] and so allowed an injunction which declared that the procedure

---

[56] P. C. Yorke, *Life and Correspondence of Philip Yorke, Earl of Hardwicke* (Cambridge, 1913), II, 469, 475-76.
[57] Journal of the House of Commons, XIX, 88, XXII, 583.
[58] *The Political State of Great Britain,* XLIV (1732), 114.
[59] *Session Papers,* 1735, pp. 164 ff.; 1736, p. 40; 1739, pp. 63, 187.
[60] Thomas Peake, *Nisi Prius Cases* (London, 1795), p. 137.
[61] Atkyns, *Reports,* I, 515–16.

of the ecclesiastical court, already noted, was contrary to equity and con-science, and thus the seducer was prevented from proceeding further in her suit. In other cases the property of minors who had been abducted and married at the Fleet was protected by the courts and tied up in such a way that the parties to the marriage were unable to benefit from it. Furthermore those Fleet clergy who came before the courts charged with such offences were treated in an equally rigorous manner.

The judicial comments made by Hardwicke at these and other cases obviously articulated public opinion: in the course of *Harvey v. Ashton* (1737) he called clandestine marriage 'one of the growing evils, introductive of much calamity and ruin to many families and complained of by consider-able men as highly wanting a remedy',[62] and in *Middleton v. Croft* (1736) he stated, 'therefore we have thought it our duty not to weaken any power whereby it may be reformed and seasonably punished'.[63] Dr. Gally warned his readers that clandestine marriage was 'a disgrace to any civilised nation',[64] and others complained in the public papers about the scandals that resulted, the dissolute life of the parsons, and that through the continued existence of these marriages the dignity of marriage itself was being perverted. By this time, it was clear, public opinion was ready for a change in the law in order to end once and for all the scandals and misfortunes these marriages created; while in the same way Hardwicke, having presided over many of the trials in which the casualties of these marriages presented themselves for legal redress, was ready to provide that change when an opportunity presented itself. In fact as early as 1741 he remarked, 'these are mischiefs that want the correction and reformation of the legislature as much as any case whatsoever, and I believe it will very shortly come under the consideration of Parliament'.[65]

Paradoxically that opportunity came with a case under Scottish law, sent on appeal to the House of Lords in 1752–3. In 1753 the House of Lords directed the judges to prepare a bill for the better preventing of clandestine marriages, but on its failure to give satisfaction Hardwicke seized the initiative and brought in his own measure. Its aim may be described as a measure to regulate the conduct of matrimony, to establish definite proof of a union and to declare which marriages the state would support as such. To achieve this objective Hardwicke made a marriage *in facie ecclesiae* the only form of marriage which the state would support and recognize, and so he enlarged upon and enforced the provisions made by canon law for regulating marriage and for its registration. Any marriage performed contrary to even one specification laid down by the Act was to be held as null and void. Those clergy who offended against the Act were to be sentenced to a term of 14

---

[62] Yorke, *Hardwicke*, II, 447.

[63] Ibid., I, 124.

[64] Henry Gally, *Some Considerations upon Clandestine Marriages* (London, 1750), pp. 28–9.

[65] Atkyns, *Reports*, II, 156.

years' transportation, and if they offended against the provisions made for registration, the sentence was to be one of death.[66] In the formulation of the Act Hardwicke accepted the then current legal notion that society had as much right as the Church to insist upon its consent being given to any particular union, and also came close to accepting the equally contemporary belief that allowed matrimony to be regarded as a form of contract, a formula directly linked to the later introduction of divorce legislation.

As the bill wound its way through Parliament it aroused enormous opposition. Many were concerned to point out that marriage was much more than a question of contract, others were deeply concerned by the theological issues involved in voiding a marriage, and some felt that the exclusion of the royal family and Scotland from its scope meant that the bill was limited in its application, though few noted in the debates that the long-standing question about the legality of nonconformist marriages had been terminated in favour of the establishment. 'The friends of Bloomsbury Square', led by Henry Fox, whose own clandestine marriage was alleged to have been the reason for his opposition, used the bill to launch a serious attack upon Henry Pelham's administration, suggesting that it was an aristocratic plot designed to overthrow lawful government and create a powerful oligarchical upper class through the family control of marriage. They claimed that the existence of clandestine marriage alone lay between the country and this threat. They argued also that the lower classes needed quick and convenient forms of marriage, or else they would not marry at all. Indeed, they suggested that the real title of the bill should be amended to read 'an act to prevent marriage' and so to encourage immorality. Their attack meant that the bill had to be pushed through by the government, whereas, with more reflection, some of its more obvious blemishes might have been remedied.[67]

The Act came into force on Lady Day 1754. The unique phenomenon of the Fleet was ended, and the only clandestine marriages now available, for those who could afford to travel there, were to be found in Scotland. Yet it must be remembered that for many generations of Londoners the services provided by the Fleet matrimonial trade formed one of the principal structures of the life of the community and the private life of the individual.

---

[66] The death penalty was introduced through an amendment and was not part of Hardwicke's original bill.

[67] Cobbett's *Parliamentary Debates*, XV, 12–13, 22, 69–70, 72, 82.

VII

Marriage, Fertility and Population Growth in Eighteenth-Century England

E. A. WRIGLEY

During the later seventeenth century the population of England was at a standstill. Barely a century later it was growing faster than at any other period of English history for which an estimate of the growth rate can be made. In the 1650s the long period of growth which had lasted throughout the Tudor and early Stuart period came to an end. In 1656 the national population stood at 5.281 millions. Thereafter it fell back substantially until in 1686 it was no more than 4.865 millions, and although there was some recovery in the next 30 years, there was a further fall in the wake of the epidemics of the late 1720s, so that in 1731 the population total, at 5.263 millions, was little different from that in the mid-seventeenth century.[1] Years in which deaths exceeded births, which had been fairly common in the later seventeenth century,[2] were not yet quite over. Population declined for this reason in 1741 and 1742, but in the main the growth which began in the 1730s accelerated steadily from that decade until it reached its peak rate in the decade 1811–21.[3]

In the 90-year period 1731–1821 the population of England increased by 118 per cent from 5.263 to 11.492 millions. In the first 30 years of the nineteenth century when English growth rates were at their highest the English population was growing more rapidly than that of any other European country for which tolerably reliable statistics are available.[4] From being a country with a population well below that of the major European countries, England was rapidly approaching a near equality with other large

---

[1] The totals quoted were obtained by back projection. The method itself and the derivation of the totals of births and deaths which constitute the prime data needed to carry out back projection are described in E. A. Wrigley and R. S. Schofield, *The Population History of England 1541–1871. A Reconstruction* (London, 1981). The quinquennial population totals between 1541 and 1871, including those quoted here, may be found in table 7.8.

[2] There were 17 years in which deaths exceeded births in the period 1650–99. Since this was also a period of substantial net emigration population declined in an even larger number of years. On certain assumptions about the even flow of emigration within each quinquennium in the half-century, there was a fall of population in a total of 31 years. See Wrigley and Schofield, *Population History of England,* table A2.3 and A3.3.

[3] For details see table I below, p. 139.

[4] The following statistics to illustrate the point are derived from population totals given in B. R. Mitchell, *European Historical Statistics* (London, 1975), pp. 19–23, apart from the English data which are taken from Table I.

countries apart from Russia.[5] The change was momentous, yet until its later stages it was not greatly remarked by contemporaries. Indeed its existence was not beyond challenge. In the debate between Price, Arthur Young, Wales, Howlett and others in the 1770s and 1780s the balance of argument lay with those who were convinced that the population was growing but Price was able to continue to find reasons to suppose that there was a decline.[6] Not until after the first census had been held was it clear beyond reasonable doubt that numbers were rising rapidly. Even then Cobbett still found himself able to write in 1822, 'I am quite convinced, that the population upon the whole, *has not increased, in England, one single soul since I was born*' (Cobbett's italics: he was then 56 years old).[7]

The first census of 1801 was intended not simply to discover the size of the population then living but also to chart its progress in the previous century. Each Anglican minister was asked to make a return of baptism, burial and marriage totals in his parish for certain years from 1700 onwards. With these data before him John Rickman, who was in charge of the census, was able to make estimates of population totals at ten-year intervals during the eighteenth century. He concluded that growth was slight in the first half of the century but thereafter accelerated.[8] Subsequently many others have

	Compound annual rate of growth	Indexed to the English growth rate
England	1.434 (1801–31)	100
Germany	1.301 (1816–34)	91
Finland	0.963 (1800–30)*	67
Norway	0.894 (1801–35)	62
Denmark	0.857 (1801–34)	60
Sweden	0.694 (1800–30)	48
Italy	0.631 (1800–33)	44
France	0.584 (1801–31)	41
Portugal	0.128 (1801–35)	9

* Three additions to the area included in Finland were made in this period and a rough allowance was made for this in calculating the growth rate.

[5] For example, the populations of Italy and France in 1700 were 13 and 20 millions at a time when England's population was 5.1 millions. By 1851 the respective totals of the three countries were 24.3, 35.7 and 16.7 millions. In 1700, therefore, the population of Italy was 2.55 times that of England, while the ratio for France was 3.92. By 1851 the comparable ratios were 1.45 and 2.14 (and the ratios to Britain as a whole—England, Wales and Scotland—were 1.17 and 1.72). Or, to express the contrast differently, during the period of 150 years in which the Italian and French populations grew by 87 and 79 per cent, the English population grew by 227 per cent. M. R. Reinhard, A. Armengaud and J. Dupâquier, *Histoire générale de la population mondiale*, 3rd edn. (Paris, 1968), pp. 221, 241, 340, 384. The English totals are taken from table I.

[6] See D. V. Glass, *Numbering the People* (Farnborough, 1973), especially ch. 2.

[7] W. Cobbett, *Rural Rides* (Penguin Books, Harmondsworth, 1967), p. 67.

[8] In the 1801 census he published estimates based on the ratio of the baptism totals in any given year to the baptism total in 1801 and concluded that the totals in 1700, 1750 and 1801 for England and Wales were 5.475, 6.467 and 9.168 millions respectively. In the next two censuses he repeated the decennial totals given in the 1801 census, but in 1831 replaced these with estimates made by Finlaison. In Finlaison's series the corresponding totals were 5.135, 6.040 and 9.187 millions (the last total being for 1800 rather than 1801). Finally, after Rickman's death, further estimates based on his second inquiry of 1836 were published in the 1841 census, this time using baptism,

studied the same issue using the data originally collected by Rickman (for example, Finlaison, Farr, Brownlee, Griffith, Ohlin)[9] and all came to conclusions about the scale and phasing of the growth which occurred that were sufficiently similar to Rickman's original estimates to leave the broad outline unaltered. Recently, exploiting the fact that annual totals of births and deaths have for the first time become available from the mid-sixteenth century onwards, and using a new technique for their analysis, new estimates of population totals throughout the period have been made. Decadal totals and growth rates for the period 1651 to 1851 obtained in this way are set out in Table I. In some important details they modify the picture of change which can be obtained from Rickman's data,[10] but the gross pattern is

Table I: English population totals and growth rates 1651–1851

	(1)	(2)	(3)
1651	5.228		
1661	5.141	−1.66	−0.17
1671	4.983	−3.07	−0.31
1681	4.930	−1.06	−0.11
1691	4.931	0.02	0.00
1701	5.058	2.58	0.26
1711	5.230	3.40	0.34
1721	5.350	2.29	0.23
1731	5.263	−1.63	−0.16
1741	5.576	5.95	0.58
1751	5.772	3.52	0.35
1761	6.147	6.50	0.63
1771	6.448	4.90	0.48
1781	7.042	9.21	0.89
1791	7.740	9.91	0.95
1801	8.664	11.94	1.13
1811	9.886	14.10	1.33
1821	11.492	16.25	1.52
1831	13.284	15.59	1.46
1841	14.970	12.69	1.20
1851	16.736	11.80	1.12

(1) Population total (millions)
(2) Percentage growth over preceding decade
(3) Compound percentage rate of annual population growth over preceding decade

Source Wrigley and Schofield, *Population history of England,* table 7.8.

Note The totals shown are those derived by back projection and differ slightly from the census totals of 1801, 1811, etc. All totals refer to England (less Monmouth).

burial and marriage ratios between a given date and 1801 rather than baptism ratios alone. This exercise yielded estimates of 6.045, 6.517 and 8.873 millions respectively. *1801 Census,* Observations on the results of the Population Act, 41 Geo. III, *Parl. Papers* 1802, VII, p. 9. *1831 Census,* Enumeration abstract, Preface, *Parl. Papers* 1833, XXXVI, p. xlv. *1841 Census,* Enumeration abstract, Preface, *Parl. Papers* 1843, XXII, p. 37.

[9] These estimates are discussed in Wrigley and Schofield, *Population History of England,* appendix 5.

[10] For example, the very substantial increase of population in the 1730s is missed by all those using Rickman's data, though Rickman himself in his 1801 estimate is a partial exception to the rule.

139

unaltered, as may be seen in Figure I. Since Rickman's day, in short, there has been near unanimity that from a standing start about 1700 population growth in the course of a century accelerated to the point where it was growing at about 1.5 per cent annually, at which rate population would double in under 50 years.

*   *   *

But if there has been agreement about the extent of the change, there has been no matching consensus about the causes of the change, either in the proximate sense of the changes in fertility and mortality which conspired to produce it, or in the more general sense of the social, economic or other circumstances which may have prompted it. In this chapter I shall concentrate primarily on the former category of cause, and will seek to show that the dominant reason for the dramatic acceleration in growth rates lay in changes in marriage behaviour, broadly understood. I shall also attempt to show how distinctive a social institution English marriage was in the eighteenth century by comparing it to marriage in France in the same period.

We may begin by noting that the *explicandum*, the transition from a zero growth rate to an annual growth rate of 1.5 per cent, is not a small but a very large change, and implies radical alterations in the demography of the country. For example, if the entire change had been caused by improvements in mortality alone it would have required an increase in expectation of life at birth for the sexes combined from about 25 to about 42 years assuming that the gross reproduction rate (GRR) had been constant at 2.5. On the other hand, if expectation of life had remained unaltered throughout at, say, 40 years, its approximate level in the mid-nineteenth century when the first national life tables were constructed, the GRR would have had to rise from about 1.7 to about 2.6.[11] Since the requisite change is so great if either one of the two major variables determining growth rates is fixed, it is natural to suppose *a priori* that both must have changed in a complementary manner. A majority of those who have interested themselves in the issue, aware of the intrinsic likelihood that mortality must have fallen and fertility risen conjointly, have opted for an explanation which combined these two changes, though with differing emphases on their relative importance. Only occa-

---

[11] These estimates of expectations of life at birth and gross reproduction rates are those obtained using the model North variant of the Princeton regional model life tables and on the assumption that the mean age at maternity was 31 years. A. J. Coale and P. Demeny, *Regional Model Life Tables and Stable Populations* (Princeton, 1966).

Fig. I: Population growth in eighteenth-century England
Source Wrigley and Schofield, *Population History of England*, table A5.3.
Note The upper and lower bound estimates have been adjusted to refer in all cases to England (less Monmouth). In some instances they refer to 1700 rather than 1701, etc. For details see table referred to in source note.

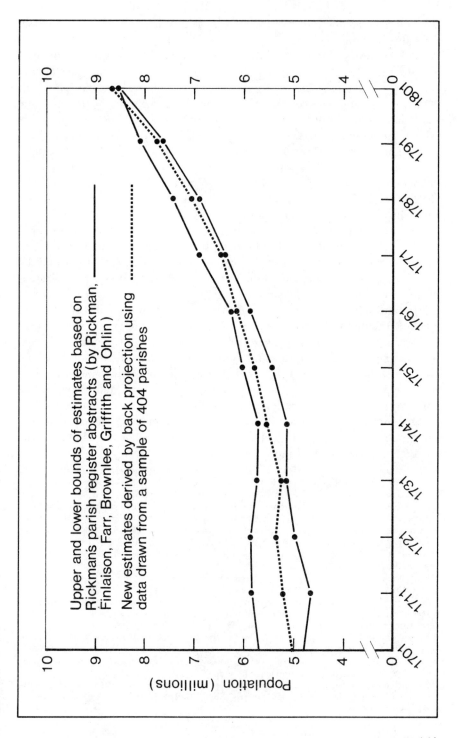

Upper and lower bounds of estimates based on Rickman's parish register abstracts (by Rickman, Finlaison, Farr, Brownlee, Griffith and Ohlin)

New estimates derived by back projection using data drawn from a sample of 404 parishes

Population (millions)

sionally have bolder spirits opted for a mortality fall so great as to exclude a fertility rise, or *vice versa*.[12]

With continuous national birth and death series it is possible for the first time to pin down the changes in fertility and mortality taking place during the period with some precision, and to assess their relative importance in changing population growth rates, as may be seen in Figure II. The individual estimates of expectation of life and gross reproduction rates upon which the figure is based were derived using a technique called back projection which has been fully described elsewhere.[13] They are set out in the form shown in the figure in order to make it easy to see how far the changes in fertility and mortality influenced the intrinsic growth rate between the late seventeenth century when it was nil and its high point in 1821 when it reached 1.76 per cent per annum.[14]

The diagonals in the figure represent different levels of the intrinsic growth rate. Each diagonal shows all the combinations of fertility and mortality which will yield the same intrinsic growth rate. Thus it may be seen from the diagonal representing a zero rate of growth that an expectation of life at birth of 30 years combined with a gross reproduction rate of about 2.3 implies a zero growth rate, and that an expectation of life of 35 years combined with a GRR of about 1.95 produces the same result. The vertical element in the movement between any two points in the figure represents a change in fertility; the horizontal movement a change in mortality; and the figure is so constructed that the relative proportion of vertical and horizontal movement between two points represents the relative importance of the contributions made by fertility and mortality change to the change in the intrinsic growth rate. Predominantly vertical movements therefore imply the greater importance of fertility change; predominantly horizontal movements the greater importance of mortality change.[15]

[12] The leading proponent of the view that falling mortality was the predominant, almost exclusive cause of the increased growth rate in the eighteenth century is McKeown. His arguments are summarized in the second chapter of his recent book: T. McKeown, *The Modern Rise of Population*. No one has taken so strong a line in favour of rising fertility, but after Habakkuk had reopened the issue in the early 1950s, Krause provided evidence tending to show that fertility change was of substantial importance in raising growth rates: H. J. Habakkuk, 'English population in the eighteenth century', *Economic History Review*, 2nd series, VI (1953), 117–33, and J. T. Krause, 'Changes in English fertility and mortality, 1781–1850', *Economic History Review*, 2nd series, XI (1958), 52–70.

[13] See Wrigley and Schofield, *Population History of England,* appendix 15; there is a brief, generalized description of the technique in ch. 7, especially pp. 195–9.

[14] The intrinsic growth rate is the growth rate implied by the prevailing fertility and mortality schedules of a population and will eventually establish itself if these schedules continue to characterize it for a sufficient period. But the intrinsic growth rate need not be equal to the current growth rate at a given point in time because the current age structure of the population may differ from the stable age structure implied by its current fertility and mortality. For a fuller, mathematical treatment of this point, see A. J. Coale, *The Growth and Structure of Human Populations* (Princeton, 1972), especially chs. 2 and 3.

[15] The method of construction used in figure II is fully described in Wrigley and Schofield, *Population History of England* pp. 235–40. The approximations involved in using such a method are also discussed in the same passage.

It is clear from Figure II that the acceleration in growth rates in the eighteenth century owed far more to fertility increase than to mortality fall. The GRR at the time of population stagnation in the late seventeenth century was about 2.0, and expectation of life at birth was about 35 years. By the second and third decades of the nineteenth century the comparable figures were about 2.9 and 40 years, and the intrinsic growth rate had reached 1.7 per cent per annum (it should be noted that all these data refer to the female population only: expectations of life for the sexes combined would be slightly lower[16]). The rise in the GRR accounted for the great bulk of the total change (i.e. the ratio of the vertical displacement to the horizontal displacement between clusters of points representing the late seventeenth and the early nineteenth centuries was roughly 3:1). It follows, therefore, that a satisfactory explanation of the remarkable rise in growth rates in the eighteenth century will turn largely upon attaining a fuller understanding of the fertility changes of the period.

An increase in general fertility could have occurred either because marital fertility had risen; or because of an increase in extra-marital fertility; or because of an increase in the proportion of women of child-bearing age who were married; or, of course, from any combination of these three reasons. It is worth noting, incidentally, that although all three causes of an increase in general fertility are logical possibilities at all times it is nevertheless true that England, and early modern western Europe more generally, were very unusual in that the third factor could be so influential in changing fertility. In most, if not all, traditional societies other than western Europe women married very young and very few remained single.[17] To be a sexually adult woman normally meant to be married or widowed. For the same reason, the second possible cause of higher fertility (an increase in extra-marital fertility rates) was also unlikely to be of much importance. Only a shortening of birth intervals among married women would be likely to induce a significant increase in general fertility.[18]

In view of the unusually large potential importance of factors other than marital fertility in the English case, it is particularly interesting to note that the available evidence suggests that fertility within marriage did not change significantly over the period of accelerating population growth rates. In Table II the averages of the age-specific marital fertility rates found in 12 English parishes are set out. They are well scattered geographically and

---

[16] The reason for concentrating on the female population only when displaying data graphically as in figure II is explained in Wrigley and Schofield, *Population History of England,* p. 235–8.

[17] Both the quantitative evidence of this pattern and its implications were discussed in Hajnal's classic article on the subject. H. J. Hajnal, 'European marriage patterns in perspective', in D. V. Glass and D. E. C. Eversley, *Population in History* (London, 1965), pp. 101–43.

[18] In principle an increase in the length of the child-bearing period reflected in an increase in the mean age of women at the birth of the last child might also result in a rise in general fertility. In practice this appears to have varied very little among pre-industrial populations in western Europe. Reconstitution studies of French, German and English communities consistently suggest that a mean age very close to 40 years was widespread.

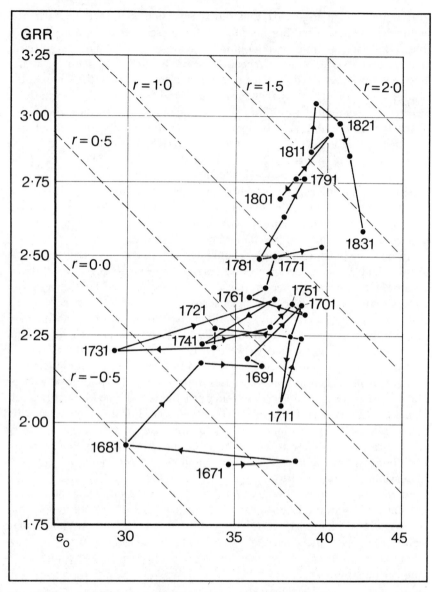

Fig. II: The combined effect of fertility and mortality changes in determining intrinsic growth rates 1671–1831 (quinquennial data)

Source Wrigley and Schofield, *Population History of England,* fig. 7.11.

Notes The years indicated are the central years of the 5-year periods centring on the dates shown.

GRR gross reproduction rate

e_0 expectation of life at birth

r intrinsic growth rate (per cent per annum)

comprise places with widely different socio-economic characteristics, including an archetypal proto-industrial village (Shepshed), a market centre with a wide range of craft and service employments (Banbury), a very remote and purely agricultural parish (Hartland), places whose economies were early influenced by proximity to London (Aldenham, Terling), and so on.

Table II: Age-specific marital fertility rates (live births per 1,000 women-years lived): means of 12 reconstitution studies

	20–4	25–9	30–4	35–9	40–4	45–9
1650–99	376	347	295	241	125	53*
1700–49	382	352	287	224	108	21
1750–99	411	338	283	234	118	17

*This high figure is the result of a freakishly high rate in a very small parish: the mean of the other 11 parishes is 34.

Source Cambridge Group reconstitutions.

Notes The 12 parishes to which the data relate are: Alcester (Warwicks.), Aldenham (Herts.), Banbury (Oxon.), Colyton (Devon), Gainsborough (Lincs.), Gedling (Notts.), Hartland (Devon), Methley (Yorks., W.R.), Shepshed (Leics.), Southill and Campton with Shefford (Beds.), Terling (Essex), Willingham (Cambs.). I am deeply indebted to the following scholars who each carried out one or more of the reconstitutions: Mr. J. D. Asteraki, Mrs. L. Clarke, Mrs. P. Ford, Prof. D. Levine, Mr. W. Newman Brown, Miss G. Reynolds, Mrs. S. Stewart, Prof. M. Yasumoto and Mrs. J. D. Young.

In several cases the reconstitutions did not extend sufficiently far into the nineteenth century to enable reliable rates to be calculated for 1800–49 and therefore no comparable rates could be set out for the half-century after 1750–99.

The stability of the average rates shown in Table II does not occur because of a cancelling out of opposing fertility trends in the several parishes. Rates in individual parishes were less stable than in the group of parishes when averaged, of course, but there is little sign in the individual rates of major changes being muffled by averaging. It would be premature, in view of the small sample of parishes involved, to exclude the possibility that national marital fertility rates rose somewhat. Nevertheless, present evidence is strongly against the possibility that changes in marital fertility can take us very far towards an explanation of the huge rise in fertility over all.

This leaves changes in illegitimate fertility and in nuptiality to be considered. Of the two the former is clearly incapable of accounting for more than a fraction of the total rise in fertility since illegitimate births were never more than about a fifteenth of all births in England during the period in question.[19] The bulk of the increase in fertility must therefore be attributable

[19] Laslett presents a number of estimates of the absolute level of the illegitimacy ratio in England in the parish register period in P. Laslett, *Family Life and Illicit Love in Earlier Generations* (Cambridge, 1977), ch. 3, especially fig. 3.2.

The demographic logic underlying a figure of this type depends on the link between the proportion of women surviving to the mean age at maternity and expectation of life at birth. This issue is discussed in Wrigley and Schofield, *Population History of England*, pp. 236–40.

145

to changes in age at marriage and in the proportions never marrying, which between them determine what proportion of women of child-bearing age is married or was once married.

* * *

At this point it is convenient to consider how far changes in illegitimate fertility and changes in the timing and incidence of marriage were independent phenomena in early modern England. Analytically they are distinct, yet in early modern England the social and economic forces which regulated marriage trends in the restricted sense (its timing and incidence), also appear to have induced changes in a number of related phenomena (illegitimacy and pre-marital pregnancy), *which reinforced the effects to be expected as a result of the marriage trends.* Marriage in the broad sense may indeed be regarded as encompassing them all. If this usage is allowed, it suggests that all aspects of marriage should be studied conjointly. Marriage changes, understood in this broad sense, explain the great bulk of the remarkable spurt in population growth rates in eighteenth-century England. Age at marriage fell and with it the proportion of men and women who never married, and yet at the same time illegitimate fertility rose sharply and the proportion of pregnant brides also increased. The rise in the illegitimacy ratio occurred in spite of the fact that unmarried women were a smaller fraction of all fecund women and that those who married were doing so at an earlier age. It might have been thought likely that in Restoration England when marriage came late in life and many women never married, illegitimate births would have been frequent and those who married would be unusually likely to be pregnant; and that by the end of the eighteenth century with earlier and more universal marriage the swifter transition to the married state would have reduced both illegitimacy and pre-marital pregnancy. The opposite was the case. Whatever constrained men and women to marry late also constrained them to avoid extra-marital intercourse, but when earlier marriage was countenanced, inhibitions on intercourse outside marriage were also relaxed. If marriage is regarded as a social licence to reproduce then it seems fair to say that at times when society issued few such licences it also took care to keep licence evasion to negligible levels, but when few had long to wait for a licence there was much less concern if its issue was anticipated.

Having sought to collapse all causes of fertility change other than the level of marital fertility into a single complex but articulated category, we may now turn to consider how far the empirical evidence sustains this suggestion, while at the same time discovering whether the magnitude of the observed changes in each aspect of marriage is sufficient when their effects are cumulated together to explain the rise in the gross reproduction rate shown in Figure II. Unfortunately, some of the phenomena which are of greatest importance can be measured only indirectly, and in other cases information is available for only a small sample of parishes. In particular back projection yields no direct evidence about nuptiality other than crude marriage rates, and as a result it is less fully and reliably covered at present than fertility and mortality. Nevertheless there are sufficient data available to enable the main outlines of marriage behaviour in the broad sense to be drawn with fair confidence.

We may begin by considering nuptiality *sensu stricto* before turning to what might be termed the fringe phenomena of marriage. There are three measures available which throw light upon the changing timing and incidence of marriage. Family reconstitution studies yield evidence about age at first marriage, but not about the proportion of men and women who never married. The latter can, however, be estimated indirectly by using mortality estimates obtained by back projection in combination with a knowledge of birth and marriage totals. And marriage totals can also be related to totals of population of marriageable age derived from back projection to yield a modified crude marriage rate whose secular fluctuations will largely reflect the combined effect of changes in marriage age and proportions marrying.

Table III: Age at first marriage: means of 12 parishes

	Male	Female
1675–99	27.7	26.6
1700–24	27.6	26.9
1725–49	27.4	25.7
1750–74	26.5	25.3
1775–99	26.1	24.7
1800–24	25.5	23.7

Source Cambridge Group reconstitutions (for list of the 12 parishes see table II).

In Table III the changes in average age at first marriage in the 12 parishes listed in Table II are set out in quarter-century periods cohorted by date of marriage. Between 1675–99 and 1800–24 mean age at first marriage fell from 27.7 to 25.5 years for men, and from 26.6 to 23.7 years for women; falls of 2.2 and 2.9 years respectively. The sample is too small for much reliance to be placed either on the absolute ages shown in the table, or on the absolute size of the fall in marriage age; but it is significant that the fall occurred with marked consistency, as may be seen in Table IV. In the case of men the maximum age at first marriage was evenly spread between the first three quarter-century periods while the minimum age was usually found in 1800–24. In only four parishes did the minimum occur in another quarter-century. The pattern was similar but more pronounced in the case of women. The maximum age in all but one of the parishes fell either in the first or second of the six quarter-century periods; 3 in 1675–99, 8 in 1700–24. The minimum was almost always found in the last period or in the penultimate period (10 in 1800–24, 1 in 1775–99). The near universality of the trend towards earlier marriage in parishes of considerable diversity in economic and social constitution encourages the belief that more extensive information would simply confirm the observed pattern. The extent of the fall was not uniform, however. In Table V the difference in marriage age between the first and last quarter-centuries is set out for each of the 12 parishes. Bearing in mind the small number of marriages on which the means are based in some parishes the picture is fairly consistent. Change was slight in the large market towns (Banbury and Gainsborough) but significant and often substantial elsewhere except in Terling where marriage age rose for both men and women between the late seventeenth and early nineteenth century.

Table IV: Quarter-century periods between 1675–99 and 1800–24 within which maximum and minimum mean ages at first marriage occurred in 12 parishes

	Maximum		Minimum	
	Male	Female	Male	Female
1675–99	4	3	1	0
1700–24	4	8	1	0
1725–49	4	0	0	1
1750–74	0	1	1	0
1775–99	0	0	1	1
1800–24	0	0	8	10
Total	12	12	12	12

Source Cambridge Group reconstitutions (for list of 12 parishes see table II).

Table V: Fall in mean age at first marriage between 1675–99 and 1800–24 (in years)

	Male	Female
Alcester	3.7	3.3
Aldenham	3.6	4.5
Banbury	0.5	2.2
Colyton	1.9	3.6
Gainsborough	0.3	0.4
Gedling	4.0	1.4
Hartland	3.2	3.4
Methley	3.0	5.7
Shepshed	4.9	4.2
Southill and Campton with Shefford	2.0	1.4
Terling	−1.9	−1.0
Willingham	1.3	5.8

Source Cambridge Group reconstitutions.

Over all the evidence of Tables III and IV suggests that during the period in which intrinsic growth rates rose from zero to 1.67 per cent per annum (the average level in the first quarter of the nineteenth century), age at first marriage of women fell by about three years. Since the middle twenties is in the period of peak fecundity for women, a fall of three years in marriage

age is sufficient to make a substantial difference to over-all fertility,[20] but it is convenient to postpone a fuller examination of the implications of changes in each aspect of marriage behaviour until all have been discussed.

It is widely recognized that female age at marriage and proportions marrying tend to be associated with one another. Where marriage is late, many never marry; where early, few remain single.[21] Change over time follows a similar pattern with rising marriage age accompanied by an increase in celibacy, and *vice versa*. Women who never marry are peculiarly difficult to trace satisfactorily in family reconstitution studies, though where, as in some French registers, age and marital status are routinely recorded in burial registers, an estimate of the proportions never marrying may be made by discovering what percentage of all deaths above the age of 50 consisted of women who had never married.[22] English registers do not provide

---

[20] This point deserves to be stressed as it is sometimes claimed to have a relatively minor effect on fertility. McKeown, for example, remarks that 'a moderate increase in mean age at marriage would not have a very marked effect on fertility'. He depends on late nineteenth-century Irish evidence to sustain his assertion. McKeown, *Modern Rise of Population*, p. 38. It is true that marriage duration is frequently found to exercise an influence on fertility (i.e. in two groups of women of equal age but having married at different ages, that group which married the older will tend to have the higher fertility), but the remaining difference may none the less be substantial. As may be seen in the following table, McKeown lighted upon a population (rural Ireland) in which both the proportional and absolute difference in completed family size between women marrying 20-4 and 25-9 was unusually modest.

	(1)	(2)	(3)	(4)
	Completed family size of women marrying			(2)/(1)
	20-4	25-9	(1)−(2)	×100
Rural Ireland (1911 census)	8.04	6.79	1.25	84.5
South-east France (1670–1769)	7.35	5.56	1.79	75.6
North-east France (1670–1769)	8.26	6.23	2.03	75.4
North-west France (1670–1769)	7.10	5.45	1.65	76.8
South-west France (1720–69)	6.61	5.28	1.33	79.9
10 German villages (before 1850)	7.02	5.42	1.60	77.2
12 English reconstitutions (late sixteenth to early nineteenth century)	5.84	4.27	1.57	73.1

Sources McKeown, *Modern Rise of Population*, p. 38. L. Henry, 'Fécondité des mariages dans le quart sud-est de la France de 1670 à 1829', *Population*, XXXIII (1978), 866. J. Houdaille, 'La fécondité des mariages de 1670 à 1829 dans le quart nord-est de la France', *Annales de démographie historique*, 1976, p. 353. L. Henry and J. Houdaille, 'Fécondité des mariages dans le quart nord-ouest de la France de 1670 à 1829', *Population*, XXVIII (1973), 895. L. Henry, 'Fécondité des mariages dans le quart sud-ouest de la France de 1720 à 1829', *Annales, E.S.C.*, XXVII (1972), 983. J. Knodel, 'Natural fertility in pre-industrial Germany'. *Population Studies,* XXXII (1978), 493. Cambridge Group reconstitutions (parishes listed in table II).

Note Where the data were given by sub-periods, as in south-east and north-east France, each sub-period was given an equal weight in calculating a figure for the period as a whole. The dates for the French data refer to cohorts of marriage. After 1770 the beginning of family limitation in France makes the fertility information unsuitable for the present purpose.

[21] Data bearing on this point are presented graphically by P. Festy, *La fécondité des pays occidentaux de 1870 à 1970*, p. 29, fig. 8.

[22] See, for example, E. Gautier and L. Henry, *La population de Crulai* (Paris, 1958), pp. 74–6. Even in such cases, however, there is often a wide margin of uncertainty.

this combination of information and so estimates of proportions never marrying must be sought in other ways.

The estimates of proportions never marrying shown in Figure III were obtained by making use of national birth and first marriage totals in conjunction with mortality estimates derived from back projection. They are both imprecise and fallible because of difficulties arising from the data used, which are unavoidable but imply substantial margins of error round any estimate.

In principle the method used should be capable of producing approximately accurate results. Its logic is simple. Back projection provides quinquennial 'censuses' in which the population is divided into five-year age groups, so that the number of persons aged 40–44 at each 'census' is known. If the proportion of all first marriages contracted by those aged 15–19, 20–24 ... 40–44 is known approximately and all such marriages are assumed to occur below age 45, the total of first marriages allocable to any given cohort in each five-year period is also calculable, and the total relating to the cohort can be cumulated age group by age group as it grows older. Each new influx of married people is subjected to the same wastage by mortality between their age group of entry and age 40–44 as is the population as a whole. In this way the total of those within the cohort who have married and survived to age 40–44 can be estimated and compared with the over-all total surviving to that age. The difference between the two totals will represent those who have remained permanently single.

In practice, however, there are several reasons why the graph shown in Figure III traces an uncertain path. They have been discussed in greater detail elsewhere but may be rehearsed briefly here.[23] First, the logic of the operation demands that the basic data should refer to those marrying for the first time and not to the over-all total of brides and grooms. English parish registers seldom provide consistent information about the marital status of individuals at marriage before Hardwicke's Marriage Act of 1753. There is sufficient information scattered in individual registers to enable rough estimates of the prevalence of remarriage at different periods to be made but their use involves heroic assumptions about their representativeness and about the smoothness of change over time. The problem eases with the passage of time and by the mid-nineteenth century the position is clear because of the data published by the Registrar-General. Second, the English population was not closed and the 'census' totals produced by back projection

[23] Wrigley and Schofield, *Population History of England,* pp. 257–65.

Fig. III: Proportions never marrying (sexes combined)
Source Wrigley and Schofield, *Population History of England*, table 7.28.
Note The data refer to the percentages never marrying of those surviving to the age group 40–4 in cohorts born in the quinquennial periods ending at the dates indicated. Each reading represents a 5-point moving average of such proportions.

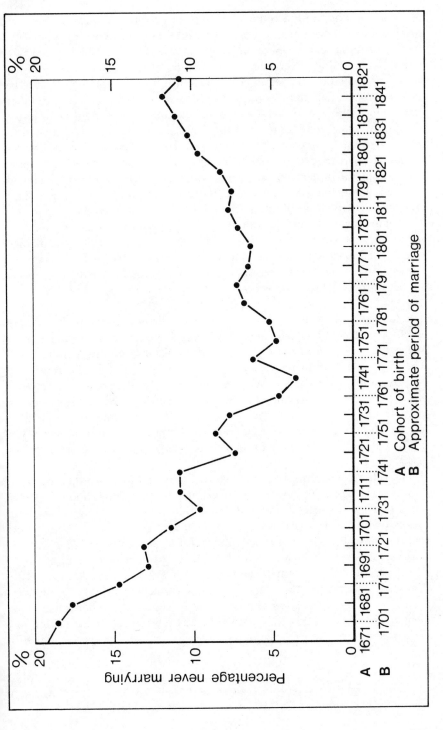

take net migration into account, but married persons were assumed not to migrate. Since they almost certainly displayed a markedly lower propensity to migrate than single people at all periods of English history, this is a defensible procedure. Nevertheless to the degree that married couples did indeed emigrate the proportion of permanently single people will tend to be underestimated, and more so at times of substantial emigration than at other times. Third, the mortality of the married and unmarried populations in the age groups 15–44 was assumed to be identical. Fourth, in the half century or so immediately following the Civil War clandestine marriage was widespread and marriage totals based on Anglican registration are misleadingly low, causing the proportions never marrying to be overstated. Fifth, it should be noted that no allowance was made for short-term increases in remarriage proportions in the wake of heavy mortalities. This will cause the proportions never marrying to be underestimated, an effect visible in Figure III in the years following the very high death rates of the late 1720s. Sixth, the age schedule of marriage used in allocating marriages to birth cohorts can influence the estimated proportions never marrying. Extreme assumptions on this score would raise or lower the line shown in Figure III by about 2–3 per cent.[24]

Before discussing the evidence about nuptiality contained in Figure III one further point should be mentioned. The back projection exercise from which the data used in the figure were derived made no distinction of sex. The birth and death totals used were for the sexes combined. Therefore the estimates shown are also for the sexes combined. But the proportions of men and women never marrying were not necessarily the same. When census tabulations by sex, age and marital status began to be published in the mid-nineteenth century, there were significant differences between the two sexes in this respect, and it is very probable that this was also the case in earlier periods.[25]

The cohorts whose history is traced in Figure III are identified by their quinquennium of birth. Since each cohort married on average about 25 years later, the figure suggests that the proportion never marrying reached its lowest point among the cohorts entering marriage late in the eighteenth century, probably about the beginning of its final quarter. The various sources of uncertainty which have been listed prohibit precision, but it is safe to assume that the proportion never marrying began to rise again with the cohorts marrying at the very end of the eighteenth century or early in the new century, having been at a low level among the cohorts marrying during the preceding 30 years or so. The last few cohorts, born during the early nineteenth century and marrying in its second quarter contained a

[24] Ibid., fig. 7.15.

[25] For example, in the age group 50–54 in 1851 the proportion never married in England was 10.66 per cent for men but 11.99 per cent for women. *1851 Census,* Population tables. II Ages, civil condition, occupations, etc., *Parl. Papers* 1852–53, LXXXVIII, i, pp. cxciii, ccii, cciii.

substantially higher proportion of men and women who remained single. Since the survivors from these cohorts were still living when the mid-nineteenth-century censuses were taken, the accuracy of the estimated figures for them can be checked. The agreement between the estimates and the census data for the cohorts born during the last 30 years shown in Figure III proves to be close.[26]

The prolonged and steady fall in the proportions never marrying from the late seventeenth to the late eighteenth century is the most striking feature of Figure III. In late Stuart times many people remained single all their lives. The prevalence of clandestine marriage would have tended to boost the estimated proportion remaining single above its true level but the rather high level of net emigration at the time would have acted in the opposite sense, and therefore the true proportions may not have been greatly different from those shown in the figure. Their level in the earliest cohorts was not much different from that obtaining just before the outbreak of the First World War.[27]

The over-all pattern of change in the incidence of marriage (proportions never marrying) therefore conforms to that of the timing of marriage (age at first marriage), except that the change in the former appears to precede that in the latter. The fall in marriage age was not clearly visible until the second quarter of the eighteenth century whereas the incidence of marriage had been falling for some time, while equally marriage age did not reach its lowest point until the first quarter of the nineteenth century by which time the proportion never marrying was probably already past its nadir and tending to rise. Both the measures of the timing and of the incidence of marriage, however, are suspect. The former is based on data from only a dozen parishes, while the latter is subject to several influences which impair its accuracy, as we have seen. There remains a third measure which has the advantage of reflecting changes both in the timing and in the incidence of marriage. It is a modified crude first marriage rate, which expresses the total of first marriages as a rate per 1,000 population aged 15–34, the years of life during which first marriage is most likely to take place.[28] A 25-year moving average of this rate is shown in Figure IV.

The rate shown in the figure suffers from some of the drawbacks listed in relation to the measurement of proportions never marrying. First marriages are separated from total marriages in the same arbitrary fashion. And short-term changes in the remarriage proportion can distort the pattern of

---

[26] Wrigley and Schofield, *Population History of England*, pp. 262–3.

[27] The average level in the first six cohorts born in the last three decades of the seventeenth century was 16.0 per cent. At the time of the 1911 census the comparable figure was 13.9 per cent (using a simple average of the separate male and female percentages never marrying: Wrigley and Schofield, *Population History of England*, table 10.4).

[28] It is preferable to relate marriages to those in the age groups in which marriage was commonest rather than to the total population because the age group 15–34 formed a changing fraction of the total population.

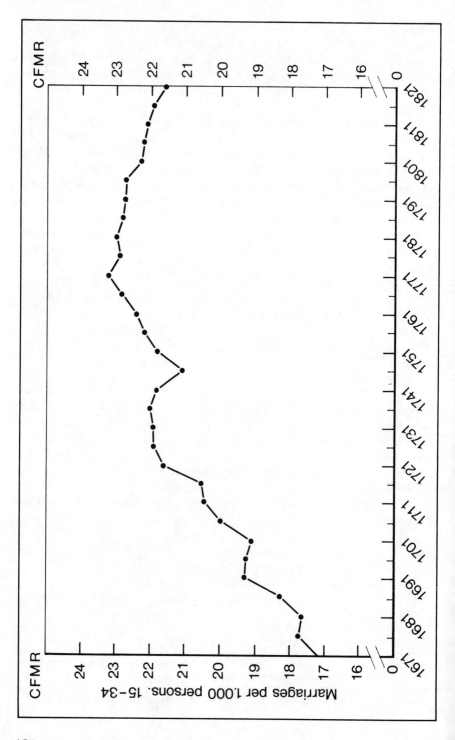

change. The bulge in the rate in the quarter-century centring on 1731, for example, is the spurious product of the surge in the remarriages following the very heavy mortality of the period 1727–31.[29] Furthermore this measure is not termed crude without reason. In periods of rapid increase in nuptiality crude rates may be driven up to misleading heights by the 'telescoping' effect of a fall in marriage age and a decrease in the proportion remaining permanently single. The converse happens during a period of sharply declining nuptiality.

In spite of these drawbacks and limitations, however, the information contained in Figure IV is a valuable supplement to the data on the timing and incidence of marriage, as well as a useful summary of them. From the 1670s onwards nuptiality increased from a very low level to reach a peak at the end of the eighteenth century which was higher than at any period for about two centuries on either side. Clandestine marriage caused the rate in the later seventeenth century to be understated, and the problem of successfully identifying first marriages within total marriages together with the 'telescoping' problem make it hard to identify the peak of nuptiality with precision. There can be no doubt, however, that there was a marked and steady rise in nuptiality between the late seventeenth century and a date about 1800, nor that there was subsequently a fall in nuptiality (which however reversed itself soon after the end of the period covered by Figure IV).

*   *   *

The potential impact of the changes in the timing and incidence of marriage upon general fertility levels, given invariant age-specific marital fertility rates, was very substantial, but before analysing them it is convenient to consider fertility outside marriage. We may begin by noting that although an individual child was either legitimate or illegitimate in the eyes of the law, normally according to whether or not his or her mother was married at the time of the birth (though the English law of marriage was involved and could give rise to substantial ambiguity[30]), illegitimacy is better regarded as embracing a wide range of situations rather than as a simple, categorical alternative to legitimacy. A child born to a couple living together in a stable union who married shortly thereafter might be formally illegitimate, but the

[29] The crude death rate in the years 1727 to 1731 was 35.5, 39.8, 44.7, 36.2 and 34.1 per 1,000. For a fuller discussion of this and related points see Wrigley and Schofield, *Population History of England*, p. 426.

[30] A. Macfarlane, 'Illegitimacy and illegitimates in English history', in P. Laslett, K. Oosterveen and R. M. Smith (eds.), *Bastardy and its Comparative History* (London, 1980), especially pp. 73–5.

Fig. IV: Crude first marriage rate (marriages per 1,000 persons 15–34)
Source Wrigley and Schofield, *Population History of England*, fig. 10.11.
Note The rates shown are 25-year moving averages of the annual rates centred on the dates shown. Points are plotted at 5-year intervals.

attitude of society towards both the child and the parents was widely different from its attitude towards child and parent when the child was the outcome of a casual encounter and the mother had little prospect of marriage. The former case is not significantly different from that which arose when a child was prenuptially conceived though born in wedlock, whereas the latter might presage great stress and difficulty for the mother and poor prospects of survival for the child.

Inasmuch as many births that were formally illegitimate were not clearly distinct from a proportion of formally legitimate births, it is not perhaps surprising that there were strikingly similar trends in the illegitimacy ratio and the proportion of first births prenuptially conceived as may be seen in Figure V.[31] In both cases the level of the measure was low in the early decades but rose steadily to reach very high levels by the end of the eighteenth century, after which both series moved uncertainly with a hint of incipient decline.

In the later years of Charles II's reign the illegitimacy ratio was slightly under 1.5 per cent, and the proportion of brides who were pregnant at marriage stood at about 15 per cent. By the early decades of the nineteenth century the illegitimacy ratio had more than tripled to over 5 per cent and the proportion of pregnant brides had also grown markedly. In both series the increases may be found in almost every parish for which data exist.[32]

[31] The illegitimacy ratio expresses illegitimate births as a proportion of all births. An illegitimacy rate, which relates illegitimate births to the total of unmarried women of child-bearing age, would be a preferable measure but the latter is not known accurately before the 1851 census. It is clearly possible for the two to tell very different stories. For example, if the rate were constant, or even declining gently in a period of falling nuptiality the ratio might rise substantially. Fortunately this is not a serious problem in early modern England since the illegitimacy ratio fell in periods of falling nuptiality and rose when nuptiality was increasing. The ratio therefore consistently tends to *understate* the changes in illegitimacy which would be recorded by a better measure. For an excellent discussion of this issue see M. Drake, 'Norway', in W. R. Lee (ed.), *European Demography and Economic Growth* (London, 1979), pp. 284–318, especially pp. 299–306.

[32] It is worth noting that the trends in illegitimacy in the reconstitution parishes were very similar to those found in the larger sample of parishes on which the illegitimacy graph shown in figure V was based. Illegitimacy was recorded in the aggregative tabulations of eight of the 12 reconstitution parishes (the missing parishes were Terling, Willingham, Shepshed, and Southill and Campton with Shefford). The average difference in the illegitimacy level between the eight reconstitution parishes and the 98 parish sample of figure V was 0.46 per cent over 30 quinquennial

---

Fig. V: Illegitimacy ratios and prenuptial pregnancy proportions
Sources Illegitimacy ratios: P. Laslett, 'Introduction', in Laslett *et al.*, *Bastardy and its Comparative History*, table 1.1(a).
Prenuptial pregnancy proportions: Cambridge Group reconstitutions.
Notes The illegitimacy ratios are based on data from 98 parishes except for the period 1805–19 when the number falls to 74. The prenuptial pregnancy proportions are derived from the 12 reconstitutions listed in table 2 and are unweighted averages of the proportions in each parish for each period. The data for both series refer to the 5-year periods beginning at the dates indicated. No data are shown for prenuptial pregnancy after the quinquennium 1810–14 because in three parishes the reconstitutions finished before the beginning of the next quinquennium.

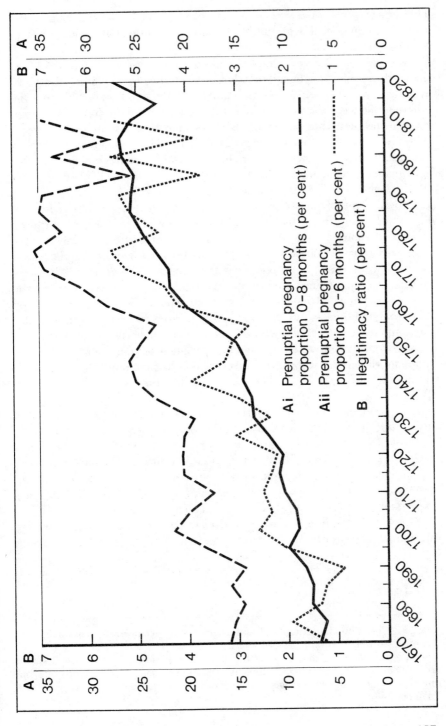

The change in behaviour was so widespread as to be almost universal in the general population, though not necessarily in certain small groups such as the Quakers.

Two lines relating to prenuptial pregnancy are shown in Figure V. One shows the proportion of all first births occurring within nine months of marriage; the other within seven months of marriage. It is notable that the difference between the two was much the same throughout the whole period. Pregnancies occurring within the last two months before marriage were a virtually constant proportion of all first births. Thus, the great increase in prenuptial pregnancy was not due to more couples marrying shortly after a pregnancy had taken place, but rather to a precipitous rise in the proportion of marriages contracted later in pregnancy.

The changing pattern of prenuptial pregnancy may be seen more fully in Figure VI where the distribution of the baptisms of prenuptially conceived children is shown by the number of elapsed months after marriage for the quarter-century period 1670–94 and again 100 years later during the period 1770–94 when prenuptial pregnancy had risen to its peak level. The overall prenuptial pregnancy proportion rose from 15 to 35 per cent between the two periods, but in 1670–94 the first seven months (0–6) contributed only 7 per cent and the last two months (7–8) 8 per cent, whereas a century later the comparable percentages were 26 and 9. The whole rise was concentrated among women who were three months pregnant or more, and the bulk of it among those who were three to seven months pregnant (baptism two to six months after marriage). The percentage for this last group rose from 6 to 22.

It is probable that two different types of circumstances gave rise to prenuptial pregnancies, depending on the temporal sequence between pregnancy and the decision to marry. For some couples the recognition that a pregnancy had occurred provided a reason to consider matrimony. For others a prior decision to marry might occasion the beginning of intercourse. In the one case pregnancy provoked an expectation of marriage; in the other expectation of marriage provoked a pregnancy.

Many of the children who were baptized in the ninth month after marriage must have been conceived only after the banns were first called. And in

---

periods, and the average difference when sign is taken into account was only 0.05 per cent. The figures for the eight parishes as a whole were taken as simple averages of the figures for the individual parishes.

Fig. VI: The changing level and character of prenuptial pregnancy
Source Cambridge Group reconstitutions.
Note For details of the derivation of the data see notes to fig. V. The graph shows the percentage of all first births (baptisms) within marriage which took place during the first 9 months after marriage. The intervals are indicated on the horizontal axis (months 0–8).

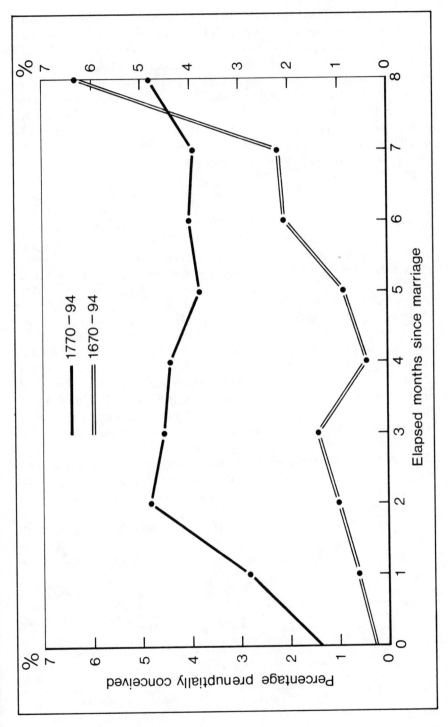

almost all the pregnancies which resulted in births in the eighth and ninth month after marriage (7–8 in Figure VI), the fact of the pregnancy would have been unknown, or at most only suspected, at the time of marriage.[33] Figure VI shows that the incidence of this type of prenuptial pregnancy remained unchanged during the eighteenth century, and there was thus no similarity between its secular trend and that of the illegitimacy ratio. Figure V shows, however, that there was a remarkably close similarity between the behaviour of the illegitimacy ratio and that of the other category of prenuptial pregnancy where a knowledge that a pregnancy had become established may be presumed to have antedated marriage plans, which may conveniently be termed 'long' prenuptial pregnancy.

The sympathetic movement in illegitimacy and 'long' prenuptial pregnancy stems from a common background.[34] Most illegitimate births were probably conceived in circumstances essentially similar to those which produced pregnancies many months before marriage. Viewed *ex post facto* there may appear to be a clear distinction between a conception outside wedlock followed by a birth also outside wedlock, and a conception outside wedlock followed by a birth within it. Seen *ex prae facto*, on the other hand, the distinction must often have been impossible to draw. Many parents of children who were in the event born outside marriage may have contemplated matrimony in much the same light as did those whose marriages comparatively late in pregnancy produced a peak in baptisms a few months after marriage. Where it was the fact of a pregnancy which raised the question of marriage, rather than *vice versa,* there were many circumstances which might conspire to prevent marriage in time to ensure the legitimacy of the child. The failure to find accommodation in a society which expected married couples to have their own household played a part in some cases; the hostility of parents or of the parish authorities in others. Refusal by the man or a change of mind about her prospective spouse on the part of the woman might also make marriage impossible. Occasionally, too, the death of the man (or his removal by *force majeure* in the shape of the courts or the press gang) prevented marriage.

Frequently, however, marriage was postponed rather than forgone by the parents of an illegitimate child. Evidence on this point is fragmentary but enough exists to show that it was common for this to happen. In this

[33] The measurement of the timing of the prenuptial pregnancy interval after marriage in English reconstitution studies involves, of course, in most cases an overestimate of the true period because the time measured is from marriage to first baptism rather than to first birth. There is evidence that the interval from birth to baptism tended to grow during the eighteenth century, and averaged about a month by the end of the century. It is probable, however, that the general pattern revealed by figure VI would not be greatly altered with more accurate information, even though the absolute percentages would be changed. B. M. Berry and R. S. Schofield, 'Age at baptism in pre-industrial England', *Population Studies,* XXV (1971), 453–63.

[34] Although the two measures are calculated on different bases (percentage of all births and percentage of all legitimate first births), it is not seriously misleading to compare their relative changes (as opposed to their absolute levels) since first births were a fairly constant proportion of all births.

connection it should be recalled that the Church held that children born to couples who married were legitimate whether or not their birth took place after their parents' marriage; and also that there is suggestive evidence that the age of the mothers of illegitimate children was virtually identical to that of married women at the time of the birth of their first child.[35] If liaisons had been widespread among those who were sexually adult but unmarried, mothers of illegitimate children would have been younger than mothers of first-born legitimate children. Equally, if bearing an illegitimate child had frequently been the result of the exploitation by their masters of girls in service or in employment, it is reasonable to expect that they would have been younger than women bearing a first legitimate child, since their period of risk came at an earlier point in the life cycle than marriage. Even if most illegitimate children had been conceived during a period of experimentation prior to settling down with a single partner, their mothers might well have been on average somewhat younger than women who first bore a child after marriage. But where there is no gap in average age between the two groups, it is reasonable to suppose that, at least for many mothers of illegitimate children, the onset of reproduction was determined by influences similar to those which led more directly to marriage for their contemporaries.

The scale of illegitimate and quasi-legitimate fertility early in adult life deserves emphasis. In some periods of English history it was a common experience for a woman to bear a first child who was either illegitimate or conceived several months before marriage. Indeed at times this was probably the predominant mode of entry into maternity. Prenuptial pregnancy is measured as a proportion of all first births but the illegitimacy ratio relates illegitimate births to births of all parities. This tends to cause their prevalence to be underestimated. For many purposes it is more illuminating to relate illegitimate births, which are usually first births, to all first births rather than to births of all parities, a procedure which also facilitates a direct comparison of the prevalence of the two modes of entry into reproductive activity that antedate marriage.[36]

---

[35] On the legitimacy of children born before their parents' marriage see Macfarlane, 'Illegitimacy and illegitimates', p. 73. On the age of the mothers of illegitimate children see K. Oosterveen and R. M. Smith, 'Bastardy and the family reconstitution studies of Colyton, Aldenham, Alcester and Hawkshead', in Laslett et al., Bastardy and its Comparative History, pp. 107–8; S. Stewart, 'Bastardy and the family reconstitution studies of Banbury and Hartland', in ibid., pp. 130–31; and D. Levine and K. Wrightson, 'The social context of illegitimacy in early modern England', in ibid., pp. 160–2. The evidence is too slight and scattered for it to be reasonable to claim that the issue is settled, but such data as exist show no consistent tendency for motherhood outside marriage to begin earlier or later than motherhood inside marriage.

[36] Smith provides a valuable review of the available evidence about the frequency with which mothers of illegitimate children bore two or more such children. He does not present the data in a way which makes it easy to estimate the proportion of all illegitimate children who were not first births. However, he presents a table in which the proportion of unmarried mothers producing two or more children is given for 12 parishes during the period when repetitive bastard-bearing was at its height in the later eighteenth century. The mean proportion for the 12 parishes is 16.3 per cent. On the assumption that each such unmarried mother bore 2.5 illegitimate children, the

In rough-and-ready terms the two were-of equal importance. At the end of the eighteenth century when both were rising to a peak the illegitimacy ratio was about 5.5 per cent and the proportion of all first births baptized within seven months of marriage was about 26 per cent. Since first births were approximately a quarter of all births, the two categories between them comprised a half of all first births.[37] On the other hand in the later seventeenth century when the illegitimacy ratio was only 1.5 per cent the prenuptial pregnancy proportion at seven months from marriage was about 7 per cent, again a similar proportion of all first births. The two categories between them comprised only about an eighth of all first births (since fertility was much lower in the late seventeenth than the early nineteenth century, the percentage of first births was higher and *ceteris paribus* any given level of the illegitimacy ratio bore a lower relationship to all first births). The notable contrast in this regard between the beginning and end of the 'long' eighteenth century affords persuasive evidence of the effectiveness with which extramarital and pre-marital fertility were limited when marriage itself came late or not at all in the lives of many men and women. Conversely in an era of early and well-nigh universal entry into matrimony regulation of forms of reproduction which took place outside or in advance of marriage was far more perfunctory.

It sits well with this pattern that in the period 1650–99 not only was prenuptial pregnancy rare, but it was rarer among young brides than among older ones, whereas after 1750 prenuptial pregnancy was both generally rife and also commonest of all when the bride was young (Table VIII). The rate for brides under 25 roughly quadrupled while that for older brides only doubled. The control of all methods of youthful entry into reproduction was the dominant characteristic of the demography of late Stuart England. A century later a far higher proportion of women married in their teens or early twenties, yet though fewer of their contemporaries were unmarried in this age range they bore several times as many illegitimate children as their great-grandmothers had done. And whereas only about a twentieth of women marrying under 25 bore a first child within seven months of marriage in late Stuart England, the comparable figure was above a quarter in the decades close to 1800. Throughout all the changes in the level of illegitimate and 'long' prenuptial fertility, however, 'short' prenuptial fertility was constant. Even though the timing and incidence of marriage might vary substantially from period to period, once the decision to marry had been made and the ceremony was imminent intercourse was common.

---

proportion of all illegitimate children who were not first children would still be just under a fifth of the total. In other periods the proportion was much smaller. R. M. Smith, 'Introduction' (to ch. 3), in Laslett *et al.*, *Bastardy and its Comparative History*, p. 87, table 3.1.

[37] The two categories were not mutually exclusive, of course. A woman might bear an illegitimate child and then marry when again pregnant. The scale of this phenomenon is at present unknown, however, and for simplicity's sake it is ignored here.

The available evidence about the circumstances in which women came to bear a first child, therefore, suggests that there were some notable similarities between the four types of circumstance which have been distinguished. Whether the first child was conceived and born outside marriage, conceived before marriage plans had been made but born after the wedding, conceived before marriage but only after the decision to marry had been taken, or conceived and born after the marriage, the age at which reproduction began was much the same and long-term trends were in harmony with one another. The four forms are best regarded as all embraced within a sufficiently broad definition of marriage. When nuptiality was at a low ebb in the late seventeenth century, illegitimate births were comparatively rare and 'long' prenuptial pregnancy was uncommon especially among young brides. The converse held true by the late eighteenth century. The pattern of 'short' prenuptial conceptions did not change over time, nor did the pattern of first births postnuptially conceived, but since both were tied to marriage, and marriage itself underwent great changes of timing and incidence, the social regulation of fertility appears to have been at once flexible, consistent and effective.

*   *   *

Since the dissimilarity of reproduction inside and outside marriage is often stressed, it may not be out of place to consider one further aspect of fertility in which there was a marked similarity between intra- and extra-marital behaviour; another feature of English eighteenth-century demography which suggests that many unions which were not—or had not yet become—marriages nevertheless had much in common with unions which had been blessed by the Church. The seasonal distribution of illegitimate births sometimes contrasted strongly with that of legitimate births. In eastern Sweden, for example, Gaunt found that in both urban and rural areas the seasonal pattern of illegitimate conceptions differed widely from that of conceptions within marriage. In rural areas it was 'obviously related to harvest festivities in July and August': more generally, 'illegitimates were conceived in the warm months from April to August while the colder months did not allow privacy outdoors'. Legitimate conceptions, on the other hand, reached a peak in the depth of winter in December and January.[38]

In England legitimate and illegitimate conceptions shared a common seasonal pattern.[39] Evidence from five reconstitution parishes for which detailed studies of illegitimacy have been made suggests that the seasonal pattern was virtually identical for the two categories. Table VI summarizes

[38] D. Gaunt, 'Illegitimacy in seventeenth- and eighteenth-century east Sweden', in Laslett *et al.*, *Bastardy and its Comparative History*, p. 324.

[39] The pattern was substantially different from that described by Gaunt for east Sweden. In the eighteenth century the seasonal distribution of baptisms suggests that conceptions were most frequent in June and least frequent in October, with a fairly regular fall and rise from peak to trough and back again. Wrigley and Schofield, *Population History of England*, table 8.1.

Table VI: The relative seasonal distribution of illegitimate baptisms and all baptisms in five English parishes 1661–1820 (percentage deviations)

	(C)	A	M	J	J	A	S	O	N	D	J	F	M
	(B)	J	F	M	A	M	J	J	A	S	O	N	D
Alcester		+10	−11	+2	+56	+10	+34	−9	−31	−4	−20	−19	−18
Aldenham		+3	+22	+48	−73	+30	+2	−14	−16	−19	+34	+11	−31
Colyton		−18	+2	+2	+10	−5	+12	−1	−19	+21	−15	−9	+20
Gainsborough		−24	+5	−30	+3	+20	−18	−20	+20	+13	−24	+8	+45
Hawkshead		+24	+19	−13	+11	+9	−20	+10	−20	−9	−47	+20	+16
Total		−5	+37	+9	+7	+64	+10	−34	−66	+2	−72	+11	+32
Average deviation		−1	+7	+2	+1	+13	+2	−7	−13	0	−14	+2	+6
Corrected		−1	+6	−1	−3	+13	0	−5	−11	+4	−13	0	+8

(C) month of conception
(B) month of baptism

Source Cambridge Group aggregate tabulations and special studies of illegitimacy in certain reconstitution parishes.
Note For explanation of method of calculation and estimation of corrected figures see text.

the available data. They were derived after first having converted the absolute monthly totals of all baptisms and illegitimate baptisms to index figures where 100 would indicate that the number occurring in the month in question was the number to be expected if baptisms were evenly distributed throughout the year taking the number of days in each month into account. The numbers set out in Table VI show the difference between the index figures for illegitimate and all baptisms. Thus in Alcester the index figures for January in the two classes were 136 and 126 and the figure of +10 in the table shows that the index level for illegitimate baptisms was 10 higher than that for all baptisms.

In the individual parishes the figures for certain months in the table are very high. In Aldenham, for example, the April figure is −73 (the index figures in this instance being 55 and 128). Wide discrepancies are, however, to be expected in occasional months having regard to the comparatively small numbers of illegitimate baptisms at issue. The total number of illegitimate baptisms in Aldenham over the period 1661–1820 was only 132 and in April only 6.[40] If, however, there were a systematic tendency for illegitimate children to be conceived following a different seasonal rhythm from that of births in general, deviations of the same sign, if not of the same magnitude, would appear in each column with some consistency, and the cumulative totals at the foot of each column would reflect this tendency. But the average deviations are relatively small and show no consistent seasonal pattern. Furthermore they slightly overstate such difference as may have existed, and

[40] The total number of all illegitimate baptisms and of all baptisms in Alcester, Aldenham, Colyton, Gainsborough and Hawkshead were respectively 173 and 5,621, 132 and 5,084, 277 and 5,873, 247 and 17,551, and 193 and 5,200 (in each case for the period 1661–1820).

for an interesting reason. The seasonal distribution of legitimate births of different birth parity showed little variation except in the case of first births whose timing was quite strongly influenced by the seasonality of marriage. The marked peak in marriages in the late autumn (October–November), for example, caused first baptisms in high summer and early autumn (July–October) to be relatively more frequent than baptisms of higher parity births. If the seasonal distribution of illegitimate baptisms is compared with that of all baptisms after making an adjustment to exclude the distorting influence of first legitimate births, the corrected deviations shown on the last line of Table VI result. The deviations are now slightly reduced and the pluses and minuses are interspersed without a seasonal pattern.

Marriage, indeed, might be described as the social institution which most disrupted an otherwise regular seasonal pattern of reproduction. Not only did conceptions taking place within a few months of marriage have a distinctive seasonal pattern related to the seasonal distribution of marriage itself, but so also did those taking place immediately before marriage and presumptively arising because of a prior decision to marry. In the 12 reconstitution parishes listed in Table II the seasonal pattern of marriages which were followed by a baptism in the eighth or ninth month after marriage was broadly similar to that of marriages in which the first child was postnuptially conceived. As a result the seasonal distribution of the associated baptisms was substantially different from that of baptisms of children whose birth parity was two or more. The strong surge of marriages in the late autumn (October and November) produced a corresponding surge in prenuptially conceived baptisms of this type in midsummer (June and July) at a time when there were relatively few births in the 'natural' seasonal pattern. Conversely there were relatively few marriages in July and August and correspondingly few baptisms about eight months later in March and April. The same pattern is found in marriages of January and February and the associated baptisms of September and October; here, too, the seasonal pattern of marriages caused this category of first births to fall short of the normal seasonal level.[41]

[41] The relationships described in this paragraph are summarized in the following percentage figures which show the extent to which baptisms associated with prenuptial conceptions occurring in the last two months before marriage differed in their seasonal pattern from that found among legitimate baptisms of second or higher parity (the 'natural' seasonal pattern of conception). The February figure of −21, for example, represents the difference between a figure of 95 for the former type of baptism and a figure of 116 for the latter type.

J	F	M	A	M	J	J	A	S	O	N	D
+19	−21	−29	−34	+10	+34	+36	+27	−23	−12	−6	−5

The data were obtained from the 12 reconstitution parishes and represent a comparison of the unweighted averages of the individual parishes after indexing the number of events in each month so that a figure of 100 would be the number to be expected from an even distribution of events throughout the year after allowing for the varying number of days in each month. The data for the five smallest parishes were first amalgamated into a single set to reduce the effect of the very

Where prenuptial conceptions antedated the decision to marry, on the other hand, it was the seasonal pattern of marriage which tended to be disrupted rather than the seasonal pattern of baptism. Marriages associated with prenuptially conceived first births baptized within the first seven months of marriage were relatively rare in the late spring (April–May) but unusually numerous in September when compared with marriages in which the first birth was postnuptially conceived. If we assume that the fact of a pregnancy is recognized in, say, the third month, and that the couple make arrangements to marry shortly afterwards, the seasonal pattern of such marriages will be affected by the normal seasonal pattern of conceptions lagged by about four months. We have already seen that the timing of such marriages was spread out over several months and would therefore be unlikely to produce a very clear-cut pattern (Figure VI). Nevertheless the more conspicuous disparities between marriages associated with 'long' prenuptial conceptions and marriages with a postnuptially conceived first birth conform to expectation. April and May were normally popular months for marriage but the 'demand' for marriages related to prenuptial conceptions taking place principally in the period November to January was modest because these were not months in which the normal seasonal tide of conception was very high. September, on the other hand, was not a month in which marriages were generally common, yet for couples who were to baptize their first child within the first few months of marriage it was relatively popular. In late spring the level of conceptions was high and rising which would tend to create a matching demand for marriages a few months later. August and October were also months with a higher than 'expected' number of marriages brought about by a preceding pregnancy. The absolute level of such marriages was especially high in October (corresponding to the June peak in conceptions), but this was in any case a popular month for weddings.[42]

It would be premature to make too much of the apparent influence of prenuptial conceptions occurring well before marriage on the seasonal pattern of the subsequent marriages. The number of events was very small in several of the 12 parishes, both because the parishes themselves were small and because the analysis was based on a sample of the full set of marriages (only those where the age of the mother and the dates of both the beginning and the end of marriage were known). In these circumstances chance variations

---

small number of events in many months, so that the data for eight rather than 12 units were averaged (7 individual parishes plus the amalgamated set).

[42] Using the same method described in note 41 the difference between the seasonal pattern of marriages which were followed by a postnuptially conceived first birth and that of marriages followed by a baptism within seven months is summarized below. A plus sign indicates that the latter type of marriage was relatively more numerous; a minus sign the opposite. The absolute figures for the latter type of marriage are shown on the bottom line.

J	F	M	A	M	J	J	A	S	O	N	D
−20	+17	+17	−29	−32	−2	+4	+7	+39	+5	−29	+24
74	105	67	101	95	92	97	70	107	148	118	128

in numbers may distort the 'true' pattern. A comparison of the seasonal distribution of births of the second or higher parities with the corresponding distribution of prenuptially conceived births baptized within seven months of marriage, for example, which ought to be similar to each other on the assumption that both were influenced by a 'natural' rhythm of conception, shows some substantial discrepancies from month to month, though without any revealing pattern. Further work is needed before it can be regarded as clear that the two types of prenuptial pregnancy and their related marriages were associated in the manner just adumbrated.

We have noted that changes in measures of illegitimate and prenuptial fertility were closely in accord with each other, and also that in several respects they displayed characteristics similar to those to be found in the study of legitimate fertility. It is appropriate to conclude this section by considering how far the secular trend in general fertility (which is, of course, principally determined by changes in legitimate fertility) paralleled the change in illegitimate and quasi-legitimate fertility already set out in Figure V. Changes in the gross reproduction rate have already been given in Figure II but under a different guise. In Figure VII they are shown in a form which makes for easy comparison with the changes in the illegitimacy ratio and prenuptial pregnancy proportion already shown in Figure V.

Since the three lines in Figure VII do not have a common origin (the GRR starting at 1.8) the unwary eye may be deceived by the close correspondence between their behaviour. The *proportional* rise in the gross reproduction rate is, of course, far less than the rises in the other two measures. Nevertheless the correspondence between the trends in the three measures of different aspects of fertility is remarkable. And if the figure had been extended backwards to the sixteenth century or forwards into the nineteenth it would then be clear that the turning points in the three series coincided closely with one another, in some ways an even more persuasive evidence of their common patterning.

*   *   *

We have now reviewed the timing and extent of changes in marriage and certain marriage-related phenomena during the 'long' eighteenth century, and have noted the stability of marital fertility and the scale of change in general fertility as reflected in the gross reproduction rate. We are therefore in a position to consider the relative contributions of the several aspects of changing marriage behaviour to the over-all changes in fertility. This may conveniently be achieved by constructing two models intended to exemplify the situations obtaining in the late seventeenth and early nineteenth century. They embody in a stylized form the contrasting marriage characteristics of the English population before the surge of population growth began and when it reached its high point early in the nineteenth century.

167

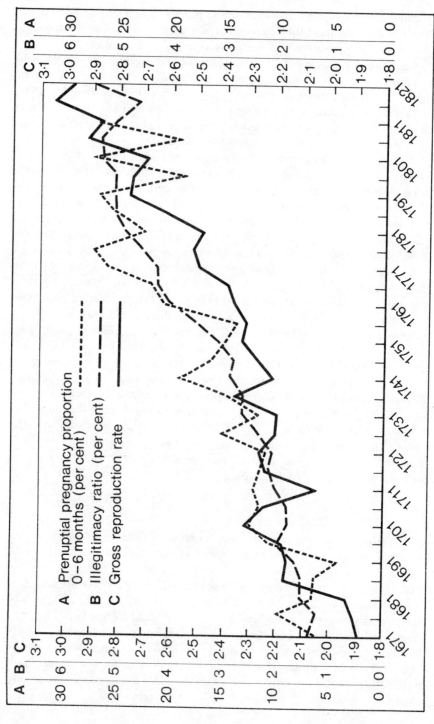

A Prenuptial pregnancy proportion
   0–6 months (per cent)
B Illegitimacy ratio (per cent)
C Gross reproduction rate

Table VII: Two models designed to illustrate the effect of changes in marriage and marriage-related behaviour in changing intrinsic growth rates between the late seventeenth and early nineteenth century

Model	(1) Total marital fertility rate	(2) TMFR with different ages at marriage	(3) Correction for celibacy	(4) Correction for illegitimacy	(5) Convert to GRR	(6) Convert to NRR	(7) Convert to intrinsic growth rate
I	4.42	4.42	3.76	3.81	1.86	1.00	0.0000
II	4.42	5.50	5.12	5.44	2.65	1.46	0.0126
I	100	100	100	100	100	100	
II	100	124	136	143	143	146	

This table is closely similar to that used in Wrigley and Schofield, *Population History of England*, table 7.29. Further details of its construction may be found in the text accompanying table 7.29.

In the lower panel of the table the figure relating to model II is indexed on model I=100.

Notes Column 1. Marital fertility rates in both models are averages of the rates in the 12 reconstitution parishes listed in table II and cover the whole parish register period. Female mean age at first marriage assumed to be 26.5 years.

Column 2. Female mean age at first marriage assumed to be 26.5 years (model I) and 23.5 years (model II).

Column 3. Proportion never marrying 0.15 (model I) and 0.07 (model II).

Column 4. Illegitimacy ratio 1.5 per cent (model I) and 6.0 per cent (model II).

Column 5. Sex ratio at birth 105 males per 100 females (i.e. column 5 = column 4 × 100/205).

Column 6. Mortality in both models as in Princeton model North female tables, level 8 (e_0 = 37.5 years).

Mean age at maternity 33 years (model I), 31 years (model II).

$NRR = p(\overline{m}).GRR$, where $\overline{m}$ = mean age at maternity.

Column 7. Intrinsic growth rate $r = \log_e NRR/t$.

Mean generation length , $t \doteq \overline{m} - \dfrac{\sigma^2 \log GRR}{2\,\overline{m}}$

In order to enable the effects of changes in marriage-related behaviour to be identified easily both the model populations shown in Table VII share the same marital fertility and mortality, as explained in the notes to the table, but in other respects they differ considerably. The object of the table is to quantify the effects of changing marriage characteristics in terms of their relative contribution in raising the intrinsic growth rate.

Fig. VII: Gross reproduction rates, illegitimacy ratios and prenuptial pregnancy proportions

Sources GRR: Wrigley and Schofield, *Population History of England*, table A3.1. Illegitimacy ratios and prenuptial pregnancy proportions: see source note to fig. V.

Notes The GRRs refer to 5-year periods centring on the years shown. The data for illegitimacy and prenuptial pregnancy both refer to 5-year periods beginning a year before the years shown (i.e. 1670–4, etc.): thus the GRRs refer to periods offset by one year from those for the other two series (1669–73, etc.).

The first column shows the average number of children born to a married couple on the assumption that the female age at marriage was 26.5 years and that all couples survived to the end of the wife's reproductive period. The figures were derived by using the average age-specific marital fertility rates found in the 12 reconstitutions listed in Table II. In column 2 female marriage age is reduced to 23.5 years for the model II population; that is, marital fertility was held constant but marriage age in this case was reduced roughly as indicated by Table III.[43] In column 3 both figures are reduced but in differing proportions. At the beginning of the period (represented by model I) 15 per cent of all women were assumed to have remained single, but by the end (model II) only 7 per cent. The first figure is therefore reduced by a larger percentage than the second $(4.42 \times 0.85 = 3.76;$ $5.50 \times 0.93 = 5.12)$. The disparity between the figures representing the two model populations therefore increases. The ratios at the foot of the table show that difference in marriage age alone would cause fertility in model II to exceed that in model I by 24 per cent. Taking proportions never marrying into account increases the disparity to 36 per cent.

The disparity is still further increased when allowance is made for the very different levels of illegitimacy in the two populations (column 4). The rise in illegitimacy during the eighteenth century was sufficient to raise the ratio between fertility in the two model populations to the point where the level of fertility in model II was 43 per cent higher than in model I.

The figures in column 5 differ from those in column 4 only in that they relate to female children rather than to all children. The conversion is a necessary step towards calculating the intrinsic growth rate via the female net reproduction rate but the ratio figure on the bottom line of the table remains unchanged.

In column 6 the net reproduction rates are given. They represent the ratio between the size of two successive female generations in a stable population and are therefore determined by prevailing levels of mortality as well as fertility. In order to isolate the effect of marriage changes during the eighteenth century mortality was assumed to be identical in the two model populations, but the ratio between the model II and model I figures is nevertheless higher in column 6 than in the previous column. This occurs because the earlier marriage age in the model II population implies an earlier mean age at maternity, and this in turn ensures that with constant mortality a higher proportion of women survive to reproduce.[44]

---

[43] Details of the marital fertility rates used may be found in Wrigley and Schofield, *Population History of England,* table 7.25. The use of over-all age-specific marital fertility rates may lead to a slight overstatement of the difference in total marital fertility between the two model populations, but the use of rates derived from different age at marriage cohorts was a refinement ignored in this exercise.

[44] This and other related points are examined in greater detail when the same pair of model populations is described in Wrigley and Schofield, *Population History of England,* pp. 265-9.

The absolute level of the figures in the top panel of column 6 are as significant as their ratio to one another. In model I, representing schematically the state of affairs towards the end of the seventeenth century, the net reproduction rate (NRR) is exactly 1.00. Such a population will display no tendency either to rise or decline in the long run as long as its fertility and mortality remain unchanged. In contrast in model II the NRR is 1.46. Each succeeding generation in these circumstances would be almost half as large again as its predecessors.

Net reproduction rates can be converted into intrinsic growth rates, and these are given in the final column of Table VII.[45] They show that the changes which occurred in marriage and marriage-related behaviour in the course of the eighteenth century were sufficient to have raised the annual rate of growth of the population from zero to 1.26 per cent, *even though there was no change in either mortality or age-specific marital fertility.* The intrinsic growth rate reached its maximum level in England in the decades 1811–21 and 1821–31 when it was about 1.63 and 1.72 per cent per annum respectively.[46] Thus, assuming that the stylized representation of change between the late seventeenth and early nineteenth centuries set out in Table VII accurately epitomizes the course of events, it shows that about three-quarters of the acceleration in the growth rate which took place over the period is attributable to the increase in fertility brought about by changing marriage behaviour, a finding which accords well with the empirical data on fertility change and the intrinsic growth rate set out in Figure II.

*   *   *

The gap between the increase in growth rates attributable to marriage changes and the total increase in growth rates is explained by the improvement in mortality in the eighteenth century.[47] Although mortality accounts for only about a quarter of the over-all acceleration in growth rates, its influence was none the less conspicuous since the mortality changes were not evenly spread throughout the period. Even if the increase in the intrinsic growth rate had been purely a function of fertility change, there would have been some acceleration in the rate of change between the last quarter of the seventeenth century and the first quarter of the nineteenth, but the change

---

[45] For an explanation of the relationship between the net reproduction rate and the intrinsic growth rate see A. J. Coale, *The Growth and Structure of Human Populations*, pp. 16–25.

[46] Wrigley and Schofield, *Population History of England*, table A3.1.

[47] Marital fertility, which might also have entered into the picture, appears to have changed very little. There was, however, a slight rise in the age-specific marital fertility rate for women aged 20–24 between the first and second halves of the eighteenth century (table II). The rise may be regarded as, in a sense, spurious since what it reflected was not a change in fecundity, pregnancy wastage, lactation habits, or some other factor affecting fertility, but rather an even sharper fall in age at 'marriage' than that shown in table III since a far higher percentage of young brides were pregnant at the time of their wedding.

would not have been very marked. The improvement in mortality was strongly concentrated towards the end of the period as a whole and plays a major part in explaining the very striking acceleration in population growth rates in the later decades of the eighteenth century.

This phenomenon is clearly visible in Figure VIII. In this figure the information given in Figure II is recapitulated but in the form of a 5-point moving average (so that each reading refers to a 25-year rather than a 5-year period centring on the date indicated). Presenting the data in this form reduces the impact of short-term movements in fertility and mortality and makes it easier to pick out changes in secular tendency. Consider the points for 1681, 1741 and 1816 (and therefore referring to the periods 1669–93, 1729–53 and 1804–28). Between 1681 and 1741 the intrinsic growth rate grew from slightly above zero to just under 0.5 per cent annually, or by about 0.45 per cent, and this change was due virtually entirely to rising fertility. Mortality had fluctuated considerably between 1681 and 1741 but ended almost exactly where it had started. Between 1741 and 1816 the intrinsic growth rate rose from about 0.5 to about 1.7 per cent annually, but if mortality had continued at the level of 1681 and 1741 the increase would have been only from about 0.5 to 1.25 per cent annually (as may be seen by transferring the point representing 1816 horizontally to the left until it lies vertically above those for 1681 and 1741). The difference of nearly one half per cent (1.7–1.25) is attributable to the significant improvement in mortality occurring over the 75 years between 1741 and 1816.[48]

Using the same years it is also easy to appreciate the effect that would have been produced by improving mortality between 1741 and 1816 if fertility had remained constant but mortality had followed its historic path. By inspection it will be seen that the intrinsic growth rate would have risen from just under a ½ per cent to rather less than 1 per cent per annum. Had this happened the demographic history of England over the next two generations would have been very similar to that of Sweden. Fertility, mortality and intrinsic growth rates in the two countries would have borne a marked resemblance to each other.[49]

Too much should not be made of the precise relative contributions of fertility and mortality to changing growth rates during the 'long' eighteenth century. By dividing the period in a different way, or by taking another

[48] The increase in the intrinsic growth rate attributable solely to fertility increases was 0.45 per cent in the first period (1681–1741) and 0.75 in the second (1741–1816). Since the first period covered only 60 years and the second 75 years, the average annual increase in the intrinsic growth rate due to fertility change was fairly modest (from 0.0075 to 0.0100). The increase in the intrinsic growth rate attributable to mortality, in contrast, was nil in the earlier period but 0.45 per cent in the second, or 0.0060 per annum. This was still only 60 per cent of the comparable figure stemming from fertility increase, but it served to make the general contrast between the two periods far more pronounced, since the over-all average annual rise in the intrinsic growth rate went up from 0.0075 in 1681–1741 to 0.0160 in 1741–1816.

[49] This is readily visible in Wrigley and Schofield, *Population History of England,* fig. 7.13.

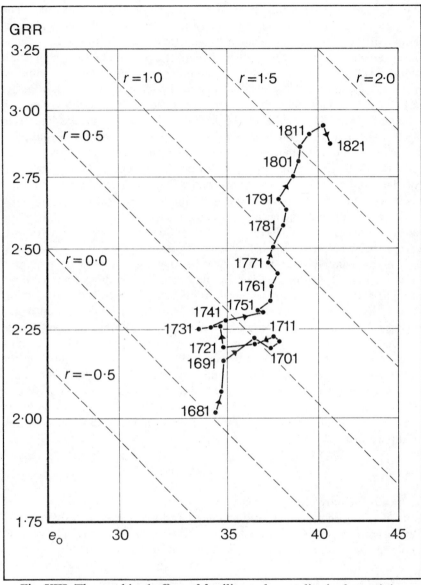

Fig. VIII: The combined effect of fertility and mortality in determining intrinsic growth rates 1681–1821 (quarter-century data)

Source Wrigley and Schofield, *Population History of England*, fig. 7.12.

Note The years indicated are the central years of the 25-year periods to which they refer.

GRR   gross reproduction rate

e_0 expectation of life at birth

r intrinsic growth rate (per cent per annum)

See also notes to fig. 2:

starting date, a somewhat different impression might be conveyed. The digression into this issue, however, is a convenient introduction to a wider issue which may serve to provide a context for the English experience. The improvement in mortality which took place in England in the later eighteenth century was probably no greater than in other western European countries; nor was expectation of life unusually high. Estimates of expectation of life at birth are available for only two other countries, France and Sweden, and then only from the middle of the century. Figure IX shows data from 1750–1830 to illustrate the broad similarity of tendency in the three countries. In all three countries mortality moved indeterminately between the 1750s and the 1780s. Thereafter there was mild improvement in England and Sweden, and a truly remarkable mortality fall in France which brought about a gain of 10 years in expectation of life over the next four decades. By the 1820s the three countries were broadly on a par with each other, whereas in the third quarter of the eighteenth century mortality in France was exceptionally severe by English or Swedish standards.

It is immediately clear from Figure IX that the exceptional population growth rates reached in England by the early nineteenth century were not brought about by a distinctive mortality history. Paradoxically, although it is true that the improvement in mortality explains a large fraction of the increase in the second derivative of population growth in the later eighteenth century, it was not this feature which appears to have distinguished England from other countries so much as her fertility history which accounted for the bulk of the first derivative of population growth throughout the 'long' eighteenth century, and for virtually all of it until about 1740. We have seen that the rise in fertility in turn was almost entirely a function of changes in marriage behaviour. How then did England compare with other countries in this regard?

*   *   *

France is the only other country with which a tolerably full comparison of nuptiality and related topics can be made. Perforce, therefore, attention will be concentrated on France with occasional reference to Sweden. The contrast between the history of marriage in England and France in this period is

---

Fig. IX: Female expectation of life at birth in England, France and Sweden
Sources England: Wrigley and Schofield, *Population History of England*, table A3.1 (female expectation of life was assumed to be 1.5 years greater than that for the sexes combined). France: Y. Blayo, 'La mortalité en France de 1740 à 1829', *Population*, XXX (1975), numéro spécial, Démographie historique, p. 141. Sweden: E. Hofsten and H. Lundström, *Swedish Population History. Main Trends from 1750 to 1970*, Urval no. 8 (Stockholm, 1976), p. 54 (the e_0s were read off from fig. 3.8).

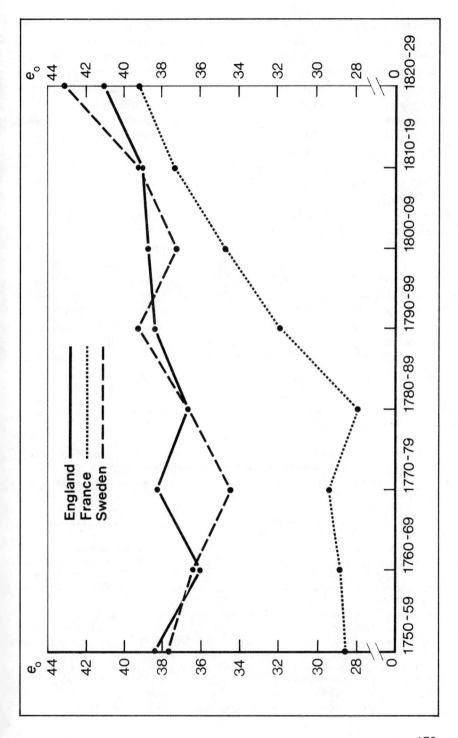

remarkable. While men and women were marrying earlier and more universally in England, both age at marriage and the proportion never marrying were rising in France. In England when nuptiality rose, illegitimate fertility also rose: in France the relationship was reversed, for the illegitimacy ratio rose steadily as nuptiality declined. In both countries changes in prenuptial pregnancy proportions tended to parallel those in the illegitimacy ratio, but even here there were major differences, and not simply in the prevailing level of prenuptial pregnancy but also in its structural character. In France prenuptial pregnancy was more prevalent among older brides than among younger ones, whereas in England the opposite tended to be the case.

The main nuptiality trends in the two countries are summarized in Figure X. The pattern of change in England will already be familiar from its earlier description. Women married at younger and younger ages from the late seventeenth to the early nineteenth century though marriage age was probably rising by the second quarter of the nineteenth century.[50] Until late in the eighteenth century the proportion never marrying also fell. It is possible for reasons discussed above that the fall continued a little longer than is suggested by the graph but the incidence of marriage was probably declining before the end of the eighteenth century, having changed trend before there was a comparable change in the timing of marriage. In radical contrast age at first marriage for women rose steadily in France until the last quarter of the eighteenth century while the proportion never marrying (sexes combined)

[50] The singulate female mean age at marriage in England, based on 1851 census data, was 25.8 years, more than two years higher than the figure for 1800–24 given in table III. The two are not properly comparable since the latter was based on information from only 12 parishes, but it is probable that age at marriage rose, and certain that the crude first marriage rate fell over this period. Wrigley and Schofield, *Population History of England,* table 10.3 and fig. 10.11.

Fig. X: Female age at first marriage and proportions never marrying (sexes combined) in England and France

Sources England: Age at first marriage, table 3. Proportions never marrying, fig. 3. France: Age at first marriage, L. Henry and J. Houdaille, 'Célibat et âge au mariage aux XVIIIe at XIXe siècles en France. II. Age au premier mariage', *Population,* XXXIV (1979), p. 413. Proportions never marrying, ibid., 'I. Célibat définitif', *Population,* XXXIII (1978), pp. 50, 57.

Notes The French data relating to proportions never marrying used in this figure were originally calculated in relation to cohorts of birth. They are here presented by their approximate dates of marriage on the assumption that the average age at marriage was 25 years. Thus the birth cohort data for the decades 1670–79, 1680–89 onwards are represented by readings at 1700, 1710, and so on. They were obtained by taking simple averages of the male and female figures. For the birth cohorts 1740–65 no estimates for males were published, and for this period it was assumed that the male figures differed from the female figures by the average difference between the two series over the preceding 16 quinquennial birth cohorts.

The English age at marriage data were cohorted by date of marriage and are represented by the midpoints of the quarter centuries to which they refer. Thus 1675–99 is shown at 1687, and so on. The English proportions never marrying refer to cohorts who would on average have been 25–9 at the dates shown.

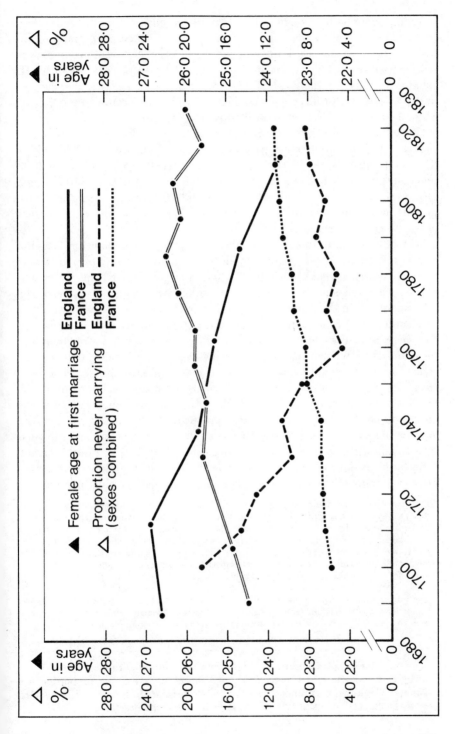

rose uninterruptedly, though it had virtually levelled out at the end.[51] The combined effect of changes in the timing and incidence of marriage in England between the beginning and end of the 'long' eighteenth century was sufficient *ceteris paribus* to have raised fertility by 36 per cent (Table VII, column 3). A comparable calculation for France suggests that the changes in the timing and incidence of marriage occurring between about 1700 and about 1800 would have reduced fertility by 19 per cent.[52]

Trends in the illegitimacy ratios in England and France are shown in Figure XI. Data for France are available only from the 1740s by which time the English ratio had already risen considerably from its very low level two generations earlier (Figure V). The ratio in France was initially well below the English figure but rose more rapidly, especially after the 1790s, to reach much the same level as the English in the second and third decades of the nineteenth century.

If a more accurate measure of illegitimacy were available for England which related the total of illegitimate children to the numbers of single women, its trend would be similar to that of Figure XI but the rise would be more marked since the illegitimacy ratio rose strongly in spite of the concurrent fall in the proportion of unmarried women of child-bearing age. The ratio is a more dubious measure of the trend in the illegitimacy rate in France because it rose steeply while nuptiality was falling and when therefore the number of women at risk was rising. Yet it is probable that a more refined measure would show a similar, if more subdued rise, and it is very clear that the relationship between marriage and illegitimate fertility in the two countries was strikingly dissimilar. In England whatever sanctions operated to delay or inhibit marriage were also effective in reducing fertility outside marriage, and conversely easy entry into marriage was accompanied by a relaxation of constraints upon illegitimate fertility. In France, on the other hand, as the waiting time to marriage grew longer and more uncertain there was some tendency to more widespread liaisons outside marriage, as

[51] For reasons explained above the proportion never married can be calculated only for the sexes combined when using English back projection data, and the French data for men and women have been combined in figure X to preserve comparability, but it may be of interest to note that the percentage of persons never marrying rose far more for women than for men, rising from 5.2 per cent in the generation marrying about 1700 to 13.6 per cent in that marrying about 1820. The loss of male life during the revolutionary and Napoleonic wars largely accounts for the contrasting trends for the two sexes. Henry and Houdaille, 'Célibat et âge au mariage. I. Célibat définitif', p. 50.

[52] The calculation was made using the same marital fertility rates as those used for the model populations in table VII, and embodying the assumption that female age at first marriage rose from 24.5 to 26.5 years while the percentage never marrying rose from 5.7 to 11.2.

Fig. XI: Illegitimacy ratios in England and France
Sources England: see source note to fig. 5. France: Y. Blayo, 'La proportion des naissances illégitimes en France de 1740 à 1829', *Population*, XXX (1975), numéro spécial, Démographie historique, p. 68, table 4 (first hypothesis).

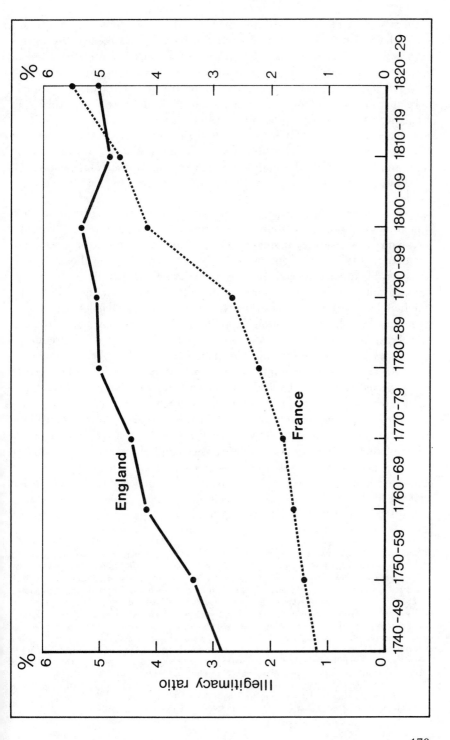

if there were a pent-up pressure which could no longer be met by unions which had been sanctioned by church and society. It is noteworthy in this regard that when the control of fertility within marriage grew common in France in the course of the nineteenth century it was closely accompanied by a fall in marriage age, as if unions were formed earlier and more freely once such action no longer necessarily tended to increase family size.[53] In England, once more in strong contrast, when the control of fertility within marriage became more and more widespread from the 1870s onwards, it was followed for a full generation by a *decline* in nuptiality.[54] Though family limitation reduced substantially the danger of impoverishment through excessive fertility it did not tempt English couples to embark on marriage earlier.

Where so much else concerning the history of marriage differed between England and France it will occasion no surprise that patterns of prenuptial pregnancy also displayed points of contrast. Table VIII shows that prenuptial pregnancy was far less common in France than in England though it rose considerably during the eighteenth century broadly in parallel with the rise in illegitimacy. The rates were not greatly different in the four major subdivisions used by the Institut National d'Etudes Démographiques in grouping French reconstitution data except that if the north-west quarter is subdivided into northern and western sectors, the level of prenuptial pregnancy proves to be very high in the north (exceeding 200 per thousand in 1790–1819) and substantially below the national average in the west. In every period shown in Table VIII the national rate for older brides was higher than for younger brides. In the south-east and south-west this was true throughout but in other regions the pattern weakened over time. In the north-east and north-west the rate for younger women was the higher in 1740–69 and 1790–1819 (and in the northern half of the north-west quarter this was true continuously from 1740–69 onwards). Until the end of the eighteenth century, however, the positive relation between the age of a bride and her likelihood of being pregnant was fairly strong and consistent. Henry permitted himself the speculation that 'les jeunes filles avaient moins de mal

---

[53] National trends in marital fertility and in the proportion of women in the child-bearing age groups who were married are set out in E. van de Walle, *The Female Population of France in the Nineteenth Century* (Princeton, 1974), table 5.5. Van de Walle also demonstrates very high negative correlations between marital fertility and proportions married by department in France 1831–51, and shows that 'the largest increases in proportions married tend to occur in those areas where marital fertility has dropped most' over the same period. He is cautious about the conclusions which may properly be drawn from the observed correlations. E. van de Walle, 'Alone in Europe: the French fertility decline until 1850', in C. Tilly (ed.), *Historical Studies of Changing Fertility* (Princeton, 1978), table 7.2 and p. 277. Earlier, however, he and Lesthaeghe argued, because of evidence that the fall in marital fertility tended to precede changes in nuptiality, that 'traditional checks to marriage were relaxed where marital fertility was being controlled'. R. Lesthaeghe and E. van de Walle, 'Economic factors and fertility decline in France and Belgium', in A. J. Coale (ed.), *Economic Factors in Population Growth* (London, 1976), p. 213.

[54] Wrigley and Schofield, *Population History of England,* tables 10.3 and 10.4.

Table VIII: Prenuptial pregnancy in England and France (children born/baptized 0–7 elapsed months after marriage: rates per 1,000)

	England				France		
	under 25	25 and over	all		under 25	25 and over	all
1650–99	82	114	95	1690–1719	44	74	62
1700–49	212	148	178	1720–39	52	75	64
1750–99	303	250	283	1740–69	70	78	72
1800–49	342	244	314	1770–89	93	123	107
				1790–1819	116	136	124

Sources Henry, 'Fécondité . . . dans le quart sud-est', p. 881; Houdaille, 'Fécondité . . . dans le quart nord-est', p. 385; Henry and Houdaille, 'Fécondité . . . dans le quart nord-ouest', p. 918; Henry 'Fécondité . . . dans le quart sud-ouest', p. 998. Cambridge Group reconstitutions (parishes listed in table II).

Notes The French rates are unweighted averages of the four quarters of France used by INED. It should be noted that for south-west France only the rates for the under- and over-25s were published. It was assumed that the over-all rate in this instance was the mean of the two sub-categories. No data were published for south-west France for the period 1690–1719. It was assumed that the rates for the south-west in 1690–1719 bore the same relation to the average of the other three quarters in this period as was the case in the next period 1720–39. The English rates are unweighted averages of 12 parishes. The numbers of cases in some small parishes are rather restricted, and the individual rates therefore unreliable, though the problem is greatly alleviated by averaging. Since several reconstitutions finish early in the nineteenth century the rate for 1800–49 refers chiefly to the first two decades of the half-century.

à observer la chasteté que les veuves dont le mariage avait éveillé les sens' as a possible explanation of the observed pattern.[55]

The very different over-all level of prenuptial pregnancy in England will already be familiar (Figure V). Entry into a reproductive career and the timing of marriage were more loosely connected with each other than in France. The over-all proportion of couples whose first child was baptized within eight months of marriage was always much higher in England.[56] The English figure was between two and three times the French except in the later seventeenth century when nuptiality and fertility were both at a very modest level in England. As in the case of illegitimacy, the rising figures for prenuptial pregnancy in the two countries in the eighteenth century took place against contrasting backgrounds. Marriage in England became more widespread and took place at younger ages; in France nuptiality was declining. Early and universal marriage in England was associated with very widespread anticipation of marriage on the part of the couples concerned, whereas in France the rise in prenuptial pregnancy marched in step with a rising marriage age and an increasing level of permanent celibacy. Perhaps in France prolonged courtship may have tended to increase the proportion

[55] Henry, 'Fécondité . . . dans le quart sud-ouest', p. 999.
[56] The English data in table VIII are given for 0–7 months after marriage rather than 0–6 or 0–8 as in figure V, to enable a direct comparison to be made with the French data.

of pregnant brides; or marriage may have been necessary to make good an increasing number of casual lapses.

The age pattern of prenuptial pregnancy in England further underlines the contrast between the societies on either side of the Channel. When pregnant brides were relatively rare in England the pattern resembled that found in France but as nuptiality increased and age at marriage fell the rate of prenuptial pregnancy among young brides rose very rapidly but among older brides the rise was less marked. After 1700 younger brides were more likely to be pregnant than those who married later; among the former the rate roughly quadrupled between the late seventeenth and the early nineteenth century, whereas among the latter it barely doubled.

*　　*　　*

Fifteen years ago Hajnal published an essay which proved widely influential in heightening our consciousness that the demography of pre-industrial western Europe was highly unusual if not unique among traditional societies. He showed that nuptiality was characteristically much lower than elsewhere both because couples married late and because a substantial proportion of both sexes never married. Since then there has been ample confirmation both of the accuracy of his observations and of their importance.[57]

The west European marriage pattern is significant not only because it implies—or at least is consonant with—demographic rates, economic structures, patterns of co-residence and household structure, systems of service, and structures of familial authority notably different from those found in other traditional societies, but also because it is so flexible. When the timing of female marriage is no longer largely a function of physical maturation (as in societies where reaching menarche means marriage), and many women never marry, marriage behaviour may be responsive to social and economic influences which alter its timing and incidence from one period to the next. Furthermore, differences in economic organization and social norms may cause different communities to respond very differently to similar pressures or circumstances. The west European marriage pattern, in short, is better described as a repertoire of adaptable systems than as a pattern.

A comparison of England and France in the eighteenth century is very instructive in this regard. Both possessed nuptiality characteristics clearly within Hajnal's 'European' canon, but they differed so substantially as to demonstrate that there were significantly variant forms within it. The same comparison also illustrates a related point. European marriage systems must be understood to connote not simply the characteristics of marriage *sensu*

[57] The findings of the Princeton fertility project as they come to be published have established the accuracy of Hajnal's judgement both of the general characteristics of the 'European' marriage pattern and of his view that a line drawn from Leningrad to Trieste would roughly mark the boundary of the west European pattern. Hajnal was at pains to stress the extent to which his essay represented a development of Malthus's original insight into the issue. Hajnal, 'European marriage patterns', p. 130.

stricto but also of reproduction generally whether within or outside marriage. Laslett's advocacy of the notion of a procreative career is of value here.[58] English eighteenth-century fertility history could be only imperfectly understood if marriage were treated in isolation from illegitimacy and prenuptial pregnancy. Certainly the history of marriage should not stop short with matters such as changes in marriage age and incidence but should embrace illegitimate and quasi-legitimate unions.

There is an important sense in which this chapter, though now in its concluding paragraphs, should be regarded as having reached only the end of its first phase. Space does not allow any but the most cursory attempt to explain what has been described. The *explicandum* has been set out but what explanation can be offered for it? Why should nuptiality have increased so remarkably in eighteenth-century England? Why should illegitimacy and prenuptial pregnancy have such a distinctive relationship with nuptiality? And why should what is observable in England have contrasted so markedly with the parallel phenomena in France in the same period?

There is evidence that the secular changes in nuptiality which took place in England over a period of more than three centuries between Elizabethan and Victorian times were closely associated with the secular trends in real wages, with the former taking place some 20–30 years later than the latter.[59] The issue, however, is too complex to be treated more fully here. Nor indeed, even if the demonstration of such a relationship is valid, does it explain how economic changes became transmuted through social norms in a manner which resulted in an 'appropriate' change in individual decisions about marriage and reproduction both within and outside marriage.

Comparisons of different national marriage characteristics raise even more complex issues. The changes in marriage age and proportions marrying which took place in France in the eighteenth and early nineteenth centuries were broadly paralleled in Sweden. Population in both countries was increasing and the growth in towns and cities, though substantial, was not so large as to prevent a steady rise in rural population. It is tempting to see in the nuptiality history of these two countries a 'peasant' variant of the European marriage system while in England a 'wage' variant was firmly established. In the former the number of viable holdings might be supposed to be growing less rapidly than the population, which might make matches harder to make, while in the latter a system of 'ecological niches' had given way to one in which current and prospective earnings had replaced access to land as a criterion for eligibility to marry. But such speculations should at present be regarded as no more than a hypothesis to be tested and its plausibility may prove superficial.

[58] P. Laslett, 'Illegitimate fertility and the matrimonial market', paper to the International Colloquium on Historical Demography, *Nuptiality and Fertility: Plural Marriage and Illegitimate Fertility in Historical Demography*, Kristiansand, September 1979.

[59] Wrigley and Schofield, *Population History of England*, table 10.2 and accompanying text.

Although the contents of this chapter may represent only the first step towards a fuller appreciation of the characteristics of English society and economy which allowed marriage to exert such a powerful influence on population trends in eighteenth-century England, at least an examination of the more strictly demographic aspects of marriage behaviour may have clarified what might be termed the mechanics of growth and the cluster of attributes whose close interrelation is so evident. English society was so constituted that at times of low over-all fertility every aspect of the reproductive careers of women up to the point of marriage was conducted conservatively. Marriage itself was postponed until the later twenties and many never married. Illegitimacy was rare, especially when the very large proportion of unmarried women in the prime reproductive age groups is borne in mind. And very few women became pregnant until after a decision to marry must already have been made. Such pregnancies were not merely rare over all but rarer among young women, who might then go on to have a large family, than among older women whose families were necessarily smaller.

There was an equal, if opposite consistency of behaviour when over-all fertility was high. Women married in their early twenties on average and teenage brides were common. Few remained permanently single. Illegitimate births were common. Up to a quarter of all women began their reproductive careers with an illegitimate birth, and as many again started with a prenuptial conception which must have antedated any firm decision to marry. Fertility within marriage varied little if at all, but the combined effect of the changes in marriage, understood broadly as the act of embarking on a reproductive career, was sufficient to account for the lion's share in the acceleration in the population growth rate in England which over a period of little more than a century moved from stagnation to a brief spell as the country with the fastest growth rate in western Europe.

Malthus, at the beginning of his first *Essay on Population*, offered as one of his two basic postulates the rule that 'the passion between the sexes is necessary, and will remain nearly in its present state'.[60] He did not then argue that fertility was constant. Indeed, very few of his successors have appreciated as clearly as he did the immense importance of marriage in moderating population growth rates in western Europe.[61] Yet it remains remarkable, and a worthy subject for far more investigation than has been undertaken hitherto, that changes in marriage behaviour in England in the 'long' eighteenth century were sufficient to raise the gross reproduction rate from under 2.0 to more than 3.0, a change as remarkable, if opposite in direction, as that which occurred in Ireland during the nineteenth century.

[60] T. R. Malthus, *An Essay on the Principle of Population* (London, 1798), p. 11.
[61] The accuracy of Malthus's understanding of this issue is discussed in E. A. Wrigley, 'Malthus's model of a pre-industrial economy', paper to the International Congress on Historical Demography, *Malthus Yesterday and Today*, Paris, May 1980.

A contemporary of Malthus, Sir Walter Scott, remarked in a very different connection that 'that which gratifies the impatience of the human disposition will be practised in the teeth of danger, and in defiance of admonition'.[62] If one were to combine the thoughts of Malthus and Scott, it might seem remarkable to the modern eye that men and women in the late seventeenth century, in an age when the Puritans were in retreat and the court allegedly licentious, should have regulated their reproductive lives with such prudent forbearance, and in such striking contrast with the behaviour of their great-grandchildren. Until such matters are better understood, it will be easier to demonstrate the importance of marriage in late pre-industrial England than to explain the patterns of individual behaviour which underlay it and gave rise to the delusively simple movements of trend lines on a graph.

[62] Sir Walter Scott, *The Heart of Midlothian* (Everyman's Library, London, 1956), p. 16.

VIII

Women, Work and Marriage in Eighteenth-Century France[1]

OLWEN H. HUFTON

In April 1766 a servant-girl named Marie Caton died in the Hôtel-Dieu at Lyons. The cause of her death was most probably tuberculosis. She left in a portress's charge the clothes she had brought in a bundle, a pair of shoes, a buckle and a notebook, the last never retrieved by her relatives. In this little book, her *carnet,* she, like others of her kind, either recorded or had recorded for her, the sums she had earned from four successive employers and the deductions made by these whenever she dipped into her wages to buy shoes or clothing or for any extraordinary expenditure she might make.

Marie Caton was born in Varacieux in Dauphiné. She had come to Lyons in 1758 and in the eight years between her arrival and her death she had held three jobs. First she had been a *servante* at a satin manufacturer's. Next she had spent two to three years as a maidservant in the house of the parish priest at Saint-André-en-Bresse, finally returning to Lyons to work as *servante* to two silk manufacturers. Her labours, all deductions made, had resulted in an annual saving of 15 to 18 *livres*—the lesser sum accumulated while servant to the priest, the larger while in the joint employ of the two silk manufacturers. When death abruptly terminated her endeavours Marie Caton had saved about 100 *livres*.[2]

There was not a working-class girl in eighteenth-century France who would not have recognized what Marie Caton was about. Indeed, her story is unusual only in its detail for few *carnets* survive among the annals of the poor. She was involved in the serious business of accumulating a dowry, a

[1] The most exciting studies of all aspects of marriage and family life in eighteenth-century France are J. L. Flandrin, *Familles. Parenté, maison, sexualité dans l'ancienne France* (Paris, 1976), now translated in abridged form, *Families in Former Times* (Cambridge, 1976); *Amours paysannes* (XVIe–XIXe siècles), coll. *Archives* (Paris, 1975); 'Mariage tardif et vie sexuelle', *A.E.S.C.* (1972); and 'L'attitude à l'égard du petit enfant et les conduites sexuelles dans la civilisation occidentale: structures anciennes et évolution', *Annales de Démographie historique* (1973). Much of what follows is based on the magisterial local studies of the society and economy of specific regions. Of these F. Le Brun, *Les hommes et la mort en Anjou aux 17e et 18e siècles* (Paris, 1971), P. Goubert, *Beauvais et le Beauvaisis de 1600 à 1730* (Paris, 1960), G. Bouchard, *Le village immobile. Sennely-en-Sologne au XVIIIe siècle* (Paris, 1972) and M. Garden, *Lyon et les Lyonnais au XVIIIe siècle* (Paris, 1970) are particularly instructive.

[2] Archives Départementales Rhône, F302. Such *carnets* are only very occasionally found in hospital records. Sometimes the sums were registered by a notarial act at the end of the girl's employment, e.g. G. Bouchard, *Le village immobile,* p. 253.

preoccupation shared by 100 per cent of other country girls and one which was pursued by them with an impressive single-mindedness, for upon their success in laying hold of a capital sum, however small, depended their own future well-being and that of the family unit of which they would form a part. A dowry was the necessary preliminary to a successful rural marriage. Why this should be so reflects the overriding concern of a society of smallholders, whether leasers or owner-occupiers, who recognized the paramount necessity of a little capital to hire and stock a farm and, as Flandrin also insists, were cognizant that marriage and child-rearing needed whatever financial security several years of effort could achieve. In the particularly difficult conditions of the second half of the eighteenth century the continuing preoccupation of the young with laying hold of something in the way of reserves goes a long way towards explaining the rising age of marriage to what were in historical terms very high levels (26–28 for a woman and 28–30 for a man).

The largest category of women in eighteenth-century France was that of the daughters of smallholders or of agricutural labourers, village artisans and casual odd job men. As such, these women could expect to become wives of men in roughly the same position unless conspicuous success in the dowry stakes made an aspirant master weaver or tradesman cast covetous glances towards their little dowries. They lived in a society in which 50 to 90 per cent of holdings, depending on the region, were insufficient to maintain a family of even two or three children; where agricultural labourers were chronically underemployed except at the peak periods of the agricultural year; and where industrial wages, except in a very few favoured industries in exceptional times, were not calculated with the support of a family in mind. Perhaps as much as a third of the population on the eve of the Revolution lived under the threat of imminent destitution and a fifth had crossed into the twilight world of the perpetually hungry.[3] In such a society a young country girl embarking on her working life at about the age of 12 had behind her enough experience to endow her with visceral appreciation of the utter fragility of the economy of the working classes. The odds were heavy that she was illiterate and she was probably also undernourished and the victim of vitamin-deficiency diseases. She might already know how to spin or make simple lace or how to wash raw cotton or wool. She might know how to unwind silk from a cocoon or how to embroider ribbons. Such experience would depend on her family's use of industry as an ancillary income to the smallholding. Certainly in her young life she had been accustomed to gather grass and weeds to feed scrawny cattle and rabbits, to feed poultry and pigs, to search for firewood and to comb the hedgerows for

---

[3] O. Hufton, *The Poor of Eighteenth-Century France* (Oxford, 1974), pp. 25–68, gives in greater depth the socio-economic background of this section of French society. See also O. Hufton, 'Women and the family economy in eighteenth-century France', *French Historical Studies,* 1976, pp. 1–22.

fruit, herbs and firewood, to look after younger children and to make the daily soup from herbs, vegetables, a little animal fat and hard bread. She was, to a limited degree, mistress of some of the arts which would assist her in the business of survival. She also knew with total clarity that she would have to provide for her own future and (as she surveyed her parents and her relatives) she could have few illusions about that future. All the evidence pointed to her having to labour unremittingly throughout her life, though in adolescence the form that work would take in adulthood was not always clear. Even so, this teenager was aware that her own efforts were about the only thing she could rely on. She could, for example, expect nothing or next to nothing from her parents. In emancipating her to earn her own living and expecting no remittances to them from her labours, a rural family considered they had done their bit to help their daughter on her way. Only the few parents with something to spare (an insignificant proportion in the social sector with which we are concerned) would contribute money to swell a girl's dowry or give a bed or linen, and the laws regulating inheritance made her a very puny beneficiary from whatever patrimony there was to be had. The parents of such a girl had nothing to spare and few possessions other than a scrap of land, a ramshackle cottage, bed, chair, table, cupboard, cooking pots, utensils and perhaps a few scrawny cattle or poultry. If she had brothers no land would come her way, and if her brothers were supposed to pay her compensation (as a few local *coutumes* suggest) one has little evidence to indicate that such payments were invariably honoured. If her father was one of the small minority of industrial workers who owned their own equipment, it was unlikely to pass to her if there was a male heir.

One can perhaps exaggerate the degree to which the country girl was disadvantaged *vis à vis* her brothers. Boys too were usually despatched from their homes in early adolescence with a view to putting a little aside which would contribute towards hiring and stocking a farm upon marriage or acquiring an industrial skill which would help in later life to buttress a frail family economy. In any case the family inheritance was of limited extent, often insufficient to maintain a family. Yet the smallholder's son, at least where the father was owner of his land, knew that something might one day come his way, while the daughter knew she could rely on nothing but her own efforts.

Female earning potential was, of course, severely restricted—a generalization applicable not merely to the 12-year-old girl but to women at all stages of their working life. Female industrial wages were not calculated to permit any woman a fully independent existence. They were pitched as low as possible and the meanest creature on the employment market, least able to defend her economic interests, was the married woman who already had a roof over her head. Her willingness, indeed frequently dire need, to work—albeit at derisory rates—determined the general level of pay for female industrial work, which rarely rose above eight *sous* per day and could fall in the lacemaking areas of the Massif Central to under four (the price of two to three pounds of bread). Such sums might feed and clothe a girl. They might even purchase candles and fuel, but they certainly would not both feed her *and* keep an independent roof over her head.[4] The girl who failed to marry and so obtain that independent roof faced a predictably bleak future. She could anticipate nothing but destitution. Historically she might be described as the woman most likely in old age to be found on the list of a *bureau de charité,* lacking adequate clothing, food and fuel. Such a ghost of Christmas future must have served to heighten a girl's realization that marriage was the only possible salvation. Yet to offer a viable existence, rural marriage needed the funds to hire and stock a farm and this was regarded as a joint venture. How could the country girl come by capital?

The simple answer was by domestic service, but one must understand this term in its full eighteenth-century sense as comprehending not merely the resident domestic drudge but anyone who lived and worked on someone else's premises, and in towns or cities involved in textile production this could mean and was most likely to mean that the girl was a resident industrial employee. Residence and payment on leaving service (hence the justification for running an individual *carnet*) were the only common characteristics of the *servantes*—a group so large that in cities they could reach 13 per cent of the total population.[5]

We can categorize domestic service in the following way: firstly, substantial farms employed a *servante* whose job was largely, though rarely exclusively, concerned with agricultural tasks; secondly, noble and bourgeois families in the towns or in the country *châteaux* had a demand for household servant-girls in the sense that we can most readily understand; thirdly, craftsmen and shopkeepers employed girls as maids-of-all-work, helpers in the shop or café-bar, etc.; lastly, textile manufacturers in most of the major industries were dependent on cheap, resident female labour to perform most of the tasks preparatory to the weaving and finishing of cloth.

Given an open choice, which rarely existed, the young country girl aspired in the first instance to become a farm *servante* on a modest if perhaps more substantial holding than that of her parents but one essentially in the same neighbourhood. Over all, work in the local *château* was a poor second though such a statement demands regional qualifications. Many seigneurs were impoverished. Others were not only of modest standing but targets of community ire. A girl in Bas Languedoc, for example, could find that in working for the seigneur she had crossed a frontier which isolated her from

---

[4] J. Merley, *La Haute-Loire de la fin de l'ancien régime aux débuts de la troisième République (1776–1886)* (Le Puy, 1975), pp. 123–5; M. Garden, *Lyon et les Lyonnais*, pp. 304–5; F. Braudel and C. E. Labrousse, eds., *Histoire économique et sociale de la France* (Paris, 1969), II, 669–70; A. Lefort, 'Salaires et revenus dans la généralité de Rouen au XVIIIe siècle' *Bulletin de la Société d'émulation de la Seine Inférieure* (1855–56), p. 219.

[5] Probably 8–10 per cent is a working norm for the north and south but a smaller percentage for the towns and bourgs of the centre.

the community and put her 'on the other side'. Such a position would have severely limited her opportunities for meeting a suitable young man, particularly where youth group cultures focused on poaching and flouting seigneurial regulations. In Brittany and the Cotentin, where seigneurialism retained a more patriarchal image and was more closely integrated with community life, work in the *château* was viewed more favourably. In regions of great farmsteads like the Beauce seigneurs were very thin on the ground and the option on such work scarcely presented itself.

As a farm *servante* the young girl would be expected to tend poultry, milk goats and cows, prepare cheese and butter, turn haymaker and gleaner when the occasion demanded it, cook meals, carry food and drink to workers in the fields, tend vegetable patches, carry water to sheep terraces or wherever it was required, wash and mend clothes and fill in any spare time with domestic industry or with extracting oil from nuts, picking oakum or chestnuts, plaiting onions and garlic and so on. Such a position carried with it multiple advantages in addition to family proximity. Paramount among these was that she would marry someone local and that her work was a superb training for the aspirant farmer's wife. She was also a relatively protected being, though she was far from totally guaranteed proof from dismissal in difficult times. Breton farmers, for example, found that keeping a girl paid only when the flax harvest was abundant and female farm labour could be turned to spinning. When the harvest failed, girls were unceremoniously shown the door and presumably had to live on their accumulated earnings at home until better times returned.[6] Notwithstanding, the turnover in farm *servantes* was much less pronounced than that in other branches of female labour and the demand for positions lagged far behind the supply. A girl's chances of finding such work were dictated by the social structure of her village, that is whether or not farms were large enough to require a farm *servante*. Similarly the girls who found work at the seigneurial *château* or were imported from rural estates to serve in town houses were dependent on the existence of substantial personages in the area. Such girls were initially employed in the least agreeable jobs as scullery maids and cleaners, but preferment to ladies' maids and nursery-maids and the multitudinous auxiliaries involved in the running of a considerable establishment was obviously open to girls who proved themselves in any way competent. To find a job in a house of social standing required contacts, and kinship above all else played its part in recommending girls to a vacancy. The *parlementaires* of Toulouse employed in their city establishments girls drawn from their estates in the Lauragais, those of Rennes from their lands in the valleys of the Rance and the Vilaine.

The presence of the États de Languedoc in Montpellier meant that girls

---

[6] Archives Départementales Ille et Vilaine, C1745. Subdélégation de la Guerche, 1785, 'bien des fermiers qui avaient des servantes les ont mises dehors par défaut de filasse . . .'. A. D. Rhône B. Maréchaussée 1733, Claudine Lambert, 1770 Marie Frinillade.

were brought into the city from the Rouergue, villages in Lodévois or the Plaine Biteroisse or wherever the delegates had rural properties. Girls stepped into positions vacated by aunts, cousins and sisters, and women in jobs were quick to recommend their relatives when vacancies occurred.[7] Employers too were dependent on such recommendations to ensure that the girl brought into the house was a known quantity rather than someone drawn from an immigrant urban sector whose standards were suspect and who might rob the house, disappear with the laundry or open the door to robbers. The girl who found work in the substantial household was also very much in a minority and the over-abundant woman-power of rural France was obliged to look towards the town.

The town offered two kinds of labour. On the one hand was the work of resident drudge. Such a girl was a carter of heavy washing to and from the local washplace, load carrier of heavy vegetables and firewood, runner of errands as well as cook and cleaner. On the other hand was the position of semi- or full-time industrial employee. (Where industry offered part-time employment, the girl combined both sets of tasks.) The heavy use by manufacturers of resident female labour is explained by economics. The cheapest and most efficient way in which a master weaver or carder in the woollen and silk industries could obtain spun thread in excess of that provided by his wife and children (it took the full-time efforts of four women to supply one full-time woollen weaver) was to have a resident girl to whom he paid a fixed sum when she left his service in addition to her board.

On the whole, the putting out system in France was of patchy extent in comparison with Britain, particularly in regions of difficult terrain south of the Loire. The Midi, broadly interpreted to include Lyons, was at this time the most industrialized part of France. In the Languedoc woollen industry, for example, especially during the period of buoyant expansion before 1750, a master weaver or carder was dependent on the services of girls from the Rouergue and housed at least one not only to spin thread but for a whole range of tasks like running errands. To this girl he would pay a fixed sum when she left his service and in the meantime he supplied her board. The masters in the traditional woollen industries of Languedoc and Normandy were very modest men and it suited them not to have to lay out wages regularly and indeed to use the girl's accumulated wages on their own account—the cause of innumerable defaultings in payment to the girl in time of slump.

The silk weaver of Lyons, Nîmes or Tours was a particularly heavy employer of female labour because the early stages of silk production were

---

[7] A. Châtelain, 'Migration et domesticité féminine urbaine en France, XVIIIe siècle—XXe siècle', *Revue d'histoire économique et sociale*, VII (1969), 506–628, remains the best survey of different levels of domesticity; L. Cahen, 'La population parisienne au milieu du XVIIIe siècle', *Revue de Paris* (1908), gives instances of the households of the ducs d'Orléans, Conti, Crozat and the *Parlementaire* family, Aligre.

labour-intensive and though not all the weaver's employees were resident, even the most modest *manufacturier* usually had a couple of young girls living on the premises, often sleeping under the loom. Most of these resident girls did the job of the *dévideuse* who unwound the silk from the cocoon, or of the *tireuse* who was a highly skilled auxiliary performing at the loom itself. Both passed under the name of *servante chez les ouvriers en soie*. The *dévideuse* had to extricate the silk threads from the cocoon. This was done over a basin of water kept at near boiling-point. The cocoons were immersed for several minutes until the sticky substance (*séricine*) binding the threads together had dissolved. The *dévideuse* plunged her hands into the water and took out a disintegrating cocoon, detaching and unwinding the filament. Once an easy and continuous thread emerged she took a second, then a third and a fourth cocoon and treated them in the same way. The four strands were then twisted and the remains of the *séricine* bound them together. As they cooled, the *dévideuse* wound the thread by hand on to a bobbin.

Even so brief a description of her labours enables us to appreciate that though the work was unpleasant—the girl suffered frequent scaldings and her clothes were perpetually damp with evil-smelling steam—it was a job easily learnt, something the immigrant girl could do immediately on arrival and at which she was, within the space of a few weeks, probably as dexterous as she would ever be. In time she might be taught the work of a *tireuse*, a task demanding much greater skill and draining her physical resources to their utmost.[8] She would not necessarily be paid more for her endeavours, but in time of textile slump a manufacturer would be more willing to retain a girl with a variety of skills.

The cotton and mixed fibre industries of the north were for many reasons less prone to use resident labour on any extensive scale. These industries were located in areas of easy communications where industrial growth was coincident with the relaxation in guild control and where all branches of textile production were gradually pushing out into the villages. Yet even in Lille, Troyes and Rouen the resident spinner cum Jill-of-all-trades had her place. Alternative solutions had to be found for girls from villages where the putting out system did not exist if they could not secure resident work. Girls came into the textile towns in groups and rented a room to share the costs of fuel and light. They sought out a manufacturer and hired any equipment and accepted raw material for spinning. Lottin's recent study of the *filles mères* of Lille suggests that such girls were in very parlous economic circumstances and that their chances of capital-accumulation were slight.[9]

In European terms, the lace industry has been a classic industry for putting out since the equipment needed and the quantities of raw material

---

[8] J. Godart, *L'ouvrier en soie* (Geneva, 1976), reprint, pp. 67–75, describes various types of female labour within the industry.

[9] A. Lottin, 'Naissances illégitimes et filles mères à Lille au XVIIIe siècle', *Revue d'histoire moderne et contemporaine*, XVII (1970), 278–322.

in question were modest. Yet in the Pays de Velay which had the most considerable lace industry in France and which was organized largely on the putting out model, philanthropic endeavour during the late Counter-Reformation had evolved an institutional framework which shaped lace-making to produce the dowry requirements of the young country girls. (We should remember that the Velay is some of the least penetrable terrain in France and that outwork deliveries to the villages could be very irregular for several months of the year.) In the 1660s a group of pious ladies (*les béates*) had formed an association, helped by funds from the bishop of Le Puy and generous lay donations, the purpose of which was both to provide rooms to serve as dormitories and working quarters for groups of eight to ten girls, and to supervise the provision of soup and bread. The girls paid for food, heating costs and candles which permitted them to work at night, but they did not pay rent, and other costs were kept down to a minimum. Although *les béates* were not involved in the marketing or business side of lace production, they assisted the young girl in all kinds of ways. They held on to payments made to her and kept records to help her in the accumulation of her all-important dowry.[10]

Village traditions were extremely important in determining patterns of female labour migration. Generally a girl might hope to find work within 20 to 50 miles of home. In Chartres servant-girls were drawn from the Beauce, in Bayeux from the Bessin, in Troyes from Champagne Troyenne. But while some villages sent girls in a single direction, others despatched them in several. The most complex mobility patterns were found south of a line drawn from Pau to Belfort which included zones of emigration like the Pyrenees, the Alps and the Massif Central, where towns were few, almost all farms insubstantial, and therefore undemanding of paid resident labour, and where the young were pushed into a variety of customary labour migrations. The regions which attracted migrants south of this line were principally the cities of the Mediterranean littoral and Lyons. But the youth of the western Pyrenees were drawn towards Bordeaux and those of the northern Massif towards Paris. Paris almost alone among northern cities had a very broad recruitment zone, receiving girls from Normandy, Picardy and Île de France, Burgundy, the Beauce and the Massif.[11]

To pick at random a village and describe its patterns of female labour mobility is somewhat invidious but such an exercise illustrates the importance of both custom and contact. The village of Saint-Geniez-d'Olt lay a few kilometres from Rodez and was remarkable for the poverty of its inhabitants,

[10] J. Arsac, *La dentelle au Puy des origines à nos jours* (Le Puy, 1975), p. 24.
[11] Arch. Mun. Bordeaux, Hôpital Saint-André, Décès, 1780–86; Arch. Mun. Marseille GG 652, Sépultures. Hôtel-Dieu 1780–86; Arch. Mun. Bayeux F., Etats de la population, An IV; Arch. Hosp. Dijon F32; J. Combes-Monier, 'L'origine des Versaillais en 1792', *Annales de démographie historique* (1970), pp. 237–51; M. Vovelle, 'Chartres et le pays chartrain, quelques aspects démographiques', *Contributions à l'histoire démographique de la Révolution Française* (Paris, 1962) pp. 129–52.

the smallness of its farms and the almost total lack of any ancillary domestic industry. A girl born here had no prospect of becoming a farm *servante* in the region. Rodez was nearby and was a diocesan centre and seat of some minor law courts, but it was an insignificant town whose population on aggregate had a relatively low demand for domestic labour and there was little industry to generate the kind of mixed economy which encouraged households elsewhere to take on a girl. A few girls from Saint-Geniez-d'Olt found work in Rodez. More were pushed, however, towards Millau, about 60 kilometres from Rodez, which had a significant domestic glove-making industry and hence heavier labour demands than did Rodez. Others walked still further, crossing the bleak Causse du Larzac to find work in the woollen industry of Languedoc centred at Villeneuvette, Clermont de Lodève and Lodève itself. The royal-protected industry at Villeneuvette had in Colbert's time actively encouraged immigrant girls from the Rouergue to work as resident spinners, and once established, the pattern persisted. But this did not represent the limits of their odysseys. The occasional servant-girl from Saint-Geniez-d'Olt is certainly to be found in the death registers of the Hôtel-Dieu of Montpellier, and perhaps even in those of the other cities of the littoral. It seems likely that the seasonal migrations of male farm labourers of the Rouergue southwards to work on the vine harvest opened up contacts and prospects which served their daughters and sisters well, in addition to providing an important safe escort for the girl walking literally hundreds of kilometres in search of work.[12]

The obstacles which lay between a girl and the realization of her coveted dowry were legion. She might fall sick and be unable to earn. She might be the victim of slump. She might become pregnant. The commonest recruit to the ranks of the unmarried mother was the servant-girl. Distant from her family, lodged in an attic, a cupboard or even expected to sleep on the kitchen floor, she was a prey for both master and apprentice. Starved of affection and given scant opportunities for leisure with which, it might be argued, she was in any case ill-fitted to cope, the wonder is that on days off more of them did not succumb to the advances of the military and employees also on holiday for whom pursuit of the servant-girl was a leisure-time activity.

Textile slumps invariably led to dismissal or laying off. Or the manufacturer himself might go bankrupt or die leaving debts to discharge and inadequate funds to cover them. Since the servant-industrial worker was paid only when she left her place of employment, she could be particularly vulnerable to such defaultings on payment. Certain cohorts (girls of the same age sharing the same working years) might be peculiarly disadvantaged by cumulative bad runs of textile slump (the experience of Lyons in 1756, 1766,

---

[12] O. Paloc, *Recherches démographiques et sociales sur Millau au XVIIIe siècle* (D.E.S. Toulouse, 1958); Arch. Mun. Montpellier 608, Hôpital Saint-Eloi, Registre de Décès; Arch. Mun. Rodez, Hôpital Général Registre de Décès.

1771, 1784 and 1787) in which layings off were frequent.[13] Perhaps also hardship back home in the form of bad harvests caused girls to part with some of their hard-earned money, or a brother or sister in need dipped into their reserves.

Disease was, of course, the most formidable and often final enemy. The textile populations of Lyons and the north were ravaged by tuberculosis, even if the disease had yet to be adequately classified, while periodic epidemics of typhus, typhoid, miliary fever, smallpox and viral pneumonia took a heavy toll.

Yet let us assume that the working girl surmounted all the obstacles in her path and emerged with something at the age of 26 or 28—let us say 80–100 *livres*. Whom did she marry? Choice of partner fell into a number of predictable categories, though one cannot offer any degree whatsoever of statistical indication as to the relative incidence of choice which would apply to the country as a whole. The dowry has its main justification in a rural context and the country girl in the first instance aspired to become a farmer's wife, using her dowry in the time-honoured way to purchase linen, utensils, livestock, and to help in the payment of the first year's rent. The girl who had been a *servante de ferme* in a modest or substantial household and who had suffered no interruptions in her labours would have no trouble in finding a *valet de ferme* whose efforts in accumulating a capital sum equalled or surpassed her own. But even if the girl had gone to town, she was not necessarily precluded from returning home with her little sum and setting up as a smallholder's wife, just as many country boys who had served an urban apprenticeship hoped to return home and become farmers. Certain smallholding societies were chronically dependent on an inflow of capital. Let us take the village of Massat in the Pyrénées Ariégoises. Here there was absolutely no demand for resident agricultural labour. Holdings were small. There was virtually no such thing as the substantial farm, and farmers in Massat were heavily dependent on seasonal migration, particularly winter movements into the Mediterranean cities for survival. Indeed, their wives and their young children were regular winter visitors to Toulouse where they begged in the porch of Saint-Sernin. What more natural step than for the young girl—and indeed the young boy—to seek a servant place or other employment in Toulouse?[14] But equally clearly, they did not lose the urge to return to their villages. Such a lure is perhaps to be explained by psychological factors, a Proustian urge to return to the paths trodden in one's youth and to the families one loved, or by more mundane considerations such as an alliance with someone who might one day own a patch of land through inheritance. For these smallholding societies the relationship with

[13] Garden, *Lyon et les Lyonnais*, pp. 298–306.
[14] J. Rives, 'L'évolution démographique de Toulouse', *Bulletin d'histoire économique et sociale* (1968), pp. 137 ff.; M. Chevalier, *La vie humaine dans les Pyrénées Ariégoises* (Paris, 1956).

the land was the crucial factor, and occupancy or ownership of a few terraced strips could appear as a greater security to the young couple than anything which could be offered in town.

The return of the children of Massat to their snow-covered, wind-swept, barren village is in stark contrast to the behaviour of the young of the Lauragais, who also came to Toulouse as adolescents in search of work but whose breach with their native village was final. The Lauragais was a *pays de grande culture,* characterized by very large farms worked by hired labour. Such farms may have employed a *servante de ferme* but their incidence was too restricted to solve the work-problem of the day labourer's daughter. Some employment was also offered by the great *parlementaire* houses whose rural estates lay in this rich region, but again such openings were limited and in any case may have been restricted to girls from certain families—estate employees, the *crème de la crème* of village society. Hence the adolescent drawn from the Lauragais towards Toulouse had no option on return: no possibility of hiring a farm on marriage in the area of origin. An exact parallel with the pattern of the Lauragais would be that of the Beauce. Standing no chance of employment locally, adolescents were driven towards Chartres (limited in its demands), Orleans (more promising), and inevitably Paris with its potentially endless resources. These adolescents would not return home to found a household, but a decade or more later whom would they marry?

A minority of servant-girls married other servants, and of these a small proportion may have remained in service. The demand for married servants of both sexes was restricted and the couple intending so to spend their lives probably had to wait for an opening. Affluent ecclesiastics preferred to employ a married couple, so as to avoid potential scandal, and substantial noble and bourgeois houses were probably relieved enough to maintain the services of a couple known to be honest. But the married couple were very much the exception among the eighteenth-century servant class. Whom then did the successful servant-girl (one who had earned a dowry) marry, and with what kind of existence in view? If she married a man from similar servant employment, what did the couple have in mind as a means of existence?

There are no comprehensive answers to such questions—marriage contracts merely record when servant married servant—but there are pointers found elsewhere, not least in the *bureau de placement* for the Parisian wet-nursing business which records the profession of both spouses, and in lists of lodging-house keepers.[15] The logical thing for a servant-girl to do on marriage with her dowry and her husband's contribution was to set up in business—running a drink-shop or café-bar—or for the pair to go into a

---

[15] Archives de L'Assistance Publique. Inventaire Fosseyeux 283. Registres pour Anne Françoise Delauney, recommanderesse de la ville et faubourg de Paris (1732–36). P. Risler, *Nourrices et meneurs de Paris au XVIIIe siècle* (D.E.S. Paris X, 1971), p. 40.

branch of the catering business. In large cities, such as regional capitals like Bordeaux, the catering trades—*traiteurs, rôtisseurs, pâtissiers,* were organized into guilds, but there was scope for the ambitious couple to try to set up in business. Many Parisian servant-girls seem to have married into the catering business—perhaps having formed contact with the apprentice making deliveries to the back door—and their dowries, however small, were a useful supplement in setting up shop. Then in the large cities there was the occupation of running apartments and lodging houses. *Servante* became *concierge,* a position which enabled her to rear her children and at the same time have an income from the tenants while her husband went out to work.

So far our concern has been with the most numerous type of girl in eighteenth-century France: the one born in a village who left home in search of a dowry. The daughter of a working-class family in the town did not leave home as an adolescent to seek work. If her family was an industrial unit or had a business such as cook shop, *cabaret* (tavern or café-bar), fish or vegetable stall, then she worked for her family. The washerwoman's daughter almost automatically became a washerwoman, the seamstress's daughter a seamstress and so on. If employed within the family she could not expect wages, and the odds on anything coming her way in the form of a dowry were remote. Otherwise, she sought employment in the garment trades as *couturière,* stay-maker, trimmer of hats and bodices and the multitudinous allied occupations, returning home in the evenings to her family. Less vulnerable than the country girl distant from her family, if she could not hope to accumulate a dowry, at least she did not share all the privations involved in dismissal when economic circumstances deteriorated. Her family did not show her the door. In textile towns and *bourgs* (2,000–5,000 inhabitants) manufacturing society (excepting silk production) was remarkably endogamous: spinner married carder or weaver, born and working but a few houses away, with conspicuous regularity. The woman could offer her husband no capital sum, but she had her skill. She expected nothing else from him, looms could be hired or purchased cheaply second-hand. Other trades required little or no equipment, and the town-girl looked to continuing her work much as before, merely changing her father's abode for her husband's.[16]

There was also a large unskilled, urban, female workforce, of flower-sellers, pedlars of haberdashery, load carriers, etc., who certainly had nothing in the way of a dowry to proffer at marriage. This indefinable category of women and girls from the country who had failed in the dowry stakes (from circumstances often beyond their control), were not precluded from finding

[16] S. Chassagne, A. Dewerpe, Y. Gaulupeau, 'Les ouvriers de la manufacture de toiles imprimées d'Oberkampf à Jouy-en-Josas, (1760–1815)', *Mouvement social,* no. 97 (1976), pp. 82–3. Perforce, such societies became less endogamous during a period of rapid growth. S. Chassagne, 'La formation de la population d'une agglomération industrielle, Corbeil-Essones (1750–1850)', *Mouvement Social,* no. 97 (1976), pp. 99–102. J. P. Gutton, *La sociabilité villageoise dans l'ancienne France* (Paris, 1979), p. 45.

a marriage partner but, lacking capital or a substitute skill, they could anticipate marriage only to a man in the same position. The girl without a dowry was certainly the model for the future, but in so far as France was still largely a society of smallholders the accumulation of a dowry to help the young couple set up a holding remained as yet the dominant ambition of the majority.[17]

The silk industry of Lyons allows one to see the immigrant girl with a hard-earned dowry set alongside the modest master silk weaver's daughter who could expect little in the way of a capital sum. The master silk weaver's daughter shunned the most arduous tasks in silk production (such as the job of *tireuse*), though she was employed within the family unit. Maurice Garden has demonstrated that the ambitious apprentice pursued the immigrant girl with a dowry, rather than the indigenous *Lyonnaise*. Hence the wife of a master silk weaver was likely to have been an immigrant *tireuse* or *dévideuse* whose efforts had produced the financial means whereby he purchased his mastership. The master's daughter, on the other hand, was likely either to marry outside silk manufacturing or to marry an apprentice without the means to buy a mastership—a future journeyman. Throughout their lives this couple were likely to remain employees.[18]

The available evidence points unmistakably towards hard economic considerations as the main determinant in choice of partner, and hence on the whole reinforces Shorter's views on the apparent absence of romantic love between the contracting parties. Shorter notes the lack of emotion on the death of one spouse and her quick replacement, and the rapidity with which a vet was brought in to tend sick cattle while a dying wife was unlikely to receive the administrations of a doctor. His picture is over-painted.[19] One must treat the emotions of the past with some circumspection and delicacy. Hard-headed financial considerations were clearly very important in determining choice of a partner, especially in smallholding societies. Physical attraction in village lore was a will-o'-the-wisp.[20] We should also remember that a woman or man who was not pock-marked, who did not suffer from a vitamin-deficiency disease, or from a congenital defect was in a small

[17] O. Hufton, *The Poor*, pp. 32–3.

[18] Garden, *Lyon et les Lyonnais*, pp. 296–7.

[19] E. Shorter, *The Making of the Modern Family* (New York, 1977), pp. 54–61. French historians reacted very strongly to Shorter's thesis—a particularly pertinent review by Emmanuel Todd, *Le Monde des Livres*, 14 October 1977: 'Il aurait mieux valu ne pas poser le problème de l'amour en termes binaires comme un ordinateur peu subtil: l'amour existe, l'amour n'existe pas. Le problème, c'est la transformation du sentiment amoureux. Le lien qui s'établit entre un homme et une femme a certainement un rapport avec l'environnement: il ne s'établit pas dans un vide sociologique. Les villageois du passé, intégrés solidement dans de petites communautés, craignaient surtout la misère. Le sentiment d'entraide devant une nature hostile devait dominer la vie du couple. Aujourd'hui dans la société industrielle, on cherche surtout à vaincre la solitude . . .'.

[20] J. L. Flandrin, *Les amours paysans* (Paris, 1975), p. 130, gives several examples of provincial proverbs denigrating beauty which are usually variants on the theme *La beauté ne sale pas la marmite* (Provence-Languedoc).

minority. Industrial malformations—the stoop of the lace-maker and her progressively deteriorating vision, the distorted limbs of the *tireuse*—were common. A girl *without* varicose veins was counted a good catch in the Franche-Comté. These were stoical people, inured to hardship; they did not readily express emotion in the form of grief or sorrow and had learnt to accept death with resignation. Yet, that said, there was a great deal of joy, pleasure and evident exuberance in the relationship between young courting couples, which readily conforms to any romantic image.

Among the levels of society which are our concern, there was virtually no such thing as the arranged marriage. One cannot perhaps in any society at any time arrange marriages for people of 26 to 28 who had laboured for 12 or more years on their own behalf. The great folklorist Van Gennep was insistent on the ubiquitous presence of free choice among couples in *la France traditionelle,* and that choice of partner depended on a combination of factors of equal importance: personal attraction, village or community traditions, and shared interests (perhaps predominantly economic) of the parties concerned.

Certain social conventions existed which provided the young with opportunities to meet and get to know each other. One such practice, the *veillée* or evening get-together, allowed them frequent contact under the close supervision of family, employers and friends, but many more were rituals devised by the young themselves—the processions, dances and celebrations of carnivals, *fêtes patronales* and holy days, the weekly meeting of youth groups in the villages of the Midi or the *promenades* of the towns and cities.[21]

The *veillée* varied a little from region to region. Above all it was an evening work session, carried on in a particular cottage in which neighbours gathered and shared the burden of heat and light.[22] Everyone did something, even if it was only to crack nuts for oil or sort pins for a pedlar's tray. In the nuclear village or the small town the *veillée* could be a nightly event in the winter. This was the scene of chap-book reading and story-telling, of ballad- and hymn-singing, and of discussion of the conduct of seigneur, priest and tax agent. But it was also the opportunity for the young to become acquainted, exchange glances, smiles, share a bench and converse a little. In regions of non-nuclear villages, *veillées* were less frequent and had to be arranged occasionally by hiring a barn. Under such circumstances they were overtly the occasion for entertainment: dancing and jollification expanded and the work element receded. In other regions, like the Velay where lace-making was the sovereign preoccupation, the *veillée* was exclusively a female sphere and the men, for whom little domestic employment existed, sought out the *cabaret*. Where male social life focused increasingly on the *cabaret,* the *veillée* provided no opportunity for girl and boy to become acquainted. The girl who intended to marry did not set foot in a tavern. This was

[21] J. P. Gutton, *La sociabilité villageoise dans l'ancienne France* (Paris, 1979), pp. 47–51.
[22] Shorter, *The Making of the Modern Family*, pp. 124–6.

emphatically a male preserve, or the haunt of the woman who had nothing to lose.[23]

Where the *veillée* was a limited occurrence, or where, as in Haut Languedoc, it drew merely the women of the village, religious festivals, processions and dances clearly assumed a predominant importance in shaping the contacts of the young. In many instances the young arranged their own entertainments for these festivals. The young parish bachelors elected a leader (*le chef*), chose one of their number to play the drum, hired a fife-player, arranged the procession and the drinking and dancing which came afterwards. Sometimes the *chef* led *dônages* (pairing). At these ceremonies the *chef* pronounced, perhaps after drawing lots, '*je dône Pierre à Marie*', whose commitment to Pierre might be no more than a dance. If it was known that Pierre wanted to get to know a certain girl then the group conspired to bring this to pass. Youth groups frequently met for short periods on Sunday night, often at dances in the village square.[24] Sometimes they engineered a more prolonged relationship. In Burgundy at the beginning of winter the *garçons de paroisse* undertook to divide up the parish girls among themselves, often drawing lots, though perhaps an element of amicable exchange took place. But, the initial choice having been made, there was no changing until the year was up. The couple had to have time to become acquainted.[25] The Counter-Reformation Church tried in vain to limit the activities of the youth groups as contrary to the aspirations of a more austere faith, but failed to refashion the mores of the young.[26]

In towns and cities the rituals of urban courtship focused on walking (*la promenade*). Time off, usually confined to a couple of hours on a Sunday, allowed the working girl and boy to dress up. In the girl's case she perhaps pinned a scrap of lace on her bodice, wore a clean kerchief and shoes rather than clogs. Thus arrayed, boy and girl sallied forth on *la promenade,* a set itinerary known to all the young of the town where girls were surveyed and accosted by young men and gradually acquaintances were built up. Sometimes *la promenade* was merely a *sortie* along the main street, sometimes a tour of squares or public buildings. The Peyrou and the Place de la Comédie served Montpellier, the Place Bellecour did the same for some elements in Lyonnais society. In the cities there were several *promenades* and it is possible that immigrant communities or certain trades had specific preferences. Maidservants met with other maidservants from their native villages and were accosted by apprentices, perhaps from back home, perhaps even distant cousins, or perhaps from the place of one of their employments. It

[23] J. Tricoire, *Libertinage et prostitution à Versailles 1747–81* (D.E.S. Paris, 1973), p. 30.

[24] O. Hufton, 'Attitudes towards authority in eighteenth-century Languedoc', *Social History,* 3 (1978), 291–2.

[25] H. Forester, 'Le "droit de garçons" dans la communauté villageoise au XVIIIe siècle', *Annales de Bourgogne,* EXIII (1941), pp. 109–14.

[26] Gutton, *La sociabilité villageoise,* pp. 244–5.

could be a remarkably small world. Groups formed which eventually gave way to pairing, but it could be several weeks before a pair were actually seen walking together as a couple, and when they were it was the first visible manifestation of courtship. The boy would be seen buying drinks or sweets—sugared almonds—for the girl. Public manifestations of affection were important in showing the serious intentions of both parties. Few presents exchanged hands and when they did they were of a rigorously practical nature. In lace-making areas pedlars found the most common gift to be lace bobbins roughly incised with the couple's initials. Combs and hairpins, handkerchiefs and ribbons lagged behind pins and needles. A couple had to save for their future. Such a procedure could go on for years. *Promenades* might be in more secluded circumstances, such as round the ramparts or in adjacent woods.[27] Sexual intercourse might or might not occur. In a few areas up to 17 per cent of first births were premaritally conceived, but a norm in the region of 8 per cent shows that couples were on the whole quite chaste.

Illegitimacy rates, except in the large cities, rarely exceeded 4 per cent in the towns, though standards were clearly declining in this respect.[28] The servant-girl, the cotton spinner and the silk worker figure largely in the *déclarations de grossesse*[29] of their regions, a fact which probably bears witness to deteriorating conditions of work in the late eighteenth century. The astonishing fact when one considers that *servantes* and textile workers lived in such close physical proximity to their employers and fellow employees is that more were not caught in this way. Among the most hard-headed girls of eighteenth-century France were those from the Midi, reared in a strong tradition of feminine chastity, of whom a small fraction demanded from their lovers *promesses par écrit*, demonstrating that before the girl succumbed she had demanded a written attestation of honourable intentions. Such an attestation would in part preserve her good name, make her seducer seem particularly despicable, and afterwards expose him to the family's vengeance, but it would also ensure some financing of her labour and the rearing of her child. The concept of honour, perhaps under onslaught as girls moved further away from home, was still a very meaningful one in eighteenth-century

[27] O. Hufton, *The Poor*, pp. 358-60.

[28] *Histoire de la France rurale*, ed. G. Duby and Armand Wallon (Paris, 1975), II, 377-8. Here Le Roy Ladurie notes: 'Les conceptions prénuptiales passent souvent de 2 per cent du total des premières naissances légitimes vers 1680-1700 à 8 à 10 per cent vers 1765-85.' In *Bastardy and its Comparative History*, ed. P. Laslett, K. Oosterveen and R. Smith (London, 1980), the egregiously high bastardy levels of Paris (over 30 per cent) and Lyons (15 per cent) are made clear, and in Blayo's contribution, 'Illegitimate births in France, 1740-1829', pp. 278-83, the considerable regional variations within the national pattern are apparent. Even by 1789, the norm in rural areas was between 2 and 3 per cent. It must also be stressed that bastardy, with special consideration given to girls who are 'repeaters', and consideration to the phenomenon of husband-getting according to established rural rules, has not received the sophisticated treatment in France characteristic of the Cambridge school.

[29] These were statutory declarations made by the unmarried mother according to the laws of Henry IV, in which she named the author (or authors) of her condition.

France. Once engaged, an event supposed to take place no earlier than 18 months before marriage, the fiancé became the defender of the girl's honour—ideally under the vigilant eyes of relatives and above all brothers.

The relationship of the couple, once they had decided on marriage, fell into a logical progression. The decision was informally made public and a verbal promise was exchanged: *la parole* or *la foi du mariage*. The next stage involved the families of the couple and was sometimes formalized by a written agreement. Next the couple were affianced and from this stage, to break the agreement needed the consent of the Church. Lastly, the banns were read and the marriage solemnized.[30]

Before the church ceremony, in the case of those couples who had succeeded in prefacing the married state with the accumulation of a little capital, a notarial act recorded the contribution of the respective parties. Where the joint effects of the couple were under about 80 *livres,* then there was probably little point in paying out the few shillings required for notarial services. All one can say about this anonymous couple is that if they were rural day labourers, they faced the threat of destitution from the onset of marriage. Their existence, however, in increasing numbers at the end of the *ancien régime*, makes it difficult to talk about the average dowry. In any given region, over 50 per cent of couples registering their assets embarked on marriage with under 150 *livres*. Such a sum would provide the couple with a bed, a table, cooking pots and linen, and sometimes the contribution of the female partner was already expended on these goods and they were recorded in kind. It might be stretched to purchase a few hens or a piglet, but it would need to be twice as much again to purchase a cow and farm tools. The rural couple needed livestock if they were to revitalize their soil and if fat and protein were to be a permanent part of their diet. In the cities, the silk worker's dowry which could—though it did so in only a small minority of cases—rise to three or four hundred *livres,* might be the means whereby an apprentice could purchase his mastership and the two with their joint skills might move forthwith into independent production. In Paris the servant girl with 100 or more *livres* to her name, the apprentice butcher, baker, *rôtisseur* or *charcutier* (dealers in cooked meats), pastry cooks and those apprenticed to the drink trade (one must presume some of these contacts were made when deliveries were made to the back door), might set up an independent shop on their joint assets and skills. Indeed, the dowry makes most sense in certain particular contexts; that of a society of smallholders on the one hand, and that of a nation of petty shopkeepers on the other, to which one might add societies in which the purchase of a mastership was still crucial and the cost of such a purchase likely to involve more capital than the aspirant master could personally command. We have no more beautiful examination of the dowry at work (*sic*) than in Garden's study of

[30] J. M. Gouesse, 'Parenté, famille et mariage en Normandie aux XVIIe et XVIIIe siècles: présentation d'une source et d'une enquête', *Annales E.S.C.,* 27 (1972), 1139–54.

Lyons. Here the master's son pursues the successful *tireuse,* whereas his sister, unable to command the type of accumulated sum to help an apprentice acquire his mastership, can expect to marry a journeyman, the two remaining employees all their lives. The successful *tireuse* and her husband with his newly acquired mastership move forthwith into independent production, renting a room, hiring a loom and employing a girl from the mountains to serve as *dévideuse-tireuse.* The lace-maker's little hoard might go towards the purchase of a few sheep and domestic utensils. In the Velay the average dowry nestled in the region of 80 *livres,* but the girl's contribution would be exceeded by that of her partner who might put up twice that amount. A scraggy sheep could be bought for 15 *livres* and the newly wedded couple, who had waited on average two years longer than couples anywhere else in France to wed, had at their disposition the framework at least of a survival economy. She would now be an outworker in the lace industry, and he a shepherd on some of the most barren hills in France. Among the utensils bought when they set up home would be a pan with holes for roasting chestnuts, the chief carbohydrate constituent of their diet.[31]

The dowry and the notarial act recording the couple's joint contribution are of much greater value to the historian than a photograph of the marriage would be because they are also a pointer to the future and they allow one to speculate on the odds of the couple's staying on the right side of the line between poverty and destitution. The more the couple could purchase in the way of livestock, the better their hopes of fertilizing their crops, of adequate nourishment and of assets to be bartered in times of poor harvest. The smallholder would never again have the opportunity of raising money to put by. The materials and cooking utensils, the bed and the linen bought by the bride were expected to last through marriage. They might, in fact, make a second appearance in the notarial records when death removed the last partner. But they would be differently qualified—*un chétif lit, du mauvais linge, de vieux outils, tous usés*—all worn out. Dearly purchased by the young in terms of human effort, carefully amassed to cope with the problems of parenthood, pawned or sold in hours of need, these vestiges remained to bear witness to a lifetime's struggle, shabby, yet eloquent relics of the passage of a marriage.

---

[31] P. Bossis, 'Le milieu paysan aux confins de l'Anjou, de Poitou et de la Bretagne', *Etudes Rurales,* XLVII (1972), 145, makes 150 *livres* the average dowry for a girl in the Mauges. See also F. G. Pariset, ed., *Bordeaux au XVIIIe siècle* (Bordeaux, 1968), p. 368; Garden, *Lyon et les Lyonnais,* pp. 304–5; Bouchard, *Le village immobile,* p. 253.

IX

Scottish Marriage, Regular and Irregular
1500–1940[1]

T. C. SMOUT

Any broad survey of the history of marriage in Scotland must touch on a number of themes and encounter various difficulties. Our starting point is the difference between the marriage laws of Scotland and England, and the tension that arose between the two halves of the United Kingdom due to these distinctions before Lord Brougham's Act of 1856. Another point of considerable interest is the law of marriage in the sixteenth century, and the ceremonial, both religious and secular, that surrounded the wedding in the period of the Reformation and immediately afterwards. A third is the growth in prominence of irregular, or 'clandestine' marriage, from the seventeenth century to the early nineteenth century, and its subsequent decline in the middle decades of the latter.

Only with the establishment of the office of the Registrar General for Scotland in 1855 is it possible to consider marriage in a quantitative manner, owing to the poor quality of Scottish church registers and the intrinsic difficulties posed by the existence of irregular marriage. Thereafter there are excellent statistics, and the focus of the final section shifts to take account of them. There was a revival in the popularity of irregular marriage following changes in the law that made it akin to civil marriage in England. What determined which type of marriage couples sought? What was the relationship with the illegitimacy rate? More generally, what determined the timing of marriages (regular or irregular), within the week, within the year, and between one year and the next?

Inevitably this paper resembles a maze of alleys, but they are not all blind: our quest is to see whether anything of the social meaning of the act of marriage can emerge from the law, the ceremonies and the statistics.

* * *

Let us consider first the problem of the difference between Scottish and English law. In 1868, the Scottish judge Lord Neave celebrated national distinctions by writing a song, 'The Tourists' Matrimonial Guide through Scotland'.[2] It began like this:

[1] I am most grateful to the following for their comments on an earlier draft of the paper: Michael Anderson, Rosalind Mitchison, Brian Outhwaite, Sylvia Price, Anne-Marie Smout, William Walker. I alone am responsible for its inadequacies and errors.
[2] Quoted in 'Claverhouse' (Meliora Smith), *Irregular Border Marriages* (London, 1934).

Ye tourists who Scotland would enter
The summer or autumn to pass,
I'll tell you how far you may venture
To flirt with your lad or your lass;
How close you may come upon marriage,
Still keeping the wind of the law,
And not, by some foolish miscarriage,
Get woo'd and married an' a'.

> Woo'd and married an' a';
> Married and woo'd an' a';
> And not, by some foolish miscarriage,
> Get woo'd and married an' a'.

This maxim itself might content ye,
That marriage is made—by consent;
Provided it's done *de presenti*,
And marriage is really what's meant.
Suppose that young Jocky and Jenny
Say, 'We two are husband and wife',
The witnesses needn't be many—
They're instantly buckled for life.

> Woo'd and married an' a'; etc.

The verses caught the essence of Scottish peculiarity and English apprehension.[3] In England the law of marriage had been determined by Lord Hardwicke's Act of 1753 as modified by Lord Russell's Act of 1836: all marriages were equally regular, but could be in either the religious or the civil mode. The former took place in church before a clergyman in daylight hours after the publication of banns or (more rarely) after obtaining an ecclesiastical licence, while the latter took place before a registrar after he had posted notice of marriage. In Scotland, however, until as late as 1940, the only *regular marriages* were those performed by the clergy (though seldom in the nineteenth century in church) after publication of banns: register office weddings were unknown, and there was no legal obligation to register a marriage even after the start of Scottish civil registration in 1855—though most marriages were so registered. On the other hand Scotland recognized the concept of the *irregular marriage,* which in origin was a marriage simultaneously illegal and valid. It was illegal, because to be married except before a Church of Scotland clergyman was technically an offence under Acts of the Scottish Parliament of 1641 and 1649, re-enacted and modified in 1661, 1695, and 1698. In practice such acts had long fallen into disuse, and the Marriage Act of 1834 recognized as regular all marriages

---

[3] For surveys see *Encyclopaedia of the Laws of Scotland,* ed. Lord Dunedin, J. L. Wark and A. C. Black, IX (1930), 402–30; F. P. Walton, *Scotch Marriages Regular and Irregular* (Glasgow, 1893); A. I. M'Connochie, *Marriage and Registration* (Aberdeen, 1909). Strictly speaking the term 'clandestine marriage' should be reserved for marriages constituted with a religious ceremony, but not otherwise regular, and 'irregular marriage' for a marriage constituted without such ceremony: but in practical terms the use is synonymous.

performed before clergy of any denomination, providing the banns had been read in the established parish church. An irregular marriage had always been valid, however, because the Scots held to the blindingly simple doctrine that if any two unmarried people of lawful age (12 for a girl, 14 for a boy) wished to get married, if they were physically capable of marriage and not within the prohibited degrees of kinship, and they both freely expressed this wish and freely accepted each other in marriage, then they were married. Consent made a marriage—not the clergy, nor the civil official—but the consent of two people wishing to marry. The marriage did not have to take place in church, nor at any particular time of the day or night, nor even before witnesses, for it to be valid, but the consent of freely contracting parties did have to be proved.

The main complication arose, of course, out of the latter fact. Consent could be proved, for example, if both parties admitted to the magistrates to having exchanged consent and were subsequently fined for an irregular marriage. This was common in the early nineteenth century in certain Scottish burghs where the baillies exacted a small penalty, and their record of having done so served as *de facto* marriage lines: such was the case in the Canongate of Edinburgh, in Rutherglen, in Dumfries, and in Annan.[4] In the mid-nineteenth century irregular marriages (between Scots) became comparatively rare, but—as we shall see—they revived in popularity again. By the late nineteenth and twentieth centuries (after the Civil Registration Acts) irregular marriages were usually formally proved by a declaration before the Sheriff, who then provided a warrant which could be shown to the local registrar and which alone could enable him to register the marriage legally: this became especially common in the large burghs and comes very close to the English concept of civil marriage.[5]

Of course, if there was a witness to verbal promises of consent to marriage at the time they were exchanged, that itself was perfectly adequate to establish the validity of the marriage in law. It was a convenience if whoever heard the consent kept a record. That was the origin of the various eighteenth- and nineteenth-century 'registers of irregular marriages' kept by laymen. But there did not have to be a written record: a marriage could be proved valid if the consent was merely heard by any one witness who was prepared to say so later on in a court of law—'the ostler, or the chambermaid, or the post boy', as Lord Brougham put it.[6] If there was an interchange of letters that was also enough if they could be construed as indicating mutual consent to marriage. Lord Neave warned his tourists in a later verse of his song:

---

[4] *Report of the Royal Commission on the Laws of Marriage*, P.P. 1867-8, XXXII (henceforth cited as *R.C. Report 1867-8)*, p. xxii.

[5] See M'Connochie, *Marriage and Registration*, pp. 23-8.

[6] *Report of the Select Committee on Marriage (Scotland)*, P.P. 1849, XII (henceforth cited as *S.C. Report 1849*), p. 9.

You'd better keep clear of love-letters
Or write them with caution and care;
For, faith, they may fasten your fetters,
If wearing a conjugal air.

Consent could even be *presumed* by Scots law, in the absence of actual proof of it. If a couple exchanged promises to marry, not immediately but at some unspecified time in the future, and then had sex, and if these promises were in writing, or if the man and woman admitted to them under oath afterwards, the act of sex was held either in itself to make a marriage or, more accurately, to indicate that further consent to marriage must have passed between the couple.[7] That was a form of irregular marriage known to lawyers as 'marriage by promise *subsequente copula*'. There was also (and finally) an unusual form of irregular marriage 'by habit and repute'. 'A promise is a thing well known,' said Lord Brougham, giving evidence before a parliamentary select committee in 1849, 'a *copula* is a thing, I believe, I may say pretty well known in practice as well as in theory; but who shall define what is habit and repute?'[8] In fact the Scottish courts made quite a business out of its definition—a couple had to be held to have been married by their neighbours or friends who would testify that they habitually treated one another as man and wife in bearing and modes of address over several years before such a proof was admitted in the courts. Marriage by habit and repute was therefore proved only rarely, usually by a widow seeking her late husband's property or children wishing to remove the stain of bastardy. It was logical enough to presume consent in this way in a country where record-keeping was so bad and entering marriage so simple.

What alarmed the English (though not, apparently, the Scots) was the threat to property implicit in this simplicity. Their attitude was illustrated by Brougham's account of the aristocracy's response to any suggestion that their sons should study at Edinburgh University.[9]

'Edinburgh!' was always the answer—'the very last place in the world we should think of sending our son to: he would be married in 24 hours; there is no saying what would happen.'

He also recounted how his great uncle, the famous William Robertson, Principal of the University in the late eighteenth century, had immediately sent a young nobleman who was lodging with him home to England on discovering 'a kind of admiration . . . springing up for one of his daughters', in case the couple should suddenly marry. For if marriage rested only on the consent of people in love, or of people who pretended to be in love for the sake of getting hold of an heiress, was inheritance safe? Lord Hardwicke's Act, which came into operation in March 1754, had been aimed at the

[7] A previous oath before witnesses was held to be sufficient before the Act of 1834—see *Encyclopaedia*, pp. 413–14.
[8] *S.C. Report 1849*, p. 10.
[9] Ibid., pp. 13, 17.

English irregular marriages which up to that time had been celebrated in certain locations like the Fleet Prison in London. Even before Hardwicke's Act had passed into law, Parliament was exerting pressure on the Scots to introduce a comparable measure, ordering 'that the Lords of Session in Scotland do prepare a Bill for the more effectual preventing clandestine marriages in that part of the United Kingdom called Scotland and lay the same before this House in the beginning of the next session of Parliament'. They did so, and a bill was given a first reading in April 1755 but subsequently dropped, its opponents successfully arguing that such an act would interfere with religion, and that the inviolability of Scottish religion had been assured by the Union settlement in 1707.[10] The marriage laws of the two kingdoms thus came to diverge sharply, and any English couple who wished to marry in haste, or in secret, had only to come to Scotland to find a way round Lord Hardwicke's Act.

It was this traffic in runaways that brought fame to Gretna Green, on the main west coast highway from England to Scotland, and also to other almost equally important marrying points on main roads over the Border, such as Lamberton Toll and Coldstream Bridge in Berwickshire, which received fugitive English couples and married them on the spot.[11]

Anyone, anywhere in Scotland could, of course, have witnessed the marriage, but a folk custom grew up by which the couples would drive to be married by certain individuals who kept registers, witnessed the consent, wrote out certificates of marriage and often pronounced a quasi-religious form of words over the nuptial pair. Such men were rough diamonds, though not (contrary to the popular myth) blacksmiths. The most famous in the late eighteenth century was Joseph Pasley, described as:

> a big, rough hard-drinking Borderer. At this time he was tall and spare, and so strong that he could, with one hand, bend a stout poker over his bare arm, and straighten a horseshoe with his bare hands. In his opinion the only liquid fit for a man to drink was undiluted brandy (of a stronger proof than the present excise laws allow). For the last forty years of his life he daily drank one Scots pint, equal to two and a quarter English measure.[12]

The trade in English clandestine marriages at the Border was already under way in the 1750s (indeed, one of the Fleet parsons is said to have paid his debts and advertised his removal to Gretna on the passing of Hardwicke's Act), but it took off only with the construction of the turnpikes and the coming of the express coaches on the west coast route at the end of the century. The dramatic runaway marriage in 1782 of the heir to the Earl of Westmorland and Sarah Anne Child, heiress to the fortune of a London banker who pursued the couple and shot one of the Earl's carriage horses

[10] *R.C. Report 1867-8*, Appendix p. 77.
[11] 'Claverhouse', *Irregular Border Marriages* is the best account.
[12] Ibid., p. 43.

in a vain attempt to prevent them reaching Gretna, gave publicity to the business.

Pasley's heir apparent, Robert Elliot (who married into his family and was in his own words 'appointed . . . to succeed him'), presided over the weddings of 3,758 couples between 1811 and 1840, the numbers increasing from about 50 a year to almost 200 a year at their peak.[13] He was only one—though the busiest—of several 'marrying men' who competed fiercely for the trade. He issued printed marriage certificates surmounted by the Royal Arms and described himself as 'the sole and only parson of Gretna Green', though neither he nor any of his rivals ever took holy orders. One surviving register of the period belonged to one of his rivals, John Linton of Gretna Hall. It contains copies of 1,130 similar certificates issued between 1829 and 1855: the overwhelming proportion (probably 90 per cent) of these couples were English, and most appear to have come from Cumberland, although there is a wide representation from as far afield as Middlesex and County Sligo.[14]

It would be wrong, however, to imagine that all English men and women who took advantage of a Scottish irregular marriage were propertied: by the 1850s it had become so much of a working-class habit to contract marriage in this way that local northern English clergy and landowners were calling for penal legislation to stop it. A committee of the General Assembly discovered that 1,091 English couples were married in 1850 on the Scottish side of the Border, while only 6,207 underwent civil marriage by registrars in the whole of England.[15]

Nevertheless it continued to be the rich who made the headlines. The most notorious elopement of all was the abduction in 1826 of Miss Ellen Turner, a beautiful heiress of 16 years, by Edward Gibbon Wakefield, at that time attached to the British Legation in Paris, who drove the girl to Gretna Green and tricked her into marriage by persuading her that her father had already given his consent to the match. This Scottish marriage was subsequently annulled by a special Act of Parliament, and Wakefield was sent to prison.[16] (After that sobering experience he began his career as imperial theorist advocating emigration for young men who wished to marry early and start a family.) Wakefield's escapade was only the wildest of many, but until the coming of the railway wealthy English parents (at least in the south) had a sporting chance of catching their runaway children before they reached Scotland by chasing after them in fast carriages. The arrival of the iron horse tipped the advantage towards the side of the young, and Parliament in 1856 was at last stirred by the growing flood of absconders to pass Lord

---

[13] Ibid., p. 62.

[14] *Marriages at Gretna Hall, 1829–55*, ed. E. W. J. M'Connel (*Scottish Record Society*, 1949).

[15] Olive Anderson, 'The incidence of civil marriage in Victorian England and Wales', *Past & Present*, LXIX (1975), 68 n. 29.

[16] 'Claverhouse', *Irregular Border Marriages*, pp. 80–5.

Brougham's Marriage Act, which decreed that couples had to reside for 21 days in Scotland before they could undertake marriage. This shielded English parents from the worst menace of Scottish law, as three weeks was ample time to apprehend most erring sons and daughters. Lord Brougham's Act, however, did not abolish Scottish irregular marriage nor indeed affect the institution of marriage in Scotland itself in any way. One of the ironies at the time of Brougham's Act was that irregular marriages among the Scots themselves had (for the moment) become rare. The English felt that Scottish marriage law was a threat to property and to the seemly control of children by their parents, but the Scots had always operated their system of marriage by simple consent without feeling that society was in any way threatened. One reason for the more relaxed attitude in Scotland could be that entail played a less important part in inheritance than in England: it was impossible to disinherit a child from succession to an entail, but in all other circumstances in both countries one could threaten to cut an erring son or daughter off without a penny. Perhaps Scottish middle-class and landed families were in any case habituated to a greater degree of parental control: one should certainly not assume that the native marriage law rested upon a tradition of respect for lovers or had ever led to libertarian tendencies among the young.

*   *   *

The Scottish marriage law of the nineteenth century was itself a medieval survival, and to understand it we shall in this section trace its legal and ecclesiastical history back to the sixteenth century.[17] The canon law on marriage, as expounded in the 1530s by William Hay,[18] the Vice-Principal of King's College, Aberdeen, stressed that there were three essential qualities for the validity of marriage: first, 'a true consent to the mutual giving of the body for matrimonial acts'; second, an outward sign of the first, which could be given 'in words, writing, gesture or anything else which adequately expresses mutual consent'; third, proof that the persons involved were lawfully capable of contracting marriage and not disbarred by impediments—of which the most notable were consanguinity and affinity up to the fourth degree, and spiritual relationship (the last-named ruled out, for example, marriage to a god-mother's child).

Hay described three kinds of marriage, ranged in theological distinction from the least perfect to the most perfect. The first and least perfect was betrothal or handfasting, described as 'incomplete marriage', when consent was made in words referring to the future—'I shall'. Though not in itself constituting a valid marriage, it was a solemn and legally enforceable contract

---

[17] I am extremely grateful to John R. Hardy for permission to draw unreservedly on his unpublished M.Phil. thesis, 'The attitude of the Church and State in Scotland to sex and marriage, 1560–1707', Edinburgh University, 1978. This section depends heavily on his work.

[18] William Hay, *Lectures on Marriage,* ed. J. C. Barry (Stair Society, 1967). Hardy, thesis, ch. 3.

to proceed to a full marriage that could not lightly be set aside. Such betrothals often took place before a priest and with customary ceremonial. There is no sense at all in which such a handfasting was (as has sometimes been alleged) a form of trial marriage that could be dissolved at the will of either partner: on the contrary, a medieval promise of marriage was almost as difficult to dissolve as marriage itself.[19] Hay's second type of marriage was a valid marriage in which mutual consent was given in words of the present time ('I do') but without subsequent sexual intercourse—the validity of a marriage was not affected by impotence or the refusal of one partner to have sex. The third and most perfect type was a valid marriage made in the same way but subsequently consummated.

Marriages to be valid did not, however, have to be performed in church nor by a priest: it was better if they were, and sin was incurred if they were not, but the legality of a 'clandestine' or 'irregular' marriage was not in doubt. In the Middle Ages, as later (in fact as late as 1 July 1940) intercourse subsequent on a proven handfasting, alias promise of marriage *per verba de futuro,* amounted to proof of marriage in law. For this reason more emphasis was sometimes placed on the earlier betrothal ceremony than on the marriage itself. The latter (when not irregular and private) took place after the publication of banns (to help ensure that there was no impediment) at the church door, as described in a Stirling record where the priest 'put the right hand of the said William in the said Annabella's hand and, *per verba matrimonii de presenti,* as use is, fully conjoined the said William and Annabella in nuptial covenant and contract of marriage, who in name of matrimony kissed each other'.[20] The essence of marriage is again seen as the simple exchange of consent: the priest blessed the sacrament of marriage, but the couple themselves performed it, and could have done so without his presence had they chosen.

It was this medieval code of marriage that the Reformers inherited when they came to power in 1560: but at virtually the same time, in the Catholic world, the European law on marriage was altered so that no valid marriage

---

[19] A. E. Anton, ' "Handfasting" in Scotland', *Scottish Historical Review,* XXXVII (1958), 89–102, deals authoritatively with this question. But, as Anton explains, peasants might form temporary or trial sexual alliances and sometimes these seem to have been formalized by folk custom into trials 'for a year and a day' and even occasionally described as 'handfastings'. An example of such behaviour not cited by Anton is described by E. W. Marwick, *The Folklore of Orkney and Shetland* (London, 1975), p. 86: 'At Kirkwall, Lammas Fair, in past centuries the most important event of the Orkney year, couples who had agreed to be sweethearts for the period of the Fair were styled Lammas brother and sister. Although the attachment might be temporary, they were allowed the freedom usually reserved for permanent relationships.' A further problem is raised by the prevalence of what was generally referred to as 'concubinage' in the western Highlands, where 'wives' might be taken for a period by an important member of the clan, and then discarded without the children either of that alliance or any subsequent one being regarded as illegitimate by their fellows. This irregularity was attacked by the Statutes of Iona in 1609, and the formal *legal* position was, of course, no different there than elsewhere in Scotland. What was distinctive was the weakness of formal law in that region before the seventeenth century.
[20] Quoted in Anton, pp. 92–3.

could be performed except in the presence of a priest.[21] It was a change with revolutionary implications designed to stop the scandals associated with promises of marriage *per verba de futuro,* but it had the effect of taking the power over marriage from the hands of the laity and placing it exclusively in the hands of the clergy. The militant lay kirk sessions of Scotland were most unlikely to play any tune called by the Council of Trent, particularly one that devalued the rights of the laity, and their inclination was naturally to keep to the old definitions of marriage.

The new kirk nevertheless had to define a Protestant attitude to marriage, and they made some changes in the medieval law which they believed made it more consonant with scripture.[22] The old impediments of consanguinity and affinity were drastically reduced, and nothing more was heard of the impediment of spiritual relationships. Divorce for adultery was also introduced, by far the most radical change to the old code, which had held that the bond of marriage was dissolved only by death. Otherwise the Reformers were distinctly conservative: in particular, marriage remained based on the simple consent of the two contracting parties.

This did not mean, however, that the Church of Knox and Melville took the affairs of the flesh lightly. Its ambition was to establish a Godly Commonwealth purged of sin by the vigilance of the kirk and the strong arm of the state, and few sins were held so foul as fornication: sex after betrothal was considered as fornication, even though it was clearly very commonly practised.

This put the Reformers into a dilemma: were couples to be handfasted in the face of the kirk, by a minister, reader or elder, after the old fashion? If so, the ceremony might unwittingly appear to condone sex afterwards by making handfasting the most prominent social symbol. Aberdeen had trouble in this respect in 1562, when the kirk session complained that couples were living in 'manifest fornication and huirdom' six or seven years after being handfasted, never having bothered with a second formality. Actually, if their handfastings had been witnessed, the act of sex presumably made the marriage legally complete, but the Church persisted in regarding such behaviour as sinful until another ceremony had been undertaken. Six years later Aberdeen kirk session decided for these reasons 'that nether the minister nor reader be present at contractis off mariage-making, as thai call thair handfastinis'. The General Assembly itself was puzzled to know what to do. In 1570 it proposed that handfasting should take place in church 'according to the ordour of the reformed Kirk' but with the proviso of 'takeand caution for abstinence till the marriage be solemnizit'. But in 1575 there was a change and the Assembly decided that there should be 'no farther ceremonies usit' before the actual solemnization of marriage.[23] Thereafter kirk sessions

---

[21] See *R.C. Report 1867–8,* Appendix p. 83.
[22] Hardy, thesis, ch. 4.
[23] *Selection from the Records of the Kirk Session of Aberdeen* (Spalding Club, 1846), pp. 11, 14; *Acts*

regularly took caution money from couples who came to ask for their banns to be read, and the cash was forfeited if the untimely appearance of a child should reveal that they had not been chaste before marriage. But no ceremony was used to mark a betrothal and the notion of a 'handfast' marriage passes into the twilight of folklore.[24]

The corollary of a slight emphasis on engagement was a greater one on the wedding itself. One innovation made by the Reformers was the introduction of a prescribed and set marriage service, and the earliest, from the Book of Common Order of 1562, began with the words:

> Dearlie beloved Brethren, we are gathered together in the sight of God, and in the face of his Congregation, to knit and joine these parties together in the honorable estate of Matrimony.[25]

This emphasized the public nature of marriage, that it should be performed by the minster in church before a congregation, in a way that was certainly not common in Scotland during the nineteenth century and the first part of the twentieth. The reference to the congregation implied that a marriage should take place on a preaching day, and Sunday was the obvious choice—but it was probably not popular either with the kirk session or the couple concerned since the festivities afterwards would appear unseemly on the Sabbath. The Synod of Aberdeen in 1620, for example, ordered that marriages were not to be solemnized on either Saturdays or Sundays unless the parties gave a 40 lib. Scots bond that there would be no dancing or other profanation of the Lord's Day. Other days therefore became popular. Andrew Symson who was a minister in Galloway, writing in 1684, said that in his parish he had married almost 450 inhabitants, of whom all but seven couples had been married on a Tuesday or a Thursday.[26]

Another problem that vexed the sixteenth and seventeenth centuries was that of parental assent to a marriage.[27] Traditional thinking from Catholic times held that it was not seemly for children to marry without parental consent, but the validity of a marriage was not impaired by its absence. The Council of Trent held that marriages without parental consent were unlawful but not invalid. The first Book of Discipline maintained this general Christian attitude when it spoke of the duty of a couple who 'have their heart touched with the desire of marriage' being bound to ask their parents' permission to proceed: it is not envisaged that fathers would tell their children whom they should marry, but they did have a veto over that choice which they should not use lightly or for a worldly purpose ('to wit, lack of goods, or because they are not so highborn as they require'). Should they wish to marry in the

---

and Proceedings of the General Assemblies of the Kirk of Scotland from the Year 1560 to 1577 (Maitland Club, 1839), pp. 195-6, 343.

[24] See above, n. 19.

[25] John Knox, *Works,* ed. D. Laing (Edinburgh 1846-64), VI, quoted in Hardy, thesis, p. 120.

[26] Hardy, thesis, pp. 110, 113.

[27] Hardy, thesis, ch. 4.

face of their parents' opposition, they were to call upon the minister of the church or the civil magistrate to arbitrate and these authorities would do so bearing in mind the affection of the couple: 'the work of God we call, when two hearts (without filthiness before committed) are so joined that both require and are content to live together in that holy bond of matrimony.'[28] If, however, the couple should eventually overrule their parents' veto, or even ignore the kirk and magistrates, that might be sinful and deplorable, but the Church admitted it did not ultimately affect the validity of the marriage. From time to time, however, there were moves to go beyond this position. For instance in 1581 the Synod of Lothian wished that 'all marriages without consent of parents, proclamations of bands or utherways without the awin solemnities according to the ordour of the Kirk be decernit null'—apparently far too radical a departure from traditional principles to appeal to churchmen and lawyers.[29] In 1644 there was a proposal to annul betrothals between minors under 21 if parents did not approve, even if (or especially if) they had already had sex. The preamble to the overture to the General Assembly explained the context. It had been:

> found by experience that some young men being put to colledges by their wel-effected parents, that they may be instructed in the knowledge of arts and sciences, to the intent that they may bee more able for publick imployments in the ecclesiastick and civill state, that the said children has committed fornication; and the woman and her friends has seduced the foresaid schollers, being minors, to make promise of marriage to the party with whom they have committed fornication; and thereupon intends to get benefite of marriage with the said young men; not onely without the consent of their parents, but to their great grief, and to the great appearance of the ruine and overthrow of their estate; which may be the case of noblemen and gentlemen's children, as well as of these other estates and degrees within the kingdom.[30]

Despite such powerful special pleading this also came to nothing: had it become the law of Scotland the form of irregular marriage *per verba de futuro* would have been altered out of recognition.

In the event, under Scots law before the Union of 1707, a parent whose child had married against his wishes had no means of annulling the match unless he could raise an action before the Commissary Court on the grounds of force and fear—he had to prove that the consent the couple gave to each other was not freely given but was based on, for example, rape, abduction or threats—and couples similarly could (and sometimes did) use the same plea to escape from matches that parents had tried to force on them against their wills.[31] There were also criminal laws against such offences, of course, as well as against the seduction of minors, and parents had the additional

[28] John Knox, *History of the Reformation in Scotland,* ed. W. C. Dickinson (London, 1949), II, 316–17.
[29] Hardy, thesis, p. 137.
[30] *Acts of the General Assembly of the Church of Scotland, 1638–1842,* ed. T. Pitcairn et al. (Edinburgh, 1843), pp. 110–11.
[31] Hardy, thesis, pp. 146–7.

private sanction of being able to disinherit those who disobeyed their wish in choosing a marriage partner. Altogether, the moral and economic force of Church and parent combined to make a powerful social sanction on the young, and there is no reason to think many children defied it just for love.

It is indeed worth pausing to ask what was the role of affection in making a sixteenth-century Scottish marriage, especially in the light of recent discussion of possible fundamental changes in western European attitudes to love between the sixteenth and eighteenth centuries.[32] Clearly the sources are not amenable to any satisfying analysis of attitudes, but the tenor of the language in the Book of Discipline, as we have seen, makes it clear that, on the one hand, marriage was too important to be left to the couple concerned alone but, on the other, that the 'desire of marriage' or 'affection' was God-given and not something that fathers simply arranged for their children. Thus 'no persons under the power and obedience of others, such as sons and daughters ... contract marriage privily and without knowledge [of their parents]: which if they do, the censure and discipline of the Church [ought] to proceed against them'. But the 'desire of marriage' was 'the work of God' that 'ought not to be hindered by the corrupt affections of wordly men', even by parents who might try to stop the marriage for purely material reasons.[33]

Thus a rather sympathetic view of a couple's rights, rooted in their affection, ran alongside a belief that they must obtain consent or be guilty of unnatural and sinful behaviour. The reality and character of sixteenth-century love in one case and in one socio-economic group can be gauged from the letters of James Melville to his uncle, Andrew Melville, when he was planning his second marriage and trying to overcome his uncle's reservations about their ages:

> Nor do I deny that I am in love: but it is legitimate, holy, chaste, sober love ... I do not pretend that I am not under the influence of the affections, for how then could I be in love? ... She indeed is in the flower of life, being only nineteen years of age. And who that is wise would not prefer for a partner one who is sound in mind and body, modest, yielding, humble, affectionate, open-hearted and thus in every way qualified for rendering life agreeable?[34]

Even if Melville seems (to modern ears) to regard his girl as a cross between a heifer and a poodle, his self-justification is in terms of the affections. It was as though a compromise had to be struck: as a minimum, parents or guardians were expected not to force matches on couples who had no affection for each other, and couples were expected not to go to the lengths of running

---

[32] Notably, J. L. Flandrin, *Families in Former Times* (Cambridge, 1979); L. Stone, *The Family, Sex and Marriage in England* (London, 1977); E. Shorter, *The Making of the Modern Family* (London, 1976).

[33] Knox, *History of the Reformation*, II, 316–17, Hardy, thesis, pp. 134–5.

[34] Quoted in Hardy, thesis, p. 164. This was a second marriage and R. Trumbach, *The Rise of the Egalitarian Family* (New York, 1978), has suggested that affection often played a larger role in second than in first marriages.

away to contract clandestine or irregular marriages if they could not obtain parental consent.

Despite the continued legal toleration of irregular marriage it was apparently not very common in the first century after the Reformation, simply because the hegemony of the Church of Scotland was so complete that the risk of censure was not to be lightly defied. The only references in the General Assembly (before its temporary suspension in 1619) were to marriages considered clandestine or irregular because they were performed by those who were not Chuch of Scotland ministers, especially 'popish priests'. The first general Act of the Scottish Parliament on the matter in 1649 mentioned disaffection 'to the religion presently profest in this kingdome' as the prime motive for irregular marriage, and then added as motives a desire 'to eschew the censures of this kirk, or to falsifie their promise of marriage formerlie made to others, or to decline the concurrence and consent of their parents'. But there is no reason at all to suppose that the overwhelming majority of marriages were not celebrated publicly by the minister in the presence of consenting parents and an interested community.

*　　　*　　　*

Marriage was in essence, then, a civil contract, the nature of which was determined by lawyers; it usually also involved a religious ceremony, specified by the Church. But for the couple and the community it was also an important occasion for a social celebration. The traditions that surrounded the Scottish wedding of the pre-industrial centuries are worth examining for the way in which they confirmed and emphasized the essentially public nature of marriage. Many of them were described and collected by amateur ethnographers in the nineteenth century, though obviously of great antiquity. All stressed the place of the community in the wedding and the place of the wedding in the community.

In Orkney and Shetland, for example, the solemnities were initiated on 'speiring night', when the prospective groom brought a bottle of whisky to the bride's father and asked his permission for the match. That was followed by 'booking' night or 'contract' night when the families went to enter the names of the couple in the session-clerk's books so that banns could be proclaimed: this was obviously a folk survival of the church betrothal, and interestingly (despite the risk of forfeiting the caution money) in Shetland the couple were expected to sleep together that night as a seal of the contract, but not to have intercourse again until after the wedding. On the wedding eve the friends of the bride and groom entered their houses and forcibly washed their feet with a good deal of horseplay. Next day the couple went in separate processions, headed by a fiddler or a piper, to the manse where the minister married them. Afterwards, the entire village was invited to the celebration, with dancing, feasting and drinking continuing for several days. Nor did it end there: 'next to her wedding day, the bride's finest hour was on "kirking Sunday" when in fine clothes bought specially for the occasion she and her groom marched to church accompanied by their attendants. Not until she was kirked did she consider herself completely and effectually married'.[35]

Customs reported from the opposite end of the country, the west of Scotland, contained many of the same elements, such as washing the bride's feet, the public procession to the minister, the subsequent celebrations and (in addition) on the morning after the wedding some of the married women of the neighbourhood met at the bride's house and placed on her head a *curtch* or mutch cap as a token of the married state.[36] Similarly on the north-eastern mainland there was a 'beuckin nicht' when the groom and the bride's father gave in the names for the banns. Here, in the processions to the church, bread and cheese and a bottle and a glass were carried to treat the first person the couple met,[37] while guns were fired to keep away evil spirits (occasionally, to great scandal, they were fired in the church itself). When more than one couple were married at the same time, it was regarded as lucky to get out of the church before any other married couples: thus at Rathven kirk in 1750 'there happened a very disorderly thing' when two couples and their freinds made a dash for the door without waiting to hear the last prayer, 'Angus Cormach taking out his sister, one of the brides, out of her seat, and John Runcie calling on the brides to go out of doors hand in hand', presumably so they could share the good fortune.[38]

Seventeenth-century and early eighteenth-century written records provide echoes of many of these customs.[39] For instance, one English traveller in the Lowlands noted that 'after marriage there will be continuing feasting and mirth for some four or five days', another that only unmarried women went bareheaded, a third that in the marriage procession the 'man and his company walked first, and the woman led by two men, with her train of women followed. Before the man went a curious concert of music, consisting of a bagpipe and a fiddle; but before the woman and her attendants was only a single solemn bag piper'.[40]

Official records, however, dwelt above all on what the authorities regarded as the excesses of the celebrations after the marriage. Nothing disturbed Church and magistrates more, nor involved the community more deeply,

---

[35] Marwick, *The Folklore of Orkney and Shetland*, pp. 87–8; W. T. Dennison, *Orkney Weddings and Wedding Customs* (Kirkwall, 1905), *passim*.

[36] James Napier, *Folklore: or Superstitious Beliefs in the West of Scotland within this Century* (Paisley, 1879), pp. 47–53.

[37] J. M. McPherson, *Primitive Beliefs in the North-east of Scotland* (London, 1929), pp. 116–19.

[39] Ibid., pp. 119–20.

[39] Hardy, thesis, pp. 186–204.

[40] W. Brereton, 'Journal', *North Countries Diaries,* ed. J. C. Hodgson (Surtees Society, 1914), II, 30; C. Lowther, 'Our Journey into Scotland', *Hist. MSS Comm. Report on the MSS of the Earl of Lonsdale,* Appendix, Part VII (HMSO, 1893), p. 83; T. Thomas, 'A Journey', *Hist. MSS Comm. Report on the MSS of the Duke of Portland,* VI (HMSO, 1901), 125, quoted in Hardy, thesis, pp. 188, 203.

than the institution of the 'penny wedding', by which guests brought to the celebrations food, drink or money (called the *lawin*), so that even the poorest could have a notable festivity, with very often scores of people eating, drinking and dancing together at the town cross. On these occasions there was a clash of interest. The authorities generally wished to limit both the number of people allowed to be present and the extent of the *lawin* because they regarded penny weddings as 'fruitfall seminaries of all lasciviouseness and debaushtrie'. The commonalty, on the other hand, plainly treated every wedding as a community affair and a suitable occasion for a binge. The very repetition of regulations suggests that community spirit was too strong to be easily quenched, but the acts were not dead letters—for example in 1688 54 people, including the minister, were fined at Peebles for contravening the Act of 1681, which had forbidden more than four friends on either side to join with the couple, their families and servants to celebrate a wedding.[41]

*   *   *

It is clear from all this that most weddings were highly public—and if they were public, they could not have been simultaneously clandestine or irregular, especially as such marriages came (by the legislation of the Scottish Parliaments in 1649, 1661 and subsequently to 1698) to be theoretically punishable by fines and imprisonment, with banishment for the celebrator.

Nevertheless, the end of the seventeenth century does mark a significant turning-point: certainly from the Restoration of 1660 onwards there was always within Scotland a significant minority of Scots who, while Protestant, did not desire the ministrations of the established Church and would go to considerable lengths to marry in secret if they could thereby be married by a clergyman of their choice. The law in the seventeenth century tried to punish this; in the eighteenth century it turned a blind eye to nonconformity, but not until 1834 did it admit as a regular marriage any ceremony performed except before a Church of Scotland clergyman (or a juring Episcopalian clergyman after the Act of Toleration of 1711). The Act of 1834 accepted the legality of the ceremony performed before any member of the clergy regardless of sect, but until that time a nonconformist (e.g. any Catholic, non-juring Episcopalian or Seceding Presbyterian) had to undertake an irregular marriage if he or she wished to marry within their faiths. This naturally increased enormously the number of irregular marriages. No one knows how many there were, but James Stark (Superintendent of Statistics at the Registrar General for Scotland's Office in 1865) estimated that 'during the whole of the eighteenth century, a third of marriages had been irregular', and he was as well placed as anyone to guess.[42]

The rise of nonconformity and popular irregular marriage must, therefore, have gone some way towards undermining the community nature of the

[41] Hardy, thesis, p. 193.
[42] *R.C. Report 1867–8,* p. xxi.

wedding celebrations: not only was the community often split, like the Church, but a couple could hardly celebrate something illegal without drawing attention to their misdemeanour. Of course, as toleration spread after 1700, this sanction on public celebration weakened again, but it is perhaps significant that one hears less of the 'abuses' of penny weddings in the towns, though they plainly continued in the more unified communities until well on into the eighteenth century, or even well beyond in some places.

What is not yet altogether clear is how far the irregular marriages which came to be so popular in the eighteenth century were solely an artefact of nonconformity, or whether they contained an element of genuine social revolt by those who cared for no church, were indifferent to parental consent and could avoid community sanctions. Stark's remarks, combined with the apparent rarity of irregular marriage for many decades after the Act of 1834 had regularized the ministration of dissenting clergy, would suggest that nonconformity was the main cause of irregular marriage.

Doubts, however, remain, at least about certain localities and particular classes within them. This is best illustrated by a perusal of the *Calendar of Irregular Marriages at South Leith, 1697–1818*.[43] Leith was a seaport, a garrison town and a satellite to the capital, growing fast in the eighteenth century. Here irregular marriages noted in the kirk session minutes exceeded by the 1740s the numbers of regular marriages, even though the kirk ignored a portion of the irregular marriages, as it took no notice of those celebrated by the local seceders. The interest of the kirk session in recording such marriages was that the Church was entitled to use the subsequent fines for poor relief and the couples were prepared to pay a modest fine as a means of having their marriages placed on record. Most couples were of tradesman status or lower—soldier, sailor, servant, barber, smith, wright, maltman, shoemaker, cooper, porter, gardener, etc. A few were distinctly more upper class. The session records are usually silent about the reasons for marriages, which were often celebrated outside the parish (in the City of Edinburgh or elsewhere) and frequently before individuals whose names recur so frequently that they must have made a profession of it, like the 'marrying men' of Gretna of a slightly later period. One such was George Blaikie who 'lodges at the head of the Bow, Edinburgh'. Certainly by the eighteenth century they seem to have operated with virtual immunity from the law, just as the Gretna Green celebrators did. Perhaps they were seen as performing a certain social service in giving a form to a type of marriage that could otherwise be dangerously unstructured.

Occasionally there is detail which shows how chaotic and informal an irregular marriage could indeed be. Three examples must suffice. In October 1698 an entry was made concerning the marriage of Alexander Hendersone,

[43] *Calendar of Irregular Marriages in the South Leith Kirk Session Records, 1697–1818,* ed. J. S. Marshall (Scottish Record Society, 1968).

younger, cordiner in Caltoun, and Isobel Philp, by Mr. James Kirk: the groom 'had no testificat to produce but said he knew him [Mr. Kirk] not, neither did Mr. Kirk know him nor sought no testificat from him, and said that for anything Mr. Kirk knew the woman he married might have been his mother'. Was the marriage valid in the absence of proof that the couple were legally free to marry (i.e. not already married and not too closely related)? Hendersone was ordered to produce 'the testimonial of marriage'.[44] In 1716 there was the case of a soldier who married a servant girl: 'it was not a minister that married them, but one Dowart, a corporall . . . who had on a black coat when he married them . . . and they promised to be dutifull to each other as man and wife'. Was this a case of a soldier posing as a minister?[45] Finally, in 1719 a couple appeared who could not agree if they were married or not. The husband, William Beveredge:

> deny'd that he was married, but she (Helen Spence) affirmed and owned she was irregularly married to him and produced the testificat thereof . . . To which he answered that if he was married he knew nothing of it for he was mortally drunk, and that the man who married them was as drunk as he was, and said that he never cohabited with her as wife, and that he did not bed with her that night, which she acknowledged also, but averred that he did cohabit with her since as her husband.

The session rebuked the husband for his drunkenness and ordered the wife to produce the witnesses (a cooper and a tailor in Edinburgh) the following day in order to validate the marriage beyond further doubt.[46]

These incidents and others like them indicate the existence of a subculture basically urban and irreligious, treating marriage in a much more casual way than either Church or peasant community. Indeed, the opponents of irregular marriage often averred that it was only too convenient an institution for rogues of either sex. For example, a soldier might seduce a respectable girl by an irregular marriage performed before witnesses taken off the street who could be relied upon to disappear again, and then desert her without leaving adequate proof of there ever having been a marriage. Or an unscrupulous girl could inveigle an acquaintance into marriage by getting him drunk in a pub, taking him upstairs to a convenient marrying man, and having the testimonial to wave in his face when he awoke next day. Such things did go on: how much of irregular marriage even in South Leith was of this character is hard to say, for along with the seamy side there were a great many respectable irregular marriages undertaken for religious scruple or other reasons.

*   *   *

Because of the poor quality of church records and the complexities introduced by irregular marriage, it is virtually impossible to attempt a quantitative

[44] Ibid., p. 2.
[45] Ibid., p. 13.
[46] Ibid., p. 17.

study of Scottish marriage before 1855, whether regular or irregular. In that year, however, the establishment of the office of the Registrar General for Scotland transformed the situation. The remainder of our examination will try to examine the statistical aspects of the problem from that date until the virtual abolition of irregular marriage in 1940.

It is important to recognize, however, that the law relating to civil registration of marriage was not identical in Scotland and England.[47] In the south there was a legal obligation to register every marriage, whether undertaken in church or in the registrar's office. In Scotland there was no such legal obligation, and no provision for civil marriage in a registrar's office. We need not doubt that all regular marriages (defined after 1834 as marriages celebrated by a clergyman of any church) were registered, but it remained awkward to register an irregular marriage. Lord Brougham's Act of 1856 provided that within three months of contracting an irregular marriage the couple could, if they chose, make a joint application before the Sheriff; and the Sheriff, on being satisfied with the legality of the procedure, then issued a warrant to the registrar in whose district the marriage had taken place, instructing him to register the marriage. This process was not expensive (there was a five-shilling registration fee) and it was simpler and cheaper than the alternatives of obtaining a decree of declarator from the court (which cost 20 shillings to register) or a conviction under the old statutes against irregular marriage (which also cost 20 shillings). But it was certainly cumbersome, and those who saw no particular advantage in obtaining a record of their marriage might conceivably omit to go to the trouble of doing so.

This gave rise to a controversy between the Registrars General for Scotland and England.[48] It was quickly established in the Scottish office that the marriage rate was lower in Scotland than in England: in 1875, for example, it was 8.40 per 1,000 people living in England and Wales, but 7.43 in Scotland; but the average fertility of marriages (measured by the annual average number of legitimate births divided by the annual average number of marriages) appeared to be higher in Scotland. The Registrar General for Scotland was inclined to explain this in terms of various social differences—the low marriage rate being partly explained by the lower density of the population, and the higher fertility by a smaller incidence of what he termed 'diminished vitality' in a more rural population. The English Registrar General, however, believed that the registration of marriages north of the Border was deficient, and that numbers of irregular marriages were going unnoticed while their offspring were being registered as legitimate, thus depressing the recorded marriage rate below what it should have been and inflating the ratio of legitimate births to marriages.

[47] G. T. Bisset-Smith, *Vital Registration* (Edinburgh, 1907), p. 34.
[48] *Fortieth and Forty-first Annual Reports of the Registrar General for England; Twenty-first and Twenty-second Detailed Annual Reports of the Registrar General for Scotland* (1875 and 1876).

221

The Scottish Registrar General made a sharp reply to this slur on his office: 'it is quite certain that marriage hardly ever escapes registration in Scotland, and that within a week of its consummation or celebration. Be the process regular or irregular, if it be a marriage in legal acceptation, registration follows as a matter of course'.[49] In fact, he said, very few irregular marriages were registered because very few took place.

How, it might be asked, could he possibly know this if he did not have a legal obligation to register them? The plausibility of his case rested, firstly, on the fact that without exception experts on Scottish marriage in the third quarter of the nineteenth century held the same view—that irregular marriage was extremely rare except in a few Border parishes and among such people as tinkers, and, secondly, that as Registrar General he received a stream of regular quarterly reports from local registrars, who commented on all aspects of demographic behaviour in their districts and were, as a class, well-informed and astute men.[50] A careful perusal of their remarks indicates that they also thought irregular marriages were rare, and that they were tending to die out even in Border parishes. Whereas, for example, in Eyemouth in 1856 the registrar had reported 'that the marriage register for the last year is blank, although from 20 to 30 parties have been married "at the Toll" who are domiciled in this parish', only seven years later he was writing that irregular marriages at Lamberton Toll 'are the exception now'. 'I believe that in a few years they will be among the things that were.'[51] So, while it is possible that the Scottish Registrar General overstated his case, it is difficult to find any good evidence that in the third quarter of the nineteenth century irregular marriages were anything but uncommon once more. Between 1855 and 1870 only about one marriage in every thousand registered was irregular.

If this conclusion is correct, it makes even more dramatic the increase in the proportion of irregular marriages that took place in the following half century, as Table I demonstrates.

Table I: Irregular marriages as percentage of all Scottish registered marriages, 1861–1939

1861–1870	0.18	1901–1910	6.39
1871–1880	1.04	1911–1920	14.90
1881–1890	2.51	1921–1930	12.74
1891–1900	4.78	1931–1940	12.70

Source Hundredth Annual Report of the Registrar General for Scotland (1954).

These irregular marriages were almost all registered on a Sheriff's warrant. Since no clergy were involved, they were a close equivalent to civil marriage

---

[49] *Twenty-first Detailed Annual Report*, p. xxii.
[50] *R.C. Report 1867–8*, Appendix; Quarterly Returns of the Births, Marriages and Deaths . . . of Scotland.
[51] Quarterly Returns, No. 8 (1856), p. 52; No. 36 (1863) p. 51.

in England. The Act of 1834 had made marriage before any clergyman regular if banns had been read, and further impediments to regular marriage had been removed by the Act of 1878 which allowed publication of a notice in the local registrar's office to replace banns (which had had to be read in the *established* parish church after 1834 even if the wedding was to be celebrated by a Free Kirk minister or in a Catholic chapel).

If irregular marriage had become like civil marriage, however, it was (until the First World War) still nothing like as popular as its English equivalent, as Table II shows.

Table II: Civil marriage in England and irregular marriage in Scotland as percentage of all marriages in each country

	England	Scotland
1864	8	0.1
1874	11	0.8
1884	15	2.4
1894	15	4.2
1904	18	5.8
1913	22	9.1
1919	23	19.0

Source O. Anderson, 'Incidence of civil marriage' in *Past & Present,* LXIX (1975), 55; *Detailed Annual Reports of the Registrar General for Scotland.*

What was the geographical context of this new popularity of irregular marriages?

Olive Anderson, in her study of civil marriage in England and Wales, found that in the nineteenth century 'the association of big cities and conurbations with a high rate of civil marriage, so well established in the twentieth century, did not then exist'.[52] At first sight this was not true in Scotland, as Table III (overleaf) shows clearly, despite all the confusing alterations to urban classification by the Registrar General's office.

Irregular marriage in Scotland had become an urban phenomenon, and especially a feature of the largest burghs, as Table IV shows (in this case we show 1915 rather than 1914, to indicate the distribution when the irregular marriage boom of the First World War was at its height).

Not too much should be made of regional or even urban/rural distinctions, however, as very many couples now came to the towns, and especially the larger towns, to get married—and their marriages were registered in the place of marriage, not in their place of normal residence to which they returned after the ceremony. This was as true of regular marriages as of irregular, and seems to have gone hand in hand with a preference for a quieter wedding than the community-centred affairs of an earlier age, as the registrar of the Hebridean island of Tiree explained in 1868:

[52] Olive Anderson, 'Incidence of civil marriage', p. 58.

The registered Marriages are no criterion of the number who are led to the hymeneal altar in the district. A good many prefer, after getting the certificate of proclamation of banns, a trip by steamer to the low country, where they get married, rather than stand the turmoil, revelry and bustle of a real Highland marriage. And considering all things, the public morals gain more than they lose by the change.[53]

Table III: Irregular marriages as percentage of all marriages in urban and rural areas in Scotland

1864		Towns		Mainland rural	Insular rural	All Scotland
		0.14		0.05	0.00	0.1
	Principal burghs	Large towns	Small towns			
1874	1.94	0.16	0.10	0.00	0.00	0.8
1884	4.61	1.22	0.33	0.02	0.00	2.4
1894	7.91	1.62	0.52	0.02	0.00	4.2
1904	10.35	1.92	0.45	0.09	0.25	5.8
	Large burghs			Others		
1914	19.9			2.1		12.6
1924	19.2			1.7		12.2
1934	16.9			1.9		11.7

Source Detailed Annual Reports of the Registrar General for Scotland.

Table IV: Irregular marriages as percentage of all marriages in the four largest cities

	Glasgow	Edinburgh	Dundee	Aberdeen	All Scotland
1894	10.7	8.8	6.0	4.1	4.2
1915	32.2	42.3	31.1	36.5	20.5
1934	18.9	26.6	16.7	16.6	11.7

Source Detailed Annual Reports of the Registrar General for Scotland.

That more traditional modes of celebrating a marriage did survive into the twentieth century, however, is amply demonstrated by the account of an Aberdeenshire wedding quoted in the Appendix below, and Dr. Walker of Dundee University informs me that up to 30 years ago weddings in the working-class tenements of that city were often very like seventeenth-century 'penny weddings', with all the neighbours coming to celebrate with their own drink and dancing continuing in the back green if the parlour was too small.

Why did irregular marriage become more popular after 1870? Table I shows that the change came in two stages—a long, steady growth until c.1910 followed by an extraordinary surge. The actual breakpoint was a jump from 9 per cent in 1913 to 20.5 per cent in 1915. After 1920 the level

[53] Quarterly Returns, No. 55 (1868), p. 46.

of irregular marriages falls again but never to pre-war figures, and shows a tendency to rise steeply again in the late 1930s.

The growth in wartime (the maximum numbers were reached in 1915 and 1919) is best explained by the speed of irregular marriage compared to regular marriage, as the former could be performed instantly but the latter had to wait for the publication of banns or notices in the registrar's office. No doubt those departing for the trenches were eager for instant marriage so that they could have a brief and blissful honeymoon before Armageddon: and many of those returning saw no reason to wait for marriage a moment longer after the frustrations and miseries of war. Table V shows how the First World War affected marriages both regular and irregular.[54]

Table V: Marriages in Scotland, 1912-1924

	All marriages	Irregular marriages	% Irregular
1912	32,506	2,555	7.8
1913	33,676	3,051	9.0
1914	35,028	4,399	12.5
1915	36,233	7,420	20.5
1916	31,419	5,962	19.0
1917	30,421	4,982	16.3
1918	34,529	5,943	17.2
1919	44,060	8,351	19.0
1920	46,754	7,848	16.8
1921	39,243	6,135	15.7
1922	34,375	4,675	13.6
1923	35,200	4,296	12.2
1924	32,328	3,935	12.1

Source Detailed Annual Reports of the Registrar General for Scotland.

More difficult to explain than the wartime growth is the steady increase of irregular marriages from 1870 to 1939. It is tempting to account for it partly by secularization, in the sense that fewer couples felt that the union of marriage needed blessing by the Church.[55] Perhaps there was also for some people a new quest for privacy and economy: an irregular marriage gave an opportunity for greater secrecy and avoidance of fuss than even a quiet wedding performed by a minister. A glance at irregular marriages in any register in a large town at the end of the nineteenth century shows the kind of people who, for various reasons, might want to avoid publicity and fuss: those for Dundee in 1890,[56] for example, include an 18-year-old

[54] A similar trend in the total number of marriages was evident in the Second World War in Scotland—a marked increase at the outbreak, followed by a reduction below the levels of the pre-war years with so many men away from home; then a considerable jump when peace returned, followed by a more gradual return to former levels.

[55] The best studies of the Scottish churches' contest with secularizing forces in the period are A. L. Drummond and J. Bulloch, *The Church in Victorian Scotland, 1843–1874* (Edinburgh, 1975) and *The Church in Late Victorian Scotland 1874–1900* (Edinburgh, 1978).

[56] New Register House, Civil Marriage Registers of St. Peter's, St. Mary's and St. Clement's, Dundee, 1890.

ploughman of St. Andrews marrying a 35-year-old domestic servant of Strathkinness; a 56-year-old 'commission agent' of Paradise Cottage, Carnoustie, marrying a 24-year-old spinster of the same address; a 22-year-old actor from London marrying a girl of the same age from Liverpool; a 29-year-old railway stoker marrying a 35-year-old widow of an engine driver; an illiterate butcher widower aged 48 marrying a 28-year-old domestic servant and so on. An irregular marriage was also speedy—20 out of 61 such marriages in Dundee in 1890 were of merchant seamen who probably wanted the convenience of a quick marriage before setting out to sea again. An irregular marriage could also be cheap: although you could have a party after a Sheriff's warrant just as easily as after a church wedding. Nineteenth-century marriage was probably more expensive than marriage in the seventeenth century if you did want a celebration, at least wherever the old community tradition of a 'penny wedding' (where all paid for themselves and contributed to the couple's expenses) had been replaced by an individualist world (where the bride's father was expected to pay for the celebrations). And an immigrant girl—perhaps a domestic servant—in a nineteenth-century town might have no father at hand to pay and know few guests to invite.

An additional explanation for the growing popularity of irregular marriage might be that marriage itself had become a more important institution for those who intended to have children. It would be difficult to argue that marriage became more widely popular: in 1871 the proportion of men in their early fifties who were married was 87 per cent; by 1931 it was 84 per cent; for women the corresponding figures were 80 per cent and 79 per cent. But increasingly child-bearing took place within the context of the family. There was a drop of 22 per cent in the illegitimacy ratio: whereas in 1871, 9.4 births in every 100 had been illegitimate, by 1931 it was 7.3. There was an even more dramatic drop of 55 per cent in the illegitimate fertility rate; in 1871 there had been 23 births per 1,000 unmarried women aged 15–49, by 1931 there were only 9.7. Evidently there was a diminishing chance that women would risk bringing a family of bastards into the world.[57]

In 1906 the well-informed commentators C. J. and J. N. Lewis noted that 'In Scotland a large proportion of the illegitimate births are the product of conditions akin to ordinary marriage, and are indeed rendered legitimate by subsequent marriage ...'.[58] The Registrar General had made similar observations in 1874: investigation showed that 'in numerous instances the parents of these illegitimate children were true to each other, that the woman had borne several children by the same man, and that frequently the children were legitimized by the subsequent marriage of the parents'.[59] It was perhaps

---

[57] *Scottish Population History from the Seventeenth Century to the 1930's*, ed. M. W. Flinn (Cambridge, 1977), pp. 325, 327, 352–3.
[58] C. J. and J. N. Lewis, *Natality and Fecundity* (Edinburgh, 1906), p. 120.
[59] *Supplement to the Registrar General's Reports, 1861–1870* (1874), p. 13.

couples like these who were increasingly anxious to secure marriage lines at a relatively early stage in their relationship, choosing irregular marriage as a way to do so partly because it was informal and easy, partly because it involved no inquisition or moralizing by a minister of religion about the previous quality of their private lives. The suggestion is not that couples had earlier 'thought' themselves married: there is little evidence that the popular definition of marriage then differed from the legal one, or that those who lived in 'concubinage' (as the Victorians called it) did not know perfectly well that they could terminate their liaison and begin a new one without penalty, just as people in a similar position today know that 'living together' is not the same thing as 'being married'.[60]

The point is rather that couples may wish to swap the ambiguities of an unmarried alliance for the certainties of marriage for good social and economic reasons. Even before 1870 there had been some reasons for getting married, though this might trouble the bureaucrats more than the couple themselves. Dr. Strachan of Dollar in 1866 commented on the problems created by vagrants who 'go and live as man and wife without any ceremony' but whose position remained ambiguous until they fell onto the poor law through sickness. If they could be proved to have been married 'by habit and repute', then the man's parish was responsible for the woman and children—if not, then the woman's parish: 'that leads to very great confusion and trouble in the management of the poor's funds'.[61] After c.1870, the inconveniences fell more directly upon the couple. For one thing, education became compulsory, and this possibly put pressure on a child and its parents who did not belong to a 'respectable' family. For another, the poor law in the early twentieth century began increasingly to elaborate separate categories of need within the family: as the dependants of a man became eligible for a wider range of relief (for example a striker in the 1920s came to be able to obtain relief for his wife and children)[62] it was more important to establish legal dependence, which could most conveniently be done by producing proof of marriage. Lastly, the welfare state itself gave another series of benefits that could be claimed by the married—for example, the 'respectable' family, properly married and with children, would certainly be given priority over the unmarried woman with babies in the allocation of council houses, and from the end of the First World War the unemployment benefit scheme involved allowances for dependants for which legal dependence had to be claimed. The expansion of the state into people's lives brought with it an

---

[60] For a discussion on this, see Ian Carter, 'Illegitimate births and illegitimate inferences', *Scottish Journal of Sociology*, I (1976), 125–34; T. C. Smout, 'Illegitimacy—a reply', ibid., II (1977), 97–103.

[61] *R.C. Report 1867–8*, Appendix, p. 173.

[62] Ian Levitt, 'The Scottish Poor Law and unemployment, 1890–1929', in *The Search for Wealth and Stability: Essays in Economic and Social History presented to M. W. Flinn*, ed. T. C. Smout (London, 1979).

increased convenience in the married state: it literally made respectability pay.

*   *   *

The painstaking work of the Scottish Registrar General's office also enables us to examine various other interesting aspects of marriage in the second half of the nineteenth century apart from irregular marriage, especially the problem of timing. For instance, there was a remarkable bunching of marriage during the week. The wedding, under the nineteenth-century Presbyterian system, now seldom took place in church—a ceremony at the home of the bride or a private visit to the manse tended to replace the marriage *in facie ecclesiae* of John Knox's day. The most popular day for a wedding was a Friday, in total contrast to England where Sunday was still the favourite day, as the Registrar General demonstrated in an interesting investigation in 1862 (set out in Table VI).

Table VI: Percentages of marriages conducted on each day of the week in Scotland and England, 1862

	Scotland	England
Sunday	1	32
Monday	13	21
Tuesday	18	11
Wednesday	7	8
Thursday	12	9
Friday	43	2
Saturday	7	17

Source Supplement to the Registrar General's Reports 1861–1870, p. 40.

The choice of Friday was not because of a lingering 'Druidical superstition', as some romantic ethnographers averred, but because the Presbyterian churches in their nineteenth-century puritan phase abhorred the desecration of the Sabbath and the Sabbath eve implied by a Sunday or a Saturday wedding, and because a wedding on a Friday evening after work gave working men a chance to spend the Saturday half-holiday and the Sunday with their brides.[63]

The same considerations meant that during the year marriages peaked on 31 December (because New Year's Day was invariably a holiday, with high absenteeism tolerated on the following days as well) and to a lesser extent at the time of the annual summertime fairs at Glasgow, Greenock, Dundee, etc. Nationally, the monthly pattern showed fewest marriages in May (5 per cent in the decade 1861–70) but most in December (17 per cent), June (14 per cent), July and November (both 10 per cent). The avoidance of May probably was partly connected with superstition, but it was also an inconvenient month since two terms occurred in it—one for changing servants of

---

[63] *Supplement to the Registrar General's Reports, 1861–1870* (1874), pp. 40–1.

all kinds on 15 May, and one for changing houses and farms on 25 or 27 May: those intending to marry therefore left at their half-yearly term and prepared for entry into a new home, marrying the following month or the one after. There was a similar fee-ing term at Martinmas (11 November), but no general winter house-changing: this also tended to lead to marriages at the end of the year. Winter was particularly popular in the north, for it was the quiet time in fishing and agriculture and a period when, with the sale of the catch and the earnings of the harvest workers, young men and women were prosperous. In many parishes in Shetland, Orkney and the western Highlands there were over long periods no summer marriages at all. Generally, in the north-west, there was a heavy preference for winter marriages; in the rural south-east, marriages in June after the fee-ing market exceeded those in December and January.[64]

In the fluctuations in the annual sum of marriages, too, economic considerations were paramount. The correlation between plentiful harvests, cheap food and marriage had been observed as far back as the seventeenth century. Nicoll's diary noted in 1665 that 'this last harvest . . . producit great numberis of cornes and very cheap, quhilk wes the caus that a number of feyet servandis, both men and women did marry at that Martimes thairefter, be way of penny bridelis, both within the Town of Edinburgh and uther pairtes of the cuntrey'.[65] This relationship still held true in the nineteenth century: in 1856 the registrar of Daviot in Aberdeenshire noted 'the numbers of marriages below the average, which may be accounted for by the high price of provisions';[66] and in 1868 the registrar of Lochbroom in Wester Ross observed that 'after a successful herring fishing there is generally a matrimonial rush'.[67] This was true of servants and fishermen, but not applicable to crofters or tenants waiting for land in an overcrowded countryside for whom, as the Registrar General for Scotland observed, 'room is only made for a new family by the death of an old'.[68] The abnormally late mean age of marriage in the Highland counties, 32.8 years for men and 28.6 for women in 1911, compared to a Scottish average for that year of 29.4 and 26.7 respectively, was explained by this.[69]

In industrial areas, the main determinant of the timing of marriage was the state of trade, and years when business was interrupted were years of low numbers of marriages. Thus the prolonged mining strike of 1856 was noted by registrars in several coal-mining communities, like Muiravonside and Slamannan in Stirlingshire, Hamilton in Lanarkshire and Kilbirnie in Ayrshire, as having discouraged marriage; and when late in the following

[64] Ibid., pp. 41-2. See also Alan Gilloran, 'Seasonality of marriage', a project for M.A. Honours Sociology, University of Edinburgh, 1978. The project report is held by the department.

[65] J. Nicoll, A Diary of Public Transactions, ed. D. Laing (Bannatyne Club, 1836), pp. 441-2.

[66] Quarterly Returns, No. 5 (1856), p. 43.

[67] Quarterly Returns, No. 53 (1853), p. 44.

[68] Fourth Detailed Annual Report, (1858).

[69] Scottish Population History, ed. M. W. Flinn, p. 332.

year the Western Bank collapsed in Glasgow 'our whole commercial system was deranged' and the marriage rate for Scotland dropped sharply from 7.14 per thousand to 6.52 per thousand.[70]

For this reason there was even a statistical relationship between the annual number of marriages celebrated and the annual number of convictions for drunkenness, as Figure I shows. In the quarter-century after 1875, for example, each of the years of severe slump, 1879, 1885, 1886 and 1893, saw a marked fall in both the marriage rate and the drunkenness rate, while the good years like 1883 and 1899 saw a peak in both. This was not because the Scots got especially drunk when they were married, nor married when they were drunk, but because the prosperous years of the Victorian trade cycle put cash in a workman's pocket but the crashes carried away his savings. Weddings and whisky were as much alternative goods as complementary ones.

Slumps were also reflected in short-term fluctuations in the illegitimacy rate. Though there has been no recent research on this subject, many well-informed contemporaries believed that most working-class Scottish girls were already pregnant on marriage.[71] Dr. Strachan believed that nine out of ten brides in the agricultural districts and 30 per cent of those in woollen manufacturing towns either already had illegitimate children or (much more commonly) were already 'in the family-way at the time of marriage'.[72] These findings correspond with the observations of many local registrars, for instance at Crail in Fife in 1863, that 'antenuptial unchastity is quite proverbially "the fashion" ',[73] and at Barry, Angus, in 1873 that there was an 'opinion among *the young folks* that the illicit intercourse of the sexes is neither *a sin* nor *a shame*'.[74]

In these circumstances one might expect the onset of a sudden commercial crisis to increase the illegitimacy rate, if marriages planned to take place later in the year and anticipated by sexual intercourse after betrothal were suddenly cancelled (or at least postponed) when the man lost his job and his savings in the ensuing crash: and registrars sometimes noted that dull trade led to rising illegitimacy.[75] Figure II shows the relationship. The years 1868,

[70] Quarterly Returns, No. 6 (1856), pp. 46–7, (1866), pp. 45–6; *Fourth Detailed Annual Report* (1858). For England, William Ogle in 1890 successfully correlated marriage rates with the volume of exports: see 'On marriage rates and marriage-ages, with special reference to the growth of population', *Journal of the Royal Statistical Society*, 53 (1890), 253–66.

[71] T. C. Smout, 'Aspects of sexual behaviour in nineteenth century Scotland', in *Social Class in Scotland*, ed. A. A. MacLaren (Edinburgh, 1976), pp. 62–81.

[72] *R.C. Report 1867–8*, Appendix, pp. 171–2.

[73] Quarterly Returns, No. 33 (1863), p. 45.

[74] Quarterly Returns, No. 77 (1873), p. 45.

[75] For example, Quarterly Returns, No. 35 (1863), p. 46.

Fig. I: Marriages and convictions for drunkenness, 1876–1900
Sources Detailed Annual Reports of the Registrar General for Scotland; G. B. Wilson, *Alcohol and the Nation.*

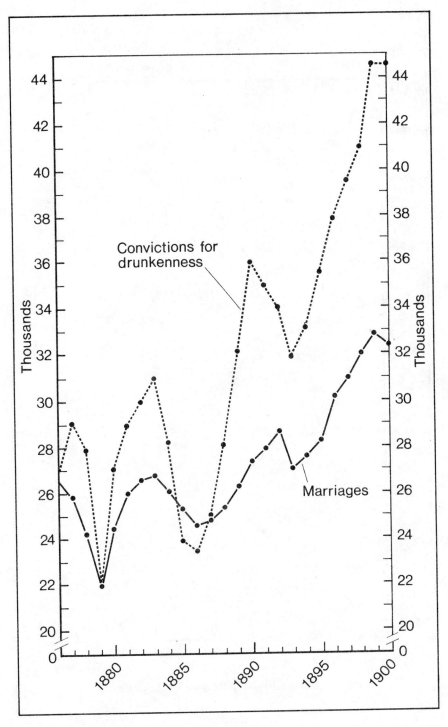

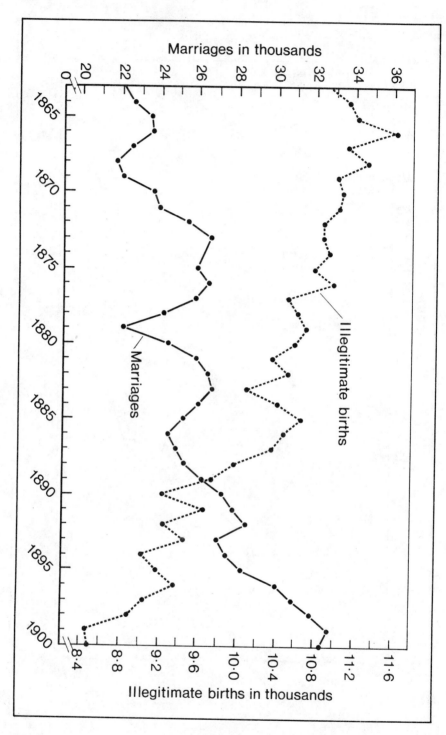

1878–79, 1884–85 and 1893 were all times of depressed trade when illegitimacy rose at the same time as marriages fell, despite the general trend of the number of marriages to rise over time and the number of illegitimacies to fall. But the relationship is not a particularly clear one because some years of *good* trade, like 1866 and 1876, also saw peaks of illegitimacy. Perhaps, in the latter case, too many trusting girls were seduced by men with cash in their pockets who subsequently refused to marry them. Dr. Strachan believed from his Stirlingshire experience that at least a third of the pregnant girls were not subsequently married, though promises 'are generally kept by young men of good character, rather the better class of persons, where the parents probably interfere, and where probably the girl has more respectable parents ... Young men who have no particular connexions ... very often abandon the girl and leave the place'.[76]

The Scottish law that legitimized bastards on the marriage of their parents was believed by Strachan and others positively to encourage both illegitimacy and eventual desertion of the pregnant girl, because it was easy for an unscrupulous man to promise marriage (without witnesses) to the girl, and then leave her in the lurch. Some indication of the differing proportions of honest men and dishonest is given by the proportion of cases in which the father of the illegitimate child is known, since registrars were forbidden 'to enter the name of any person as the father of an illegitmate child save at the joint request of the mother and the person acknowledging the paternity, who must attend at the Registration and sign the Register along with the mother'.[77] This very explicit social act was a public acknowledgement of parenthood and alliance that might well precede a marriage, but when the father refused to sign the register one might have considerable doubt about his intentions. An inspection of 679 illegitimate births in selected counties in 1861 showed that in only a quarter of the cases was the father's name entered, ranging from 38 per cent on Orkney and 34 per cent in Banff to 15 per cent in East Lothian and 10 per cent in Wigtown.[78] The north evidently held rather fewer irresponsible men than the south, but even in the north-east two-thirds of fathers did not sign.

* * *

What conclusions might now be drawn about the nature of Scottish marriage in the long run? The main available sources—legal and demographic—are not illuminating over a whole range of problems where the historian has a right to be inquisitive. Did people enjoy marriage, for example? They were

[76] *R.C. Report 1867–8,* Appendix, p. 173.
[77] G. T. Bisset-Smith, *Vital Registration,* p. 17.
[78] T. C. Smout, 'Aspects of sexual behaviour', p. 68.

Fig. II: Marriages and illegitimate births, 1863–1900
Source Detailed Annual Reports of the Registrar General for Scotland.

initially discouraged from the idea of sex as pleasure not by Calvinism but by medieval canon law, which stressed that its only purpose was procreation: William Hay described intercourse as an act bound up with 'modesty and sadness, so that it should not take place for the sake of lust, but in virtue and justice'.[79] No doubt the reformed Church re-emphasized this opinion, which finds echoes down to the nineteenth century in the views of the physicians who believed that it was unnatural for a woman to have orgasm. But such views were only the effusions of male theologians and doctors, and tell us nothing of how ordinary people felt.

Was marriage for love? The sixteenth-century view was that it was bound up with God-given affections, but needed the approval of parents. This surely has continuity in the Georgian world of fashion in the New Town of Edinburgh where marriages were not so much arranged as artfully contrived: the carefully-chaperoned balls in the Assembly Rooms and elsewhere were the arena where 'suitable' couples were introduced and encouraged to fall in love, much as happened later in the drawing-rooms of the Victorian bourgeoisie. The expectation is never that parents have the right to oblige children to marry someone whom they do not hold in affection. This was strongly and clearly reinforced by the Scottish doctrine that consent makes a marriage—the consent of the couple, not the consent of the parents, who in the last instance had no right of veto. On the other hand the expectation is also, especially where property is concerned, that the children will consult their parents and not act without their blessing. Even where there was no property, parents might still have an interest: would their son marry a girl who seemed suitable to look after them when they became old and helpless? When, in the nineteenth century, marriage often became associated with young people moving to a town, parental consent was no doubt less important. But 'respectable' parents continued to have a role in the marriage of their grown-up children even in very humble strata of society, as Dr. Strachan shows in his remarks on how they could enforce marriage on couples who had already made their affection for each other only too visible.

All these things suggest features of continuity from the sixteenth century to at least the end of the nineteenth. Perhaps the most significant sign of change was that in some circles marriage appeared to become more of a private and less of a public event. In the sixteenth and seventeenth centuries, and in places to the end of the eighteenth and well beyond, the community participated in a marriage. The dancing at the town cross in the burghs, the processions with pipers and carrying food and drink to offer to passers-by, the firing of guns and unseemly rushing for the door in church were public demonstrations of the involvement of the couple in the society around them. As late as the early part of the nineteenth century the miners of rural

[79] Hay, *Lectures*, pp. 115, 135, 139.

Lanarkshire celebrated 'pay weddings' with the old customs of public processions for the bride and groom headed by a fiddler, guns fired in celebration, and a feast that culminated in putting the lucky couple to bed.[80] The social importance of a traditional wedding was demonstrated, for example, in the Highlands in 1792 when the marriage of John Ross Davidson to Helen, daughter of Donald Munro MacAdie, was chosen by agitators to concert their plans to expel the lowlanders' sheep from Ross-shire and Sutherland, because the occasion would bring together all the people of Strathrusdale and the surrounding districts.[81]

By the nineteenth century, however, marriages seem to have become in certain cases much more private. The more extravagant public demonstrations became matters for folklorists to write about as quaint or rough habits of the past, even if it was still the case that celebrations in the countryside or in the slums often continued to have a very public and communitarian aspect. But now there were other kinds of wedding. An irregular marriage registered on a Sheriff's warrant was an act done away from the eyes of the community; no less was a wedding in a manse of a strange town of a couple from a Hebridean island who did not wish to face the stir of a traditional wedding. Celebrations there would always be, but they were increasingly by written invitation to family and friends. If nothing else, this shift from community involvement in a wedding to individualist privacy, though by no means total or all-pervasive, does seem to reflect a social reality that distinguishes the Scotland of John Knox from that of the industrial revolution and after. No doubt it was itself a reflection of changing social values which allowed people greater freedom from community control in deciding how to run their lives. There is a sense in which 'private life' is itself a worthwhile invention of modern times.

APPENDIX

The following description of a traditional community-centred Scottish wedding in the bride's home is from John R. Allan's semi-autobiographical novel *Farmer's Boy* (London, 1935), pp. 156–7. The wedding is set in 1914, but the emphasis is very much on the survival of traditional modes in the conservative rural society of the north-east. The 'greybeard' referred to was a five-gallon jar of whisky. The ceremony was followed by a feast of memorable proportions, the description of which is too long to quote.

> The company assembled in the dining room at three o'clock. As if indeed to celebrate the end of an epoch, Dungair had invited all his old friends, some of whom were like himself, farmers of the third and fourth generations in those

[80] Alan B. Campbell, *The Lanarkshire Miners: A Social History of their Trade Unions* (Edinburgh, 1980), p. 36.
[81] K. J. Logue, *Popular Disturbances in Scotland, 1780–1815* (Edinburgh, 1979), pp. 60–1.

parts. He sat in his easy chair in the corner between the window and the fire with the greybeard between his feet and a tray of glasses and a jug of cold water from the pump on a small table at his side. As the old men came in with their wives, they walked over to shake his hand and he, without rising, gave them a stiff dram from the greybeard while the maid helped their ladies to a glass of wine. They then sat down in a wide circle around him. The younger guests, friends of Sally and Peter, disposed themselves in odd corners and laughed among themselves while Peter stood in the middle of the room and was congratulated after the coarse fashion of the countryside by all who came in. The minister arrived last of all and, after taking a little wine, turned to Dungair and said they might begin.

Sally came in with her mother, wearing a plain tweed skirt and a white blouse on which she had pinned a black cat that Tom the second horseman had given her at the games. The company stood up, the minister took his position on the hearthrug with Sally and Peter before him, the Old Man made sure that the greybeard was safe between his knees, and the service began. We sang the Hundredth Psalm, led by Uncle Scott, whose rolling bass was like the elemental let loose in that crowded room. Then the minister prayed and began to read the ancient and somewhat pagan service. When he asked who gave the woman to be married, the Old Man replied from his chair with a wave of his staff, Sally and Peter swore to love and cherish each other for the good of their souls and the comfort of their bodies, the minister blessed them, and so they were married. It was usual for the company to have to endure a long discourse on the more refined joys and the less obvious responsibilities of marriage, but it was cut mighty short on this occasion, which was just as well, for the Old Man was quite capable of putting a sudden end to the address if it had lasted one minute over the five. So the minster talked briefly if not to the point, the papers were signed, the benediction pronounced, and the healths of the man and wife were drunk in noble bumpers.

X

Marriage and Fertility in Nineteenth-Century Ireland

L. A. CLARKSON

The stereotype of marriage and fertility in nineteenth-century Ireland is well known. Before the Famine Ireland was a country of young marriage, high nuptiality, and consequently high marital fertility. After the Famine Ireland was characterized by postponed marriage and a uniquely high level of permanent celibacy. Age-specific marital fertility, however, continued to be high by western standards. In so far as the crude birth rate fell in Ireland in the later nineteenth century, it was through the combination of low marriage rates and high fertility and not, as in Britain, by a reduction in marital fertility.

Accompanying this stereotyped description is a stereotyped explanation, essentially economic in character. Early marriage in pre-Famine Ireland was made possible by the existence of extensive waste land, the ease with which holdings could be sub-divided, and the ubiquity of potato cultivation: thus the economic conditions for marriage and the setting up of a new household were readily available. Futhermore, so enduring was poverty in pre-Famine Ireland, and so hopeless the future, there was little point in postponing marriage to more propitious times: two could live as miserably as one and children were both a comfort to ageing parents and labour for tilling the potato patch. The Famine sent these mechanisms into reverse. The potato could no longer be relied on, landlords successfully resisted sub-division, and consolidated farms and commercial farming on compact hold-ings offered the best hope of material gain. The tenancy passed undivided to the eldest son, whose marriage was delayed until the father died or was ready to surrender possession. The younger children had the choice of remaining single or leaving the land. Only the persistence of high marital fertility seems to lack an economic explanation, but even here R. E. Kennedy has supplied one. Emigration, he argues, was an alternative to celibacy as a means of attaining improved material welfare; but emigration removed from Ireland the most adventurous and resourceful in sexual as well as in economic matters, leaving behind the most conservative. Those women remaining in Ireland, and marrying, clung to behaviour patterns which continued to result in very high fertility even after such patterns had been abandoned elsewhere in western Europe.[1]

[1] Robert E. Kennedy, Jr., *The Irish: Emigration, Marriage, and Fertility* (London, 1973), p. 15 and ch. 7.

The difficulty with stereotypes is that they may fail to reveal the full picture or may even obscure parts of it. The problem with those presented above is two-fold. First, there is the question of timing. The Famine did not mark the change from young and widespread marriage to delayed marriage and celibacy. The change was in train before the 1840s, although the quality of the evidence makes the tracing of the transition uncertain. Conversely, old patterns persisted in some areas long after the Famine. Then, secondly, there is the matter of motives. If the Famine was not the dividing line between different modes of marital behaviour, then possibly the simple economic explanations offered, both for young and widespread marriage, and for delayed marriage and celibacy, are not adequate either. There is certainly a need to put marriage in Ireland into a wider explanatory social setting than hitherto has been the case.[2]

Evidential difficulties bedevil all efforts to write the demographic history of Ireland, particularly in the pre-Famine years. The first attempt at a national census in 1813 was abandoned uncompleted. The censuses of 1821 and 1831 were defective in various degrees, both probably understating the true population and neither providing direct evidence about marriage and fertility (although the 1821 census did collect data on ages).[3] The 1841 census, by contrast, was a major achievement and gathered information, *inter alia*, on marriages, and births and deaths for the previous decade. However it under-recorded those aged two years and under to the extent of about 150,000, an error that affects calculations of fertility and the crude birth rate.[4] The 1841 census, nevertheless, is the statistical starting point for the study of marriage and fertility; and censuses continue to be the only source of statistical information on these matters until the introduction of official registration of births, deaths, and marriages in 1864. For the pre-Famine years census sources may be supplemented by impressionistic literary evidence, travellers' reports, the so-called 'Statistical Surveys' of various counties commissioned by the Dublin Society, and government investigations such as the Poor Inquiry Commission of 1836, but the period remains a demographer's dream world. Parish registers, the salvation of English demographers for the pre-registration period, are sparse and inadequate in Ireland and have not, so far, been made to yield worthwhile evidence about the age or frequency of marriage, nor about marital fertility.

*　　　*　　　*

[2] I have here in mind the work on English and European marriage by such authors as Peter Laslett, Edward Shorter and Lawrence Stone.

[3] W. E. Vaughan and A. J. Fitzpatrick (eds.), *Irish Historical Statistics: Population, 1821–1971* (Dublin, 1978), pp. xii–xiii. It is commonly believed that the 1831 census overstated the population of Ireland, but Professor Lee has recently argued plausibly that it under-recorded it. (Joseph Lee, 'On the accuracy of the pre-Famine Irish censuses', in J. M. Goldstrom and L. A. Clarkson (eds.), *Population, Economy and Society: Essays in Irish Economic and Social History in Memory of K. H. Connell* (Oxford, 1982, pp. 46–53).

[4] G. S. L. Tucker, 'Irish fertility ratios before the Famine', *Economic History Review*, 2nd ser., XXIII (1970), 278, n. 1.

238

'In the two or three generations following the 1780s', wrote K. H. Connell, 'peasant children by and large married whom they pleased when they pleased.'[5] According to Connell this period of 'haphazard, happy-go-lucky marriage'[6] was the result of a unique set of circumstances. 'A settlement was the preliminary to marriage, and settlements in these years were made more readily available by a swing from pasture farming to arable, by the sub-division of holdings, by the reclamation of waste land, and by the more general dependence upon the potato as a foodstuff.'[7] However, the evidence Connell used for early marriage—essentially the Poor Inquiry Commission—and the manner in which he used it have been criticized by Professor Drake, who doubts whether Irish marriage ages before the Famine were especially low. Professor Lee, on the other hand, has argued that among the large and growing labouring class the age of marriage for males was commonly in the low twenties, higher than Connell supposed, but below the age thought to be general in western Europe.[8]

Assuming that the age of first marriage in pre-Famine Ireland was below the levels prevailing elsewhere in western Europe, it is far from clear that it was a phenomenon established from the 1780s. Connell noted evidence of young marriage in Ireland dating back to the seventeenth century, but preferred to believe that it became widespread only after 1780 when 'the economic and social scene made it increasingly possible . . .'.[9] More recently, however, Dr. Ó Gráda has pointed out that early marriage may have been common throughout the eighteenth century, while Professor Cullen has asserted boldly—and without evidence—'that Ireland was unaffected by the demographic revolution which had affected western Europe in or before 1500 in which the marriage age rose progressively to around 27 for males and 25 for females'.[10] In the present state of demography in Ireland, the matter is unlikely to be resolved. But if young marriage was a long established pattern it cannot be explained simply in Connell's terms, since the conditions which he claimed produced it did not exist in the earlier decades of the eighteenth century.

It is, of course, possible to think of alternative economic explanations for low marriage ages before the 1780s. In the late seventeenth and early

[5] K. H. Connell, 'Catholicism and marriage in the century after the Famine', in *Irish Peasant Society: Four Historical Essays* (Oxford, 1968), pp. 114-15. This is merely the last of a long line of similar statements by Connell, commencing with *The Population of Ireland, 1750-1845* (Oxford, 1950).

[6] Connell, 'Catholicism and marriage', p. 114.

[7] Connell, *The Population of Ireland.* pp. 52-3.

[8] M. Drake, 'Marriage and population growth in Ireland, 1750-1845', *Economic History Review*, 2nd ser., XVI (1963), 301-13; Joseph Lee, 'Marriage and population growth in pre-Famine Ireland', *Economic History Review*, 2nd ser., XXI (1968), 283-95.

[9] Connell, *The Population of Ireland*, p. 53.

[10] Cormac Ó Gráda, 'The population of Ireland 1700-1900: a survey', *Annales de Démographie Historique* (forthcoming); L. M. Cullen, 'Population growth and diet, 1650-1850', in Goldstrom and Clarkson (eds.), *Population, Economy and Society*, p. 93.

eighteenth centuries land was relatively abundant, tenants were in short supply, and landlords were willing to grant favourable leases to those wishing to occupy land. People wishing to marry could rent land readily enough. However, it was not tenant farmers who married very young, but the labouring or cottier class. For this group other explanations are needed. One possibility is that the great importance of family labour in the Irish economy enhanced the value of children, so encouraging early marriage; or at least making them less costly in economic terms than they might otherwise be. Family labour, for example, was important in the linen industry as it developed rapidly in Ulster from the end of the seventeenth century. But it was valuable, too, in such diverse activities as turf-cutting, rabbiting, fishing, fowling, the collection of seaweed, reeds and rushes, petty dealing, as well as in the more obvious agricultural tasks. Children were also employed as domestic servants, not just as living-in servants, but frequently as non-resident daily servants who continued to dwell with their parents, so contributing directly to parental income.[11] In the later eighteenth century, of course, the increasing number of tillage farms created as a result of the growing demand for grain, increased the demand for agricultural labour of all kinds and further raised the economic value of children; while sub-division and potato cultivation provided, as Connell suggested, greater . opportunities for early marriage.

Nevertheless, eighteenth- and early nineteenth-century patterns of marriage behaviour require a broader explanation. Marriage performs a number of distinct functions. One is as an institution for the transmission of property from generation to generation. Indeed, delayed marriage and the high level of celibacy existing in many societies, including post-Famine Ireland, are often explained as strategies designed to avoid the excessive sub-division of tenancies. Such strategies held limited attraction in pre-Famine Ireland. Among the cottier class, occupying land as under-tenants or precariously renting potato land on con-acre (i.e. on tenancies of less than one year) in return for labour services, the question of passing on property to the next generation did not arise. Even among those with tenancies to bequeath, sub-division to accommodate all the children was frequently carried to excessive lengths, notwithstanding the opposition of landlords. For many of the Irish the desire to retain the family together on the land was stronger than the desire to keep holdings to a viable size for agriculture; and the existence of dual occupations made this not merely possible but necessary.[12]

[11] For family labour in the linen industry see W. H. Crawford, *Domestic Industry in Ireland: The Experience of the Linen Industry* (Dublin, 1972). For rabbiting and similar activities see Graeme Kirkham, 'Economic diversification in a marginal economy: A case study of Magilligan, Co. Londonderry', in Peter Roebuck (ed.), *From Plantation to Partition: Essays in Honour of Professor J. L. McCracken* (Belfast, 1981, pp. 72–81). For non-resident domestic servants see L. A. Clarkson, 'Household and family structure in Armagh City, 1770', *Local Population Studies*, XX (1978), 18.

[12] In the linen industry, for example, there was division of labour in the household based on sex and age; the composition of the household was therefore crucial to its operation as an

Marriage is also a religious ceremony, although its sacramental nature does not necessarily lead to early or widespread marriage. The striking feature about eighteenth-century Ireland is the apparently universal accept-ance of Christian teaching on monogamous marriage little more than a century after sections of Gaelic and Gaelicized society had practised poly-gamy.[13] What is unclear, however, is the extent to which the Catholic population submitted to, or was able to submit to, the disciplines of their Church on the subject of marriage. Catholic marriages were required to be celebrated in the presence of a priest 'privately or publicly, at any time or place, and in any form or manner the celebrating priest thought proper'.[14] During the period of the Penal Laws when the Church operated with a suppressed episcopate and with a low ratio of priests to people, it cannot have been easy to organize even an informal priestly ceremony in the more remote areas of the country, to impose regulations relating to consanguinity, nor to supervise patterns of sexual behaviour. Yet there is a widespread impression in the literature that the desire to marry early was not frustrated by a shortage of clergy; and the low level of illegitimacy and pre-nuptial pregnancies apparent in pre-Famine Ireland suggests that lawful marriage, at least as a prelude to raising children, had a strong hold on the population.[15]

For whatever reasons, pre-Famine Ireland displayed a generally lower age of first marriage than in England; and a level of marital fertility which at the time of the 1841 census was about 20 per cent higher.[16] Marital behaviour, nevertheless, was changing even before the Famine. From as early as about 1815 the age of first marriage had been rising in some regions of the country and the proportion of the population married was falling. The consequent restriction of fertility was a major cause of a decline in the rate of growth of population.[17] Between the 1790s and 1821 population in Ireland may have been growing at around 1.5 per cent per annum and the rate of growth could have been as high as 2.0 per cent; but between 1821 and 1841 the annual rate of growth, based on Lee's revision of the census figures, had fallen back to about 0.8 per cent.[18]

economic unit. See Brenda Collins, 'Irish emigration to Dundee and Paisley during the first half of the nineteenth century', in Goldstrom and Clarkson (eds.), *Population, Economy and Society*, pp. 202–4.

[13] Kenneth Nicholls, *Gaelic and Gaelicised Ireland in the Middle Ages* (Dublin, 1972), pp. 73–7; Edward MacLysaght, *Irish Life in the Seventeenth Century* (Cork, 2nd edn. 1950), p. 49.

[14] W. Harris Faloon, *The Marriage Law of Ireland* (Dublin, 1881), p. 9. See also Nicholls, *Gaelic and Gaelicised Ireland*, p. 74.

[15] K. H. Connell, 'Illegitimacy before the Famine', in *Irish Peasant Society*, pp. 51–86; S. J. Connolly, 'Illegitimacy and pre-nuptial pregnancy in Ireland before 1864: the evidence of some Catholic parish registers', *Irish Economic and Social History*, VI (1979), 5–23.

[16] Tucker, 'Irish fertility ratios', p. 280.

[17] S. H. Cousens, 'The restriction of population growth in pre-Famine Ireland', *Proceedings of the Royal Irish Academy*, LXIV, section C, no. 4 (1966), 85–99.

[18] L. A. Clarkson, 'Irish population growth revisited, 1687–1821'; and Lee, 'Pre-Famine Irish censuses', both in Goldstrom and Clarkson (eds.), *Population, Economy and Society*.

The clearest indication of changes in marital behaviour comes from comparing in the census returns the numbers of children aged five years or younger per thousand women of child-bearing age (15–46) in different parts of Ireland. For the country as a whole in 1841 the figure was 659, but the range ran from 761 in County Mayo in the west to 469 in County Dublin in the east. These figures, in fact, minimize the contrast between west and east, since they take no account of child mortality which was also highest in the western counties. Allowing for this, births per thousand women in the remote western counties in 1841 were almost 40 per cent higher than in south-eastern Ireland.[19] The most important cause of the regional contrasts was the difference in the proportions of married women in the population, which, in turn, reflected differences in the age of first marriage. In 1841 the proportion of women in Ireland in the age range 16 to 45 years who were married was 45.3 per cent, with extremes of 53.1 per cent in County Mayo in the west and 38.5 per cent in Queen's County in the east. The census of 1821 does not contain evidence on marriage; but marked regional differences in the proportions of women aged 46 to 55 who were married appear in the 1841 census, again with the highest proportions in the west, and the lowest in the eastern and north-eastern counties of Dublin, Queen's, Wexford, Londonderry and Down. Most of these marriages had been formed when the women were in their early twenties; thus regional differences were already likely to have existed at the time of the 1821 census.[20]

In the two or three decades before the Famine, therefore, the eastern parts of Ireland were retreating from the traditional pattern of young and widespread marriage and high fertility. The pattern could not be sustained without an adequate economic basis, and this was being eroded by changes in economic and institutional conditions. From the end of the Napoleonic wars the market conditions facing Irish farmers were altering in significant ways. Grain prices that for half a century had risen and encouraged the spread of arable farming in a country so well endowed by climate and geography for pastoral farming, now moved into secular decline. Arable products remained the major component of farm output until the Famine, but the market no longer encouraged that spread of tillage which had generated the demand for cottier labour subsisting on small potato plots. In addition, the more progressive landlords were attempting to reduce the tangle of sub-letting that had made rational estate management such a nightmare. The trends away from tillage and towards eliminating sub-tenancies were more advanced in the eastern half of the country and were not entirely successful even there. In the west sub-division and the colonization of waste land persisted under the continuing pressure of population growth, giving rise to the regional differences in marriage and fertility revealed by the census of 1841.

[19] Cousens, 'Restriction of population growth', pp. 87–8, 94.
[20] Ibid., pp. 94–5.

A further undermining of old ways came from the decay of by-employments. The most important influence here was the introduction of power-spinning into the Irish linen industry in the 1820s which had the effect of concentrating spinning in the south-east of Ulster, close to Belfast and the Lagan valley. Until the 1860s there remained a continuing demand for hand-loom weavers in the countryside, using the power-spun yarn supplied by the Belfast factories, but domestic hand-spinners could not survive the competition of cheap factory-spun yarn. The effect on rural population growth depended on whether there were alternative employments to fall back on. In the Montiaghs, for example, an extensive parish on the southern shores of Lough Neagh in County Armagh, hand-spinning succumbed to competition from factory-spinning in nearby Lurgan, but reclamation of land from the lough, fishing and turf-cutting for sale in Lurgan provided other forms of livelihood, and population continued to increase in the parish until the 1860s, long after neighbouring regions were losing population.[21]

Emigration was another response to the closing of economic opportunities in Ireland. It had already reached substantial proportions by 1841. In that year 419,000 Irish-born people were recorded as living in Britain, many of them having arrived in the previous 20 years. In addition, at least 214,000 people emigrated directly to America during the 1830s, and a further 153,000 went to America via Liverpool.[22] The highest levels of emigration were from the north and north-eastern counties where the combined effects of shortages of land, restrictions on sub-division, and the contraction of the domestic linen industry were most severely felt. In the west, where traditional marriage patterns persisted, emigration was much less marked.

The effect of pre-Famine emigration on marriage and fertility is unclear since not a great deal is known about the sex and age composition, and marital status of pre-Famine migrants. Of the 2,000 to 3,000 transatlantic migrants from County Londonderry in 1834, 41 per cent were aged 20–29. Sixty per cent of all migrants were males and 40 per cent females. Probably more than half the migrants left in family groups, but there was also a considerable number of solitary males, both unmarried men and husbands migrating ahead of their wives and children.[23] Males also dominated seasonal migration which was important before the Famine.[24] Migration with these characteristics depressed the total number of marriages in the community and also the crude birth rate by removing a disproportionate number of the

---

[21] F. X. McCorry, 'The Montiaghs: A study of population in North Armagh, 1700–1901', unpublished M.S.Sc. thesis, Queen's University, Belfast, 1979, pp. 51, 70, 86.

[22] S. H. Cousens, 'The regional variation in emigration from Ireland between 1821 and 1841', *The Institute of British Geographers: Transactions and Papers,* Publication no. 37 (1965), p. 18.

[23] James H. Johnson, 'Population movements in County Derry during a pre-Famine year', *Proceedings of the Royal Irish Academy,* LX, section C, no. 3 (1959), 147, 150.

[24] Lynn H. Lees and John Modell, 'The Irish countryman urbanized: a comparative perspective on the Famine migration', *Journal of Urban History,* V (1976–77), 400–1.

most fertile from the population. Because of the sex imbalance in the stream of migration, there was also probably an increase in celibacy resulting from a shortage of marriage partners. Emigration may also have reduced *marital* fertility by separating husbands and wives. On the other hand, the *over-all* fertility rate, measured by comparing the numbers of children aged five years and under with all women of child-bearing age, might well have risen because migration tended to be concentrated on young adults, thus removing from Ireland a disproportionate number of females in the fertile age groups.

*   *   *

The trends already in motion in the 1820s and '30s help to put the trauma of the Great Famine into perspective. Famine deaths probably numbered 800,000 or more and between the two censuses of 1841 and 1851 the population of Ireland through deaths and emigration declined by 20 per cent. Mortality was highest in the west and south-west among the cottier class whose dependence on the potato was greatest. In other words, it was highest in those regions and among those groups in society where traditional patterns of high nuptiality and high fertility had continued in the pre-Famine decades. The survivors of the Famine, therefore, were principally those who were already moving towards the modern Irish pattern of postponed marriage and celibacy. The Famine did not initiate the shift in marriage and fertility in nineteenth-century Ireland.

It is misleading, nevertheless, to reduce the Great Famine to the role of catalyst speeding up events that were already taking place. The loss through starvation and disease of almost 10 per cent of the population in five years and the even greater outflow of population to Britain and America emphasized the precarious nature of an agrarian system based on sub-division and potato culture; in the second half of the nineteenth century, and particularly from the 1870s, the existing trend towards consolidation of holdings accelerated, strengthening the forces leading to emigration. Moreover, as emigration became a dominant feature of Irish life, the contrast between living standards in rural Ireland and standards in the receiving countries became better known, leading to further emigration. Of greater relevance to the present discussion, the selective nature of post-Famine emigration contributed strongly to the peculiarly Irish way of reducing the birth rate through the combination of low nuptiality and high marital fertility.

Between 1851 and 1901 the population of Ireland fell from 6.5 millions to 3.2 millions. The crude birth rate declined from over 33 per 1,000 in 1841,[25] to 26.2 in the 1870s, and to 22.4 in the first decade of the twentieth century. The proportion of men unmarried in the 45–54 age group rose from 10 per cent in 1841, to 16 per cent in 1871, and to 24 per cent by 1901;

---

[25] The figure of 33 per 1,000 has been calculated from the 1841 census, but as Tucker has pointed out, if it is correct, it is so by accident. Tucker's adjustments to the 1841 census imply a higher figure (Tucker, 'Irish fertility ratios', p. 277).

for women the proportions were 12 per cent, 15 per cent and 20 per cent. Marital fertility, on the other hand, possibly rose between 1841 and the 1870s. It fell between the 1870s and 1880s but then increased until the first decade of the twentieth century. Marital fertility in England and Wales, by contrast, was falling steadily from the 1870s, and by 1911 was 60 per cent lower than in Ireland.[26] As Walsh has pointed out, 'Ireland shared its reduction in natural increase with the countries of Europe at this time, but it was unique in its almost complete reliance on low nuptiality to achieve this reduction.'[27] It is this unique pattern of events that poses the most important demographic problem in post-Famine Ireland.

*　　　*　　　*

One possible explanation—at least in its crude form—can be quickly discarded: that the Famine exercised such a profound psychological influence on Irishmen and women that they were determined never again to allow farms to become so fragmented and the potato so dominant in the diets. In practice, from the 1850s to the 1870s, pre-Famine patterns of marriage and fertility, associated with sub-division and the potato, re-established themselves in the west of Ireland, precisely in those areas where mortality in the 1840s had been so high. Rates of natural increase of population were substantially higher in the western counties of Ireland than in the east—regional differences that were associated with regional variations in nuptiality. Between 1841 and 1871 the proportion of women who remained unmarried rose in all counties; nevertheless, a sharp contrast persisted between east and west, with the highest levels of nuptiality being found in western counties such as Leitrim, Mayo, Galway, Kerry, Clare, Roscommon and Sligo. In these seven counties, under 14 per cent of women in the age range 40–44 were single in 1871, barely half the figure found in the seven eastern counties displaying the lowest levels of nuptiality: Londonderry, Down, Wexford, Dublin, Queen's, Carlow and Antrim. Higher marital fertility in the west was not offset by higher levels of emigration. In the west of Ireland waste land was still available to be colonized and landlords remained willing to permit sub-division when the only viable alternative land use was rough grazing. The very poverty of the western communities inhibited emigration except in years of periodic potato failure when bursts of emigration occurred. Thus pre-Famine characteristics were eroded in the west only very gradually and not until the 1880s did rates of natural increase come close to those on the eastern side of the country.[28]

---

[26] Kennedy, *The Irish,* pp. 176–7, 213.

[27] Brendan M. Walsh, 'Some Irish population problems reconsidered', *The Economic and Social Research Institute,* Paper no. 42 (1968), p. 10.

[28] S. H. Cousens, 'The regional variations in population changes in Ireland, 1861–1881', *Economic History Review,* 2nd ser., XVII (1964), 301–21; Brendan M. Walsh, 'Marriage rates and population pressure in Ireland, 1871 and 1911', *Economic History Review,* 2nd ser., XXIII (1970), 148.

A psychological response to the Famine, nevertheless, appears in Connell's accounts of the development of peasant marriage in the second half of the nineteenth century, albeit combined with economic and religious influences. 'The Famine was remembered and described too starkly and too vividly for men to disregard the folly of impetuous marriage. And as people became more enlightened they became more cautious: many of them penetrated now the mystery of the social ladder; it exists, they perceived, to be climbed . . . Much of the Irishman's spiritual teaching, too, tended, if it did not aim, at deflecting his thoughts from marriage . . .'.[29] The result was a major transformation in the nature and function of peasant marriage.

Before the Famine peasant marriages (the word peasant is used loosely by Connell to refer to all in the rural community who occupied small plots of land) were 'youthful and general', with the parties themselves choosing whom and when they married. But after the Famine 'a marriage came to be heralded by commercial rather than biological advances; and until the two fathers concerned had completed their negotiations their children remained unmarried'.[30] The objective was to keep the farm undivided. To this end inheritance was restricted to one child, usually the eldest son, who was not permitted to marry until the father was ready to make over the farm. The remaining children, save perhaps for a daughter, had the option of remaining single or emigrating. The father selected his son's bride, for it was important that she bring an adequate dowry with her; this was valuable in settling the remaining children, perhaps by paying for their education or providing their fare in the case of emigration. Once the marriage had taken place, husband and wife moved into the groom's parental home, taking over the running of the farm and household, and creating in due time the classic three generational stem family said to be characteristic of Irish rural society.[31]

Several forces, in addition to the psychological shock of the Famine, contributed to the change. Market trends encouraged pasture farming on larger holdings and the shedding of under-employed family labour. These trends were reinforced, first by profit-conscious landlords, and then by the land legislation of the later nineteenth century that turned tenants into peasant proprietors, making them all the more aware of the advantages to be had from commercially cultivated undivided farms. The material benefits were made even more obvious by the spread of retail trade, which brought new consumption goods into peasant consciousness, and by the demonstration

---

[29] K. H. Connell, 'The land legislation and Irish social life', *Economic History Review*, 2nd ser., X (1958), 5.

[30] K. H. Connell, 'Peasant marriage in Ireland after the Great Famine', *Past & Present*, XII (1957), 76–91. Quotations at pp. 76, 77.

[31] K. H. Connell, 'Peasant marriage in Ireland: its structure and development since the Famine', *Economic History Review*, 2nd ser., XIV (1961–62), 501–23; P. Gibbon and C. Curtin, 'The stem family in Ireland', *Comparative Studies in Society and History*, XX, no. 3 (1978), 433–4.

effects of visiting migrant relatives with 'clothes like the Yankee's, a voice so *bizarre* and a purse so full . . .'.[32]

The material allures of delayed marriage and celibacy received unexpected support from the teaching of the Catholic Church in Ireland. The new patterns of peasant marriage imposed strains and sacrifices on the individuals involved: on the eldest son whose marriage was delayed, sometimes until well into middle age, and then to a girl not of his own choosing; on his bride whose wedding was arranged by her father with as much finesse as the sale of a cow at a market; and even more on the remaining brothers and sisters who were denied both inheritance and matrimony unless they moved right away. Loyalty to family helped to overcome the demands but, according to Connell, stronger support came from the Maynooth-trained clergy of the Catholic Church. The majority of Irish priests were themselves sons of peasants, personally familiar with the material benefits deriving from arranged marriages. Proceeding direct from rural farm to diocesan school to the seminary at Maynooth, they absorbed, undiluted, Catholic teaching on celibacy, marriage and sexual behaviour. The Church taught that marriage was good but that religious celibacy was even better; however, in Connell's view, such teaching was slanted in sermons and by other means into a suspicion of marriage and a downright hostility towards courtship and normal social relationships between young men and women. Because of their dominant position in rural society, the clergy were able to impose their views of marriage and sex on the population, so shaping attitudes that accepted the discipline of delayed marriage and celibacy.[33]

Connell's account of post-Famine marriage is plausible and persuasive, not least because of the elegance with which it is presented. Nevertheless, it poses difficulties, of which four may be identified. The least important is that of chronology. Connell writes of the post-Famine period generally, paying little attention to the persistence of old habits in the west, although not ignoring them entirely. More important, he assumes more than demonstrates the existence of the stem family, relying on descriptions collected by the Irish Folk Lore Commission and, possibly, extrapolating back from Arensberg and Kimball's famous study of the stem family in County Clare in the 1930s. As Gibbon and Curtin point out, there is little other anthropological evidence to support a belief in the widespread existence of the stem family and even less historical investigation. Their own sample survey of household schedules completed for the 1911 census suggests that the stem family was indeed more common in Ireland than in England, but not more common than simple family households of one or two generations.[34] A third set of problems arises from Connell's view of the influence of the Church.

[32] Connell, 'Peasant marriage in Ireland after the Great Famine', *passim*. Quotation at p. 86.
[33] Connell, 'Catholicism and marriage', *passim*.
[34] Gibbon and Curtin, 'The stem family in Ireland', pp. 433–9. In Ireland, unlike Britain, the household census schedules for 1901 and 1911 are open to public inspection.

Catholic critics have complained of his portrayal of Catholic teachings on marriage; but even conceding its accuracy, it does not adequately explain why, of all the Catholic countries of Europe, Ireland adopted so enthusiastically the peculiar combination of low nuptiality and high marital fertility as a means of restricting the birth rate in pursuit of higher material standards of living. Finally, more pointedly, it does not explain why the Irish Protestant population also displayed a tendency towards low nuptiality.

*   *   *

R. E. Kennedy has attempted to deal with some of these questions in his re-examination of post-Famine marriage. Kennedy agrees that marital behaviour was determined primarily by economic circumstances and assumes, with Connell, that the stem family emerged as an important social institution after the Famine. But he integrates changes in marriage behaviour with emigration in a more satisfying manner, and takes a fundamentally different view of the role of the Church. He is also more explicit about the timing of changes. Dealing with the last point first, the move towards postponed marriages took place in two stages. The first shift occurred in the 1840s and was followed by two decades in which the extent of postponed marriages actually decreased a little; but in the next period, 1871–1911, there was a very pronounced move towards later marriage, as measured by the percentage single in the 25–34-year age group, among both men and women. As far as celibacy is concerned, indicated by the percentage single among those aged 45–54, there was an increase in the 1850s, followed by another sharp increase, especially among men, between 1891 and 1911.[35]

In explanation, Kennedy argues that the Famine, by demonstrating the precariousness of life on smallholdings, prompted the move towards postponed marriages in the 1840s, with an increase in permanent celibacy emerging in the statistics a decade later. Here Kennedy follows Connell, although he largely ignores the fact that the trends could be observed in the 1820s and 1830s. The second turning-point requires a more subtle explanation, although once more economic motives dominate. After the 1870s 'the motivation to postpone marriage and remain permanently single was especially intense . . . because the gap between desired and actual standard

---

[35] Kennedy, *The Irish,* pp. 141–4. It should be noted that Kennedy's Table 50, giving the percentage of men and women aged 25–34 who were unmarried, is taken from the *Censuses of Population of Ireland, 1946* and *1951.* They show that in 1891 67 per cent of males aged 25–34 were unmarried, and in 1901, 72 per cent. However, the *Censuses of Ireland, 1891* and *1901* (H.C. 1892, XC, 1 and H.C. 1902, CXXXIX, 1) give different figures: 64 per cent for 1891 and 68 per cent for 1901. It seems then that an error has occurred in transcribing the data from the United Kingdom censuses to the Republic of Ireland censuses. The increase in the incidence of postponed marriage (and celibacy) occurring at the end of the nineteenth century, therefore, may have been less sharp than Kennedy supposed. There are also small discrepancies in the figures for single women between the Irish and U.K. censuses. I am grateful to Mrs. Brenda Collins for helping me discover the differences in the two sets of sources.

of living probably was greater than in any other European country'. Kennedy does not adequately explain why the awareness of the gap became sharper after 1870, but hints that it was connected with rapidly rising living standards in England and America. He ignores the possibly depressing effects on Irish rural incomes of agricultural imports from the New World. Emigration, too, was stimulated by the prospects of greater wealth overseas, but because of its character emigration had two conflicting influences on nuptiality. More single women emigrated than single men, creating a shortage of marriage partners for men in the countryside, so increasing the amount of permanent male celibacy. On the other hand, when the rate of emigration increased in the 1870s and '80s, a disproportionate number of unmarried people of both sexes left Ireland and nuptiality in the population that remained behind therefore actually increased. However, when the rate of emigration declined after 1891, there was once more a fall in nuptiality, especially obvious in the increasing amount of celibacy among men.[36]

The relationship between emigration, marriage, and fertility occupies a central place in Kennedy's thesis. Three characteristics of permanent emigration from post-Famine Ireland are striking. First, it was 'betterment' migration: people moved in the expectation, not always fulfilled, of better jobs or enhanced social postions. Overwhelmingly, the Irish finished up as general labourers or as unskilled workers in factories or in the service sector, but to migrants formerly underemployed and probably unpaid on small family farms, this *was* an improvement. Women, particularly, were persuaded to migrate by social considerations. In Irish households their role was subordinate to that of men, their household tasks, their social life and their matrimonial prospects determined by fathers and brothers. Emigration offered such women the prospect of independence as well as employment.[37] This leads to a second feature of post-Famine migration: the preponderance of women. Except for the years of the Boer War when army service attracted men to Britain, women outnumbered men in Irish emigration before 1914.[38] This was a reversal of pre-Famine patterns and was established early in the 1840s and '50s.[39] Depending on the employment opportunities available, the disparity could be very marked. In Dundee, for example, the linen industry generated a large demand for female labour during the 1840s and attracted many young female migrants from Ireland. As as result, the sex ratio of the Irish-born population of Dundee aged 15–24 was 551 males per 1,000 females in 1851, compared to a ratio of 738 for the same age cohort in the whole community.[40] Over the total spectrum of Irish emigration to Britain and America, the disproportion of women was not nearly so great, but its

[36] Kennedy, *The Irish,* pp, 156–8, 163–4, 209–10, 213. Quotation at p. 209.
[37] Ibid., pp. 7, 76–7.
[38] Ibid., pp. 77–8.
[39] Lees and Modell, 'The Irish countryman urbanized', p. 401.
[40] Collins, 'Irish emigration to Dundee and Paisley', in Goldstrom and Clarkson (eds.), *Population, Economy and Society,* p. 201.

existence helps to account for the high level of male celibacy in the Irish countryside.

This brings us close to the third feature of Irish migration. It was essentially a rural-urban movement; and because nineteenth-century Ireland lacked rapidly expanding urban centres, with the exception of Belfast from the 1860s, it was principally a movement from the Irish countryside to the cities of Britain and North America. The implications of this feature for nuptiality, when considered with the other characteristics of emigration, were considerable. Most notably, it produced unbalanced sex ratios in both town and country, with an excess of men in rural areas and surpluses of women in the towns. The female excess in urban areas appeared most clearly among the Irish in the cities of Britain and America,[41] but it was also apparent within Ireland. In Belfast, Ireland's one major industrial city, the sex ratio among the whole population in 1901 was 862 males per 1,000 females; and in the 15-24 age group it was 759. Among migrants (i.e. those born outside Belfast) in the same age cohort the ratio was only 707. The imbalance between the sexes was particularly marked among young Catholic migrants (15-24), where the ratio was as low as 582, compared with 750 among young Protestant migrants.[42]

Had Ireland possessed other industrial cities similar to Belfast in attracting young women from the countryside, the sex ratio in Ireland as a whole would have been close to unity. As it was, the majority of women who migrated went to the cities of Britain and America, leaving an excess of males in Ireland. In the forty years 1871-1911 the ratio of single males to females rose in every county and by 1911 was below 1,000 males per 1,000 females only in the relatively urbanized counties of Antrim, Down, Dublin and Londonderry.[43] In this way the limited extent of urban development in Ireland depressed nuptiality. And it did so in another way as well. Cities with their greater range of employment opportunities imposed fewer barriers to matrimony than the Irish countryside where land, inheritance and marriage were so closely intertwined. Thus marriage was more common and occurred at an earlier age in cities. Once more Belfast provides the clearest example within Ireland. In 1901 the proportion of unmarried men in the 25-34 age range was only 44 per cent, compared with 72 per cent for Ireland as a whole, and 36 per cent in England. For women in the same age group the figures were 44 per cent in Belfast, 53 per cent in Ireland and 34 per

---

[41] Lynn Hollen Lees, *Exiles of Erin: Irish Migrants in Victorian London* (Manchester, 1979), Table A.1.; Lees and Modell, 'The Irish countryman urbanized', p. 401.

[42] The ratio for the whole population is calculated from the *Census of Ireland, 1901* (H.C. 1902, CXXVI, 1). The age cohort sex ratios are based on an 8 per cent sample of household schedules completed for the 1901 census, covering 26,349 people. I am grateful to Mrs. Brenda Collins for making them available to me from her unpublished paper, 'Aspects of the family in Edwardian Belfast', presented to the Annual Conference of the Economic and Social History Society of Ireland, Galway, September 1980.

[43] Walsh, 'Marriage rates and population pressure', pp. 154-5.

cent in England.[44] The Irish in Belfast behaved in much the same way as the British in Britain, but very differently from the Irish in rural Ireland. The Irish in British and American towns, too, displayed habits of marriage closer to those of the host communities than to their kinsmen left behind.[45]

A major difference between Kennedy and Connell concerns the influence of the Church. There are two points of dispute. First, Kennedy argues that Catholicism encouraged early marriage and did not discourage it. 'The Church does not consider sexual union within marriage sinful, and during the nineteenth century early marriage was encouraged by the Church as a deterrent to immorality.'[46] Here Kennedy appears to ignore Connell's distinction between official doctrine and what was preached in the parishes. Secondly, he believes that what he calls Catholic sexual puritanism was a body of beliefs accepted by those who had adopted a single way of life for other reasons—for example, because they aspired to an economically or socially superior status—because 'it helped them to avoid emotional involvements which might lead to marriage'.[47] The argument is not, in fact, too far from Connell's; and does not exclude the possibility of a two-way connection between belief and action—or rather inaction.

Mention has already been made of Kennedy's explanation of the persistence of high marital fertility: that those women who remained in Ireland and who married young were more likely to acquiesce in Catholic teaching encouraging large families than those who departed. This conservative attitude to fertility was reinforced by the assumption on the part of parents that many of their children would emigrate on reaching adulthood, so ceasing to be a responsibility. Kennedy also argues that postponed marriage and emigration actually increased marital fertility in Ireland by removing from the ranks of the married those women who desired low marital fertility. At the end of the nineteenth century barely 10 per cent of women of any given age cohort of women married by their early twenties (20–24); the remainder either emigrated or delayed marriage. Kennedy assumes that those who married young actually preferred high marital fertility, whereas the women who postponed marriage or emigrated were those who desired to have small families. When the rate of emigration declined from the end of the nineteenth century more of these women remained in Ireland to marry, causing marital fertility to fall.[48]

This hypothesis rests on the assumption that desired fertility was the same as actual fertility. Indeed, much of Kennedy's discussion of marriage and fertility in nineteenth-century Ireland proceeds on the basis of assumption,

[44] The Belfast figures are taken from the *Census of Ireland, 1901* (H.C. 1902, CXXVI, 12). The figures for Ireland and England are taken from Kennedy, p. 143.

[45] Lees, *Exiles of Erin*, pp. 148, 260; Lee and Modell, 'The Irish countryman urbanized', p. 393.

[46] Kennedy, p. 146.

[47] Ibid.

[48] Ibid., pp. 192–200.

including—like Connell—his belief in the importance of the stem family. The most interesting aspect of his work, though, is its attempt to fit Ireland into a general model. Irish population history is often claimed to be unique. 'Flattering as this idea might be to the Irish', writes Kennedy, 'it is unsettling to social scientists to admit the existence of an apparent exception to so many well known and widely accepted theories concerning population growth, urbanization, emigration, age at marriage, and family size.'[49] This leads him to search for what was peculiar and what was general in Ireland's demographic history, and to the conclusion that Ireland 'is the most extreme example of the general European pattern'.[50] But at what point does a country's history become so extreme that it ceases to accord with the general model at all? When does it become unique?

*   *   *

Ever since the publication of Connell's *Population of Ireland* in 1950 the question of Ireland's uniqueness has been debated. His revised calculations of Irish population before 1821 demonstrated a rate of growth lower than that implicit in some older estimates and close to the rate of growth of population in England. Ireland seemed, therefore, to fit into an English pattern. True, the mechanism that Connell claimed caused population growth in Ireland—rising marital fertility, was different from that emphasized by English demographers, but he suggested that perhaps increasing fertility was important also in England.[51] Later, when Drake argued that a decline in the death rate was the most important reason why population grew in Ireland as well as in England,[52] the case for believing Ireland to be peculiar all but disappeared. Yet population growth in Ireland before 1821 may well have been more rapid than Connell calculated, more rapid than in England or indeed anywhere else in western Europe; and it depended on a high level of marital fertility.[53] Further, not even the most enthusiastic advocate of the importance of rising fertility in explaining English population growth has ever associated it with dietary changes. In England, moreover, population growth did not occur largely within an agrarian economy lacking industrialization and urbanization. Pre-Famine Ireland, if not unique, was certainly extreme. It is this extremeness that produced the peculiarities of the later part of the century. Because of the absence of urbanization, migration became important in taking off the surplus agrarian population. Because migration was selective in terms of sex, age and, possibly, attitudes, it contributed to the lowering of nuptiality. And because nuptiality was

[49] Ibid., p. 1.
[50] Ibid., p. 141.
[51] K. H. Connell, 'Some unsettled problems in English and Irish demography', *Irish Historical Studies*, VII (1951), 225–34.
[52] Drake, 'Population growth in Ireland', pp. 301–13.
[53] Clarkson, 'Irish population growth revisited', in Goldstrom and Clarkson (eds.), *Population, Economy and Society*, p. 28.

lowered, the crude birth rate fell. Other countries in Europe made the demographic transition to lower birth rates in the late nineteenth century, but no other country followed the Irish way. In this sense, Ireland was unique.

If the consideration of Ireland as a special case is one dominant theme running through discussions of marriage and fertility, another is the division of the nineteenth century into two periods separated by the Famine. In spite of successful attempts by Cousens and others to show that population growth was slowing down and the age of marriage rising before the Famine, and notwithstanding the demonstration that old ways persisted in the west of Ireland until the 1870s, the Famine remains the great watershed in Irish historiography. In part this is because of its proximity to the census of 1841, a source that offers historians their first really solid foothold after picking their way through what Professor Lee has recently referred to as 'the swirling hazards of eighteenth-century population estimates'.[54] As the period of speculation almost untempered by data merges into an era of solid statistical information, it is easy to assume that we are moving from one period of demographic history to another. Indeed, we are. Before the Famine the population was rising, and trends in marriage and fertility must be considered in this context. After the Famine population was falling. In this sense, too, Ireland was special, for no other nation in Europe permanently lost population in the nineteenth century, although most countries, including Britain, possessed regions in which the population declined. Only if it is argued that the population of Ireland would have declined in the nineteenth century without the failure of the potato crop does the Famine lose its role as the event splitting Irish population history in two. It has, in fact, been suggested both by Carney and by Kennedy that population might have fallen without the Famine, for Ireland was facing Malthusian pressures that would have produced preventive checks and massive emigration. Relying on a survey of population made in 1843 of the estates of Trinity College Dublin, scattered over 16 counties and comprising one per cent of the land area of Ireland, Carney believes that population decline may have already begun in the early 1840s. Kennedy believes a fall would have commenced in the 1860s or '70s, as inescapable changes in agricultural methods pushed people off the land.[55] On the other hand, Mokyr has recently denied that Ireland was in a Malthusian trap and assigns to the Famine a cataclysmic role. It is too early yet to assess the soundness of Mokyr's work, since his evidence remains unpublished.[56] But if he is correct, then Ireland is certainly unique, for the

---

[54] Lee, 'Pre-Famine Irish censuses', in Goldstrom and Clarkson (eds.), *Population, Economy and Society*, p. 38.

[55] F. J. Carney, 'Pre-Famine Irish population: the evidence from the Trinity College estates', *Irish Economic and Social History*, II (1975), 35–45; Kennedy, pp. 207–8.

[56] J. Mokyr, 'Malthusian models and Irish history', *Journal of Economic History*, XL (1980), 159–66.

population of no other country in recent times has been permanently affected by a single natural disaster.

A third feature of writing on marriage and fertility within Ireland is the narrow focus of the discussion. Marriage has been considered primarily as an economic institution conditioned by economic pressures. It is true that many other issues are hinted at by Connell, particularly in his later writings. For example he has interesting things to say about the feelings existing between husbands and wives, parents and children, and he does not ignore the biological and psychological aspects of marriage and fertility. Yet, except in his long but tentative essay on Catholicism and marriage—which he himself described as a *ballon d'essai*[57]—these issues flicker for a while before fading into the background of economic determinism. Even his discussion of the 'match' in peasant marriage is dominated by economic considerations. Kennedy, the other major contributor to the subject, claims to deal with social, economic and political issues underlying Irish population trends, but his discussion of social conditions is subordinate to the economic, consisting mainly of assumptions about the stem family and attitudes to women, and his treatment of political conditions barely exists.

A wider view of marriage has been taken by historians of Irish migrant communities; and in this respect Lynn Hollen Lees's study of Irish marriage in Victorian London is useful in providing an agenda of what might be investigated in Ireland.[58] First, there are courtship patterns. These have been studied to some extent by Connell in his examination of the swing from young and unrestricted choice of partners to older and regulated marriage in rural Ireland, but much still remains to be learned, particularly about the forms of courtship and the incidence of pre-marital sexual activity. Secondly, there are the related issues of affectivity, authority and familial roles. Very little has been written about these subjects. Pre-Famine marriages, among the lower classes at least, are assumed to have been contracted on the basis of romantic love, but we do not know how marriages so frailly rooted survived the erosions of endemic poverty. Similarly, post-Famine arranged marriages, organized around commercial rather than romantic consider-ations, are thought to have functioned satisfactorily, or at least to have endured, but little is known for certain. Arthur Young and other eighteenth-century observers frequently commented on the Irish fondness for children. What happened to such feelings after the Famine, when delayed marriage at one end reduced the number of children on which to bestow affection, and emigration at the other took them off to Britain or America, perhaps never to be seen again? As for authority, nineteenth-century Irish families are portrayed as dominated by men who played the major economic role, bequeathed and inherited the family property and made the important family decisions. To judge from the handful of household listings that have survived

[57] Connell, 'Catholicism and marriage', p. 113.
[58] Lees, *Exiles of Erin,* ch. 6.

from the late eighteenth and early nineteenth centuries and the structure of census schedules, the public face of the Irish household was strongly masculine,[59] but the workings of the family behind the façade is scarcely known.

Finally, how did the family function as a unit and how did those functions change over time? Much of what has been written about marriage in nineteenth-century Ireland implies that the family fits into the pre-industrial type identified by Young and Wilmott, whereby it was the unit of production dependent on the mutual economic co-operation of its members.[60] Lynn Lees has shown how family functions and relationships between individuals within the family changed in Irish communities established in English towns as the economic activities were transferred from the household to the marketplace, and as employment became organized through the labour market and not within the family. What similar changes occurred in the functions of the Irish rural family as land holdings were consolidated and pasture farming replaced labour-intensive tillage? And what changes developed in the relationships between its individuals—between the ageing parents cantankerously clinging onto the farm and the eldest son frustrated in his desire to marry; and between him and his siblings restricted to celibacy or emigration? Until such questions have been adequately studied, our knowledge of marriage and fertility in nineteenth-century Ireland remains incomplete.[61]

[59] L. A. Clarkson, 'Armagh 1770: Portrait of an urban community', in D. W. Harkness and M. O'Dowd (eds.), The Town in Ireland: Historical Studies XIII (Belfast, 1981), 82–3; F. J. Carney, 'Aspects of pre-Famine Irish household size: Composition and differentials', in L. M. Cullen and T. C. Smout (eds.), Comparative Aspects of Scottish and Irish Economic and Social History, 1600–1900 (Edinburgh, 1977), pp. 32–46.

[60] Michael Young and Peter Wilmott, The Symmetrical Family: A Study of Work and Leisure in the London Region (London, 1973); cited in Lees, Exiles of Erin, pp. 140–1.

[61] I am grateful to Mrs Brenda Collins and Miss Margaret Crawford for their help with this paper.

XI

Natural and Sacred Professions: Motherhood and Medicine in America[1]

MIRIAM SLATER and PENINA M. GLAZER

At the turn of the nineteenth century marriage was perceived as a dimension of one's life which was in contradistinction to professional life. Although men were expected to function in the world and at home in a highly compartmentalized fashion, women could not aspire to such dualistic behaviour. The separation of domestic and professional activity reflected an ideology which maintained that a woman's place was in the home, but the newly emerging professionals had to operate in the public sphere of the market-place. This compartmentalization of life was a trend which fitted well with male, but poorly with female, professional goals. To the extent that men became identified with the professions—scientific, objective, and active in the world, and women became identified with the domestic—emotional, subjective, and nurturant in the home, professional life became the world of middle-class men and the home became the place for middle-class women.[2]

The unusual woman who left her sphere to penetrate the outside world of work was making a rarely attempted journey whose social distance was measured in light years.[3] Such women faced a double set of obstacles. They had either to add the natural 'profession' of motherhood to their chosen one, or to reject that role actively, a difficult task in a society which increasingly emphasized motherhood as the natural choice for all middle-class women.

In traditional professions such as medicine, women professionals faced further complications. Not only did their ambitions violate strong social mores, but also they had to do battle against the increasing pressures to exclude women from the modern training and practice of medicine. Under these heavy constraints, only a few women made it into the most advanced medical schools at the turn of the century.[4] They were apt to be women of

[1] The authors wish to thank the Center for Research on Women in Higher Education and the Professions at Wellesley College and the Russell Sage Foundation for their encouragement and support in writing this chapter which is part of a larger project on women professionals.
[2] Mary Roth Walsh, *Doctors Wanted: No Women Need Apply* (New Haven, 1977); Cynthia Fuchs Epstein, *Woman's Place: Options and Limits in Professional Careers* (Berkeley, 1970), esp. ch. 2; William H. Chafe, *The American Woman* (New York, 1972), ch. 4; Elizabeth Janeway, *Man's World, Woman's Place* (New York, 1971), esp. ch. 1.
[3] Juliet Mitchell, *Women's Estate* (New York, 1971), ch. 6.
[4] Although there were a number of female medical colleges at this time, they were of very mixed quality. This is not surprising since it was rare for any medical school in the country

extraordinary drive and achievement, whose professional ambitions violated the rigid norms of a society which assumed that married women would stay at home. They found themselves competing for entrance to medical schools, coveted internships, and hospital staff positions in a profession which actively sought to eliminate them from its precincts.

Even the most successful of these avant-garde women were forced by social pressure and marital responsibilities to adjust their career goals. Their male colleagues could choose whether or not to marry; for a man either choice was acceptable, and the decision to marry normally enhanced male professional prospects. The reverse was true for women. Although their numbers were few, these extraordinary women provide a clear view of the way in which marriage practices and professional definitions interacted to move women out of the mainstream of public life. It should also be stressed that the response of these women was not passive and that their actions and success in overcoming barriers contributed to the formation of a complex culture of professionalism and to the creation of some new options for women.

In order to examine the special nature of the relationship between marriage and professionalization, this chapter will focus on two eminent women physicians in the United States who came to maturity in the late nineteenth century—Dorothy Mendenhall (née Reed) and Anne Fearn (née Walter). Their lives illustrate the nature of the structural limitations placed on even the most ambitious and talented members of their sex during a period which is noted for the expansion of opportunities for men of their class and background.

*　　*　　*

Dorothy Reed Mendenhall graduated in 1895 from Smith College, an institution which was one of the early experiments in female higher education, designed to offer women undergraduate training equal to that of the elite men's colleges and universities. She also benefited from the hard-won battle of the Women's Committee of Baltimore, an older generation of feminists whose influence and money combined to force the reluctant but needy founders of the Johns Hopkins Medical School to open its prestigious doors to women students. She entered the medical school in 1896, just three years after that institution began its pioneering effort in modern medical education,

---

to require a college education or training in the sciences. Among the more prestigious schools Harvard accepted no women, Cornell agreed to accept a few women in return for a $25,000 endowment. The biggest breakthrough came when Mary E. Garret donated over $300,000 to the $500,000 endowment campaign and thereby compelled Johns Hopkins to open that school with equal terms for women and men. One distinguished pathologist resigned in protest. Walsh, pp. 169, 176-7, also see table on female enrolment, p. 183; Simon Flexner and James Thomas Flexner, *William Henry Walsh and the Heroic Age of American Medicine* (New York, 1941), pp. 215-17.

with its curriculum modelled primarily on the German medical schools.[5] Thus, the hard work of an older group of feminists had created networks and organizations which allowed Reed and a small group of able and privileged young women to avail themselves of the best professional education the United States had to offer at that time.

Reed's subsequent career depended on this access to modern education which concentrated on laboratory methods and scientific research, and an enriched curriculum appropriate to the new discoveries in bacteriology. She went on to incorporate that learning into her professional life and achievements. In the early part of her career, Dorothy Reed made significant discoveries concerning Hodgkins disease.[6] She is also known for her work in public health, which she moved into after marriage and childbirth ended her research and hospital practice.

Anne Walter Fearn followed the more typical nineteenth-century method of entering medical school without first attending a liberal arts college. She enrolled in the Women's Medical College of Pennsylvania, one of the few remaining female institutions which had been established by women in response to being denied access to schools for men.[7] Virtually all of Fearn's professional career was spent in China where she provided medical services to Chinese populations that were otherwise without access to western-style medical care.

An examination of their lives reveals that both women struggled with the problem of being female, which for each entailed the need to confront the problem of marriage; each chose a different style of career management for coping with her own and society's attitudes toward women physicians and women in marriage. Reed's career, contrary to expectations, indicates that the greatest barriers to her professional success were to occur after she had successfully obtained her M.D. from the most prestigious school of the period.

*   *   *

[5] Ibid., pp. 91–2; William G. Rothstein, *American Physicians in the Nineteenth Century* (Baltimore, 1972), pp. 290–1. The earlier medical schools offered very poor science education, no research and little clinical instruction. It was not until after the Civil War that Harvard Medical School even acquired microscopes or stethoscopes. The new education placed a high premium on science and laboratory instruction and the bedside method of clinical instruction. A report by Abraham Flexner became very important in the early twentieth century in forcing other schools to move to scientific, research-based education and to close down the small proprietary schools. See Abraham Flexner, *Medical Education in the United States and Canada* (New York, 1910, reprinted 1972).

[6] *New York Times* (1 August 1964), 21:4.

[7] Anne Walter Fearn, M.D., *My Days of Strength: An American Woman Doctor's Forty Years in China* (New York, 1939), ch. 1; Walsh, pp. 72–3 and 178–80, discusses the importance of the women's medical colleges, founded between 1848 and 1895, in the face of bitter opposition from the male medical establishment. Once small numbers of women were accepted at the male controlled medical schools (especially Johns Hopkins, Cornell, and Tufts) the women erroneously assumed that their schools had outlived their purpose. In the early part of the twentieth century all but the Women's Medical College of Pennsylvania closed their doors.

There were any number of ways in which the pre-existing prejudice against women's equal participation could reappear in the evolving professional opportunities of the period. As the professions came to be elaborated in modern terms, the rewards of participation and the concern with territoriality and exclusivity increased concomitantly. As new standards and expectations of professional endeavour were defined, both formal and informal opportunities also arose for denying entrance to those who did not qualify, or often even to those who did qualify academically but who failed to fit the conventional mould because of race, class, or gender. For example, in the case of medicine, professional success depended on securing an appropriate internship in a prestigious specialty, approval by newly empowered licensing boards, promotion up the ranks of the expanding medical faculties, leadership positions or at least a voice in professional associations, editorships of medical journals which were the arbiters of medical knowledge and contributions—in short, all the myriad requirements and rewards of professional advancement. The fact that many of the latter were only barely emerging in the late nineteenth and early twentieth centuries did nothing to make these requisites of professional achievement less esteemed and sought after in the gathering momentum for professional expansion. Access to each of these opportunities and possibilities was hedged about with biases and restrictions against certain classes and ethnic groups.[8] But the women on whom we are focusing should have been the most likely candidates in terms of class, colour, and educational attainment. Only the blemish of gender marred their acceptability.

Preference on the basis of class, sex, or ethnic origin was nothing new and clearly was not an invention of the new professions. What made the exclusion of women particularly complex was the determination of the modern professions to wrap themselves in a mantle of meritocratic goals and scientific objectivity. The medical profession's main claim to superiority over rival healing and training programmes was based on its commitment to objectivity and science. Reconciling such meritocratic goals with the reality of ill-concealed discrimination against certain groups involved medical schools, hospitals, and individual physicians (and their counterparts in other professions) in arbitrary and often contradictory systems of exclusion which often resulted in holding out false hopes for aspiring and qualified newcomers.

The arbiters of professional ideology argued that the true professional could seldom be a woman because her temperament and training were unsuitable for the kind of dispassionate inquiry which was increasingly touted as the central component of medical training. They reasoned that commitment to scientific method made deep probing into the nature of life and death legitimate. Scientific inquiry even sanctioned the violation of taboos concerning personal modesty for the higher motives of attaining

[8] Burton J. Bledstein, *The Culture of Professionalism* (New York, 1976), ch. 3; Walsh, especially chs. 1 and 4; Magali S. Larson, *The Rise of Professionalism* (Berkeley, 1977), pp. 239–44.

greater scientific knowledge. In the healing relationship a patient could be expected to reveal not only physical problems, but also emotional and even moral concerns to the objective scrutiny of the scientifically trained medical practitioner.

Given the profession's interest in enlarging its role as an authority on moral and emotional problems, it might have been possible to argue that women's natural reproductive capacities put them directly in touch with natural functions and actually enhanced their usefulness in the new style of healing. Furthermore, there was an earlier tradition of midwives and healers which tied women to the natural world. However, the possibility that women might have natural predispositions to be healers came under attack in the late nineteenth century by male practitioners who, in the name of science, proclaimed that women lacked the higher order of intellect and reason which scientific investigation and a profound commitment to rationality required.[9]

In addition to their reputedly physiologically inferior mental equipment, there were also psycho-social barriers to keep women from the newly developed precincts of laboratory training. Just as their mental inferiority meant that they might not be able to make the logical leap from the identification of micro-organisms on the slide to some larger theoretical understanding of disease theory (of which there was very little reliable understanding by anyone), so did the supposedly fragile female constitution make it difficult to expose their delicate sensibilities to the horrors of the death house and the morgue. The myth of female sensitivity encouraged the development of a deeply held conviction that young women could not abide the stench and suggestion of the nude cadaver. However, a familiarity with the latter was an essential component of the increasing emphasis on pathology in medical training. Furthermore, to combine such morbid activity with prospective motherhood was unthinkable. Given these values and perceptions, it was not difficult to create settings which virtually precluded women's participation in the evolving profession. These emerging professional definitions and structures fit well with the larger drive towards exclusivity among the approved membership, which by the turn of the century was composed overwhelmingly of white, native born, middle-class men.

*   *   *

Despite this set of negative assumptions about women and these exclusive organizational mechanisms, some few women contrived to join the ranks of the modern, scientifically trained physicians. In attempting to qualify themselves as legitimate members of this increasingly prestigious group, those women who succeeded in becoming doctors were a group whose daring and ambition evoked ambivalence in others as well as in themselves.

Dorothy Reed's memoirs, one thousand pages of her recollections set down

[9] Barbara Ehrenreich and Deirdre English, *For Her Own Good: One Hundred and Fifty Years of the Experts Advice to Women* (Garden City, 1978), pp. 84–8.

over a period of almost a decade and a half (1939–53) near the end of her life, reveal something of the private experience of a woman of Faustian ambition who tried to be both a dedicated physician and a devoted mother. With characteristic frankness and insight she tells us that there will be some omissions and unexplained passages 'for I am a woman and a Victorian but I shall write for my great granddaughter of the way my world was made, and what happened to me in the making and unmaking of it'.[10] Her unpublished memoirs provide an unusually unsentimental, poignant, literate record which allows us considerable access to the private satisfactions and stresses as well as to the public accomplishments of this extraordinary woman.

These papers are an unusual source and could be the basis of a major biography. It is not our intention to present biographical studies of the two women we are considering. Rather, the Reed papers and the Fearn autobiography allow us to explore certain critical themes. We will focus on the way in which their professional development was inextricably bound up with their maturation as women. Although they were ideologically committed to the idea that excellent performance would ultimately overcome any lingering prejudice against female participation, they were forced to come to terms with the considerable pressure which resulted from their deviant female behaviour.

The position of token which they came to occupy was a very difficult one. On the one hand, it provided some possibilities for ambitious and talented persons. At the same time it evoked uncertainty and doubt about their proper role, both as physicians and as women. This ambivalence had a serious impact on their decision to marry. Most of their contemporaries chose not to combine the two separate and contradictory sets of demands which came from family and work. Colleagues like Florence Sabin, Alice Hamilton, and S. J. Baker all remained single and devoted themselves entirely to their careers. Reed and Walter were among the very few who embraced both domestic and professional life. Although they did ultimately marry, they still had some reservations about the appropriateness of the decision for professional women.[11] They struggled to create a family life which was satisfactory but which did not stifle their professional ambitions. Although devoted to their husbands and children, they found domesticity quite disagreeable and even painful at times. They never became fully enmeshed in the appropriate activities of conventional, middle-class wives—charity, church, and clubs. Work was their most satisfying and demanding outlet, yet it always filled them with unrelenting conflicts.

Reed's memoirs begin with the description of a childhood in a middle-class family of conventional Victorian sensibilities. Although her father died

[10] Dorothy Reed Mendenhall, unpublished autobiography (1939–53), Sophia Smith Collection, Smith College, Northampton, Mass., Folder A, p. 1 (hereafter referred to as DRM).
[11] Reed was 32 years old; Fearn was 29.

when she was still quite young, there was enough money for Dorothy to be educated in Europe by private tutors, as befitted young ladies of her class. There was very little encouragement from her mother or other family members to break away from prevailing social conventions and little else in her background that would have pointed to her career choice and lifestyle. When she undertook the study of medicine it was still considered a highly questionable occupational choice for women. The medical training of the period involved a violation of Victorian standards of female modesty regarding bodily functions. Even the men of the period examined these mysteries rather self-consciously, and familiarity with such matters was considered to be totally unsuitable for women. The ramifying influence of these attitudes surfaced in any number of ways. For example, Dr. Hurd, Superintendent of Johns Hopkins Hospital, and a man of considerable influence at this most advanced institution, accused Reed of being 'a sex pervert' when the new intern expressed a willingness to work in the male wards.[12]

Ironically, he made the accusation to a woman whose own family would probably have shared his evident repulsion towards her behaviour. When Dorothy's elder sister had installed her at Smith College as a freshman a few years earlier, the sister immediately wrote home to their mother that 'it was no place for a well-brought up girl to stay'. Her sister 'disapproved of the girls crowding the streets, calling out joyously to one another, hatless, and acting with a freedom and abandon' which the well-protected Dorothy 'had never seen before'.[13]

That these strict standards of female decorum were not some peculiarity of the crabbed New Englander's sense of propriety, is confirmed by the experience of Reed's southern contemporary, Anne Walter Fearn. Dr. Fearn, who was subsequently to practise medicine in China for 40 years, had been a southern debutante who had her fashionable coming-out party at the Governor's mansion at Jackson, Mississippi.[14] When this proper young belle announced to her family that she intended to study medicine, they were horrified because 'Dr. Mary Walker in gentlemen's attire was our idea of a woman doctor', and the latter was considered to be 'a sacrilege against womanhood'.[15] Anne's mother wired her daughter, who was visiting in California, to consider that 'No disgrace has yet fallen upon your father's name. Should you persist in carrying out your mad determination to study medicine I shall never again recognize you as my daughter'.[16] Anne's previous behaviour appears to have been quite unremarkable. The young socialite's career decision drew the observation from a physician friend of the family that 'as a social butterfly Miss Walter would be a great success, as a

---

[12] DRM, Folder F, part 1, p. 3.
[13] DRM, Folder D, p. 1.
[14] Fearn, p. 6.
[15] Ibid., p. 11.
[16] Ibid., p. 12.

physician never—there is nothing to her'.[17] Apparently, there was little indication at that stage of her development that she would persist in her goal and ultimately found and administer a hospital in China.[18]

Reed's experience with her family showed marked similarities. It took 'nearly ten years to accustom my mother to my being a doctor, which she had bitterly opposed'.[19] And society's judgement of the impropriety of medical practice for women can be seen in her aunt's accusation that Dorothy's example contributed to the delinquency of her younger female cousin. Her aunt believed that the aspiring physician was 'loose moraled like all women doctors'.[20]

This stamp of social disapproval followed her up to the time of her marriage. Her future in-laws were not very pleased that their son had decided to marry a doctor. 'As far as the Mendenhalls were concerned, I was a professional woman—a type they disliked. Father Mendenhall never spoke of me or introduced me to anyone as a physician. Mrs. Mendenhall, always subservient to his every wish, was not the first vice-president of the anti-suffrage association for nothing. So I certainly was not wanted as an in-law.'[21]

Like most women trained at the end of the century, Reed had to prove herself repeatedly against the prejudices regarding female frailty. A generation had passed since 1878, when the Association for the Advancement of Medical Education of Women found it necessary to defend the then daring proposition that women physicians could work in the Infirmary as 'faithfully, steadily, and perseveringly, as it could have been done by men' and further that 'it is very rare that the health of any of these [female] physicians fails under the work'.[22] Nevertheless, Reed felt it necessary to remain on duty at Johns Hopkins during the full twelve months of ward duty, rather than the usual ten which her male colleagues thought sufficient. She worked those wards in the suffocating heat of a Baltimore summer when the male interns had sensibly left for cooler climates and a brief rest. She was spurred to remain because of 'something Dr. Hurd [the hospital superintendent] had said of woman's being irresponsible and not to be trusted to see things through'.[23]

Although Reed resisted seeing herself as a trail-blazer and always preferred to minimize the differences between herself and her colleagues, she was caught up in the pioneer's unavoidable obligation to perform heroically.

[17] Ibid.
[18] Ibid., ch. XXIV.
[19] DRM, Folder G, p. 61.
[20] DRM, Folder F, part 2, p. 21.
[21] DRM, Folder G, p. 61.
[22] Emily Blackwell, 'Women in the regular medical profession', an address printed in the *Report of the Association for the Advancement of the Medical Education of Women*, delivered 26 March 1878 (New York, 1878), p. 10.
[23] DRM, Folder F, part 1, p. 29.

Numerous accounts by women physicians corroborate their sensitivity on this point and their determination to prove that women were as able as men. And it was always the male defined standard that women believed they must match. No task was too arduous, no personal risk too high or frightening, no patient too threatening, contagious, or vile. This super-woman style can be understood partially as a counter-phobic attempt by these path-breakers to offer opposing evidence to long and deeply held beliefs concerning the stereotyped female—that weak and neurasthenic fragile flower.[24]

The women who are the central focus of this study were committed to basing their sense of achievement and professional attainments on male models of activity. Hence they believed that the highest priority was to be given to one's work over one's personal life. They considered their femininity an intrusion on their pretensions to be taken as experts of some substance and consequently wished to make their physical differences as unnoticeable as possible.

The challenge of trying to be like men manifested itself in every area of life. Their excessive concern with dress was a manifestation of the unspoken assumptions about their need to be accepted as equals. Dr. S. Josephine Baker, an eminent contemporary of these women, articulated the lengths to which she went so that her feminine appearance might not prove a distraction.

> The Gibson Girl [style of clothing] was a great help to me when I started work in the public health field: It is difficult to realize today how curious it seemed then [first decade of 20th century] that a woman should hold my position. [When she was made assistant to the Commissioner of Health] they made me print my name on the letterheads as 'Dr. S. J. Baker' to disguise the presence of a woman in a responsible executive post. The Gibson Girl played a part in the situation because shirt waists and tailored suits [became] a conventional feminine costume . . . if I was to be the only woman executive in the New York City department of Health, I badly needed protective coloring . . . I could so dress that, when a masculine colleague of mine looked around the office in a rather critical state of mind, no feminine furbelows would catch his eye and give him an excuse to become irritated by the presence of a woman where, according to him, no woman had a right to be.

She appreciated also the convenience of tailored clothing because it required very little time or energy to care for, and

> in the process of convincing myself that my work must be a success and equal to the best that might be done by a man in that man-made world, I invariably took home a brief case full of trouble every night and worked at it until the small hours

[24] The period was noted for its production of advice manuals aimed at women of this class, frequently written by male doctors, which warned of the dangers of strenuous activity. Women professionals clearly broke with this tradition and flouted these dicta. Jill Conway, 'Stereotypes of femininity in a theory of sexual evolution', in M. Vicinus, *Suffer and Be Still* (Bloomington, Indiana, 1973), pp. 140–54, documents the theories concerning the belief in the innate differences between men and women; Barbara J. Harris, *Beyond Her Sphere: Women and the Professions in American History* (Westport, Conn., 1978), ch. II, contains a detailed summary of 'The Cult of Domesticity' in the late nineteenth-century United States; Sheila M. Rothman, *Woman's Proper Place: A History of Changing Ideals and Practices, 1870 to the Present* (New York, 1978), pp. 23–6.

of the morning. Dr. Mary Walker wore trousers to startle men into recognizing that a woman was demanding men's rights. I wore a standard costume—almost a uniform—because the last thing I wanted was to be conspicuously feminine when working with men.[25]

The uncritical adoption of male values, which judged femininity as a distraction to professional work, tended to engender considerable ambivalence in women. Marriage often served to exacerbate their guilt and doubts rather than to resolve them. Marriage forced them to face all the realities of being a woman, some of which might be side-stepped by those who remained single. But even if they chose not to marry, they had to be careful not to lean too far in the other direction and call attention to themselves for being too mannish. In fact they had to be prepared to try the impossible task of not being enough of either sex to be noticed on that account. They were afraid that notoriety of that kind would result in the speedy withdrawal of the tenuous sufferance on which their participation was based.

By contrast, an earlier generation of feminists, of whom M. Carey Thomas (President of Bryn Mawr College) and her friends on the Baltimore Women's Committee were typical, tended to base their feminism on their sense of separateness from men. Thomas and her friends rejected marriage as a trap for a professional woman. In some ways they were more sophisticated in their assessment of the impossibility of being accepted on equal terms with men. One gets a sharp sense of this in Thomas's and the Baltimore Committee's insistence, for example, that women be accepted on 'the same' terms as men at Johns Hopkins, rather than the proffered 'equal terms' which the male leadership thought generous in exchange for the endowment donated by the Women's Committee.[26] These older women had seen the value in establishing separate institutions for women when necessary, and they also spent considerable energy in promoting their younger colleagues. Women like Reed, on the other hand, were uncomfortable with this concentration on the special strengths and possibilities of women. They preferred to gravitate toward the exhilarating but elusive goal of merging themselves and their work with those of male colleagues, and to minimize differences. They continued to believe that they would gain acceptance, if only their performance were good enough. That is why they criticized the behaviour of the older generation of women for a style which they viewed as pushy and querulous.[27]

Reed recalled with amusement bordering on disdain that Thomas and the Women's Committee were eager for her and her colleague, Florence Sabin, to march in the Johns Hopkins academic procession, because the elder

---

[25] S. Josephine Baker, M.D., *Fighting for Life* (New York, 1939), pp. 64–5.

[26] Flexner and Flexner, pp. 217–19.

[27] In her memoirs Reed comments that she did not like Miss Wald (Lillian Wald, the Settlement House leader) because the latter overworked her staff. DRM, Folder F, part 1, p. 10. She goes on to say that 'women do not stand authority well', and 'women in positions over other women tend to become tyrants'. Ibid., p. 12.

feminists 'wanted the world to know that there were women on the Johns Hopkins University faculty—though she stretched it a bit to put two simple interns in high places'.[28] Reed's attitude contrasted markedly with Miss Thomas's view of the matter. The younger woman revealed an uncritical acceptance of the faculty hierarchy, and was loath to pass herself off as an equal. As a mere intern she felt outranked and inferior. To a feminist like Thomas, the public spectacle of two women marching with an all-male faculty was seen as a visible gravamen against their token position in that estimable institution. In her desire to see the two interns turn out, Thomas was seizing the occasion for a public reminder that there were in fact no women on the university faculty, nor in the undergraduate student body for that matter. If Thomas and the Committee had not previously intervened with their generous gift, there would have been no women in the medical school either.

Although Reed was one of the beneficiaries of these efforts, any gratitude she might have felt was vitiated by the personal repugnance with which she regarded these feminist reformers. Years later, when Reed met the educator Thomas again, she 'was thankful that my life was not that of an administrator or pioneer in any profession for women'. She believed that 'being in the limelight continuously and exercising authority over the young and immature is a fearful responsibility and one that develops unpleasant characteristics'.[29]

Reed seems to have lacked that sense of individual connection with other women which might have made her more charitable towards the acerbic excesses of their leaders, since women understand that the occupational disease of the female path-breaker is sometimes a shrill insistence on her authority. Although Reed had many women friends she confessed to not having any to 'whom I ever felt like unburdening myself'.[30] In this she differed from many accomplished women, including Carey Thomas, who enjoyed life-long, profound, and sustaining friendships with other women.[31] Still, Reed realized that her men friends could not be much help in that regard either because she knew that 'the problems of a man's life are so essentially different from those facing a woman that it would be difficult for him to put himself in her place and see the straight path'. She ended by usually making decisions on her own and 'prayed a lot' that her solitary choices would be the right ones.[32]

Even in the late life recollections of her memoirs, Reed's ambivalence about herself as a woman is still discernible. For example, she thought it important enough to record the fact that the female interns at Hopkins did not go into the doctors' lounge in their rest periods but visited the nurses'

[28] Ibid., p. 23
[29] DRM, Folder F, part 2, pp. 11–12.
[30] Ibid., p. 12.
[31] Edith Finch, *Carey Thomas of Bryn Mawr* (New York, 1947), describes these friendships in great detail.
[32] DRM, Folder F, part 1, p. 12.

sitting room because '46 years ago we still felt on sufferance and wished to be unobtrusive'.[33] She is then moved to the comforting generalization that 'on the whole we women at Johns Hopkins were treated very well. Some over-attention while in school and a little horse play'. Presumably their positions even improved when they became interns for then she asserted that 'there was no discrimination against us'.[34] But the ambiguity surrounding these judgements became apparent when, on the next page, she reconsidered once more, and revised the view to include the reservation that 'we were tolerated and on the whole treated well—but we were distinctly not wanted'.[35]

This barely perceptible awareness of prejudice was reinforced by her experience after finishing medical school when she applied for an internship at Johns Hopkins. Florence Sabin and Dorothy Reed were third and fourth in class rank respectively. Professor Osler, the head of Medicine, advised Reed that there were only four available internships in medicine, the most coveted specialty, and that he could not accept two women, even if their grades made them otherwise eligible. He suggested that Reed take surgery or obstetrics instead, but both of these were less desirable appointments. She refused to compromise and encouraged the less assertive Sabin to do the same. In the end they were both awarded the desired placements, but not without some cost in colleagueship. Those who had earned lower ranking in the class proved to be jealous and put off by the fact that half the available places in medicine had been allocated to women.[36] To Reed, 'this animosity was a blow. It was the first time that I personally was made to feel that I was not wanted in the medical profession and my first realization of the hard time any woman has to get recognition for equal work'.[37]

This lesson learned early in her career was to be repeated in numerous settings. Reed's work as a doctor required continual resistance to the overwhelming prejudices which forced most women to the margins of the medical profession in that period. In the course of her struggle to continue her professional life, she held fast to the conviction that talent would ultimately prevail, even when faced with prejudice that was clearly based on considerations other than ability.

Indeed it was hard for her to surrender her belief in meritocracy. Had she not been admitted to one of the finest institutions in the United States on the same terms as male students? Had not the medical profession demonstrated its own commitment to meritocratic ideas by upgrading the curriculum and by providing an education which centred on scientific and rational achievement? Johns Hopkins' claims to superiority were based on open, verifiable, objective criteria. If excellence were the basis of the admis-

[33] Ibid., p. 4.
[34] Ibid., p. 18.
[35] Ibid., p. 19.
[36] DRM, Folder E, pp. 58–63.
[37] Ibid., p. 63.

sions policy for students as well as for faculty appointments, then surely the demonstration of superior achievement would lead to recognition and success in the field. Reed and her female contemporaries had imbibed these ideas along with their laboratory work, and they optimistically believed that the fight to get women admitted to the medical profession had been won. However, their internship experience did not bear out this optimism and they continued to struggle with a set of beliefs which did not always fit the evidence.[38]

The response to Reed's application for a fellowship in pathology also reflected prejudice against women. She was confirmed with only 'a perfunctory question or two. Dr. Gildersleeve, Professor of Classics, rose and said before affirming [her] appointment he would like to ask Dr. Welch [Dean of the Medical Faculty] one question, "Was the candidate good looking?" The meeting broke up in confusion and with Dr. Welch all hot and bothered.'[39] Even the best women could turn into an embarrassment.

Reed was less than confident about being the token and highly visible woman in a predominantly male institution. The young pathologist believed she was always 'conspicuous anyway as one of the few medical women employed in the medical school or hospital', and she 'felt often as if [she], too, were under the microscope'.[40] This sense of vulnerability to special scrutiny in part accounted for her subsequent decision to keep her impending marriage a secret from hospital superiors because she feared that it might engender unwarranted comments about her neglect of her work, presumably through some romantic distraction on her part.[41]

*   *   *

Dorothy Reed's determination to keep her matrimonial intentions a secret was but the first and relatively minor sign of the more radical disruptions of her career which were to result from her decision to marry. She was already in her early thirties and by then she understood that marriage had consequences not only for her own professional career, but also for other women in succeeding generations, whose prospects for success would be determined by a judgement of her accomplishments.

As she matured the stability of married life had a great and increasing appeal to her. A series of family deaths and problems made the prospect of 'a family and normal home life very attractive and necessary in that context

---

[38] They were not the only ones who believed that coeducation had been assured. This conviction resulted in the closing of almost all the women's medical colleges only to find that women applicants were not given equal consideration and that their numbers were generally kept to a quota of 5 per cent. Harvard University did not admit women to its medical school until after the Second World War, despite repeated efforts to challenge its policy. Walsh, ch. 6, also tables on pp. 193 and 245.

[39] DRM, Folder F, part 2, p. 2.

[40] Ibid., p. 3.

[41] DRM, Folder G, p. 62.

of personal uncertainty'.[42] By this time she had had some professional success at leading hospitals both in Baltimore and in New York City. Dean Welch had become very supportive of her work. On at least one occasion he had praised her publicly 'and said as I closed [the lecture] that the audience had had the privilege of hearing a description by the leading authority on the [Hodgkins] disease', a subject for research which he had originally recommended to her.[43]

Her marriage was viewed as a kind of apostasy. It was construed by her mentors and certain colleagues as a rejection of professional commitment on her part. Now, whenever she saw Dr. Welch, 'usually in Washington at the meetings of the National Academy he always asked anxiously, "Are you keeping up with your reading?" '[44] The reiteration of that patronizing question and the succession of embarrassments that became part of her annual experience at professional meetings, must have been very difficult for her. Behind that seemingly solicitous query was the unspoken accusation that she was wasting her training which made her 'suppose I was a great disappointment to him'.[45]

As if this were not sufficient punishment for her lapsed condition in the profession, she also learned that her marriage was used as justification for keeping women out of other medical schools. Dr. Alice Hamilton, the only female faculty member at Harvard Medical School, told Reed that the latter was cited as an example of a wasted education when the Harvard faculty debated the possibility of admitting female students. It was characteristic of that institution's determined and successful efforts (until 1946) to keep themselves free of women that they should seize on Reed's example 'as an able woman who had married and failed to use her expensive medical education'.[46]

In her 1,000-page memoir there is nothing to match the bristling anger of her comments on this particular point. She admitted 'that it always hurt, but now I know it was a damn lie, and I can claim honestly that I think that I can give evidence of the use of medical knowledge much wider and deeper than that shown by the average physician, whether in practice or teaching'. And the aged doctor, still smarting from the affronts of decades past, added for good measure, 'This is why I am writing this section on my work after marriage'.[47]

By any standards that work was considerable, but it evoked nevertheless an ill-concealed disdain from erstwhile colleagues. However painful such rejection was, it did make her more willing to develop a healthy scepticism

---

[42] DRM, Folder H, p. 10.
[43] DRM, Folder F, part 2, p. 9.
[44] Ibid.
[45] Ibid.
[46] DRM, Folder I, part 1, p. 1.
[47] Ibid.

towards their 'expert advice' and judgement. As it turned out this scepticism became professionally useful when she went to work for the Children's Bureau and turned her attention to the radical idea of preventive medicine.[48]

It never seems to have occurred to her critics to consider the role that the profession itself played in creating an environment which made it virtually impossible for her to pursue their idea of professional work. It was difficult enough for single women. In all of New York City, for example, 'there were less than a dozen places open to women as interns'.[49] She had been fortunate to secure a staff position in a hospital there, but after she married she was expected to follow her husband and his work to Madison, Wisconsin, a small and medically backward town. Her first child and only daughter was delivered there by a man whom she had to remind to wash his hands before approaching the delivery table. This was a macabre turn of events for the sophisticated Hopkins graduate, supine and terrified, who later blamed the infant's death in parturition on the primitive obstetrical care she had received.[50]

In Wisconsin in this period, male practitioners, however questionable their training, did not welcome her competition, and her superior education at Johns Hopkins did nothing to lessen their antagonism toward a better trained competitor. When the stresses of married life and the grief attendant on her infant's death made her depressed, she thought that professional work would provide her with some much needed activity and a sense of purpose. But all that was available to her was the impossible fantasy of returning to the east and taking up practice there. She writes that she 'thought of it every day and made all sorts of plans' which were totally impossible if she wished to maintain her marriage.[51]

She of course remained with her husband in Wisconsin. But even when she forged some professional connections there, this was accomplished by moving into the most marginal professional areas—health education and hygiene. The regular physicians had little interest in these areas for they wished to pursue the more lucrative treatment of the ill in private practice. She justified seeking professional engagements on the grounds that she was badly in need of additional income in order to educate her sister's orphaned children. She took to the lecture platform in the rural cow towns of Wisconsin to speak to audiences on basic nutrition, child care, and infectious diseases. Travelling in harsh mid-western winters to speak to 15 or 20 mothers was physically demanding, but she found this paid work exhilarating and personally rewarding. She viewed it as 'an answer to my prayers, for besides

---

[48] For a discussion of tensions in the Children's Bureau between professionals and nonprofessionals, see Nancy P. Weiss, 'Mother, the invention of necessity: Dr. Benjamin Spock's baby and child care', *American Quarterly*, 5 (Winter 1977), 530 n.

[49] DRM, Folder G, p. 64.

[50] DRM, Folder H, pp. 13–14.

[51] Ibid., p. 15.

the money I made, it gave me a needed outlet and a way back into professional work'.[52]

This type of activity was a far cry from the fee-for-service, one-to-one medical practice of her male colleagues, and at the absolute opposite end of the professional spectrum from the research activity of her Hopkins mentors. Yet its very marginality afforded her the possibility of a critical posture in regard to the conventional paths to professional success. This was the beginning of a career which culminated in 20 years of work for the Children's Bureau, a newly formed, federal agency which focused on issues in public health. That this was theoretically, ideologically, and empirically at odds with conventional private medical practice did not deter her from eagerly seeking out such a position when her husband moved to Washington, D.C. during the First World War. She was already working in the most marginal areas and had few vested interests to protect.

A paper which Reed wrote entitled 'Prenatal and Natal Conditions in Wisconsin' typified the nature of the work and the aims of her career in public health. The paper, which dealt with infant mortality in childbirth, illustrates both the subject of her developing interests and the adversarial role which public health women professionals began to take toward their male colleagues in private practice. At that time physicians rather glibly blamed the high incidence of puerperal deaths of 5.6 per thousand on the participation of female midwives and nurses, whom they claimed were not trained to handle deliveries in modern scientific fashion. It was partly a measure of Reed's disaffection that she proclaimed quite forthrightly the discomforting conclusion that the high infant mortality rate was more the fault of the physicians than any other group involved in childbirth attendance. She went on to insist that the preventive measures advocated by the Children's Bureau—visiting-nurse services, nutritional education, sensible pre-natal care—were critical to the health of the mother and the baby. Physicians of that period had become increasingly wedded to disease theory and generally ignored preventive pre-natal and post-natal care. They also rejected natural childbirth techniques in favour of forceps and similar interventionist methods which allowed them to demonstrate their individual expertise. This may have made their presence at childbirth seem more indispensable, but it also tended to put mother and child at risk. Reed's research made her more cynical about their claims to expertise. She insisted that her data showed that their methods were responsible for the high death rates and that though 'the shoe fitted the doctors did not want to put it on'. Not surprisingly the paper was received with little enthusiasm when she read it at the seventieth annual meeting of the Wisconsin State Medical Society.[53]

---

[52] Ibid., p. 26.
[53] DRM, Folder I, part 1, p. 12. No copy of the paper is left in the collection of Reed's published work in the Sophia Smith archives.

Reed also realized that being a 'woman and from the east' played a part in the cold reception which she had received from the doctors at the Madison meeting, 'but public health work was new to most physicians and seemed to the majority of the profession in Madison a distinct effort to undermine their means of livelihood'.[54] These elements of market competition, which tended to intrude on the more noble aims which the profession publicly espoused, were confirmed privately by some of the more forthright physicians. One of her colleagues, a Dr. Harper, who was also Secretary to the local Board of Health, pointed out to her that she 'was wrong in considering that medicine was a profession when it was really a business'.[55] Despite the many disclaimers from medical spokesmen, this kind of unvarnished self-interest was prevalent among the aspiring and upwardly mobile groups that comprised the profession in the early twentieth century. Dr. S. Josephine Baker reported on the testimony of a male physician who was representing a New England Medical Society before a congressional committee hearing that was

considering the appropriation of funds for the newly founded Federal Children's Bureau. I was down there testifying too—on the other side. This New England doctor actually got up and told the committee: 'We oppose this bill because, if you are going to save the lives of all these women and children at public expense, what inducement will there be for young men to study medicine?' Senator Sheppard, the chairman, stiffened and leaned forward: 'Perhaps I didn't understand you correctly,' he said; 'You surely don't mean that you want women and children to die unnecessarily or live in constant danger of sickness so there will be something for young doctors to do?' 'Why not?' said the New England doctor, who did at least have the courage to admit the issue; 'That's the will of God, isn't it?'[56]

Her comments were significant not only for what they revealed about the morality of some physicians but also for what she unmasked about the structure of the profession. On the one hand the medical establishment set goals for practitioners that emphasized the mastery of disease theory, the commitment to interventionist treatment, and fee-for-service patient interaction. The doctors at the top of the professional hierarchy touted the superiority of this style of treatment. On the other hand, women doctors, excluded from the medical elite, often supported community public health and emphasized preventive treatment, and enthusiastically endorsed the benefits of health education for all classes of persons.

In founding public health agencies women professionals created a very different model of treatment. Their concerns were more comprehensive and their style of organization more collective. This kind of collective and public enterprise afforded women like Dorothy Reed Mendenhall the flexibility of meshing the demands in their personal and professional lives more easily. This kind of service also had the advantage of providing an arena in which

[54] DRM, Folder I, part 2, p. 12.
[55] Ibid.
[56] Baker, p. 138.

272

it was acceptable for a woman to be ambitious because she was also ameliorating the suffering of the poor, who were largely ignored by the conventional practitioner. Nevertheless, for a graduate of the elite, research-oriented Johns Hopkins, this kind of service was considered to be an inferior endeavour, made barely respectable by its altruistic goals.

The slight rewards from the medical establishment, and considerable personal tension which resulted from family and professional obligations, contrasted markedly with the attitudes of the female social reformers. They were unreserved in their appreciation of the services given by the female physicians. For example, Julia Lathrop, that indefatigable head of the Children's Bureau, was eager to have women like Reed on her staff because she had a double set of credentials; as a married woman with children she justified, through personal and direct experience, the public concern with improving maternal and child care; as a doctor she could offer impeccable qualifications in testifying before Congressional committees or making other kinds of public appearances. Josephine Baker, the eminent director of the first Bureau of Child Hygiene in New York City, recounts similar appreciation for her title of M.D.

> I was always going down to testify at hearings on Children's Bureau appropriations because Miss Julia Lathrop, the Bureau's brilliant first chief, thought I was a good ally. I was called Doctor instead of Miss and so could escape from the eternal remark always coming up among Congressmen about giving money to an old maid to spend.[57]

As the work of the Children's Bureau and its physicians became better known, the women's accomplishments as professional physicians became increasingly suspect and demeaned by those representing the private physicians. Dorothy Reed Mendenhall described the growing antagonism when she recalled that 'The medical profession (with few exceptions) belittled all the work of the Children's Bureau and questioned our statistics, or at least our presentation of them'.[58] She, in turn, sought to express her displeasure with them by refusing to join the local branch of the powerful American Medical Association. This gesture was the futile recourse of the marginal person and tended to confirm her lack of affiliation and her inferior status as a professional outcast. In retrospect she decided that this action might have been a tactical error, because it rendered her completely powerless to challenge the leadership that she detested.[59] In fact, even if such women had become members, there were not enough of them in the profession to have provided sufficient leverage to influence any of the policies of that organization. Reed under-estimated the obdurate resistance that any considerable female incursion of their ranks would have provoked; a challenge from those

[57] Ibid.
[58] DRM, Folder J, p. 17.
[59] DRM, Folder I, part 2, p. 16.

questionable women who had created the anathema of public health would have been most repugnant.[60]

For her part Dorothy Reed Mendenhall did not hesitate to make connections between her personal experience and her professional choices. Her work at the Children's Bureau focused almost exclusively on maternity issues. She believed that 'the tragic death of my first child, Margaret, from bad obstetrics in 1907, was the dominant factor in my interest in the chief function of women'.[61] It was not atypical for the married woman professional to justify her professional work in highly personal and feminine terms. In the same vein, Reed viewed the Child Health Centers of Madison, which she was instrumental in founding, as 'a monument to my boy, Richard [who died accidentally at the age of two], all the writing and teaching on safe maternity, I have thought of as a memorial to Margaret, my first child and only girl'. She ended that touching recollection with an underscored and revealing observation that '*A mother never forgets*'.[62]

This represents something more than the unique sentiment of a particular mother's grief. It is hardly coincidence that Dr. Anne Walter Fearn, whose career pattern was totally different, also attributed her work with children to the death of her only daughter at five years of age. In her memoirs she suggests that 'If Elizabeth's visit with us had not been so brief I might have been content to relinquish my practice and stay at home. I do not know'.[63] Yet there is nothing else to indicate that she would have retired from practice if her daughter had lived, nor does she seem to have enjoyed curtailing her activity while her daughter was still alive. What is significant here is that both these women justified their work as something more than conventional professional engagement by elevating it to a kind of memorial to their deceased children.

In other ways Dr. Fearn's career differs substantially from that of Dorothy Reed Mendenhall. Fearn represented the professional style of combining marriage and family in a quasi-institutional setting—a departure which permitted a more egalitarian relationship with her husband and somewhat greater professional options for her. This unusual woman, whose family had expected her to live the conventional life of a wealthy southern wife, instead prevailed upon them to use their influence to obtain a place for her in the Women's Medical College of Pennsylvania. Her prominent family obtained reference letters for her from her 'father's friends, Governor Stone, Governor Robert Lowry, and one or two others'. A friend of hers, Dr. Elizabeth Yates, helped her to meet her financial obligation at the medical college, and Fearn named her only daughter after this early supporter.[64]

---

[60] Anti-female acts had a long tradition among the medical associations. See Walsh, pp. 25–34, 106–46.
[61] DRM, Folder entitled 'J? (or part of H or I)' (*sic*), p. 19.
[62] Ibid., p. 20.
[63] Fearn, p. 104.
[64] Ibid., p. 103.

She described her student experience, in the very different female environment of Pennsylvania, as largely positive. She became the protégée of Dr. Joseph Price, 'a Southerner and one of the world's greatest surgeons and obstetricians'. He took a 'a fancy' to her and 'had unlimited faith in my future success'. In the fashion of that period, Dr. Price had his own hospital, the Preston Retreat, 'one of the largest maternity hospitals in the United States'. She served as his nurse and assistant and received a valuable apprenticeship in return.[65]

When she finished medical school she viewed her decision to go to China with a kind of adolescent casualness as 'a wonderful chance for me to see the world', but the decision came as 'a shock' to her mother. The young doctor was careful to point out to family and friends that she would 'not go as a missionary'. In what was becoming a fairly typical pattern for late nineteenth-century professional women, religious commitment was no longer a driving force in her work. She recalled with some degree of satisfaction her announcement to her family that she was not a missionary, 'not even a church member'; rather she insisted, 'I'm a physician'.[66] By 1893 she had begun her work in China at the Soochow Women's Hospital. The hospital had originally been organized by another female physician, Dr. Mildred Phillips, who had left when she married. The hospital had been forced to close for lack of staff. When Anne arrived it was reopened.[67]

Within a few years she had met and married Dr. John Burrus Fearn. Since her husband was a missionary their marriage 'definitely settled my fate as far as my return to the United States was concerned, for my husband expected to make China the field for his life work; as for me I had grown to love the country so well that I welcomed the prospect of exile'.[68]

The young couple appeared compatible in many ways. He, too, was a Southerner and they had in fact both been raised in neighbouring Mississippi towns. Nevertheless their marriage was marked by dissension and conflict from their earliest days together. According to the wife, the source of their difficulty came from the fact that 'my husband had grown up in the Church. I had not. For every hour he had spent in Sunday School and church I had spent two in dancing and similar pleasure'.[69] In many ways his austere Christianity was repugnant to his wife.

But the fact that she did not share his religious enthusiasm could not alone account for their estrangement. Her own evidence indicates that it was not her commitment to 'pleasure' which was at the core of their disaffection, but rather something quite different and perhaps more divisive—her commitment to work. She tells us that she 'honestly endeavored to follow his wishes' and that 'one of his obsessions was that the day should begin with

[65] Ibid., pp. 17–18.
[66] Ibid., p. 18.
[67] Ibid., p. 28.
[68] Ibid., p. 87.
[69] Ibid., p. 95.

prayer and Bible reading, and that the Bible should be read through methodically once or twice a year'. None of this was especially aberrant for a missionary, and would hardly have been difficult for a conventional wife. However, in Fearn's case this practice made her late for rounds and hence interfered with her care of her patients. One morning, when the pressure of work seemed particularly acute, she lost control, seized the Bible, threw it to the floor, and rushed out of the room, screaming 'I wish I'd never seen the damned thing'.[70] Not surprisingly, 'this little flare-up ended the Bible readings'. The subject was never mentioned again but her husband 'never forgave nor forgot, and I lost forever my taste, if I ever had any, for the Old Testament'.[71]

Within the first year of their marriage she became pregnant and in addition her husband was transferred to a different assignment. She followed him to his new appointment, but she returned to Soochow for her confinement and the child was delivered in the facility which she 'had built in the compound of the Women's Hospital'.[72] After several years the child died. The family returned to the United States for several months, and subsequently her husband accepted employment with the Associate Protestant Mission in China and was reassigned to Shanghai.

She viewed the change of city with little enthusiasm, for 'after the first excitement of settling a new home had subsided I found that I missed Soochow and my own work with a poignancy that made me restless and dissatisfied'.[73] She was further depressed by the prospect that 'a period of apparently endless drifting was opening for me, although I was never without some work to do'. She tried to patch together volunteer and charity work into an activity that would substitute for full-time professional work. Her husband became the chief financial support of the family and she undertook the role of housewife and active volunteer. 'For several years I was to expend my energy on various activities without finding the one channel into which they could flow with complete satisfaction. It was a new experience for me and not wholly a happy one.'[74]

With the outbreak of the First World War she wanted to move into a more demanding life. She tried to enlist in the Red Cross, but the anomaly of her position precluded that. They took only female nurses and male doctors. This was a great disappointment, because the intervening years in Shanghai did not give her the opportunity to 'practise medicine in good earnest' although that had been her intention. She worked at a local clinic several hours each day, but even this and her American Women's Club activities could not fill her day. They could not ease the 'rankling sensation

[70] Ibid., p. 96.
[71] Ibid.
[72] Ibid., pp. 102–3.
[73] Ibid., p. 143.
[74] Ibid.

276

that something more important, to me at least, lay waiting around the corner; and I must find it or remain forever only half a person'.[75]

Although the Red Cross failed to offer her new opportunities to become a whole person, the war did alter the circumstances of her personal life with far-reaching consequences. Her husband was called to serve in France, and in his absence she set up her own hospital. She apparently did this with some trepidation for she was aware that 'all of our married life was tinged by the merest shadow of professional jealousy. He had a strong sense of masculine protectiveness . . . and he was never so completely himself as when helping the sick and the weak. But in marrying a woman who took life with both hands and people as she found them, this protective instinct was more or less frustrated. He would much rather have had his wife sit at home and be managed by him'.[76] Yet this forthright analysis led her to conclude that 'for her devotion to duty as a doctor, however, he had only admiration'. It was his 'admiration' which she was to count on to gain his acceptance of her continued operation of her own hospital after his return. This acceptance, she reported with some satisfaction, was mixed with ambivalence as they became 'rivals in good earnest'.[77]

On his return he assumed the Superintendency of the Shanghai General Hospital. She continued to work at her own hospital and to maintain her own apartment there. She did sleep in his living quarters at the hospital, she tells us, in part because it provided some change for her. This arrangement had some obvious drawbacks from her husband's point of view. Despite his 'admiration' of her work as a doctor, he 'condemned my lack of interest in the religious life, and felt that my independence was unbecoming to a woman'.[78] She did add, with some relief, that when he died in 1926 he forgave her for opening the hospital because of the care and comfort which she had provided for the sick.

For her part, Dr. Fearn finally left her hospital with great reluctance, remarking that 'it was the last day of a decade spent in that beloved hospital-home'.[79] She claimed to have closed it because a newer facility had opened which provided a similar service and also because her husband's failing health made it increasingly difficult to continue her work. Even she was not prepared to insist that her decision was made solely in terms of her husband's needs.

The establishment of her own hospital had been the high point of her life and that was made possible by the special circumstances of life in China and by the institutional setting which the hospital/home provided. If she had been living in the United States the medical establishment would not easily

[75] Ibid., pp. 179–80.
[76] Ibid., p. 216.
[77] Ibid.
[78] Ibid., p. 261.
[79] Ibid., p. 263.

have acquiesced in the establishment of her own facility, nor in her assuming sole control of all the phases of its management. But even the exotic circumstances of the Orient did little to change the conventional expectations of her husband, whose wishes she flouted with some success and considerable ambivalence. She had embarked on her project while he was in France, and the separateness of their working lives after his return probably alleviated as much conflict as it engendered.

There was always something suspect about married women practising medicine. In part, these women dealt with the reservations by emphasizing the humanitarian and altruistic dimensions of their medical practices. The exaggerated reiteration of women's peculiar role in alleviating misery was bolstered by the definition of medicine as a 'sacred' activity which sustained the value of life. But the sacred was understood to have two dimensions: one was the discovery and penetration of the mysteries of life by recourse to the scientific method; the other was the altruistic component. The most eminent male practitioners had already arrogated the former activity to themselves by monopolizing control of the medical schools, teaching hospitals, and scholarly journals.[80]

This left the other dimension of the sacred, 'an ideal of service and devotion to human welfare',[81] which female practitioners and their supporters tried to claim for themselves. Their appropriation of this exclusive and elevated concern was necessary in order to legitimize their intrusion into sacrosanct areas of physiological functioning, which men were claiming as their exclusive territory.[82]

Fearn's commitment to a cause as noble as healing probably placated the worst resentment in her missionary husband. But in the end, it was he who had to forgive her for devoting her life to alleviating the misery of the sick. Female professionals defensively offered the apologia of sacrifice and service when they predictably assumed that it was their responsibility to explain and legitimize their professional ambitions.

Although the careers of Anne Walter Fearn and Dorothy Reed Mendenhall differed substantially, there were also several important similarities. As married women they were forced to do marginal work among remote and/or socially subordinate clienteles. It is not that the work which they did was unworthy or unnecessary; in the long run it probably turned out to have a greater social impact than most private practices. It was simply that those who interpreted professional reality chose to define that work as inferior and less deserving of reward. Like most women they were excluded from the powerful, financially rewarding, and prestigious positions.

[80] Larson, pp. 163–6.
[81] Ibid., pp. 38–9.
[82] Ibid., pp. 40–4. For an analysis of the French case see Haroun Jamous and B. Peloille, 'Changes in the French university-hospital system', in *Professions and Professionalization*, J. A Jackson, ed. (Cambridge, 1970), pp. 111–52.

As women professionals, their marriages had additional complications which impeded career development. Whereas for men, marriage and family supported and sustained their professional endeavours and augmented their chances for success, for women marriage was an obstacle to conventional definitions of achievement. Marriage was a central factor in the female life cycle, but it also became an insuperable barrier to achievement because it made incompatible demands on their time and energy. Since home and work were viewed as irreconcilable obligations, women ordinarily had to choose one or the other.

Fearn and Reed shared more than the similarity of being married; in both cases their professional goals put serious strain on their relations with their husbands. Both women chose their future spouses well after they had embarked on their professional careers. The extant evidence reflects only the wives' assessment of their husbands' personalities and the relationship of the partners. Even by their accounts it appears that these men were unusual for their time in their willingness to choose wives who did not fit the traditional expectations for this group. Yet they emerge in the wives' portrayal as very conventional, late Victorian men. For example, Reed describes her husband's almost stereotyped suspicion of pleasure by recalling that

> when I married him, Charles had never danced, smoked, played cards, or indulged in any of the usual pastimes of youth ... what was really true was that his straight-laced upbringing had made him question every harmless pleasure—if he enjoyed a thing he had a feeling it must be wrong.[83]

Here and elsewhere she implies a sombreness and conventionality which was so different from her own personality. Fearn made similar observations.[84]

Although it is impossible from the surviving evidence to tease out all the personal tensions from the professional frustrations, both women's memoirs recount, at disproportionate length, the dissensions in their conjugal relationships. They vacillate between expressing their hostility to their husbands and lacerating themselves in guilty confessions of their wifely inadequacies. A quarter of a century after Charles Mendenhall had died, his wife was still debating the wisdom of her decision to marry him in terms which reflected the complexity of her feelings.

> There had been several times, especially in the Spring of 1904, which [sic] it seemed impossible for me to carry on the arrangement [engagement] or to think of marriage with him or any man. Gradually Charles' devotion, tenderness for me and innate goodness conquered my doubts ... I felt that I could go through with it and with his help and understanding make him a fairly decent wife. I have always had my doubts, if it were fair to him.[85]

[83] DRM, Folder H, p. 7.
[84] Fearn, pp. 95–6, 260–1.
[85] DRM, Folder G, p. 6.

In another section of her autobiography she writes:

> Neither the years before I was married, or those of my early married life were happy ones and yet I struggled through them, and after 1917 I worked out a way of living and a plan for the boys' training and education that gave me satisfaction at the time and has made the early decades of 1900 seem worthwhile—in spite of the agony.[86]

It is of course extremely difficult to generalize about the quality of marriage in a given society. Obviously there were other unhappy marriages, in which the wives were entirely conventional. A number of scholars have concluded that the many ailments—neurasthenia, hysteria, back problems—found among this class of married women probably can be attributed to dissatisfaction with their domestic lives.[87] What is distinctive about these two physicians is their willingness to write so frankly about their anger and frustration. It is equally relevant that they resisted the more common recourse to hypochondria and invalidism. Instead they drew on the kind of emotional resources which allowed them to develop as professionals and also as autonomous women.

[86] DRM, Folder H, p. 4.

[87] Ehrenreich and English, ch. 4; Carroll Smith-Rosenberg and Charles Rosenberg, 'The female animal: medical and biological views of woman and her role in nineteenth century America', *Journal of American History*, LVII (1970), 332–56; Carroll Smith-Rosenberg, 'The hysterical woman: sex roles and role conflict in 19th century America', *Social Research*, XXXIX (Winter 1972), 652–78.

Index